FOURTH EDITION

POLITICAL IDEOLOGIES

Their Origins and Impact

Leon P. Baradat

Mira Costa College

PRENTICE HALL, *Englewood Cliffs, New Jersey 07632*

Library of Congress Cataloging-in-Publication Data

Baradat, Leon P.
    Political ideologies : their origins and impact / Leon P. Baradat.
  -- 4th ed.
        p.   cm.
    Includes bibliographical references.
    ISBN 0-13-684275-5
    1. Political science--History. 2. Ideology. .I. Title.
JA83.B248   1991
320.5'09--dc20   89-49331
                                                         CIP

Editorial/production supervision
  and interior design: Shelly Kupperman
Cover design: Bruce Kenselaar
Manufacturing buyer: Bob Anderson

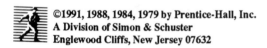 ©1991, 1988, 1984, 1979 by Prentice-Hall, Inc.
A Division of Simon & Schuster
Englewood Cliffs, New Jersey 07632

Printed in the United States of America
10 9 8 7 6 5 4 3 2 1

ISBN   0-13-684275-5

PRENTICE-HALL INTERNATIONAL (UK) LIMITED, *London*
PRENTICE-HALL OF AUSTRALIA PTY. LIMITED, *Sydney*
PRENTICE-HALL CANADA INC., *Toronto*
PRENTICE-HALL HISPANOAMERICANA, S.A., *Mexico*
PRENTICE-HALL OF INDIA PRIVATE LIMITED, *New Delhi*
PRENTICE-HALL OF JAPAN, INC., *Tokyo*
SIMON & SCHUSTER ASIA PTE. LTD., *Singapore*
EDITORA PRENTICE-HALL DO BRASIL, LTDA., *Rio de Janeiro*

To Elaine:

Wife, Partner, Friend

And to the memory of:

Henry Meier, colleague and mentor
Kevin Muldoon, student and friend
Richard Frizzell, student and friend

Contents

Preface

Since the first edition of this book, we have witnessed many changes in the tides of political turmoil throughout the world. Now, as the communist states have become more moderate, and as the strident ideologues of the Reagan administration are no longer in power, the world's political climate becomes increasingly temperate. Still, however, we find ourselves confronted with a threatening environment. Over 50,000 nuclear warheads are deployed in Soviet and American arsenals; the Middle East festers politically; terrorists murder hundreds of innocent people; famine emaciates millions in the underdeveloped world; racism and nationalism divide people against themselves; air pollution is rampant; water everywhere is increasingly adulterated; and the globe apparently is warming in response to the chemicals released into the atmosphere.

These problems, and many others demanding solutions, confront us and our national leaders. To resolve our difficulties, we realize that we must work together with other people in the world, since many of our problems traverse national boundaries and exceed the capacity of single states to successfully address them. In order to cooperate in the salvation of humankind, we must learn to deal with people who have values, biases, views, and ideas that are different from our own. Hence, we must confront a number of basic questions if we hope to successfully meet the challenges of the last decade of this century. What, for example, are the fundamental concepts in modern politics? What ideas serve as the foundation of our political system? How does our system differ from others? What is socialism, and how does it relate to democracy and to communism? Is fascism moribund, or does it survive, awaiting another chance to take hold in a society confused and disoriented by the complexities of modern life? Why don't people of the world see things *our* way? How do they view the world, and why do they value the things they do? What are their assumptions and objectives? These and hundreds of other questions must be addressed if we are to face intelligently the political controversies which loom before us. These questions can be ignored only at great peril, and the study of political ideologies is perhaps the best context in which to begin to find answers.

Although the emotional debate among the world's leaders has somewhat quieted recently, the substance of the differences expressed remains fundamental. Ideological assumptions become the premises for the approaches different societies take to resolve their internal problems and their international difficulties.

Traditionally, the American people have been impatient with theoretical concepts. Finding such concepts abstract and uninteresting, they prefer more tangible, practical approaches to politics. Moreover, the American approach to politics has usually been isolationist. We have either tried to ignore the rest of the world—as in the early part of this century— or we have expected the world to conform to our attitudes and policies —as has been the case since World War II. But such isolationism is no longer possible—if indeed it ever was. The United States must face the fact that it is only one player, albeit an important one, in world politics, and we must learn to cooperate with the rest of the world in the resolution of global problems. To do so, we must understand the other peoples of the world. We must comprehend their views of politics, and we can start by comprehending their ideologies as well as by developing fuller appreciation of our own identity. A clear understanding of the current ideologies, therefore, is essential for anyone who hopes to grasp the political realities of our time.

A NOTE TO THE READER

One of the most gratifying things about writing a text book is the knowledge that it is a vehicle for teaching; it reaches students whom the author will probably never meet and thus influences the lives of strangers, if only slightly. With this in mind, I have designed this book as a teaching mechanism and have included several features which should help the reader learn its contents more easily.

Each chapter is preceded by a preview of the material to be covered in that chapter. The preview is designed to alert readers to the principal ideas developed in the text that follows. Thus you will find that, equipped with this overview, the details in the chapter become more meaningful. If after finishing the chapter, you feel you need a review, reread the preview.

The text also includes terms in boldface or italicized words and phrases. When encountering these words, take special note of them; it is my way of saying that that material is particularly important. The glossary and the index at the end of the book should also be especially useful.

As a final note to the reader, I would like to say just a few words about general education courses. Our society has recently adopted a much more materialistic attitude than existed in the past. Responding to economic and social pressures, students today are anxious to complete their studies so that they can begin to make a living. Courses which do not immediately translate into dollars are often viewed by students as superfluous impositions on their time. The course for which you are reading this text may be one of those offerings. Yet, there is more to life than materialism, and we must learn to appreciate and enjoy what we are and who we are while we make a living. In fact, it is likely that we will make a better living, or at least live better, if we appreciate and understand the world in which we live.

An education is more than a ticket to a higher salary. A college education brings perspective, ideas, thought, history, art, literature, logic, science, and more to those who pursue it. Education is the custodian of civilization, and its function is to transmit the knowledge of our civilization to each succeeding generation. General education courses are the principal vehicle by which this function is executed in college. They offer you priceless treasures of knowledge and wisdom. Immerse yourself in them, savor them, absorb them, enjoy them. Let general education courses expose you to the wonders of our world, expanding your vision and deepening your appreciation of life so that, as Stephen Bailey recently wrote, "Later in life when you knock on yourself, someone answers."

The views of students and professors are important to me. Hence, I encourage you to write me, offering criticisms, reflections, and suggestions for future editions of this book. Your letters will be answered. I can be reached at Mira Costa College, One Barnard Drive, Oceanside, CA 92056.

ACKNOWLEDGMENTS

While any inaccuracies in this book are completely my own responsibility, several people have made such substantial contributions to this work that I take pleasure in mentioning them here. My deepest gratitude belongs to my family: Elaine, who shares my dedication, and our two boys, Pierre and René. They have unselfishly sacrificed time we might have spent together in pleasurable pursuits so that this book could be written.

For the lucidity the first edition enjoyed, all credit and many thanks go to Professor Julie Hatoff. Spending untold hours reviewing the manuscript, suggesting improvements, and correcting errors, Professor Hatoff was of invaluable assistance. I am similarly indebted to Professor Patricia Valiton and Mary Murphy for their services on the subsequent editions. Their conscientious attention to my misplaced modifiers, arbitrary punctuation, and eccentric spelling has been very helpful, and I am most grateful to them. For the excellent artwork embellishing this edition, my deep appreciation goes to Professor Dan Camp, who graciously consented to interrupt a busy schedule to do the drawings. I am also very grateful to my colleague and friend David Ballard for his help on this edition. Additionally, Myles Clowers of San Diego City College deserves special recognition for his many comments and suggestions about this book. I would also like to take this opportunity to thank Stan Wakefield, Karen Horton, Shelly Kupperman, and Walter Welch of Prentice Hall. Without their help and encouragement this book probably would not have been written. I appreciate the fine copy editing job done by Steve Hopkins. Thank you to the Prentice Hall reviewers for their helpful suggestions: Philip Abbott, Wayne State University; James L. Troisi, Rochester Institute of Technology; and Vernon D. Johnson, Western Washington University.

Besides those who did so much to make this book a reality, I would like to take this opportunity to express my gratitude to the people of California for providing an excellent and free public education system to its youth. Were it not for the opportunity to attend state-supported schools, I would almost surely not have received an education. In addition, I would like to single out three teachers who have had particular influence on my professional life and whose scholarly examples have been important inspirations. To N. B. (Tad) Martin, formerly professor of history at the College of the Sequoias, who has a grasp of history and a teaching ability worthy of emulation, my sincere appreciation. To Karl A. Svenson, professor of political science at Fresno State University, whose lectures were memorable and whose advice was timely and sound, my heartfelt thanks. Finally, and most important, to David H. Provost, professor of political science at Fresno State University, my lasting gratitude for the help, encouragement, scholastic training, and friendship he so abundantly extended. His example has been particularly meaningful to me.

Leon P. Baradat

1

Ideology and Nationalism

PREVIEW

Ideologies were made necessary by the Age of Enlightenment belief that people could improve their conditions by taking positive action instead of passively accepting life as it came. This new belief was accompanied by the great economic and social upheaval caused by the mechanization of production. Indeed, one of the major themes of this book is that *ideologies are the result of attempts to develop political accommodations to the economic and social conditions created by the Industrial Revolution.*

Political scientists do not agree on the exact definition of the term *ideology,* but their opinions have enough in common to allow us to develop a five-part definition for our purposes:

1. The term *ideology* can be used in many contexts, but unless otherwise specified, it is proper to give it a political meaning.
2. All ideologies provide an interpretation of the present and a view of a desired future. The anticipated future is invariably portrayed as materially better than the present and as attainable within a single lifetime.
3. Each ideology includes a list of specific steps that can be taken to accomplish its goals.
4. Ideologies are oriented toward the masses.
5. Ideologies are simply stated and presented in motivational terms.

Nationalism is the theory of the nation-state, and as such it has had an enormous impact on the modern world. The terms *nation* and *state* are often confused.

Nation is a sociological term referring to a group of people who, because of blood relationships, linguistic similarities, common cultural patterns, or geographic proximity, have a sense of union with one another. *State* is a political term that includes four elements: people, territory, government, and sovereignty.

The state probably evolved when societies exchanged their nomadic lifestyle for farming. Yet, several theories of the origin of the state have had an important impact on nationalism as an ideology. The natural theory actually based its definition of humanity on the existence of the state. The divine theory suggested that a particular people was chosen by God, while the divine right of kings theory regarded the monarch as the personification of the state. The social-contract theory equated the nation-state with the individuals in it, suggesting that the people are the source of all political power; the force theory went further toward viewing the state as an amoral institution with few, if any, limits.

Each of these theories contributed to nationalism as the most powerful of contemporary ideas. While *patriotism* is an act, gesture, or expression of loyalty to the state, *nationalism* is the theoretical definition and basis of the state. It tends to divide people along territorial lines, and people use it as a frame of reference for their own identity as well as a yardstick by which to measure other people. Being primarily property-oriented, nationalism is firmly rooted in the conservative tradition.

IDEOLOGY

Prior to the modern era, people were discouraged from seeking solutions to their problems. They were expected to do what they were told by their spiritual and temporal superiors. Politics had not yet become democratized. Ordinary people were not allowed to participate in the political system. Politics was reserved for kings heading a small ruling class. The masses were expected to work, producing material goods to sustain the state, but they were not mobilized for political activity. Frederick the Great (1712–1786), a Prussian ruler and great general, once said, "A war is something which should not concern my subjects."

This attitude would be viewed as arrogant by contemporary observers, but only because every modern society is democratic in at least one sense of the word. *Every modern political system is motivational*; that is, the leaders attempt to mobilize their citizens to accomplish the political, economic, and social goals of the society. The United States, Great Britain, France, the Soviet Union, Japan, the People's Republic of China, and every other modern national political entity, regardless of the differences among them, share at least one major feature: They are all intensely interested in involving their citizens in efforts to accomplish the objectives of the state; and ideologies are among the major tools used by modern governments to mobilize the masses. Consequently, modern ideologies call upon people to join in collective efforts. The goals of each ideology and the precise methods used to reach these goals are different, but they each call for mass mobilization and collective efforts to accomplish desired ends.

The Source of Ideology

Knowledge, as it was commonly understood before the Enlightenment, was to be revealed by a superior wisdom; people were to understand and conform to such

Galileo Galilei (1564–1642)

knowledge as best they could. Consequently, little questioning or challenging took place, and, naturally, change came very slowly. Tradition was the repository of knowledge, and people were expected to comply with customs, laws, and teachings that had always been accepted.

Gradually, however, people began to challenge the established mode. Some, such as Galileo, were punished for doing so. Yet they persisted, and in time their efforts led to discoveries that revolutionized human existence. I will not catalog these accomplishments here but will simply state that the net result was the development of science and its application, technology. Success in early attempts to solve problems through the application of science, such as curing a disease or developing an important labor-saving device, encouraged people to apply human reason to an ever-widening range of problems.

In time, innovators developed machines that greatly increased productivity and drastically changed people's relationship to the things produced. Whereas production was once limited to the quantity a person could fashion by hand, the new technology produced goods in quantities that no one had ever imagined before. At the same time, however, the worker was no longer personally involved in the production process. Machines were weaving fabrics, forging steel, and carving wood. Workers found themselves tending the machines instead of making goods.

These changes in productivity had enormous social effects. People who once led a relatively healthy, albeit poor, life in a rural setting were brought together to live in the cities. The workers' neighborhoods were crowded and unsanitary. Life became less social as people found themselves psychologically estranged from their neighbors at the very time when they were forced to cohabit the same city block. Doing for others became passé, and doing for oneself alone became increasingly necessary as society became more competitive. For millennia people had depended on a close relationship with the soil for the necessities of life. Now, suddenly, they found themselves divorced from the land. The full effects on people in industrial societies being wrenched from the land and self-sufficiency in such a brief period of time has not yet been fully studied. We do know, however, that urbanization and industrialization as accomplished by the brutal methods employed during the eighteenth and nineteenth centuries caused massive confusion and insecurity among most people. Scholars, philosophers, and politicians launched themselves into efforts to comprehend these events, to explain them, and to rationalize them. Some of the rationalizations became ideologies. The ordinary people were disoriented and frightened. No longer could they produce most of the things they needed themselves. They had become dependent for their well-being on people they did not know, in places they had never seen.

If the mechanization of production, the urbanization of society, and the separation of people from an intimate relationship with the land had been all that people had to face, the impact on human life would have been great indeed. However, even more turmoil lay ahead. Economic dislocation became a severe problem. Unemployment, depression, and inflation began to plague society and to disrupt the order of things to a degree previously unequaled. Workers became disoriented as the skills that had once been a major source of self-identification and pride were made unnecessary by automation. It became necessary to learn a new set of skills to fit the new technology. At the same time, the workers became divorced from owners. Capital investment necessary to buy machines, factories, and resources became so great that owners had to spend their time managing their money (becoming capitalists); they were no longer able to work alongside their employees. Eventually, companies were financed by stockholders, people who could own the business without even knowing where it was located, or even what it did. Absentee ownership necessitated a corps of professional managers whose relationship with the workers was detached and impersonal. Hence, the workers, lulled by the monotony of the assembly line, became estranged from their work, alienated by impersonal managers, and separated from their employers.

Meanwhile, as family farms and businesses have disappeared, society has become increasingly mobile. Roots have disintegrated. People are in constant motion as a result of a technology which affords rapid, comfortable travel. Families, the most basic of all social units, have become dislocated from ancestral foundations, and the institution of the family itself seems to be dissolving before our eyes. While we are being crowded closer together, we seem to be losing concern for one another. We are becoming increasingly isolated in a world filled with people. Ironically, we are developing a self-oriented world at the very time that we are becoming more and more dependent on others for our most basic needs. As the pace of change quickens and the basic institutions of society are weakened, the generation gap, which must always have existed in some form, has widened. This separation can be found even within a single generation. A husband and wife, for example, may be members of the same generation, but the world each experiences may be greatly different from that encountered by the other. As a result, each grows at a different rate until after a few years two people who may once have had much in common no longer share compatible ideas.

Our economic success has tended to make our social problems worse. Industrialization has produced great wealth for those who are fortunate enough to profit from it. For others, however, it has produced a new kind of slavery. The new slaves, be they industrial workers or neocolonial suppliers of cheap raw materials, are exploited more fully than those of previous eras because of the efficiency of the modern system. The gap between the user and the used, between the haves and the have-nots, is also increasing, threatening frightful results for a world that remains insensitive to it. In addition, industrialized economies have become voracious consumers of natural resources. Some of these vital commodities are, in fact, reduced to very short supply. The competition for the remaining fuel and mineral resources increases the tension between industrialized and developing nations as well as among the industrialized nations themselves.

Not only have many technical advances increased the demand for resources, but they have also tended to increase the population and thus further escalate the demand for resources. Medical and nutritional discoveries have lengthened life expectancies and eradicated certain diseases so that today the world's population is close to five billion, a figure which will almost certainly double within the next half century. Housing, clothing, and feeding these multitudes aggravates the drain on basic resources, causing scarcity and stimulating greater competition for control of those goods.

Prior to the present era people relied on religion for answers to adversity, putting their faith unquestioningly in their God and in their priests. However, as rationalism developed and science seemed to contradict certain basic tenets of the Church, people began to rely on science for solutions to their difficulties. The world became increasingly materialistic, decreasingly spiritualistic. Unfortunately, however, science brought humanity mixed blessings. For each problem it solved, it created new difficulties. Automobiles give us mobility, yet they also visit air pollution on their owners; birth control pills prevent unwanted children, but now ancient moral scruples are rejected and society faces venereal disease and AIDS in epidemic proportions; preservatives keep food from spoiling for months, while cancer and other maladies plague users of the embalmed commodities; nuclear energy offers cheap and virtually inexhaustible energy, yet, as the accident at Chernobyl attests, a mishap at a power plant can be disastrous; and while nuclear deterrence has kept an uneasy peace, the use of nuclear weapons could produce the ultimate holocaust.

As if these problems were not enough, their impact has been magnified because they have been forced on us over an extremely brief period. Most of the developments just mentioned have occurred during the span of a few generations. People have never before experienced the rate of change they face today. Not only is the speed of change faster than in any previous era, but it is also increasing at an alarming rate. We find ourselves catapulted into the future before we can fully understand the present or the recent past. We are overwhelmed by new things before existing goods have become obsolete, old, or even familiar.

Such fundamental change, to say nothing of the rate at which it is occurring, has tended to disorient and confuse people. Values and institutions have become temporary. The industrialization of our economy has caused social upheaval and political change. It is, of course, political change with which we are concerned in this book. However, the political developments of the past several centuries have been stimulated by economic and social conditions. The political ideologies described in later chapters may be viewed as *attempts to find a political accommodation to the social and economic conditions created by the Industrial Revolution*. Madison, Marx, Mussolini, and others developed their ideas in response to the conditions confronting them. If those conditions had been different, political thought would have been different. The two factors most responsible for the world in which we now live are (1) *the belief that people can take active steps that will improve their lives* and (2) *the mechanization of production*. Almost every modern social condition and political idea is supported by these two factors. The phenomenon of political ideologies is unique to our era because it is a response to a unique set of circumstances.

Because I believe that a political idea can be understood completely only if it is considered in its historical perspective, some space will be devoted to sketching the circumstances surrounding the development of each political ideology. The reader will then be able to grasp the full impact of that ideology. For the same reason, I have organized this book chronologically, so that the reader is exposed to the various ideologies in the order in which they were conceived. Our task here is not simply to learn *what* Hobbes, Marx, Hitler, Dewey, and others have said, but to understand *why* they said it. What stimulated their ideas? What did they hope to accomplish? And, most importantly, how do their ideas relate to us? Before we turn to specific ideologies, however, let us investigate exactly what ideology is.

IDEOLOGY DEFINED

The meaning of the word *ideology* is frequently debated. Dozens of different definitions have been suggested, and each has been challenged and contradicted. Indeed, political scientists cannot agree on whether ideology is a positive, negative, or neutral feature of modern society. While I have no hope of settling this controversy here, I do wish to discuss the origins of the term, explain the varying definitions of the word, and arrive at a definition that will be useful to us during the rest of this study.

The Origin of the Term

It is generally agreed that the term *ideology* was first used by the French in the early nineteenth century, but we do not know for sure who coined the term. Most of the evidence, however, indicates that the French scholar Antoine Louis Claude Destutt de Tracy (1754–1836) probably originated the word. Writing between 1801 and 1815, he used the word *ideology* in his systematic study of the Enlightenment. Like other thinkers of his time, Destutt de Tracy believed that people could use science to improve social and political conditions. To him ideology was a study of the process of forming ideas, a "science of ideas," if you will. *Ideas,* Destutt de Tracy believed, are stimulated by the physical environment. Hence, *empirical learning* (the kind that is gained through experience) is the only source of knowledge. Supernatural or spiritual phenomena play no part in the formation of ideas.

While Destutt de Tracy and his followers, the *ideologues,* were perhaps the first to use the term *ideology,* they were not the first to study the question of how ideas are formed. The most dramatic statement of the new empirical reasoning was made by Francis Bacon (1561–1626) in the *Novum Organum*. In this work Bacon argued that knowledge should come from careful and accurate observation and experience. He

Francis Bacon (1561–1626)

believed that any knowledge deduced from less scientific methods of inquiry was distorted by false impressions or "idols." Bacon's theory of knowledge persisted through English intellectual history until John Locke (1632–1704) refined it further. Locke believed that we know nothing at birth; our minds are "blank slates." Ideas gradually develop in the mind after we encounter experiences that lead to particular thoughts. Thus, the argument that some knowledge is present at birth is false. "Facts" based on anything other than the empirical method, such as belief in good or evil spirits or the notion that bleeding cures illness by ridding people of bad humors—that is, ideas accepted on faith alone—are not true knowledge. These distinctions had been made before Destutt de Tracy refined the "science of ideas," producing the concept of ideology.

Although the thrust of Destutt de Tracy's thought is psychological, and hence not of immediate concern to us, two aspects of his theories should be noted. The first is *materialism*. Thought, according to Destutt de Tracy, is stimulated by material things only, and the formation of an idea is a physical rather than a spiritual or mystical process. The scientific and materialistic basis of ideology will be pointed out later. For now it is sufficient to note that materialism is a dominant theme in the concept of ideology.

The second important aspect of Destutt de Tracy's thought is that social and political improvement was its main goal. Destutt de Tracy wanted to apply the knowledge developed from his "science of ideas" to the whole society and thereby attempt to improve human life. Thus, ideology has been closely associated with politics from the beginning. It is therefore appropriate to give the word a political connotation unless a different context is indicated.

Karl Marx and Friedrich Engels developed the first theory of ideology. Ironically, they perceived ideology as the exact opposite of what Destutt de Tracy thought it to be. To them an ideology was simply a fabrication used by a group of people to justify themselves. The concepts in an ideology, according to Marx and Engels, are incorrect and usually work to the benefit of the ruling class. In short, ideology becomes part of the *superstructure* of the society. (See Chapter 7 for a further explanation.)

Karl Mannheim also studied ideology. While he basically agreed with Marx's conclusions, Mannheim contributed an analysis of ideology from a historical perspective. He compared the ideology of one historical era to that of another, arguing that no ideology could be fully understood unless this historical relationship was clear. No ideology, in other words, can be understood unless we grasp the ideas of the previous era and investigate the impact of the previous ideology on the current one.

Contemporary Definitions

Americans tend not to view political issues ideologically. Impatient with theoretical arguments, they consider ideologies idealistic and impractical concepts. Yet, political theory gives us statements of objectives by which to guide our actions and by which to assess our accomplishments. Without theory, political policy can be shortsighted and inconsistent. Hence, most political scientists readily agree that ideology is an important factor in our lives. Alas, they are no closer than earlier authorities to an agreement on exactly what the term means. In this section we will consider the definitions of ideology suggested by some important contemporary scholars.

Frederick Watkins, in his insightful book *The Age of Ideology,* suggests that ideology comes almost entirely from the political extremes. Ideologies, he argues, are always opposed to the status quo. They propose an abrupt change in the existing order; therefore, they are usually militant, revolutionary, and violent. Watkins goes on to point out that most ideologies are stated in simplistic terms, are utopian in their objectives, and usually display great faith in humankind's potential for finding success and happiness. Conservatism, because it defends the status quo and resists change, is an "anti-ideology," according to Watkins. Ideology emerged from the rationalist tradition, in which it was assumed that most problems could be solved if people applied reason rightly. (Destutt de Tracy, after all, was one of those rationalists who tried to understand the process of idea formation.) As will be seen in the following chapter, however, the conservative rejects this optimistic assumption about the capacity of human reason. Hence, Watkins argues, the conservative is opposed to the basic assumption of any ideology.

This particular point occasions some difficulty. It is true that conservatives are very cautious about human reason. They are quick to argue that reason has its limits. Yet, they do not completely reject reason as a means by which a political problem can be solved. To argue, therefore, that conservatism is not an ideology may be to exaggerate.

Another modern commentator, David Ingersoll, suggests that each ideology includes an assessment of the status quo and a view of the future. The future is always represented as something better than the present or the past. Exactly what is better for the society is usually expressed in materialistic terms; for example, both Marx and Hitler envisioned a society of great bounty. In addition, Ingersoll asserts that each ideology contains a definite plan of action by which this better future can be attained. Indeed, the plan of action is central to any ideology, according to Ingersoll. Ideologies tend to convey a sense of urgency. Moreover, they are intended to stimulate people to achieve utopian objectives.

L. T. Sargent approaches the definition of ideology differently. He sees ideologies as based on the value systems of various societies. Yet, modern societies are complex and often contradictory. Hence, individuals within a society may not accept a single ideology; they may appropriate parts of several ideologies, or they may become completely attached to a single idea system. In any event, Sargent makes the point that ideologies are simplistic in their approach to solving problems. Ideology, he writes, "provides the believer with a picture of the world both as it is and as it should be, and, in so doing, . . .organizes the tremendous complexity of the world into something fairly simple and understandable."[1]

Even though these authorities do not agree fully, there are broad areas of accord in their positions. It is possible to extract from them a five-point definition of ideology that we can apply throughout the remainder of this book. To begin with, ideology is first and foremost a political term, though it can be applied to other contexts. The political nature of the term *ideology* stems from its historical use in political contexts. Second, every ideology consists of a view of the present and a vision of the future. The preferred future is always presented as a materialistic improvement over the present. This desirable future condition is almost always attainable, according to the ideology, within a single lifetime. As a result one of the outstanding features of an ideology is its offer of hope. Third, ideology is action-oriented. It not only describes reality and offers a better future, but most important, it gives specific directions about the steps that must be taken to attain this goal. Fourth, ideology is directed toward the masses. If nothing else, John Locke, Karl Marx, Benito Mussolini, Vladimir Lenin, Mao Tse-tung, and Adolf Hitler had one thing in common: They directed their appeal to the masses. They were interested in mobilizing huge numbers of people. Finally, because ideologies are directed at the masses, they are usually couched in fairly simple terms that can be understood by ordinary people. For the same reason ideologies are usually motivational in tone, tending to call on people to make a great effort to attain the ideological goals. This mass appeal in itself implies confidence in people's ability to improve their lives through positive action. *All modern societies are democratic in this sense of the word.*

Ideology and philosophy. Finally, it is necessary to distinguish between philosophy and ideology. Previous eras enjoyed much more stable conditions than we experience now; life moved at a slower pace. Although much was not known, almost everything was explained by spiritual or metaphysical propositions. Things were as they were because God intended them so and, consequently, to question the basic order of life was certainly inappropriate and perhaps even heretical.

Government, as has already been explained, was the province of an elite. If actions were guided by theory at all, the theoretical base was normative and lodged in relatively complex tracts that only the best educated were likely to understand. Ordinary people were not involved in politics, nor were they expected to be ac-

---

[1]L. T. Sargent, *Contemporary Political Ideologies*, rev. ed. (Homewood, IL: Dorsey Press, 1972), p. 1.

quainted with the goals or justifications for government beyond the most rudimentary principles. Hence, the philosophy that served as the theoretical base for the society was available to only a tiny percentage of the population.

Although each ideology is founded upon a set of philosophical beliefs, philosophy is composed of three basic characteristics that distinguish it from ideology. First, philosophy tends to be profound. It attempts to penetrate the veneer of human existence and to address the actual meaning of life itself. To do so, it must deal with the subject in a very complex and holistic manner. It tries to analyze the totality of human experience to find the meaning contained therein and, by so doing, to produce generalizations by which future conduct can profitably be pursued and by which actions can be assessed. Second, although philosophy can be the set of principles upon which an entire society bases its actions, it can also be taken up by a single individual. Indeed, when reading philosophy, one is often struck by the feeling that the author is communicating directly with the reader and is not necessarily trying to reach a larger audience. Third, philosophy tends to encourage introspection. The objective of philosophy is to explain the universe and help the reader find his or her place in it. Philosophy requires sustained contemplation and examines profound questions about the human condition. While philosophy may advise measures to improve society, action is not its central focus: understanding is; and it is through greater understanding that human happiness is presumably achieved.

Ideology differs from philosophy in all three of the foregoing respects. First, where philosophy is profound, attempting to deal with the intricacies of the world in detail, ideology is uncomplicated and shallow. The world is usually explained in very simple terms and little attempt is made to deal with the multitudinous variables we confront. Usually, "right" and "wrong" are made very clear, and people are simply asked to believe in them and to act accordingly. Second, ideology is addressed to huge numbers of people rather than to the individual. Ideology, as previously indicated, is the theoretical base for the mass mobilization upon which each modern nation is founded.

Third, in explaining the world (albeit simply), ideology asks for people to take definite steps to improve their lives. Unlike philosophy, ideology invariably demands that people change the world to suit themselves. People are not asked to investigate the complex and underlying variable of human existence. Instead, they are called upon primarily to act, and this emphasis on action often demands suspension of contemplation. While ideologies may ask people to transform themselves, the objective of such personal change is not limited to creating a better person. Instead, ideologies are outwardly directed. People are to change themselves in order to be better able to modify the environment around them. Happiness of people in society is often juxtaposed to the condition of the world in which they find themselves, so that the world must be made to conform to the needs and conditions of the people who subscribe to a given ideology.

NATIONALISM

Before beginning our examination of specific ideologies, we should consider *nationalism,* a phenomenon which has affected most of the important ideologies. Indeed, nationalism is often dominant over many ideological goals. It would be difficult to exaggerate the importance of this concept in contemporary politics. Nationalism is the most powerful political idea of the past several hundred years. It has had a great impact on every person in every modern society. People who have applauded policies pursued in the name of country would have condemned the same acts if committed for any other reason. Millions of people have been sacrificed and died, property has been destroyed, and resources have been plundered in the name of the state. Yet, individuals have also risen to noble heights and made great contributions to humanity for the sake of the state. As we will see in later chapters, nationalism is so powerful that it has dominated almost every other idea system. Indeed, only certain extreme forms of anarchism completely and abruptly reject the state. Before we consider nationalism itself, however, let us gain a more accurate understanding of the terms *nation* and *state*.

Nation and State

The term *nation* is often used as a synonym for *state* or *country*. This is not technically correct, but the mistake is commonly made by political leaders as well as by ordinary people. To be precise, the term *nation* does not have any political implication at all. Indeed, the concept of a nation is not political, but social. A nation can exist even though it is not contained within a particular state or served by a given government. A nation exists when there is a union of people based on similarities in linguistic pattern, ethnic relationship, cultural heritage, or even simple geographic proximity.

Probably the most common feature around which a nation is united is ethnic background. One's *nationality* is often expressed in terms of ethnic background rather than citizenship. Thus, while some people will respond "American" when asked their nationality, it is not uncommon for loyal United States citizens to answer "Dutch" or "Spanish" or "Latvian." These individuals are thinking of nationality as a social or ethnic term, not making a political comment. The fact that ethnic background can be the basis of a nation does not, however, mean that people must be related by blood to be members of the same nation. Switzerland, the United States, and the Soviet Union all include several ethnic groups. In fact, the Soviet Union contains about 120 separate and distinct ethnic groups. It is divided into fifteen union republics and several autonomous areas that reflect the territories of its most important ethnic cohorts.

Even when a nation is clearly identified by its ethnic makeup, the people of that nation can be divided into any number of different states. The German people are a good example. Basically, German people make up the bulk of the populations of East and West Germany, but the Austrian and Dutch people are also Germanic, or Teutonic, to say nothing of the inhabitants of several Swiss cantons (provinces). On the other hand, the Jews are a good example of a nation of people who, for a long time, had no country to call home. For thousands of years Jews maintained their national identity, linked by strong cultural patterns as well as by ethnic relationships, while they lived in countries dominated by other national groups. Although their folklore promised a return to the homeland at some future time, the movement to set up a Jewish state in Palestine (known as *Zionism*) did not develop until the nineteenth century. Finally, in 1948 the state of Israel was created, and many Jews left their former homes for the new country. Today there are about four million people in the *state* of Israel, yet many members of the Jewish *nation* are still living in other lands. Both the Soviet Union and the United States, for example, have large Jewish populations.

While a nation need not be organized into any particular state, it is indeed possible that a nation can evolve almost solely because its people identify with one another on the basis of residing in the same country. Few would argue that the people in the United States are not a nation. Indeed, we are a people who enjoy a very strong national identity. Yet, what factors draw us together? Being a people of enormous racial diversity, ethnicity certainly is not the focus of our nationhood. Though we speak a common language, English plays only a peripheral role in making us one people. "Baseball, hot dogs, apple pie, and Chevrolet" are hardly cultural features upon which our common bond exists. In fact, the American *nation* is founded upon the *state* itself. It is forged by popular support of concepts that can best be assimilated in the notion of the state: flag, country, democracy, liberty, tolerance, and so on. Although most Americans[2] do not consider themselves political beings, the fact that we tend to find unity with one another primarily through the context of the state makes us very political indeed.

While the term *nation* has no particular political implication, the term *state* certainly does. A description of the state normally includes four elements: people, territory, sovereignty (meaning ultimate legal authority within a given territory), and government. A nation can be located in several areas and need not be confined to any specific location. All states, however, have clear territorial boundaries. Moreover, these lands are served by governments that technically have final authority over all the people within their boundaries. The only characteristic shared by state and nation is people, who in modern societies see their state as the primary social unit. The state is a focal point around which people unify and through which they identify themselves. Thus, the individuals within the state are so closely bound together that they soon become a nation if they are not one already. Consequently, the state is converted into a *nation-state*. The term *nation* symbolizes the social unity of the people; the term *state* politicizes that union.

It should be noted at this point that while it is dominant today, the nation-state is only history's most recent political institution. Human beings have rallied to several other political organizations before adopting the nation-state. Among these earlier forms are tribes, city-states, empires, and feudal baronies. Since the nation-state is only the latest in a long series of systems used as principal organs of human political association, it is logical to expect that the usefulness of the nation-state will eventually become marginal, thus encouraging the evolution of yet another institution to replace it.

In the United States the terms *nation* and *state* have specific meanings other than those just explained. The Articles of Confederation, enacted in 1781, served as our first constitution. It was a compact among independent political entities under which the United States of America was created. In this case the name United *States* was completely justified, since the compact was indeed an agreement among sovereign entities. In 1789, however, the federal Constitution was adopted. Under this agreement the thirteen states surrendered their sovereignty to the central government.

[2]The term *Americans* is used here only because the phrase *United States citizens* is awkward and *United Statesians* sounds strange. There is certainly no intent here to deny our neighbors of North and South America their right to the same title.

Thirteen political entities, formerly independent, merged into a single state. If they had wanted to be completely correct in their terminology, the nation's founders would have renamed the union the United Provinces of America (or Cantons, or Departments). Instead, in this country as well as in several Latin American countries that have followed our example, the term *state* has two meanings. It can mean *country,* as it has traditionally, or it can be used as a synonym for *province.* To complicate matters further, we use the word *nation* to refer to the central government. Thus, we pledge allegiance to the flag, to the Republic, and to the *Nation.* Congress is our *national* legislature, and a *national* law takes precedence over the laws of the *states.*

Theories of the Origin of the State

We are now fairly certain that the state evolved because society had a practical need for it. As farming developed, people ceased their nomadic wandering and private property became important. The state probably evolved as a way of organizing society to maximize resources which had become limited when the people stopped moving. Further, the instruments of the state were used to define, protect, and transfer property. Yet, in previous eras, philosophers and theologians explained the origins of the state in several other ways. Many of these theories are probably true in particular cases; most of them, however, are demonstrably inaccurate, and some are even fanciful. True or not, however, these theories have motivated people, causing enormous impacts on political theory and on modern ideologies. Hence, we should at least consider the most important of them here.

The natural theory.   Aristotle, the father of political science, is an early prominent proponent of the *natural theory* of the origin of the state. He believed that people are basically good and that they constantly seek moral perfection, which they probably will never reach. Still, the quest for moral perfection is the noblest of human pursuits. Humans, according to Aristotle, are social beings by nature; that is, they naturally gather together and interact with one another, thus forming a community. This congregation takes place for reasons which go beyond simple biological necessity. The formal organization of the community is the state. The formation of the state is a result of people's natural inclinations to interact. Aristotle believed so firmly that the state was a society's natural environment that he claimed that people were human only within the state. An individual outside the state was either "a god or a beast," the state being the only environment in which one could be truly human. The state was the central institution in Aristotle's philosophy; it was not only the manifestation of our natural inclination to interact but also the vehicle through which the individual could achieve moral perfection.

To Aristotle the state was not merely a natural phenomenon, it took on a much more important characteristic. While it was made up of interacting individuals, it was actually greater than any single person or any group. It became an entity with a life, rights, and obligations apart from those of the people it served. This *organic theory* of the state was later supported by diverse people such as Thomas Aquinas, Rousseau, and Mussolini. Today's liberals also often refer to the organic society.[3] The

---

[3]The next chapter will establish that while individualism was the keynote of early liberalism, more recent liberal thinkers have turned increasingly toward a group, or social, orientation.

most extreme interpretation of the organic nature of society, that used by Mussolini, argues that the whole (the state) becomes something greater than the sum of its parts (the individuals within it).

The force theory. The *force theory* actually embraces two schools of thought. The original school goes back to ancient times. In this theory the state was created by conquest and force; it grew out of the forceful imposition of the strong over the weak. Therefore, the state was an evil thing that could be resisted in a righteous cause. As one might imagine, this particular attitude has been dogma to revolutionary groups through the ages: to the early Christians resisting the Roman Empire, to medieval theologians trying to make the temporal authority subject to the spiritual, to democratic insurrectionists leading the struggle against monarchical tyranny, and so forth.

The second school of thought embraced by the force theory developed in Germany during the nineteenth century. At that time almost every Western European area, except Italy and Germany, had developed into nation-states. Internal political divisions and external pressures had prevented the consolidation of these areas into modern political units. A nationalistic spirit had been growing in Germany, however, since the Napoleonic wars. It became exaggerated as a result of the frustration encountered by its proponents.

The theory of the forceful origin of the state was developed mainly by Georg Hegel (1770–1831) and Friedrich Nietzsche (1844–1900). Their theories form the basis of what is now called *statism*. They argued that the state was indeed created by force, but that rather than being evil, this feature dignified the state. Force was *not* something to be avoided. On the contrary, it was the primary value in society. It was its own justification: "Might makes right," as Nietzsche put it. The state, institutionalizing the power of the strong over the weak, simply arranged affairs as they should be. According to force theorists, the weak should be ruled by the strong.

Some students of Hegel and Nietzsche have argued that the state is the most powerful form of human organization. As such it is above any ordinary moral or ethical restraint, and it is greater than any individual. It is not limited by something as insignificant as individual rights. Although certainly neither Hegel nor Nietzsche would have been termed fascist or Nazi, Mussolini and Hitler used the force theory for their own purposes; so we shall return to a discussion of the ideas of these nineteenth century philosophers in Chapter 10. For now it is enough to remark that the force theory is probably the most extreme example of nationalism. It puts the state above the people, giving government a status that cannot be equaled or surpassed. Hence, the institution itself has power separate from that of the people under it. The state is a self-contained being, an organic personality in and of itself, all-powerful and total.

The divine theory. The *divine theory* is probably the oldest theory of the origin of the state. It is based on a fairly common assumption: Some people are God's chosen ones.

Saul, for example, was anointed by Samuel, the prophet of God, and Saul led the "chosen people" in the conquest of the Philistines. The Arabs conquered a vast empire and the Crusaders invaded the Middle East in the name of the "true religion," and Islamic fundamentalists still claim that they are the chosen ones. Similarly, the Japanese, believing they were favored by the sun goddess (Amaterasu) and convinced their emperor was her direct descendant, willingly died in the emperor's cause, thinking salvation awaited them for such martyrdom.

Early Christian theologians used the concept of the divine origin of the state to their own advantage. The early fathers of the Church, St. Ambrose (340–397), St. Augustine (354–430), and Pope Gregory the Great (540–604), argued that spiritual and temporal powers were separate but that both came from God. Each of these thinkers was ambivalent about the relationship between the state and the Church. Augustine and Ambrose implied that the state was subject to the spiritual leadership of the Church, but neither pressed the point too far. Gregory, on the other hand, believed that the Church should bow to the state in all secular affairs. Pope Gelasius I (492–496) first interpreted the *theory of the two swords* as it was to be applied during the Middle Ages. The spiritual and secular powers were both essential to human life, but they could not be joined under a single person. The primary function of each was to contribute to the salvation of people. The state helped pave the way to paradise, providing peace and order and creating the atmosphere in which people could best serve God. The Church was responsible for developing the true spiritual doctrine and giving people guidance toward their heavenly goal.

None of the early Christian fathers would have disagreed with any of these propositions. Gelasius I, however, went on to claim that the Pope should take precedence over the state. He was the first to argue that the Pope should be un-contradictable on questions of dogma. Further, he insisted that since the primary duty of both Church and state was to help people reach their eternal reward, the Church, being the *spiritual sword*, should prevail in disputes between these two basic institutions. John of Salisbury (1120–1180), a noted scholar, went even further than Gelasius I, stating that all temporal power actually came from the Church. Anyone who supported this theory would not question the superiority of the Church over the state.

The Church was generally regarded as the greater of the "two swords" throughout the medieval period, and princes normally accepted this notion, often reluctantly. Gradually, however, the intellectual advances of the Renaissance led to religious and political changes. National monarchs began to claim authority over secular affairs. At the same time, the Reformation challenged the Pope's spiritual absolutism.

Closer to home, the notion of *manifest destiny* was used to imply God's sanction for the United States conquering the North American continent and portions of the Pacific Ocean. Mormon doctrine teaches that the United States Constitution was divinely inspired, and a popular patriotic song suggests "God shed his grace on thee." Even President Reagan's 1983 assertion that the Soviet Union was an "evil empire," which threatens our survival, smacks of the divine theory born anew.

Whatever the particular notion, three generalizations can be drawn about the divine theory: (1) Virtually every group of people has, at one time or another, seen itself as chosen above all others in the sight of God; (2) Divine selection has invariably been self-recognized—the chosen people have usually discovered their privilege by themselves, rather than having it pointed out by less fortunate folk; (3) The discovery of such exalted status has usually preceded activities against other people—actions, such as conquest, which could scarcely be justified without self-proclaimed superiority.

Martin Luther (1483–1546)

Divine right of kings theory.   Inevitably those supporting absolute monarchy and those challenging the centralization of spiritual power joined forces in the *divine right of kings theory*. This contention was put forward as a counterproposal to the ancient theory of the two swords. Pierre de Belloy (1540–?), a lawyer, first expressed the divine right notion. Later it was expanded by Jean Bodin (1530–1597), who gave it philosophical respectability when he developed his theories about the origin of the state and sovereignty.

Some early Christians believed in the *original donation theory,* which is somewhat compatible with the divine right of kings theory. It was contended that Adam and Eve's fall from grace and their banishment from the Garden of Eden resulted in God granting Adam the right to rule the temporal state and that all later kings were his heirs.

Like the ancients, adherents of the divine right of kings theory believed that all power came from God, but they differ from the churchmen by suggesting that God specifically chose the king and gave him absolute power (authority unrestrained by the monarch's subjects). Here these absolutists were joined by the Protestant reformers Martin Luther (1483–1546) and John Calvin (1509–1564), who proposed the theory of *passive obedience.* The Reformation and absolutist factions agreed that political power came from God and that those who were chosen to exercise it were higher on the social scale than ordinary people. Consequently, people were duty bound to obey the prince, even though he be a tyrant, because he was God's magistrate on earth. Sinful kings would be held accountable to God.

This theory had a tremendous impact. Claiming legitimacy from divine authority as well as from civil right, monarchs became extremely powerful in this religious era. Popular refusal to obey the king was seen as heresy as well as treason. The absolute monarchy of Louis XIV of France was based on this theory, and the Stuart house of England was purged because of it. As the basis on which the national sovereign built his power, the divine right of kings theory was central to the development of the nation-state system. Perhaps equally important, the theories of popular sovereignty and democracy were developed in opposition to the divine right of kings theory.

The social contract theory. Although the idea of a *social contract* will be studied more completely later, a brief sketch of this theory, so central to our understanding of the state and the ideology of democracy, is necessary here. The idea that government was created by a contract is an old one. The notion that ruler and ruled agreed on their respective roles and had obligations to one another can be traced back through millennia. Interpretations of the contract varied from time to time, but the ruler generally benefited from the theory more than the subjects. Still, the idea that the ruler governed by the consent of the governed was always implied by this theory.

The divine right of kings theory was used by monarchs to claim that there should be no limits on their political power. Opponents of absolute monarchy needed arguments to use against this powerful theory. The social contract theory as it developed in the seventeenth and eighteenth centuries was based on the concept of *popular sovereignty,* in which the ultimate source of the power of the state was the people.

The contract, it was argued, was established when the all-powerful, or sovereign, people made an agreement that created the state and gave the ruler of the state certain powers. However, social contract theorists disagree as to the exact form of government the contract created and the limitations placed on the powers of government by the sovereign people.

The social contract theory will be discussed more fully in Chapter 3. It is important to note, however, that this theory is a major contributor to the ideology of nationalism. Under the social contract theory the state is created by all the individuals within it. Therefore, the state is of them, and at the same time they are part of it. This close interrelationship between the people and the state is fundamental to nationalism. The social contract theory gives the individual an important role. At the same time, it describes the combination of individuals into a whole that is different from, yet related to, its individual parts and, according to some theorists, has a greater power and justification than the simple sum of its parts.[4] Because of its close relationship with individual rights in some theories of the state, some scholars argue that nationalism is in the liberal tradition. In fact, nationalism is more comfortably situated on the right of the political spectrum, for the reasons developed in the next section.

---

[4]This refers to the organic theory already mentioned in this chapter and developed further in subsequent chapters.

The Theory of Nationalism

Nationalism is a relatively new phenomenon. While it began to emerge as long ago as the twelfth century, it did not become an established political institution until much later. Developing at the same time as the Age of Enlightenment, nationalism was a response to the growth of trade and communications accompanying the era, but it was not until the French Revolution that nationalism became an irrepressible idea. Since then, nationalism has grown in influence, until today it is the most powerful political idea in the world.

Nationalism is an abstraction. Rather than giving loyalty to a person like a noble or a king, people are asked to commit to an idea, to a tradition, to a history, to a notion of fraternity. Nationalism represents the union of a political phenomenon with the identity of the human being. As a frame of reference for individuals and their societies, it dominates the modern world. This is especially true of Western civilization. While oriental societies tend to see social phenomena, such as the family, as the primary institutions, we in the West are much more political in our viewpoints. For example, if one were to ask a group of people from various Western countries to identify themselves, it would not be long before they mentioned the nation-states of which they were citizens. People in Western societies identify very strongly with their home countries, and patriotism is a common phenomenon in the West.

Several attempts have been made to differentiate between *nationalism* and *patriotism*. None of these has been very successful, however, because none has taken into account the theoretical nature of nationalism as opposed to the activist nature of patriotism. Put simply, nationalism is the theory of the modern nation-state. It is the theoretical basis for the organization of the world's people into about 170 political units, each claiming to be sovereign.

Patriotism, on the other hand, is not a theory but an act or gesture of loyalty or commitment to the nation-state. Nationalism describes the nation-state and offers a theoretical justification for it. Patriotism is saluting the flag or singing the national anthem; it is a feeling of commitment to the institution that is expressed by nationalism. Put differently, patriotism is to nationalism what religious worship is to theology. Patriotism is a form of secular worship of the nation-state.

The emotional attachment to nationalism is so strong because nationalism gives the individual an identity and extends that identity into something greater than the self. Nationalism does more than simply describe a political entity. It creates a mirror in which individuals see and define themselves. It is also a prism through which the individuals observe, assess, and react to events and to other people.

Nationalism has certain transcendental qualities, evoking a sense of history and purpose for its followers. As Edmund Burke put it, "it becomes a partnership not only between those who are living, but between those who are living, those who are dead, and those who are to be born." It requires that its followers sacrifice everything—family, fortune, even life itself—for the good of the state if necessary.

L. T. Sargent points out that the emotional nature of nationalism makes it the most powerful of all political ideas. It affects the individual more deeply and needs less reinforcement than any other political idea system. It unifies people and gives them a common basis for identifying themselves and one another. It sets up a value system and provides a mechanism through which the needs of the society can be met. And as mentioned earlier, it has stimulated some people to perform extraordinary deeds.

At the same time, however, nationalism establishes an artificial barrier between groups of people. Human beings are identified on a territorial basis, a property division if you will. Nationalism encourages people to define their interests and values in terms of something less than the good of humanity as a whole. Hence, it tends to work against the ethic of human rights. Because of its emphasis on the values of property at the expense of human values, nationalism, as I mentioned above, is found on the conservative side of the political spectrum. It is to this spectrum that we now turn our attention.

SUGGESTION FOR FURTHER READING

BARON, S., *Modern Nationalism and Religion*. New York: Meridian Books, 1960.

BREUILLY, JOHN, *Nationalism and the State*. Manchester, England: Manchester University Press, 1982.

BROWN, L. B., *Ideology*. Baltimore: Penguin Books, 1973.

CHRISTENSON, REO M., ALAN S. ENGEL, DAN N. JACOBS, MOSTAFA REJAL, and HERBERT WALTZER, *Ideologies and Modern Politics*, 3rd ed. New York: Harper & Row, 1981.

ECCLESHALL, ROBERT, VINCENT GEOGHEGAN, RICHARD JAY, and RICK WILFORD. *Political Ideologies*, London: Hutchinson, 1984.

GELLNER, ERNEST, *Nations and Nationalism*. Oxford, England: Basil Blackwell, 1983.

GOULD, JAMES A., and WILLIS H. TRUITT, *Political Ideologies*. New York: Macmillan, 1973.

HACKER, ANDREW, *The Study of Politics: The Western Tradition and American Origins*, 2nd ed. New York: McGraw-Hill, 1973.

JENKINS, THOMAS P., *The Study of Political Theory*. New York: Random House, 1955.

KOHN, HANS, *The Idea of Nationalism: A Study in its Origins and Background*. New York: Collier Books, 1967.

KOHN, HANS, *Nationalism: Its Meaning and History*. Princeton, NJ: Van Nostrand, 1955.

SMITH, ANTHONY D., *Nationalism in the Twentieth Century*. New York: New York University Press, 1979.

SYMMONS-SYMONOLEWICZ, K., *Nationalist Movements: A Comparative View*. Meadville, PA: Maplewood Press, 1970.

THOMPSON, J., *Studies in the Theory of Ideology*. New York: Macmillan, 1966.

2

The Spectrum
of Political
Attitudes

PREVIEW

The terms *radical, liberal, moderate, conservative,* and *reactionary* are among the words most often used in political vocabulary. Besides referring to places on a spectrum of political attitudes, these terms bear such important political significance that no discussion of political ideologies is complete without reference to them.

    The concepts of political change and political values must be discussed in relationship to these five terms in order to gain a clear understanding of what these words represent. Radicals, those farthest to the left, are people who find themselves extremely discontented with the status quo. Consequently, they wish an immediate and profound change in the existing order, advocating something new and different. Radicals differ from one another in many ways but most importantly in the means they would employ to attain the desire modification.

    Considerably less dissatisfied than the radicals, but still wishing to change the system significantly, are the liberals. Liberalism enjoys a philosophical base which is divided into classical and contemporary eras. Although classical liberals tended to focus on the individual and on property rights while contemporary liberals see society as collective and emphasize human rights, both share a belief in the equality, intelligence, competence, and goodness of people.

    Moderates tend to find little evil in the existing society, and their reluctance to

Note: The drawing at the top of the page portrays Jeremy Bentham in the foreground and Edmund Burke in the background.

change it is exceeded only by that of the conservatives. Differing from the liberals in almost every respect, conservatives have little confidence in human morality or intelligence. Consequently, though the world may not be as pleasant as the conservatives might wish, they are dubious about efforts to change it for fear that incompetent meddling might, indeed, make things worse.

While each of the previous positions on the spectrum differs as to the speed, depth, and method of change necessary, they all advocate progressive modifications of society; that is, they propose changing society with new and different innovations. Only the reactionaries propose that policy be reversed, that institutions of previous eras be reinstated. Rejecting modern values, reactionaries would see society retrace its steps and adopt former political systems.

Simply knowing the intensity of dissatisfaction one feels for the status quo and what specific change he or she advocates is not always enough to accurately place a person on the political spectrum. The objective sought from a particular change is often more revealing than the degree of dissent expressed by the individual. This factor involves us in questions about the values held by people on the right or left of the spectrum. Basically, people on the right of the political spectrum revere authority, elitism, and property rights, while those on the left emphasize liberty, human equality, and human rights.

Beyond these philosophical convictions, there are several other motivations that cause people to lean to the left or right. Psychological factors are also important. Some people need stability in their lives and thus tend to oppose change. Others need change for its own sake, so they find themselves on the left. Still others, nostalgically, want things to be as they were in a former time. Economics also plays a part. The poor who have little to lose from change may hope to gain from liberal egalitarian policies, while the well-to-do may see proposals for change as threats to their best interests, thus aligning themselves on the right. Age is another factor. Generally, young people, having little stake in the status quo, are prone to the left. On the other hand, older individuals are inclined to support the preservation of society as it is.

Each of these factors predisposes people's political advocacies to certain policy alternatives. The controversy in the United States in the 1980s over the conservative "supply side" economics as opposed to the "demand side" economics favored by liberals is an excellent case in point.

UNDERSTANDING THE SPECTRUM

Before going further in our discussion of ideologies, it is a good idea to develop an understanding of certain basic political concepts. The terms *radical, liberal, moderate, conservative,* and *reactionary* are among the most commonly heard words in politics. Indeed, it is incumbent upon all who study, discuss, or participate in politics to truly understand them. Unfortunately, however, those who would learn the meaning of these terms may encounter some initial confusion because some of these words are often used incorrectly. To compound matters, some of these words have different meanings in ordinary parlance than they do when used in a political context.

Being used in political debate, these terms are often employed to convey the speaker's or writer's bias. A leftist politician is not likely to use the term conservative in a sympathetic or even objective manner. Nor is a reactionary political commenta-

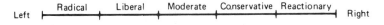

FIGURE 2–1   The Political Spectrum

tor prone to be kind when referring to liberals or radicals. In these pages, however, no value judgments are implied in the use of any of the terms. Our objective is to understand the terms, not to label them as necessarily good or bad. Later, you may choose to ascribe your own values to each term, but for now let us satisfy ourselves with determining what each means in political context.

Actually, any valid explanation of these political terms must include consideration of two basic concepts: *change* and *values*. We will begin with an analysis of the concept of political change. We shall then turn to an investigation of the meanings of these terms as they relate to intent, or political values. Before proceeding, however, we should arrange the terms *radical, liberal, moderate, conservative,* and *reactionary* along a continuum in order to gain a pictorial perspective on them. (See Figure 2–1.)

When they are arrayed from left to right in this fashion, we can see certain relationships among the terms with which we are concerned. For instance, the radical is at the far left of the spectrum, and the reactionary is at the opposite extreme. This alignment tells us something important. In politics the term *radical* means an extremist of the left but not of the right.[1] In everyday conversation, on the other hand, the term *radical* is usually used to refer to an extremist at either end of the spectrum. Sadly, even some political scientists use the term incorrectly in unguarded moments. Such will not be the case in this book. The term *radical* will be used only to indicate the far left of the political spectrum.

CHANGE

People at each point on the political spectrum have an attitude toward change in the existing political system (the status quo). Political change is fundamental to any society. By learning the attitude of each group toward change, we will be taking a large step toward understanding what the terms radical, liberal, moderate, conservative, and reactionary means. Be careful to note, however, that change is only one of the concepts with which we must deal in defining these terms, and that our definition will be complete only when we have also considered the basic values of various groups.

Political change is a complex subject, and we must actually learn four things about it. First, we must determine the *direction* in which the proposed change would carry the society. Put differently, is the change progressive or retrogressive? At this point the reader should be on guard. Our society generally has a favorable bias toward progress. This is so because our ideological origins are rooted in eighteenth-century British liberalism. But, in fact, progress is not necessarily good or bad. It has

---

[1]The terms *left* and *right* come to us from the French political tradition. Those who generally supported the policies of the monarch were seated to his right, and those who proposed changes in the system were arranged to his left.

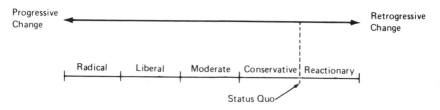

FIGURE 2–2   The Position of Status Quo on the Political Spectrum

no intrinsic value at all. *Progressive* change simply means a change from the status quo to something new and different. Conversely, *retrogressive* change refers to a return to a policy or institution that has been used by that society in the past. For instance, if one were to support the adoption of a compulsory public medical-insurance program, or "socialized medicine," if you will, such a position (in the United States) would be a progressive attitude toward the government's role in the field of public health. On the other hand, one might favor returning the present United States Postal Service to its previous status within the President's cabinet. Such a position would clearly be retrogressive in this society. The watershed between progressive and retrogressive change lies between the conservative and reactionary sectors, and the line between these two sectors can be taken to represent no change at all, or continuation of the status quo. (See Figure 2–2.) In other words, everyone to the left of reactionary is progressive—even the conservatives. Only the reactionary wants a change from the status quo to something that existed previously.

At this point some people might protest that they consider themselves conservative, but that on a given issue they would prefer a previous institution to the present one. Does this make them reactionaries? Yes, it does—in relation to that particular issue. Although they might correctly consider themselves conservative as a general rule, they—like most of us—will find themselves at several different places on the spectrum in relation to a variety of specific issues. Few of us are absolutely consistent in our views, nor is there any particular reason to be so. Indeed, upon careful scrutiny most people will find it difficult to place themselves in any single category because their attitudes on various issues will range over two or even three sectors on the spectrum. Typically, however, we can identify a general pattern; that is, we might find ourselves supporting liberal policies more frequently than any other position on the spectrum, and consequently we might correctly characterize ourselves as liberals.

The second thing one must determine is the *depth* of a proposed change. Would the desired change amount to a major or a minor adjustment in the society? Would it modify or replace an institution that is fundamental to the society as it now exists? If so, what is the likelihood that the proposed change will cause unforeseeable and uncontrollable effects once it is implemented? For example, a proposal at the state level to require a course in introductory political science for graduation from college would undoubtedly inconvenience and annoy some students. However, such a policy change would probably have almost no disruptive effect on the society as a whole. On the other hand, if a state were to greatly reduce its funding of the college system, the impact of such a policy would be enormous, changing thousands and perhaps millions of lives and eventually affecting the society as a whole. Further, although it is

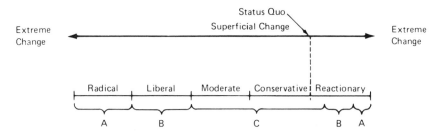

FIGURE 2-3   The Desire for Change as Shown on the Political Spectrum

possible to anticipate some of the consequences of such a policy change, it is impossible to accurately predict all, or even most, of the subsequent changes, problems, or benefits that might result from such an action. As a general rule, the more basic the change, the more unpredictable, disruptive, and uncontrollable its effects will be.

Once again, as with the direction of change, the watershed for the depth of change is at the line between conservative and reactionary, or at the "status quo" point on the spectrum. The farther people find themselves from the status quo, the more dissatisfied they are with the existing order and the more intense their desire for change. (See Figure 2-3.)

Individuals in the areas labeled A are extremely dissatisfied with the existing system and propose changes that would strike at the foundations of the society. In short, such change would revolutionize the society. People in the areas labeled B basically support the existing system but see many problems in it. They propose changes that would significantly modify the society but would leave its foundations intact. Those in area C are fundamentally content with the society as it is and would support only superficial changes. It should be noted here that the foregoing is meant only to show the intensity of dissatisfaction that the As and Bs have with the *status quo* and to demonstrate that the Cs are basically satisfied with it. With regard to how they would like to change the *status quo,* the radical As are completely at odds with the reactionary As and the liberal Bs oppose the reactionary Bs.

The third aspect of change that we must consider is the speed at which people want it to occur. Obviously, the more upset people are with the status quo, the more impatient they are likely to be and, therefore, the more rapidly they would like to see the existing order modified. Hence, although it cannot be claimed that there is an absolute correspondence between the depth of change people desire and the speed at which they would like to see modification occur, it is possible to argue that there is often a general correspondence between the two. Because both attitudes relate to a common factor (the status quo), the intensity with which people feel alienated from the existing system usually corresponds with the depth and rapidity of the change they desire.

The last factor we must consider regarding the concept of change is the method by which it occurs. Political change can take place in a multitude of ways: officially or unofficially; legally, illegally, or extralegally; peacefully or violently. It is tempting for some people to conclude that those who would use violence to gain their political objectives are extremists. This, however, is not necessarily the case. True, violence is a major tool of certain extremist political groups. However, *violence is used by people at practically every point on the political spectrum.* The death penalty, property expropriation, and warfare itself are examples of forms of violence supported by people distributed all along the political continuum. Thus, it is unwise to jump to conclusions about the methods others use to accomplish their political goals.

It is possible, however, to make some generalizations about the methods employed for political change. For example, the farther we are from the status quo on the political spectrum, the more likely we are to find ourselves in opposition to the laws of the society. This is so because the law is a form of communication that sets forth the purposes, goals, and structure of the society. People who are opposed to those purposes, goals, or structure will necessarily be at odds with the law. Hence, it is usually easier for conservatives to be law-abiding and patriotic, since they are satisfied with the system. Radicals, liberals, or reactionaries, by contrast, find it much more difficult to abide willingly by all the laws or to wave the flag as enthusiastically as their conservative counterparts.

Nevertheless, one should not assume from this discussion that conservatives would never violate the law to gain their political objectives. It sometimes happens that even those who control the laws of a society may not benefit from them at a given time. In such circumstances it is not unlikely that an otherwise upstanding "pillar of society" would ignore or even violate the law. Examples include the incredible career of the "law-and-order-man" Richard M. Nixon, the refusal of corporations to comply with legislated health and safety requirements, and the scheme of landlords to paint their homes in the suburbs and write off the cost as maintenance for their rental properties in the central city. Even the administration of President Reagan, the most conservative in decades, chalked up a record—unequaled by any in our history—for people convicted of corruption in office: witness the exploits of Lieutenant Colonel Oliver North and National Security Adviser Admiral John Poindexter, public officials who admitted deliberate violations of the law to address what they regarded as more important principles. Thus, it should be clear that the methods people use to achieve political change are complex. It is inaccurate to conclude that certain methods are the monopoly of a single sector of the political spectrum. It is usually safe to say, however, that those who identify least with the existing order are most apt to resort to illegal and perhaps violent means to bring about change.

With the preceding general guide in mind, let us now turn to a consideration of each term on the political spectrum to determine the specific attitude of each group toward the concept of political change.

Radical

The term *radical* is the most misunderstood of the five we are considering here. As explained earlier, it is often mistakenly used to refer to extremists on both the right and the left. Another common misunderstanding about this term is the belief that the radical is necessarily violent. *Not all radicals are violent.*

In general terms, a radical may be defined as a person who is extremely dissatisfied with the society as it is and therefore is impatient with less than extreme proposals for changing it. Hence, all radicals would favor an immediate and fundamental change in the society. In other words, *all radicals favor revolutionary change.* The criteria that distinguish one radical from another most clearly are the methods

FIGURE 2–4   Radicalism on the Political Spectrum

they would use to bring about a particular change. To illustrate this distinction, the radical sector has been divided into four sections in Figure 2–4. Note that these divisions are not intended to imply that there are only four different kinds of radicals. Rather, they are intended simply to point out the differences in degree with regard to the methods radicals might employ to get what they want politically.

Section A is, of course, the most extreme radical position. Individuals this far out on the political spectrum are extremely dissatisfied with the existing order and are probably greatly frustrated by it. Therefore, they propose not only that the system be *immediately* changed at its *foundations* but that it be changed by *violent* means. They believe that the society is so corrupt and so perverted that only fire will cleanse it. They argue that if change were to occur by any method short of violence, the reformers would have to compromise with the very people who are corrupting the present system, and that such a compromise would infect the new system with the same evils that made the previous one unacceptable. Hence, one must "burn [the system] down and rebuild on its ashes."

Sections B and C are variations on the same theme. People in these sections are displeased and frustrated by the existing system. Yet, since their position on the spectrum is slightly less distant from the status quo, one can expect that the intensity of their frustration, impatience, and extremism is somewhat tempered. Each group proposes basic change in the society and argues that the change must occur immediately, but they differ with the people in Section A, and with each other, over the need for violence. People in Section B argue that although violence is not essential to meaningful change, it is probably necessary. Because the change they propose is so disruptive of the status quo, those in Section B believe that anyone who supports the existing order "would rather fight than switch." Yet, the people in Section B do not insist that violence is the only way of bringing about meaningful change; they simply believe that it is the most likely way.

Those who find themselves in Section C of the radical sector are very reluctant to use violence as a method of bringing about change. They would use it only as a last resort. In other words, they are also frustrated with the system, and they also propose fundamental and immediate change, but violence is to be used only if change is impossible by any other means. If, however, they were asked to choose between change with violence and no change without violence, they would opt for the former.

People in Section D of the radical sector are not usually classified as radicals by the casual observer. But, after careful consideration, one must conclude that no other logical designation can be made for people of this persuasion. These people, like other radicals, propose fundamental and immediate change in the society, but they *refuse to use violence* to accomplish their political objectives. Excellent examples of this kind of attitude can be found in the careers of Mahatma Gandhi, Dr. Martin Luther King, Jr., and farm labor leader Cesar Chavez. Each leader organized great social movements demanding immediate and profound change, yet each refused to use violence to reach his goals, even after he had suffered violence at the hands of supporters of the status quo.

At this point, let me underscore a point made earlier. Many casual observers not only equate radicalism with extremism at both ends of the political spectrum but also assume that all radicals are violent. This assumption is definitely not the case. Considering the current values of most societies, refusal to fight for one's country constitutes an abrupt break with the norm and is therefore a radical position, but it is obviously not a violent one. Political pacifists are appropriately counted among the radicals because their refusal to use violence for political objectives is founded on an extreme belief in human rights. As you will soon learn, human rights is a value held most sacred on the left side of the political spectrum.

Having established that people can be radical without relying on violence, we confront an apparent contradiction. Earlier I said that all radicals favor revolution. Yet, if some radicals are pacifists, how can all radicals be revolutionary? The answer can easily be found by clearing up another common misunderstanding. People normally believe that all revolutions are violent. But, this is not so at all. Violence is not inherent in revolution. The term *revolution* means a profound or fundamental change in a social, economic, cultural, or political system that occurs in a relatively brief period. Violence often accompanies revolution because fundamental change occurring over a short period of time is likely to stimulate deep-seated anxieties, which may erupt in conflict. Yet, bona fide revolutions have occurred which have not provoked widespread acts of violence. Hence, while the American, French, and Russian revolutions were violent transformations of the political order of those countries, the Renaissance, England's Glorious Revolution, and the Jacksonian Revolution all represented fundamental changes in society without violence. Thus, they qualify as revolutions even though they were essentially peaceful.

Even though not all radicals are violent and not all revolutions provoke conflict, radicals tend to be received by their adversaries with inordinately severe reactions. Owing a great debt to the philosophy of Jean Jacques Rousseau, contemporary radicals make the establishment terribly uncomfortable. Extreme leftists challenge the most cherished values and assumptions of society. They reject the institutions of the establishment, calling for a more humane, egalitarian, and idealistic social and political system. In fact, they demand a society which many of us desire in the ideal but which, for practical reasons or for reasons of expedience or lack of commitment, we have been unable or perhaps unwilling to create. Put differently, the radical causes us to wonder if indeed we did not fail—if we settled for a less than perfect world because it was more convenient.

The radicals' contempt for society's values is so complete, their remedies so unorthodox, and, perhaps, the establishment's feelings of guilt at the thought that it may have failed so threatening, radicals are often feared with an intensity far beyond what is necessary to deal adequately with the challenge they pose. Accordingly, even though their numbers and influence do not demand such severe action, radical movements are often abjectly and totally crushed. The emotions prevalent among the establishment as a result of the New Left activities in the late 1960s and early 1970s reached levels far beyond those that should have existed given the size and power of the movement. This exaggerated response occurred not because the challenge threatened to succeed—far from it. The establishment's response, culminating in the

In 1970, protesting students were fired upon by National Guard troops at Kent State University in Ohio.

Chicago "police riot" which put down the Yippies in 1968, the shooting at Kent State University in 1970, and the 1970 peace march on Washington, D.C., during which 10,000 people were arrested in a single weekend, assumed violent proportions for different reasons. The frightening thing about the New Left movement was that some of the nation's youth totally rejected the values of their parents. The young radicals drove home the horrifying specter that the establishment generation had built lives on a series of naive and shallow values: (1) that the adults, worshipping materialistic idols, had wasted their lives; and (2) that time, the commodity which the establishment generation had least of, had been frittered away in pursuit of false goals which the youth, the nation's sons and daughters, contemptuously rejected. Clearly, this proposition could not be quietly accepted, and it was too terrifying to ignore. The perpetrators of such a disquieting challenge had to be smashed!

One last observation is appropriate to complete our understanding of radicalism. Since most of us are not radicals, we are often tempted to think of them as people who willingly refuse to abide by the established norms of society, deliberately setting themselves apart from "right conduct," and who must therefore pay for their transgressions. In many cases this perspective is no doubt true. Yet there is another way of regarding radicals. Is it not possible that society is the culprit, that instead of the individual being at fault for not accepting the values of the larger group, society wrongs the individual by defining its norms so narrowly as to exclude that person from the possibility of voluntary compliance? For example, what choice is given a person who believes it morally wrong to take another person's life in a society which compels its young to kill during wartime? Can we legitimately condemn people who believe the annual bludgeoning of seal pups in the Arctic is an inhumane slaughter of innocent creatures and who take steps to stop it? Does society act justly when it punishes civil libertarians in South Africa for advocating their cause, or American

Indians who struggle against the white man's law that defiles sacred Indian traditions and takes their land? Is a policy moral which punishes citizens for harboring Central American refugees fleeing deadly oppression in El Salvador and Guatemala, even as our government welcomes people who escape similar injustice in Nicaragua? When looked at from the perspective that society sometimes requires people to violate the dictates of conscience, radicalism may seem somehow less offensive and intransigent. Indeed, it conjures a question that has perplexed philosophers for ages: Does society, which is to say its opinion-makers, have the right to oblige the individual to violate personal moral convictions?

Liberal: The "L" Word

Since the liberal sector is closer to the status quo point on the continuum than the radical category, the liberal is significantly less dissatisfied with the existing society than the radical. Indeed, the liberal supports the basic features of that society. However, liberals are quick to recognize weaknesses in the society and therefore are anxious to reform the system. In general terms, liberals are not nearly as frustrated with the society as are radicals, but they are impatient with its deficiencies and therefore favor *rapid* and relatively far-reaching, progressive changes in the society.

One of the most fundamental differences between the radical and the liberal is the attitude of each toward the law. Since radicals are basically opposed to the political system that governs them, they are apt to see the law as one way in which those who dominate the society maintain their control. Hence, radicals find it hard to respect the law. Liberals, on the other hand, generally respect the concept of the law, and although they may want to change certain specifics of it, they usually will not violate it. Instead, they try to change the law through legal procedures. Liberals seek change in the system by several important means, but they reject any attempt to revolutionize the system because they support its essentials.

Liberalism is one of the intellectual by-products of the Enlightenment, of the scientific method, and ultimately of the Industrial Revolution. During the medieval era, people looked heavenward for Divine relief from their wretched earthly existence. Faith in human potential, as well as esteem for humankind in general, was very low. However, the discoveries of inquisitive people such as Copernicus, Galileo, and Bacon revolutionized people's attitudes toward themselves and their function in life. Through use of the scientific method, people began to make improvements in their material existence, and in so doing they began to develop confidence in their ability to solve many problems that they had previously borne with little complaint. It was not long before people began to conclude that if technological problems could be solved through the use of human reason, the same could be done with social and political problems.

This speculation led to the theory of liberalism. Optimism about people's ability to solve their problems is the keynote of liberalism. Hence, the liberal is apt to apply reason to every problem and to be confident that this will lead to a positive solution. It is this willingness to "trifle" with "tried and true" social institutions that causes the conservative such anxiety about the liberal.

Change has remained the major tool of liberalism throughout its long history. Consequently, its specific objectives have been revised from time to time. What was once desirable to liberals may be passé and unacceptable to them today, so that the exact meaning of liberalism has evolved over the years. For example, the original, or *classical liberals,* whose principal spokesman was John Locke (1632–1704), believed that all human beings were moral, competent, and intelligent. Further, Locke asserted that *natural law* (that is, certain rules of nature governing human conduct that could be discovered through the use of human reason) applied to all people in equal measure, thus assuring their fundamental equality. Revering the individual above all things in society, classical liberals believed that government oppressed people when it had too much power—therefore, the less government the better. In addition, private property was held in high esteem. Indeed, classical liberals believed that property was a natural right and that an individual's possessions were to be protected from government confiscation. More of this theory will be explained in Chapter 3, but for now it is sufficient to say that liberals have since moved beyond Locke's views. Some people, however, still cling tenaciously to this ideology, thus seeming enigmatic in a political system almost three hundred years advanced from Locke's time. A relatively well-known Lockean political party is the Libertarian Party, which has attracted some interest in recent elections.

Contemporary liberalism, as will be seen in Chapter 4, was fathered by Jeremy Bentham (1748–1832), and its followers continue to uphold several of the notions developed by their classical predecessors. Still viewing people as essentially good and intelligent, contemporary liberals remain optimistic about our ability to improve life through reason. Change, therefore, is still a major tool of the liberal. Human equality is another concept that the liberal continues to support, but the basis for the assumption of equality has changed. Few liberals still believe in the concept of natural law. Instead, the contemporary liberal is more likely to argue that although there are a wide variety of differences among individuals, we are all equal in our humanity and therefore are all entitled to fundamentally equal treatment. In addition, contemporary liberals prefer to use government as a tool to help improve the conditions of human life, rather than insisting, as did the classic liberals, that government stay out of people's affairs. Moreover, finding that some people have used their control of property to unfair advantage over less fortunate individuals, contemporary liberals temper their belief in the individual's right to accumulate property with their concern for the happiness of the society as a whole.

A vexing difficulty has traditionally plagued the liberals, and radicals for that matter. It is their inability to unify. Although people on the left often can, albeit after considerable debate, agree on what areas need reform, they seldom agree on the specific changes that are necessary. Since liberals and radicals propose to change the status quo to something that has not been tried before in their society, they may offer a great variety of alternatives, perhaps as many possible solutions to a given problem as there are leftists. When the leftists are finally able to unite, these unions tend to be relatively short lived, and the various factions soon lapse into internal squabbling. For this reason leftist movements tend not to last long.

Moderate

Moderates are fundamentally satisfied with the society, although they agree that there is room for improvement and recognize several specific areas in need of modification. However, they insist that changes in the system should be made gradually and that no change should be so extreme as to disrupt the society. Because there is a bias toward moderation in our society, we must be vigilant in our study of this political sector. Moderation as a cultural predisposition, for example, has elicited biting criticism from the fascists, who maintain that tolerance rewards mediocrity and discourages the unusual or excellent. Meanwhile, some leftists argue that resistance to serious reform benefits the status quo at the expense of the downtrodden masses. Other critics argue that the moderate position tends to attract a large number of people who are unwilling or unable to commit themselves to a definite political position. Instead of admitting that they are unfamiliar with a given issue, they will take what appears to be an objective stance, one that allows them "to see both sides."

Ironically, it is in our study of the moderate that the consideration of emotion, not reason, is relevant. Most radicals, liberals conservatives, and reactionaries are usually informed about issues and knowledgeable about alternative policies. Presumably they have considered the available options and have concluded that the system should be either revolutionized, modified, maintained, or returned to a previous order. Many moderates also are informed about current issues and have rationally weighed the alternative policies. Yet, there are many more who appear reasonable and sensible on the surface but never really take a position at all. If a person takes a definitely liberal or conservative stance, he or she is likely to be called upon to defend or at least explain it. However, people who call themselves moderates can usually satisfy their listeners by saying, "Each side has its good points." This equivocation tends to satisfy the American values of fair play and political moderation.

The reader must be careful not to misunderstand what is being said here. I do not mean to suggest that the moderate sector is the only one in which we find people who are uninformed on current issues; far from it. Nor do I wish to suggest that all or even most moderates are ignorant on those issues, and I certainly do not wish to imply that a moderate position on an issue is valueless. I do, however, maintain that because of the basic values of American society, a large number of people who do not understand the political system, but are unwilling to admit it, take a moderate position when pressed for an opinion because that posture is least likely to engender challenge or criticism in our society.

Conservative

Conservatives are the most supportive of the status quo. Being content with things as they are does not suggest that conservatives are necessarily happy with the existing system, however. Conservatives are often accused of lacking vision, but this charge is unfair. The difference between conservatives and liberals is not founded on the fact that the latter dream of achieving a better world while the former think the status quo is the best conceivable existence. In fact, conservatives may desire a future no less pleasant than the liberals—a future free of human conflict and suffering. The essential difference between the two viewpoints rests on their respective confidence in when (or, indeed, whether) the ideal can be accomplished. Thus, conservatives support the status quo not so much because they like it but because they believe that it is the best that can be achieved at the moment. Put differently, conservatives oppose change because they doubt that it will result in something better, not because they do not desire improvement.

Lacking confidence in society's ability to achieve improvements through bold policy initiatives, most conservatives support only very slow and superficial alteration of the system. The most cautious of them often resist even seemingly minor change. They tend to see an intrinsic value in existing institutions and are unwilling to tamper with them, claiming that to do so might seriously damage that which tradition has perfected.

To say that conservatives are satisfied with the status quo is certainly not to say that they are complacent. Indeed, conservatives are active not in seeking change, like their counterparts on the left, but in defending the system against those who they believe threaten it.

Of course, not all conservatives are equally resistant to change. Obviously, those closest to the status quo point on the spectrum are the least inclined to desire change. And, although it seems unlikely that many people are absolutely content with the system and are opposed to any change whatsoever, some people do take this position, and each of us could probably find some areas in which we would prefer no change at all. Still, most conservatives will accept some deviation from the status quo, be it ever so slight, and the change they will accept is progressive.

I said earlier that because they are satisfied with the society, it is usually easier for conservatives to obey the law, though on occasion even they will violate it to attain their political objectives. In fact, some conservatives are not above using the law to suit their own purposes. Vagrancy laws are a case in point. In some parts of the country the vagrancy laws have been relaxed during the harvest season. Then, when all the fruit has been harvested, these laws have been enforced once again, thus sweeping the transient laborers off the streets and out of the sight of the "good people."

Basically, conservatives are pessimistic about our ability to improve our lot through the use of reason. While they do not deny the importance of reason, they are wary of relying too heavily on it for solutions to human problems. Liberals and conservatives agree that people have complex natures composed of moral and immoral, rational and irrational impulses. They differ, however, on which attributes dominate. As you will recall, liberals believe that people are basically good and that they can generally be trusted to do the correct thing when left alone. Conservatives have less faith than liberals that people can use reason to restrain their animalistic impulses and their emotions; they mistrust human nature. Conservatives see people as relatively base and even somewhat sinister. Hence, the conservative view tends to favor authoritarian controls over the individuals in society.

Because they mistrust reason, conservatives often rely on irrationalist[2] rather than rationalist solutions to problems. For example, conservatives are more apt to

[2]Note: The term *irrationalist* is not intended to imply that conservatives lack the rational or intellectual prowess of their opponents. In this book the term *irrationalist* only applies to persons who see severe limitations in people's ability to solve problems through the use of reason. While reason is thought useful for certain minor tasks, conservatives look instead to elements beyond their own control such as institutions, authority, tradition, and religion for answers to the most serious difficulties.

Contrary to President George Bush's statements during his 1988 presidential campaign, our society is a product of the liberal tradition. The philosophies upon which our civilization is based imply confidence in human rationality to grasp the complexities of life and to improve conditions by using thought. Consequently, to be a rationalist is usually considered a positive trait and to be an irrationalist, a negative one. These, however, are value judgments which I do not wish to ascribe to liberal and conservative camps. Indeed, no value at all is applied to the terms *rationalist* and *irrationalist* in these pages. They are used only to describe attitudes regarding the potential of human reason.

found their religious beliefs on faith alone, while liberals seek more rationalistic bases for spiritual solace. Hence, the former are likely to gravitate toward fundamentalist faith—witness the Moral Majority—while religious liberals tend toward less absolutist beliefs. One must seek long and hard to find a liberal fundamentalist or a conservative Unitarian. The former faith teaches that people are essentially evil and emphasizes that fire and brimstone await the unfaithful. The latter dwells more on the positive aspects of people, emphasizing that mutual human understanding offers rewards found in no other way. By the same token, liberals are more likely to be atheistic or agnostic than are conservatives. It should not surprise the reader to find that most religions are basically conservative. Conservatives tend to be religious, and religions tend to be conservative—and they both rely on powers beyond human reason for the answers to their problems.

To conservatives reason is of limited use in making life better. They tend to place great importance on institutions and traditions that have evolved over time. They value longevity for its own sake and resist change in social institutions. This "stay with the winner" syndrome is supported by the belief that the justification for any institution today is, in part, the fact that it was worthwhile in the past. Obviously, this attitude encourages very little change in society.

Before leaving the discussion of how human reason and private property affect the views of people on the political spectrum, let us turn to a particularly interesting contradiction. On the face of it, one might be tempted to assume that the conservatives are the most apt to support conservation of the world's resources. This surmise, however, is not correct. Equating a natural environment with a desirable lifestyle and being far less solicitous of private property than their conservative counterparts, liberals are vitally concerned with preserving the wilderness and other natural phenomena for future generations. Conservatives, on the other hand, who tend to assess living conditions in materialistic terms and who hold private property rights to be virtually uncontradictable, are prone to encourage the development of natural resources, even at the cost of some of our national parks and monuments. The Reagan Administration's policies of allowing coal mining and oil drilling in many previously protected areas demonstrate such conservative views.

The foregoing controversy involves us in an intriguing irony. As rationalists, liberals tend to have faith in the human capacity to successfully apply reason to solve problems. Such faith in humanity was, after all, incubated by human progress in science, technology, and the mechanization of production. Conservatives, on the other hand, tend to be very critical of our ability to successfully use the rational process to find answers to our greatest problems. Yet, liberals tend to be the first to decry the application of technology to nature, a development which they argue is making our world increasingly artificial; whereas conservatives vigorously encourage the use of technology, arguing that it will lead to the greatest happiness. Each position tends to contradict its own ideological premise.

Liberals and conservatives differ also with respect to the concept of human equality. The liberal assumes that all people are essentially equal even though they have widely diverse characteristics. To the conservative this position is more wish than fact. In the conservative's opinion the differences among people are so great in both quality and quantity as to make any claim of human equality absurdly idealistic.

Here again we find a difference in emphasis dominating the debate between the two antagonists. Liberals recognize that people differ from one another: Some are stronger, more intelligent, better looking than others, and so on. But, the leftist argues, these are only superficial differences. The fact that all people are human—equally human—should be the condition that predisposes our conduct toward one another. "Cut a black man and he will bleed red," they argue, emphasizing that beneath the surface all people are alike. Conservatives take the opposite view. They are quick to recognize the biological similarity among people but argue that this fact is relatively unimportant given the enormous variation of qualities among people. To the liberal protestation about everyone having red blood, conservatives respond by asking, "So what?" Emphasizing that crucial inequalities have always existed among people, conservatives insist that to attempt constructing a society on any other assumption is pure folly.

Conservatism has, of course, long been a prominent political position, but it was not until Edmund Burke (1729–1797) put pen to paper that it was given a formal philosophical base. Many people had defended conservative positions before, but no one had dealt with conservatism itself with the brilliance or thoroughness of Burke.

The well-governed society, Burke argued, is one in which people know their place. "The rich, the able, and the well-born" govern, while the people of lower social rank recognize their betters and willingly submit to their rule. Should they refuse, should the ordinary people try to govern themselves, as in France during Burke's time, the ultimate result can only be disaster, for nothing noble can come from the mediocre.

Burke was not content, however, to see the elite rule with no admonition for temperance, for while they were the best in society, they too were human and plagued with the same frailties as the commoners, albeit to a lesser degree. The elite, according to the venerable British Parliamentarian, are responsible for ruling benevolently and effectively. Power is not to be used by the rulers to suppress the masses. Still, nothing good will result if either group pretends that inferior people share equal political rights with the ruling group. Decrying the "false" values of liberalism, Burke put his case bluntly when he wrote

> The occupation of a hair-dresser, or of a working tallow-chandler, cannot be a matter of honor to any person—to say nothing of a number of other more servile employments. Such description of men ought not to suffer oppression from the state; but the state suffers oppression, if such as they, either individually or collectively, are permitted to rule.

Interestingly, the present conservative position on private property is very close to the classical liberal attitude. The conservative believes that private property is an inalienable right of the individual and that it is one of the important factors that distinguish one person from another. As we will see later, conservatives believe that the property right dominates virtually every other right. Consequently, government has no legitimate power to interfere with the individual's accumulation or use of private property unless this activity causes injury, death, or the destruction of another's property, and even these conditions are allowable under certain circumstances. For example, conservatives have for years opposed government safety regulations for the automobile industry even though such regulations would reduce the number of fatal car crashes. Conservatives suggest that if people really wanted stronger fenders and air bags to protect them in collisions, consumers would demand such improvements in the marketplace. They argue that requiring such features by

Of all the arguments made by conservatives to justify their position, clearly the most attractive is the promise of political *order*. The preference for discipline alone attracts many people who might otherwise be drawn to other parts of the political spectrum. Radicals and liberals offer change, new ideas, different institutions; but even if these were to succeed, the process of change itself would disrupt the society for a time. As it happens, large numbers of people have very low thresholds for disorder. Thus, change—even though it might be for the better in the long run—disturbs them and they resist it. They are even willing to suffer a system that is somewhat harmful to their interests rather than go through any kind of abrupt dislocation in the pattern of their everyday lives. Order, then, is a powerful selling point for the conservative philosophy.

Reactionary

Earlier we learned that the term *radical* is the most misused of the five terms we are considering here because it is often applied to both the left and right extremes of the political spectrum. For the same reason *reactionary* is the least used of these five terms. Nevertheless, of all the political positions discussed here, only the reactionary proposes retrogressive change; that is, reactionaries favor a policy that would return the society to a previous condition or even a former value system. For example, we have witnessed a reactionary revolution with the overthrow of the Shah in Iran. Without going into detail about the nature of the movement formerly headed by the Ayatollah Khomeini, we can see that his advocacy of a return to a literal application of the ancient laws in the Koran was clearly a reactionary legal posture.

Before we go further with the definition of *reactionary,* however, we should return to Figures 2–1 through 2–4 and note that they are distorted in one important respect. As explained earlier, the intensity of opposition to the status quo increases as one moves farther to the left or right of the status quo point on the spectrum. The distortion in Figures 2–1 through 2–4 is in the length of the reactionary sector. In these diagrams the reactionary sector is no longer than any other sector, leading one to believe that a person at the extreme right of the reactionary sector is not more dissatisfied with the system than a person at the leftmost point of the conservative sector. Actually, nothing could be further from the truth. In point of fact, the person farthest to the right among reactionaries is just as frustrated as the person at the leftmost point of the radical sector. To be accurate in this respect, the reactionary sector should actually be extended so that it is as long as all the progressive sectors combined. (See Figure 2–5.)

As Figure 2–5 indicates, the intensity of feelings about the status quo and the actions proposed by people at different points on the spectrum demonstrate a huge range and an enormous variety. The reactionary sector extends from basic satisfaction with the society as it is on the far left to an extremely dissatisfied and frustrated attitude toward the status quo on the far right. While a moderate might cautiously support some gradual progressive change in the existing political order, a person at the center or at the left of the reactionary sector might support a mild reform that would adopt some of the policies of an earlier time. Further, just as the leftmost radical wants to destroy the present system and replace it with a brand-new one, the reactionary on the far right would destroy the existing system and return to former values and institutions. While the radical would lead us to the "brave new world," the extreme

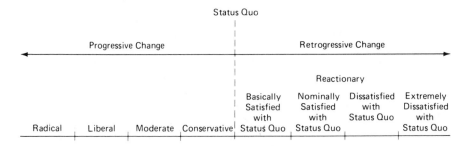

FIGURE 2–5   Reactionary Detailed on the Political Spectrum

reactionary would return us to the warrior state. Each position is equally revolutionary.

The progression in method is similar to the progression in intent. The closer people are to the status quo, the less impatient and frustrated they are and the more socially acceptable their methods. However, just as the Marxist at the far left insists that no change without violence is valid, so too the fascist at the extreme right argues that war is good in and of itself.

VALUES

Having dealt with the concept of change, the reader is now prepared to distinguish a radical from a liberal or a moderate. But the perceptive reader has probably begun to wonder whether one must not know more about people than their attitudes toward change in order to understand their political attitudes. For example, is it possible for a liberal and a reactionary to support exactly the same policy even when it proposes a basic change in the society? Yes, it is possible. The change itself is not important; what is significant is the anticipated result. Intent or expectation strikes at something much more fundamental in politics than simply the concept of change. It leads us to an investigation of basic political values and motivations.

For purposes of illustration, let us return to the question posed a moment ago: Can people on opposite ends of the spectrum favor the same change? Since World War II the United States government had deliberately pursued a policy of raising the national debt to purchase goods for which it has not paid. Generally speaking, leftists, citing the imperatives of Keynesian economics, have been less outspoken against the level of the debt, but neither side of the spectrum rejoices at the growing deficit. At the same time, administrations from both sides of the spectrum have used the debt in pursuit of their respective policies, indicating that each is willing to increase the debt in order to accomplish its ends. Indeed, Ronald Reagan, the most vociferous contemporary opponent of deficit financing, managed to borrow almost twice as much money as all previous presidents combined!

Spokespersons from both left and right have often argued against the debt, but for different reasons. Some rightists argue that being in debt is immoral and that the government should pay it off, thus setting an example for its citizens. Some leftists, on the other hand, seeing the interest on the debt filling the pockets of the rich who own the bulk of the bonds of which it is composed, argue against it on grounds that it simply represents one more device to funnel tax money from the poor into the coffers of the wealthy. Here we see two opponents advocating the same policy, elimination of the debt, but clearly their motivations and intentions differ markedly.

Perhaps the less esoteric subject of abortion can be used to underscore the same point. On what grounds might abortion be supported or opposed? Although a pro-abortion stance is usually seen as a liberal position, some conservatives have supported abortion, arguing that such a policy would reduce the number of unwanted children among the poor, thus indirectly reducing welfare costs. Liberals supporting abortion do so for an entirely different reason, claiming that a woman should not be arbitrarily prohibited from deciding her own fate by government regulations based on the establishment morality.

Yet, are there not opponents of abortion? Of course, there are many; they also come from both sides of the continuum. Taking a traditionalist stance, conservative opponents assert that pregnant women are morally obliged to bear their children to term and, except in extreme circumstances, they do not have the right to abort. Yet, liberals who oppose the death penalty because they reject society's right to take human life could oppose abortion for the same reason. Related issues, such as legalizing euthanasia, prostitution, and the use of heroin, can be argued on similar grounds by the various antagonists.

Another example of the phenomenon can be found in the 1988 congressional debate over aid to the *Contras*. With President Reagan's Central America policy in disarray, Congress vacillated on the question of continued aid to the *Contras*. At one point, an unlikely alliance of lobbyists for the *Contras* and for the Sandanistas occurred. With the congressional moderates undecided on the issue of future aid, the *Contras* supported a Democratic plan to give them $16 million for humanitarian supplies but nothing for military support. They took this position because they knew that this was their last chance to win congressional aid for some months. On the other hand, the Sandanistas supported the same policy—aid to their enemies—because they feared that the bill's failure would result in the congressional moderates supporting a military aid bill for the *Contras*.

A slightly different variation of the same theme can be seen in the congressional debate over whether or not the Constitution should be amended to prohibit defacing the American flag. The *conservatives want the change*—even though it constitutes the first amendment to the Bill of Rights in our history—while *liberals oppose the change*. Frustrated by his opponent's position, Senate Majority Leader, George J. Mitchell (Dem–ME.), said, "I can't for the life of me understand how so-called conservatives can urge amending the Constitution for one of the few times in our history and the Bill of Rights for the first time. . ." This seeming contradiction is easily explained, however. The conservatives want to protect an important patriotic symbol and favor the amendment to *preserve* the flag's dignity. Liberals, on the other hand, oppose the amendment because they feel it will deny one of the important civil liberties the flag represents, freedom of expression. Although each side is taking a different stance from their usual position regarding change, each side is completely consistent with their respective political values.

Clearly, then, intent, or political values, are important to our study and bear further inquiry. Unfortunately, the complexity of the subject is beyond the scope of this book, but it must be dealt with, at least superficially, as a conflict between *property rights* and *human rights*.

Most people in our society have a fairly good understanding of human rights, since such rights appear in general terms in the Declaration of Independence and in specific terms in the Constitution of the United States, especially the Bill of Rights. Human rights include life; liberty; the pursuit of happiness; freedom of press, speech, and religion; *habeas corpus;* and so forth. These rights and liberties were incorporated into our political tradition by the classical liberals of the seventeenth and eighteenth centuries.

As mentioned earlier, the private property[3] right was also originally thought to be a human right. Classical economists such as John Locke, Adam Smith, and David Ricardo were convinced that people could not be truly free unless they were allowed to accumulate private property. It was not long, however, before liberals observed that the control of property by some people could be used to deny liberty to others. Hence, the property right was quickly relegated to a secondary position in the priority of rights. Today it is considered a *social right,* but not a human or inalienable right, by liberals. Indeed, people as close to Locke's time as Thomas Jefferson and Jean Jacques Rousseau refused to recognize property as an inalienable right. One of the most hotly debated phrases in the proposed Declaration of Independence of 1776 was "life, liberty, and the *pursuit of happiness*" (emphasis added). People more conservative than Jefferson, its author, argued that the phrase should be changed to read "life, liberty, and *property*" (emphasis added), just as John Locke had originally written.[4] Jefferson prevailed in that debate, of course.

Liberals challenge private property as a human right on the basis that no necessary logical link exists between human well-being and *private* property. Human rights are those things which are necessary to the species in order to lead a decent human life. Consideration of the constituents of the phrase "life, liberty, and property" reveals that life is obviously an essential factor. Liberty is also fundamental if one accepts human equality as a reality. If people are equal, then no person has the moral right to subject another without consent. People, therefore, have the right to liberty. Private property, however, does not enjoy similar status since it is not essential for people to lead a decent human life. Food, clothing, and housing are, of course, necessary for people to enjoy life, but these things need not be privately owned. Yielding to this logic, and impressed by the fact that some people use their control of property to the disadvantage of others, Jefferson penned the more general phrase "pursuit of happiness," and he successfully defended it against those who wished to substitute "property" for it.

Later, however, in 1787, while Jefferson was serving as United States ambassador to France, a much more conservative group of men gathered in Philadelphia to write a new constitution. In it only scant mention was made of the rights of the people. Indeed, it was not until the Fifth Amendment was adopted that any general statement of inalienable rights appeared in the Constitution; that reference would read "life, liberty, and *property*" (emphasis added). Clearly, conservatives were in control of the country at the time.

---

[3]Please note that in this book the term *property* is being used in the broadest context. Hence, property refers not only to real estate but to all material items including money, clothing, furniture, and so forth.

[4]Locke actually used the word *estate* but *property* is commonly substituted for that term.

The term *property rights* is usually understood in the narrow sense; that is, a person may accumulate and use property without restriction so long as that endeavor does not injure anyone, damage another person's property, or unnecessarily interfere with someone else's property rights. This definition is useful for most purposes, but it is too restrictive for the distinction that follows. For our discussion the definition of property rights must be expanded to include territoriality or nationalism. As indicated in Chapter 1, nationalism, reduced to its simplest terms, is a kind of territoriality or property value. The concept of national sovereignty implies an exclusivity, an isolation of people within their respective states. Thus, there is a possessiveness about nationalism, and a personal identity with the nation, that approaches the property ethic we find on a smaller scale.

As a general rule we can conclude that those toward the left on the political spectrum tend to give the greatest emphasis to *human rights,* while those on the right tend to emphasize *property rights.* For example, if one were to ask a liberal whether a person has the right to refuse to sell a piece of property to a black, he or she would certainly say, "No! As long as the black has the money to buy the property, the seller has no right to refuse to sell." Notice that liberals are not unappreciative of the property right. Clearly, they insist that the prospective buyer have the amount of money asked by the seller. With that condition satisfied, however, the liberal would require that the sale be completed. In this case the liberal's position is predicated on the assumption that a black has the right to be treated like any other person because the black is basically equal to any other person. The emphasis is definitely on human rights.

On the other hand, if the same question were put to conservatives, their response would be different. They would probably say that while racial prejudice is unfortunate, if property owners insist on refusing to sell their property to a particular person on the basis of racial prejudice, they have every right to do so. Why? Because it is *their property.* Here the conservative recognizes the conflict between human rights and property rights, but the property right obviously supersedes the human right; property holds forth over equality. The conservative might even argue that the property right is one of the human rights. Even if that were the case, close scrutiny of the conservative's attitude toward various human rights would show the conservative insisting that the property right dominates all other rights.

Let us put another question to the same test. Should you be able to shoot a person who is breaking into your home? The conservative would say yes, if that is the only way you have of defending your property. The liberal would argue that no piece of property is worth a human life; therefore, one does not have the right to shoot a burglar (unless, of course, the life of the owner is threatened).

As already mentioned, the balance between human and property rights becomes increasingly one-sided as one moves toward the ends of the political spectrum until, at the farthest extremes, one side insists that there is no property right and the other totally denies human rights. On the far left, Karl Marx predicted that socialism would be democratic, allowing absolutely no private property or inequality. Benito Mussolini, at the opposite extreme, denied human rights entirely, insisting that people had no justification, no rights, no reason for being that was not bound up with the nation-state. Indeed, the individual's only function was to produce for the good of the state, and anyone who failed to do so could be liquidated.

To further dramatize the differences between left and right, let us consider the various goals that arise from their respective values. The left is inclined toward *egalitarianism.* Socialism, generally thought to be a leftist economic theory, tends to level the society and produce material equality because one of its main goals is to reduce the gap between the haves and the have-nots in a society. Marx envisioned a form of socialism in which all people would have all things in common. The means of production would be held by the society as a whole so that no one could profit from the labor of others.

Politically, leftists advocate an egalitarian society as well. Radicals tend to propose pure democracy. Both Rousseau, the founder of modern radicalism, and Marx demanded that political power be shared equally by all people. Liberals, on the other hand, accept representative government but insist that political power remain in the hands of the people, who control the leadership.

By contrast, the right is unabashedly *elitist.* Capitalism is today a conservative economic system. This was not always so. Adam Smith, who fathered modern capitalism, was a classical liberal of the eighteenth century. Do not forget that the liberal attitude toward private property has changed and that in Smith's day the prevailing economic system was feudalism combined with monopolistic mercantilism (see Chapter 4). Capitalism represented a liberal challenge to the status quo. Today, however, capitalism *is* the status quo; hence, support of this system in a capitalist country is necessarily a conservative position.

Capitalism tends to stratify our society. Those who are successful are respected and rewarded. Those who are not are abandoned as failures. The net result is that the society becomes hierarchical, a circumstance thought desirable by people on the right.

Politically, rightists advocate an elitist structure as well. Believing that people are somewhat unequal, animalistic, and in need of guidance, conservatives and reactionaries favor a society in which superiors command while subordinates obey. The farther to the right we look, the more structured and *authoritarian* is the desired society, until at the extreme right we come to Mussolini's fascism. Mussolini saw his society as a sort of social pyramid. At the base were the masses, whose duty was to perform their functions as well as possible. They must not fail to reach their level of greatest productivity, nor should they aspire to heights beyond their abilities. Those who underachieved, or who tried to exceed their potential, could be liquidated. At the top of the pyramid was the party and, ultimately, the leader. The leader's function was to perceive good, justice, and right, and to rule the society accordingly. The masses were expected to obey without question because the leader was considered infallible.

Finally, the left tends toward *internationalism* and the right toward *nationalism.* Leftists speak of all people being brothers and sisters, arguing that national boundaries are artificial and unnecessary divisions setting people against one another. Marx, for instance, asserted that national boundaries would disappear between socialist systems because "working men have no country." Eventually the world would become a single socialist brotherhood. In an earlier generation French revolutionaries borrowed from Rousseau, demanding a system dedicated to "Liberty, Equality, [and] *Fraternity*" (emphasis added).[5] Conversely, fascists exalt differences

---

[5] It is worth noting here that the fraternal, or social, aspects so prominent in the French Revolution were not very important in the American Revolution. Because America was blessed with an abundance of land and natural resources, opportunity was not as severely restricted in America as in the more stratified European societies. Hence, the American Revolution was almost completely political in nature. No serious attempt was made to realign the social structure or to redistribute the land in America. Because our

between individuals within a state and dissimilarities among states. As people are ranked according to their value within a society, fascists argue, so too will state dominate state until one state rises above all others.

SOME GENERAL OBSERVATIONS

Before we end our discussion of political attitudes, a few general observations should be made regarding the various factors influencing individuals to take particular positions on the political spectrum.

Motivation

Many people suspect that economic pressures are the primary motivation for choosing a particular political position. This does indeed seem to be an important factor. People who are doing fairly well in a given society usually do not want to disrupt the system. On the other hand, the poor have little to lose and much to gain from progressive change. It is tempting to resent the wealthy conservatives' defense of property rights. But are the poor, who support the redistribution of property so that they can benefit, any less selfish?

Economics is not the only factor in the choice of a political philosophy, however. There are plenty of poor conservatives, and one can easily find rich liberals. The well-to-do are often found at the forefront of the battle over issues such as integration, consumer protection, conservation, legalized abortion, and decriminalization of marijuana use, whereas the poor are often indifferent to, or even resist, liberal suggestions for reform. In fact, there is no single motivation for people's political attitudes. The list of motivations is probably as great as the number of people with political attitudes. In the following paragraphs we will discuss only a few of the most important factors influencing people's political choices.

Age seems to be a significant factor. Although Ronald Reagan attracted a large number of young people to his cause, generally speaking, youth is more likely to be liberal than the aged. This is probably because the older generations have a vested interest in the status quo that the younger generations have not yet acquired. Young people lack not only wealth but also a sense of commitment and belonging. Fifty-year-olds are likely to feel that they have a stake in the society, not only because they have become used to it, but also because they helped create it. The young have neither of these reasons to be committed to the system. As with all such generalizations, however, exceptions prove the rule. There are plenty of young conservatives, and some people grow more liberal with age.

Some people are also more *psychologically suited* for liberalism or conserva-

---

revolution simply constituted a transfer of power from the English to the American elite, it has not been a model for European revolutions. It is true that the success of the American Revolution encouraged Europeans to seek change in their lives, but the changes needed in Europe were far more sweeping than those desired on the American side of the Atlantic. European revolutions became vehicles for economic and social change as well as for political transformation. Hence, the French Revolution, the world's most influential revolution, became the model for all subsequent European upheavals. Indeed, due largely to our unique social and economic environment, American politics has never been very similar to public affairs in Europe, a fact that sometimes causes serious misunderstanding on both sides.

tism than others. To be a liberal, one must have a relatively high tolerance for disorder. Many people do not, so that while they may not benefit materially from the system, they resist change because they dislike disorder. On the other hand, some people seem to need almost constant change. The status quo never satisfies them simply because it *is* the status quo.

Perhaps the greatest single determining factor as to whether one will tend to the left or right is what he or she feels the *nature of people* to be. If one believes that people are essentially bad, selfish, and aggressive, then that person is likely to lean to the right of the spectrum. Anyone who thinks that people are inherently evil will tend to rely on strict laws and firm punishment for violators in the belief that such measures are necessary to control errant people. On the other hand, people who believe their fellows to be essentially moral and rational will lean toward the left. They will try to avoid impeding human liberty by unnecessarily severe laws and they will try to reason with offenders. Thus people on the right tend to believe that prisons should be institutions for punishment, forcefully teaching transgressors to behave, whereas leftists see prisons as institutions for rehabilitation. Believing that denial of liberty is punishment enough, leftists hope to use penal institutions to school criminals in socially acceptable behavior and to give them skills that they can use to make a living honestly, thus avoiding a life of crime. The crux of the matter rests in assumptions about human nature. Those who believe that people are fundamentally bad are likely to insist on stern measures to show that misbehavior is painful, whereas those who believe people are naturally rational and moral will try to educate transgressors with less strident techniques.

The Changing Spectrum

Just as people's views can modify over time, thus changing their location on the continuum, the spectrum can shift to the left or right while a person remains stationary. Ronald Reagan was a liberal New Deal Democrat in the 1930s. By the 1960s he had become a reactionary Republican, and as such he served two terms as governor of California (1967–1975) before becoming president of the United States in 1981. During Reagan's first term as governor a reporter asked him why he had left the liberals. His answer was, "I didn't; they left me." Reagan was arguing that the things he wanted in the 1930s had been enacted and that he was satisfied with this achievement and did not want further change. Whether Reagan's assessment of himself was accurate is not important here; the important thing is that if we were to remain unchanged in our political attitudes for thirty or forty years while the world changed around us, we might very well become reactionary after having been liberal because the status quo would have changed so much in the meantime.

It is also appropriate to point out that the political spectrum of a society bears no particular similarity to that of any other society unless the status quo is the same in both. Hence, a given policy could be conservative in one society, liberal in another, and radical in a third. (See Figure 2–6.)

Let us assume that the issue we are dealing with is labor strikes for public employees. In England, strikes by labor unions are common. While they may not be completely appreciated, they are accepted by the general public as a legitimate means by which labor can pressure for an increase in benefits. This attitude even extends to public employees. Thus, for a person in England to support strikes for most workers

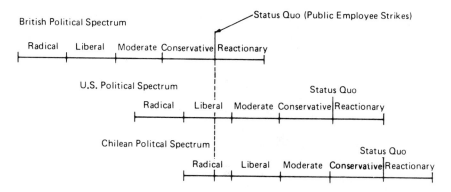

FIGURE 2–6   A Comparison of Political Spectrums

(including most public employees) would be quite conservative, since it is supportive of the status quo.

In the United States, labor strikes also are fairly common and accepted; however, the question of a public employee's right to strike is far from settled. Anyone, therefore, who supported strikes for public employees in the United States would be taking a fairly liberal point of view.

In Chile, on the other hand, all strikes are illegal. Thus, to support the legalization of strikes for workers would be very liberal and to suggest the same for public employees would certainly be radical.

SPECIFIC POLICIES

At this point, it might be helpful to translate some of the previously discussed general ideological points into practical policy as related to United States politics. Basically, the politics of any country can be divided into two main arenas: foreign and domestic. Let us assume that the goals of our society can be generalized in the form of two major objectives: peace and prosperity. Since the Great Depression of the 1930s American politics has usually fluctuated along a rather narrow area of the spectrum, between mildly liberal and conservative policy alternatives. Given this fact, what specific policies might one expect from the establishment right and left in the United States in pursuit of the goals described above?

Foreign policy.   Believing that people are self-oriented and competitive, conservatives are likely to assume a relatively suspicious posture in dealing with foreign governments. Accordingly, they are apt to rely heavily upon a strong military capability to preserve the peace. Resorting to cliché, we can readily identify the slogan "The way to preserve the peace is to be prepared for war" as a distinctly conservative approach to foreign policy.

Given the propensity among conservatives to be suspicious, we can expect that the hallmark of their relations with other states will be a strong military posture

A Peace Corps worker instructs youngsters in a third world country.

buttressed by mutual defense alliances with their friends against those whom they perceive as adversaries. Their foreign aid programs will tend to emphasize military assistance, thus strengthening their allies. The thrust of their policies will be directed at guarding against the incursions of their foes. They tend to view gains by their adversaries as losses of their own, and vice versa. Essentially, the world is viewed in adversarial terms, with the opponent seen as the aggressor. Since conflict is considered inevitable, little hope is held out for sustained amicable relations until the adversary conforms to the conservatives' views.

The liberal approach to foreign affairs is considerably different. Liberals hold that people are fundamentally moral and are capable of solving their differences rationally. Warfare is regarded as abnormal, while peace and cooperation are considered natural to human beings.

While liberals certainly do not ignore the martial aspect of foreign policy, they place much less emphasis on it than do their conservative counterparts. Their confidence in human reason is clearly displayed when they counter conservative militarism with the attitude that "the way to preserve the peace is to discover and eradicate the causes of war."

Deemphasizing military solutions, liberals tend to rely heavily on economic and technical aid to strike at what they conclude are the causes of war: poverty, disease, ignorance, intolerance, and so on. Further, liberals look to exchange programs among intellectuals, artists, and ordinary people as a means by which tensions can be reduced. This approach is based on the assumption that people will generally get along better if they understand one another; ignorance breeds fear, mistrust, anxiety, and conflict. Accordingly, liberals are likely to place great store on institutions such as the Peace Corps, the United Nations, and the World Bank, institutions which conservatives view with suspicion. Liberals support these organizations because they believe that they give the greatest promise of letting rational beings solve their problems peacefully.

Domestic policy.   As a general rule it can be assumed that, all other things being equal, liberals will spend more on domestic programs than will conservatives. This principle also pertains to foreign policy, but to a lesser extent. Liberals not only spend more money, but they release it on a broader base in the society, among people who are apt to spend it again quickly. For their part conservatives usually spend much less on domestic policy, and they release money among far fewer people—people who are also least likely to spend it again quickly. Consequently, liberal policies tend to place inflationary pressures on the economy by increasing the volume of money (the number of dollars in circulation) and the velocity of money (the frequency with which dollars are spent). Conservative policy reverses the liberal emphasis, thus exerting deflationary pressures on the economy.

Specifically, conservatives argue that ours is an industrialized economy. The health of the country is therefore dependent on a sound industrial base. Hence, although government involvement in the economy should be kept to a minimum, government should engage in efforts to secure the industrial base.

This view, referred to as *supply side economics,* calls for money to be funneled from the government directly to big business by various means, such as reduced government regulation of business, increased subsidies, increased tax write-offs, lucrative government contracts, guaranteed loans, free grants of government-funded research, high protective tariffs, low-level import quotas, and so on. The theory suggests that the captains of industry will use the added revenue to increase productivity through the purchase of new factories and machines and will also improve the condition of the workers by increasing wages, improving working conditions, and augmenting fringe benefits. Opponents refer to this as the *trickle down* effect.

These policies, however, must be paid for by someone. Hence, conservative economic policies usually increase taxes on the poor and the middle class while reducing government services to them through cuts in social programs such as government aid to education, job training programs, social security, and so on. (See Figure 2–7.)

Liberals argue to the contrary, contending that people, not industry, are the nation's principal resource. The benefits of direct government support should go to the people as a whole rather than to the wealthy. Having their spending power increased by government programs, the people will purchase the goods produced by industry, thus affording its profits to increase wages and capital investments.

However, these policies must also be paid for. Hence, liberals would reverse the policies of the supply side technique, substituting what might be described as the *demand side,* which increases government regulation and taxation of big business. (See Figure 2–8.)

Interestingly, however, since liberal policies are so much more expensive than conservative programs, reversing the flow of money alone is not enough to cover the costs. Hence, besides increasing taxes on industry and the wealthy, liberals would ask the middle class to pay more taxes as well. Comprising the bulk of the taxpayers, and being less protected than the very wealthy or the very poor, the middle class would be asked to carry the bulk of the tax burden under either plan.

The arguments by each side against the other's programs are familiar. Conserv-

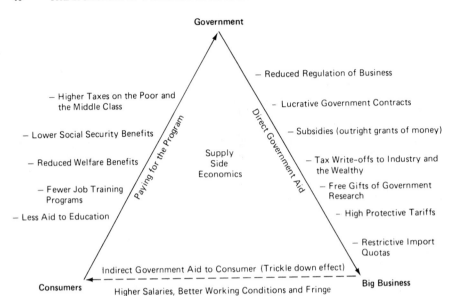

FIGURE 2–7   Supply-Side Economics

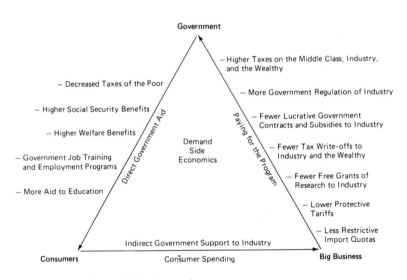

FIGURE 2–8   Demand-Side Economics

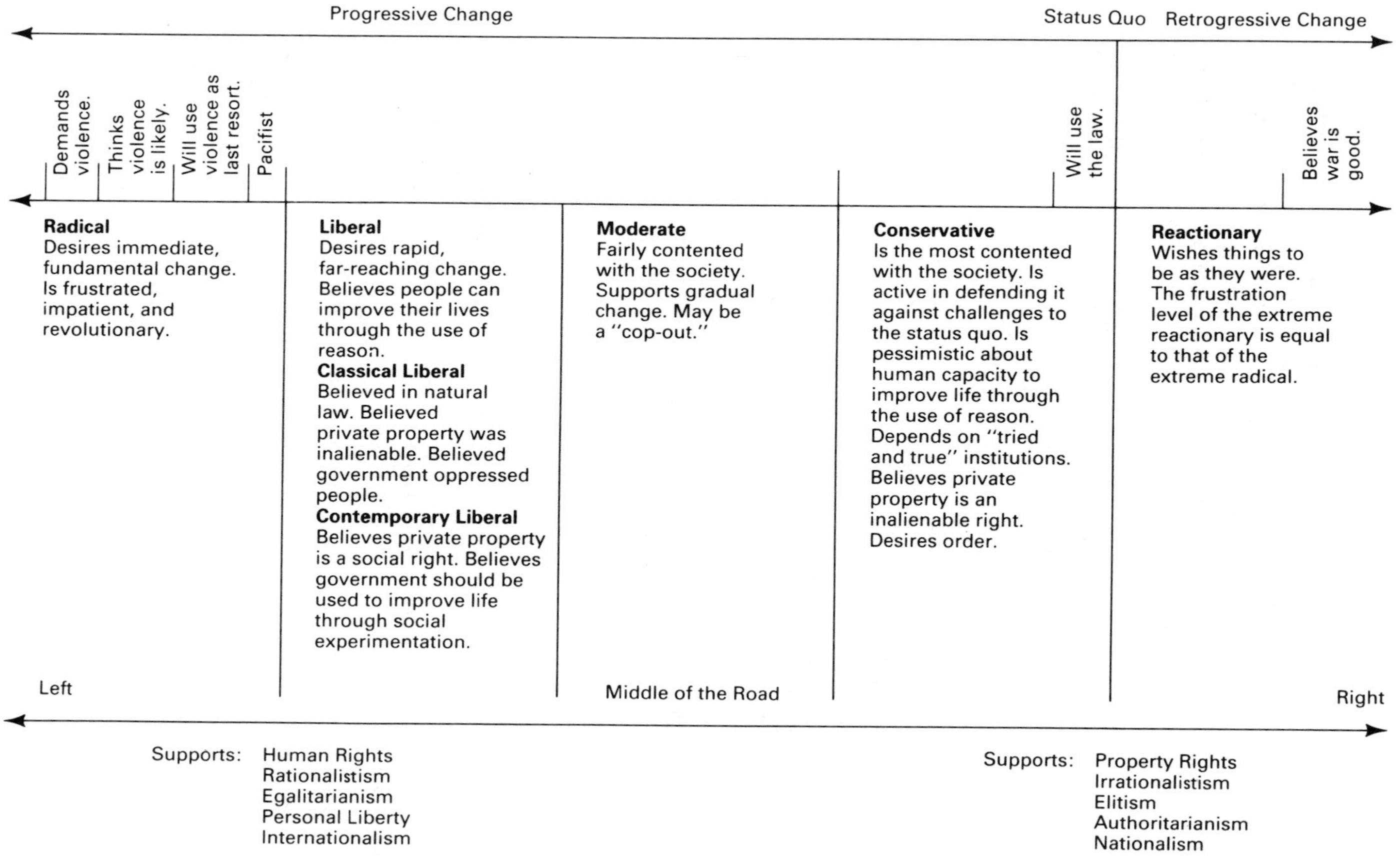

Progressive Change | Status Quo | Retrogressive Change

Radical
Desires immediate, fundamental change. Is frustrated, impatient, and revolutionary.

Demands violence.
Thinks violence is likely.
Will use violence as last resort.
Pacifist

Liberal
Desires rapid, far-reaching change. Believes people can improve their lives through the use of reason.
Classical Liberal
Believed in natural law. Believed private property was inalienable. Believed government oppressed people.
Contemporary Liberal
Believes private property is a social right. Believes government should be used to improve life through social experimentation.

Moderate
Fairly contented with the society. Supports gradual change. May be a "cop-out."

Conservative
Is the most contented with the society. Is active in defending it against challenges to the status quo. Is pessimistic about human capacity to improve life through the use of reason. Depends on "tried and true" institutions. Believes private property is an inalienable right. Desires order.

Will use the law.

Reactionary
Wishes things to be as they were. The frustration level of the extreme reactionary is equal to that of the extreme radical.

Believes war is good.

Left | Middle of the Road | Right

Supports: Human Rights
Rationalistism
Egalitarianism
Personal Liberty
Internationalism

Supports: Property Rights
Irrationalistism
Elitism
Authoritarianism
Nationalism

FIGURE 2–9 Spectrum of Political Attitudes

atives assert that liberal programs put everyone on the government dole, destroying individual initiative and making the recipients wards of the state. Liberals respond by contending that if individual initiative is destroyed by the grant of government aid, what happens to initiative in business under the supply side technique? Quoting George Bernard Shaw, who said, "American capitalism is really socialism for the rich," liberals ask whether business is not made dependent upon government protection against competition by the conservative method.

Liberals go on to argue that the supply side technique will not necessarily work. The government may release money to business in order to increase employment, for example, but business is likely to spend that money for its own purposes. Hence, the industrial owners may take greater profits from money the government meant for increasing jobs. After all, was it not just such a malfunction of the supply side approach that caused the Great Depression?

"Ah," the conservatives respond, "if the supply side is an inefficient method of releasing money into the economy—what of the demand side? The government may give the poor money with which to buy milk for the children but, all too often, it is spent on beer and cigarettes!"

Round and round go the arguments. Each of us must decide which, if either, is right. Of course, the foregoing is not an exhaustive discussion of policy options nor is the debate between supply side enthusiasts and demand side advocates complete. The material in this section was introduced only so that we might gain some insight into how the general ideological positions on the spectrum work in practice.

As a final note, the illustration shown in Figure 2–9 is offered in hopes that it will give you a more complete picture of the spectrum and thus help you understand the material in this chapter.

SUGGESTION FOR FURTHER READING

BOWLES, SAMUEL and HERBERT GINTIS, *Democracy and Capitalism*. New York: Basic Books, 1986.
BUCK, PHILIP W., *How Conservatives Think*. Harmondsworth, Middlesex, England: Penguin Books, 1975.
BUCKLEY, WILLIAM F., JR., *Up From Liberalism*. New York: Hillman Books, 1961.
BURKE, EDMUND, *Reflections on the Revolution in France*. Chicago: Henry Regnery, 1955.
CAMERON, WILLIAM BRUCE, *Informal Sociology*. New York: Random House, 1964.
CARNOY, MARTIN and DEREK SHEARER, *Economic Democracy*. White Plains, N.Y.: ME Sharpe, 1980.
DOLBEARE, KENNETH M. and LINDA J. MEDCALF, *American Ideologies Today*. New York: Random House, 1988.
FRIEDMAN, MILTON and ROSE FRIEDMAN, *Freedom to Choose*. New York: Harcourt Brace Jovanovich, 1980.
HALBERSTAM, DAVID, *The Reckoning*. New York: Simon and Schuster, 1986.
HOBHOUSE, H. T., *Liberalism*. London: Oxford University Press, 1964.
KIRK, RUSSELL, "Prescription, Authority, and Ordered Freedom," in *What Is Conservatism?*, ed. Frank S. Meyer. New York: Holt, Rinehart & Winston, 1964.
———, A Program for Conservatives. Chicago: Henry Regnery, 1954.
LEKACHMAN, ROBERT, *Greed Is Not Enough: Reaganomics*. New York: Pantheon, 1982.
NISBIT, ROBERT A., *Conservatism*. Minneapolis: University of Minnesota Press, 1986.
SIGLER, JAY A., ed., *The Conservative Tradition in American Thought*. New York: Capricorn Books, 1970.
VOLKOMER, WALTER E., ed., *The Liberal Tradition in American Thought*. New York: Capricorn Books, 1970.

3

The Evolution
of Democratic
Theory

PREVIEW

Democracy is a very old idea, dating back to ancient Greece. Eventually, however, the Greeks abandoned it for other forms of government. Centuries passed before the Protestant Reformation stimulated renewed interest in democracy.

Some contemporary political scientists think of democracy in procedural terms only, while others insist that it also includes important philosophical content. The *process democrats* contend that democracy is nothing more than a procedure by which decisions are made, while the *principle democrats* argue that democracy is much more than a formula for making policy. To them democracy also includes certain basic assumptions about people. Among these assumptions is the belief that the individual is of primary importance in the society, that each individual is basically equal to all others, and that each has a set of rights that are inalienable.

Perhaps the most basic idea in democracy is that political power comes from the people and that government, therefore, is legal only by consent of the governed. The act of popular consent to government is explained by the theory of the social contract. Both Calvinist and Jesuit theologies believed that in the distant past people had come together and agreed to form a government. This idea led to the theories of *popular sovereignty* and the *social contract,* which were opposed to the divine right of kings theory.

Note: The drawing at the top of the page portrays, from background to foreground, Thomas Hobbes, John Locke, and Jean Jacques Rousseau.

In the seventeenth century political conditions in England reached a critical juncture. An assertive Parliament and an aggressive monarch were on a collision course. As often happens, those trying times resulted in a flurry of creativity, producing the works of Thomas Hobbes and John Locke. Almost a century later the momentum had shifted to France, where Jean Jacques Rousseau made his important contribution.

Hobbes, Locke, and Rousseau had much in common. Each believed that people had lived without government at one time and that they had been governed by natural law in the natural state. Each also believed that people were capable of understanding natural law and of organizing a government that served their interests better than the natural state. In addition, they believed that people were essentially equal under natural law and that political power was derived from the people.

Nevertheless, while these philosophers agreed on many points, there were also many areas in which they differed. They agreed that the individual should be free, but they disagreed on the definition of freedom. The conservative Hobbes made a significant contribution to the development of democracy by supporting the notion that political power comes from the people and by insisting on the separation of church and state. Even so, he believed that the evil nature of people made them prisoners of their own greed. Freedom, he suggested, was possible only when the individuals in society subordinated themselves completely to the monarchs. The liberal Locke, on the other hand, thought that because people were basically good, freedom was greatest when the individual was left alone. The radical Rousseau believed that people were timid and peaceful in the state of nature. They became greedy only after they entered a society that had become perverted by private property. Freedom from the captivity of their own passion could be achieved only through the creation of a new society in which equality was the dominant principle. Like Hobbes, Rousseau argued that freedom was possible only when individuals subordinated themselves to the sovereign authority. While Hobbes held that the monarch was this authority, Rousseau asked individuals to surrender themselves to the community, or general will.

The three philosophers also varied in their attitude toward government itself. Hobbes thought that an absolute monarchy would best suit the needs of the people. Locke favored a parliamentary republic in which the government did little except arbitrate disputes between citizens. Rousseau, adopting the most radical point of view, believed the community created an infallible general will by a direct democratic vote of all the people in the society.

Although Hobbes said little about a person's right to private property, both Locke and Rousseau were fairly explicit about it. Locke argued that private property was vital to people, yet he was clearly opposed to unlimited accumulation. Rousseau's attitude toward private property is almost completely political. He argued that private property could be used by individuals to dominate others. Such inequality would destroy the community that Rousseau proposed. Hence, he was opposed to the unequal distribution of private property.

THE MEANING OF DEMOCRACY

Modern democracy evolved only after a very long period of development. The basis of democratic theory came from liberal philosophers, many of whom were not at all democratic but whose ideas could be extended logically to democratic conclusions. In this chapter we will study the thought of three early philosophers: Thomas Hobbes, John Locke, and Jean Jacques Rousseau. First, however, we should contemplate the nature of democracy. The inherent features of democracy are, even today, not completely agreed upon by the experts. Some political scientists argue that democracy is simply a way of making decisions. These scholars, sometimes called *process democrats,* claim that there is no real philosophy, or theory, of democracy. They believe that democracy is nothing more than an agreement among citizens that the majority vote will carry the issue or that one branch of government will not reach too far into the functions of another branch.

The process of democracy is, of course, very important and will be discussed in a later chapter. For now, however, let us study the ideas of a second group, the *principle democrats.* Principle democrats argue that democracy has a very important theoretical base. Although the procedure of democracy is important, they believe it is secondary to the basic intent and objectives of democracy as expressed in democratic theory. For instance, the basic principles of modern liberal democracy include the ideas that the individual is of major importance in the society, that each individual is basically equal to all other individuals, and that each has certain inalienable rights such as life and liberty. According to this notion, a person's liberty cannot be justly denied unless specific legal and administrative steps, known as *due process of law,* are followed. For example, let us say that majority assent is the procedural rule for decision making in a given society. Even if every person in the society voted to imprison a particular individual, the state could not legally do so. Why not? Because the *process* of majority rule is subordinate to the *principle* of liberty, according to this view of democracy.

While certainly not uninterested in process, principle democrats regard the ultimate philosophical goals of democracy as more important than the procedures used to meet those goals. At the very least, principle democrats insist that a democratic government be dedicated to improving the conditions of life for all its people and that some mechanism exists by which the people in the society can exercise a degree of control over their leaders and express their wishes and needs.

On its face, *liberal democracy* would certainly seem to meet the principle democrats' standards. Assuming that freedom will make people happy, its goal is to make people as free as possible. Liberal democracy includes a large list of freedoms, including freedom of press, speech, religion, assembly, and so forth.

Yet, critics of our system contend that while it allows a wide range of political liberty, liberal democracy ignores the economic needs of its citizens to the point where any effort at real democracy is destroyed. However, this view is foreign to many Americans who satisfy themselves that simply securing political liberties is enough to create a democracy. Indeed, many of our citizens equate democracy with our system and see other forms of government, those without our cherished liberties, as undemocratic.

The Soviet Union is a good example of a system that claims to be democratic while arguing that our system is not. Soviet authorities readily admit that their citizens do not enjoy the same right to criticize the government as we do. Yet, they contend that their system is far more democratic than ours because it is dedicated to freeing people from economic bondage to an ownership class, while our system actually encourages such bondage. In answer to a question about free expression in the USSR, a high Soviet authority once told me, "People who define democracy on the basis of being able to criticize the government have never been hungry." Obviously, we do not agree with this analysis. We contend that political freedoms are the very heart of democracy. We deemphasize the importance of economic freedom as the Soviets define it, preferring to equate that freedom with being able to work where one wishes and to accumulate goods as best as one can. It is true our system allows great economic diversity. Sociological studies indicate, however, that while we enjoy great social mobility in the middle class and above, the poor tend to remain poor generation after generation.

Clearly, the Soviet Union and the United States differ as to which procedures define a democracy. Yet the dispute is based upon something much more fundamental than process. The real argument revolves around the question of which principles are inherent in democracy: What is the philosophical content of democracy?

It is obvious that both process and principle are important to the meaning of democracy. Accordingly, we shall study both concepts in the next three chapters.

THE EARLY HISTORY OF DEMOCRACY

There are about 170 national constitutions in the world today, and almost all of them claim to be democratic. Democracy is currently a very popular term, but people have not always found it so attractive. Indeed, until about a century ago it was decidedly unpopular. To the ancient Greeks the word bore a sinister connotation. The Greek roots of the word seem innocuous enough: *demos* meaning the people and *kratien* meaning rule. Yet democracy was thought to describe something much more threatening. To Plato, for example, it meant rule by the masses. Plato argued that there are few people of high quality in any society and that if all the people were allowed to rule, those of low quality, who were more numerous, would dominate the state. This group would establish a government that would reflect their meanness, and the result would be a "tyranny of the majority." Further, Plato warned that democracies were usually short lived and that the mob would soon surrender its power to a single tyrant, thus destroying their own popular government. Instead of democracy, Plato preferred a state governed by the intellectual elite trained for the purpose of ruling wisely. This scheme, he suggested, would result in the most efficient and benevolent political system.

Aristotle, whose attitude toward democracy was somewhat less negative than Plato's, still clearly preferred a different form of government. He reasoned that under certain conditions the will of the many could be equal to or even wiser than the judgment of a few. When the many governed for the good of all, Aristotle accepted democracy as a "true" or good form of government. However, when the many ruled only for the benefit of themselves, rather than for the good of all, he considered the system to be "perverted" and called it *ochlocracy,* meaning mob rule. To even the best democracy, however, Aristotle preferred what he called *aristocracy,* by which he meant rule of the upper class for the good of all the people in the society. The upper class contained the people of greatest refinement and quality in the society; hence, they were best equipped to provide sound government for the society as a whole.

Eventually the ancient Greeks abandoned democracy, and serious interest in it did not arise again until the Protestant Reformation set in motion a major challenge to the Catholic Church, the authority that had brought order to medieval Europe.

Plato (428 BC–347 BC)

Among the most radical of the movements stimulated by the Reformation was that of the Puritans in England. Persecution by the British Crown, coupled with the Calvinist doctrine of "the priesthood of all believers," led the Puritans to reject any government that was not controlled by the people it governed.

Puritan agitation combined with a number of other issues to produce the social and political ferment that led to the English Civil War (1642–1649). Bitterness, disruption, and conflict continued until 1689, when the Bill of Rights was adopted by Parliament and a new monarchy under William and Mary with greatly reduced powers was established. England emerged from this trying period at the threshold of a new form of government, one that featured a limited monarchy and a politically dominant Parliament.

These events were justified and even guided by what is known as classical democratic theory. The *classical democrats* resurrected democracy as a governmental system and made the first major contributions to modern democratic thought. The issue that seems to have concerned them most is the concept of government by consent of the people.

THE SOCIAL CONTRACT

The slow progress out of the Middle Ages, into which Europe had been plunged by the collapse of the Roman Empire, was accomplished largely through the use of the scientific method, leading ultimately to the development of the Industrial Revolution itself. As I have already pointed out, success in solving their material problems gave people the confidence to take positive steps in search of solutions to their social, political, and economic problems. This new optimism, based on science and reason, led some thinkers to an exaggerated notion of individualism. Under individualism all people were essentially equal. If this were so, no one had a greater right to rule than another; hence, dynastical monarchy seemed to lose its relevance. Yet, society needed governors to maintain order, and these leaders were chosen by the community as a whole. Hence, the power to govern came from the people; the people were the source of ultimate legal and political authority. This theory of *popular sovereignty* led to much speculation about democracy during the seventeenth century. The theory that resulted, involving the actual grant of power by the people to the government, is called the *social contract theory;* that is, the social contract is the act of people exercising their sovereignty and creating a government to which they consent.

Calvinists and Jesuits

The first important utterances of the social contract theory came from two unlikely sources. The Calvinists in France, called Huguenots, were unhappy under the burdensome Catholic rule. Eventually they abandoned John Calvin's policy of passive obedience and adopted a doctrine that justified resistance to the Bourbon monarch. The basic ideas in this theory are found in the writings of Francis Hotman (1524–1590) and of Theodore Beza (1519–1605), a protégé of Calvin himself, and in the pamphlet *Vindiciae Contra Tyrannos,* whose author is not definitely known.[1] Though each of these sources had something different to say about the rights of the people in relation to their king, they agreed on this basic thesis: Spiritual doctrine and truth come from God, but political power emanates from the sovereign people. The people elect a king to serve them. Two contracts are then entered into. The first, between God and the society, requires that all people maintain spiritual truth. The second, between the king and the people, provides for civil order. The first agreement requires that both king and people abide by God's law and calls for punishment of either for any failure to do so. The second contract binds the king as well as the people to the laws of the state. If the king governs justly, the people are bound to obey him; but if he is unjust, the people may—and indeed are obliged to—put him out. The ouster of such a king must be a last resort, however.

Although the democratic implications of this theory are clear, these Calvinists did not have democracy in mind. They discouraged any popular effort to overthrow the monarch. Such an act was to be carried out by the people's representatives: local magistrates, the Estates General, or Parliament. Nor was a tyrant to be replaced by a democracy. These Calvinists were opposed to absolutism, but they believed it should be replaced by a limited monarchy or aristocracy.

Implausible as it seems, the Calvinist assault on monarchical absolutism was embellished by Jesuit theological writers. The rise of absolutism and the Protestant Reformation had combined into a powerful attack on the Church and the power of the

---

[1]*Defense of Liberty Against Tyrants,* printed in 1594, was probably written by Hubert Languet or Philippe Duplessis-Mornay. It was published under the pseudonym Stephen Junis Brutis in an obvious and successful attempt to avoid the penalty for sedition in sixteenth-century France.

John Calvin (1509–1564)

papacy. The Jesuit Order, established by Ignatius Loyola in 1534, led the Catholic Church in reforms which arrested the progress of the Protestant Reformation. The Jesuits believed, however, that all spiritual power and authority should derive from the Pope. Hence, since the absolute monarch wanted the state to control the Church, the Jesuits were opposed to the king.

The Jesuits were no more in favor of democracy than were the Calvinists, yet their ideas contributed greatly to the concept of popular government as well as to the notion of separation of church and state. Robert Bellarmine (1542–1621), Juan de Marisna (1536–1623), and Francisco Suarez (1548–1617) were the most important Jesuit writers. Suarez made a significant contribution by developing, with Hugo Grotius and others, the meaning of natural law, which would later be used by the classical liberals in their statement of democratic principles.

Like the Calvinists, these three Jesuits did not entirely agree on details but did agree on a basic theme. Generally, they distinguished between God's law and natural law, which was subordinate to God's law. Political organization and government, two natural phenomena, were granted to a ruler by the people; God did not grant such authority. God directly invested power only in the Pope. Thus, the Pope was chosen by God and was superior to all. By contrast, the king was chosen by the people and was therefore inferior to them. The Pope could overthrow a tyrant or grant the people the right to resist an evil ruler.

We should be careful not to assume that these early Jesuits favored popular government, however. They, like the Calvinists, were careful to recommend that the

Elizabeth I (1533–1603)

people depose a ruler only indirectly, through their representatives. The Jesuits also recommended that a tyrant be replaced with another monarch who was limited by the Pope and by Parliament. Even though these religious writers were not democrats, their ideas helped create the intellectual atmosphere in which democracy took form in the centuries that followed.

Thomas Hobbes

As mentioned earlier, England went through a period of serious civil disorder during the seventeenth century. Two forces competed: *absolutism*, allied with Anglican traditionalism, versus *Puritan reform*, in league with Parliamentary assertiveness. When Elizabeth I died in 1603, the Tudor line, England's most popular and powerful ruling house, also ended.

James Stuart succeeded Elizabeth to the throne. Unattractive and bookish, he believed vehemently in the divine right of kings. His unpleasant personality and unpopular politics led to conflicts with the assertive Parliament. The situation was not helped by James's death in 1625, since his son, Charles I, shared his unpopular political attitudes. Charles I pursued arbitrary and foolish policies until a civil war broke out, ending in 1649 with Charles's execution. For the next eleven years England was ruled by Oliver Cromwell and the Puritan religious minority. Upon Cromwell's death Parliament decided to restore the Stuart monarchy by placing

Charles II, the son of the executed monarch, on the throne. Thomas Hobbes (1588–1679), a mathematics tutor for the exiled prince, developed his theories in part to justify the Stuart restoration.

Hobbes believed that monarchy was the best possible form of government, yet he rejected the theory of the divine right of kings. Instead, he claimed that the social contract was the source of royal power. Though Hobbes believed that royal power came from the people, he placed few limits on the monarch.

Hobbes's view of people is not a happy one. He thought that people were basically self-serving. Although they were rational, they were not in control of their own destinies because they were driven by an overwhelming fear of death. This caused people to be aggressive toward one another. Hobbes, like all social contract theorists, assumed that there had been a time when government did not exist. In this *state of nature* people were free to act as they wished. No law governed them save natural law, and that law had no enforcement agency. Given his pessimistic views about the nature of people, it is not surprising that Hobbes believed that the state of nature was a wretched condition. Unregulated by law and government, people had given in to their baser instincts and acted aggressively toward their neighbors. They committed every kind of violence and deceit in order to raise their own status.

In *Leviathan,* his major work, Hobbes eloquently describes the hopeless chaos of the state of nature, a life without gentility or beauty, without charm or peace, without industry or culture. In this hideous state there was only human conflict, a constant "war of each against all." Hobbes complained that there was "no knowledge of the face of the earth; no account of time; no arts; no letters; no society; and which is worst of all, continual fear, and danger of violent death; and the life of man, solitary, poor, nasty, brutish and short." Clearly, Hobbes viewed the human condition in the state of nature as chaotic, irresponsible, and devoid of freedom.

Though he viewed people as prisoners of their own avarice, Hobbes believed they were rational. As rational beings, they realized the futility of their existence and hit upon a way of creating order out of the chaos endemic to the state of nature: the social contract. Though people could do as they wished and had natural rights, their evil nature had made life unbearable. Consequently, they gathered together to make an agreement. In exchange for order they agreed to surrender all their natural rights to a monarch and render to him complete obedience. Obviously, Hobbes did not consider natural rights inalienable as did later natural law theorists; but he did assert that the sole function of the king was to keep order. As long as the monarch did so, his subjects were bound to obey his laws. However, since the social contract was an agreement among ordinary people, the king was not a party to it and need not be bound by it. Only he could make the law; and because he made the law, the king could not be bound or limited by it. Indeed, the only restraint on the sovereign was his obligation to keep *order.* Only if he failed to keep the peace could the people resist him.

Hobbes believed that freedom, though limited, was possible only if people surrendered their liberty to a monarch—hardly a democratic point of view. Since people were naturally wicked, they could experience freedom only when they were restrained by a superior authority. Without such authoritarian checks people would become victims once again of their own evil impulses and would return to the chaos of the state of nature. Thus, while Hobbes believed that people were rational enough to contrive a solution to the chaos in the state of nature, their capacity to reason was not sufficient to control their own sinister impulses, so absolute power had to be given to the king. In short, human reason, according to Hobbes, was powerful enough to devise a solution to chaos, but not strong enough to allow people to become part of the solution. Only the all-powerful monarch could do that.

Despite Hobbes's antidemocratic attitude, he was not popular among monarchists. Since he denied the divine right theory and accepted, however slightly, the possibility of popular revolution, the supporters of Charles II would have nothing to do with him. Hence, his philosophy was rejected by democrat and monarchist alike. Not until Jeremy Bentham developed his thoughts on utilitarianism in the nineteenth century did Hobbes influence another major thinker.

Many students of Hobbes consider him a classical English liberal because he contributed to the development of democratic theory. It is true that he made important contributions, if unintentionally, to contemporary democratic thought by asserting that political power comes from the people rather than from God. In this theory he led his English successors to the concept of the separation of church and state just as the Jesuits and Calvinists had done on the continent. In so doing, Hobbes divorced the state from the source of morality. Morality was considered to be quite apart from the monarch. Although the divine right also held the king and the source of morality separate in theory, in practice the two were often equated. In this respect Hobbes's philosophy was an important step toward democratic theory.

Yet, Hobbes never intended his ideas to be used as the basis of popular government; quite the reverse. Even though he employed concepts normally thought to be liberal (for example, popular sovereignty and the social contract), his interpretation of these ideas led him to very conservative conclusions. Further, you will recall from Chapter 2 that liberals are optimistic about people, believing that they are basically good. Conservatives, on the other hand, hold the opposite attitude toward humanity. Clearly, Hobbes's view is closer to the conservative position. In short, Hobbes used a liberal vocabulary, which was in vogue among the intellectuals of his time, to express a conservative philosophy. The next natural law philosopher we will study, however, enjoyed indisputably liberal credentials.

John Locke

Because of the stark puritanical nature of Cromwell's Commonwealth (1649–1660), few people in England wished for the experiment with republicanism to continue after the Lord Protector's death. Accordingly, the Stuart monarchy was restored with the coronation of Charles II in 1660. Charles ruled for twenty-five years. Though he was not inactive, he heeded the lesson of his father's execution and tempered his activities accordingly and the people were satisfied with his reign.

The popular reaction to James II (1685–1688), brother and successor of Charles II, was considerably different. Not content to let his ministers bargain with Parliament, James II tried to be an active executive. Worse than that, he wanted absolute power. Such royal ambitions were not welcome in eighteenth-century England under any circumstances, but the fact that James was a Catholic sealed his fate.

In June 1687, the English rose up against the "Catholic tyranny" and James II fled to France. This episode, known as the *Glorious Revolution* because it was practically bloodless, brought to a close the long struggle between king and Parliament for dominance in England. Although virtually free of violence, the Glorious

Revolution was a true revolution because it visited major changes upon the English government, changes which ultimately led to the development of democracy in that land.

Before allowing a new king to ascend the throne, Parliament adopted a document, the *Bill of Rights,* that limited the power of the English monarchy as it had never before been limited. It guaranteed Parliament the right to hold free elections, to meet frequently, to petition the king, and to legislate. The king was not allowed to suspend an act of Parliament, and he was forbidden to tax or to keep a standing army in peacetime without Parliament's approval. These restrictions had to be accepted by the new monarchs as the "true, ancient, and indubitable rights of the people of this realm."

Just as Hobbes had tried to justify the restoration of the Stuart dynasty, so John Locke (1632–1704) tried to give a philosophical base to the Glorious Revolution and the limitations placed on the monarch as a result. Of all his works, the one with the greatest political importance is his *Second Treatise.* In it are a series of arguments that, because of their simplicity and common-sense approach, captured the imagination of Locke's fellow citizens as well as people of later generations. Though he was not the first to express such ideas, his writings were the most important statement on limited government and individual liberty yet made. His ideas caught the mood of his country and his era.

As George H. Sabine has written, "His sincerity, his profound moral conviction, his genuine belief in liberty, in human rights, and in the dignity of human nature, united with his moderation and good sense, made him the ideal spokesman of a middle-class revolution."[2] So close to the thinking of his countrymen was Locke that the resolution declaring the English throne "vacant" after James II's exile could have been drafted by him. It read, in part, "King James II having endeavored to subvert the constitution of the kingdom by breaking the original contract between the king and the people . . . " and continued to its conclusion in typical Lockean prose. Though his work obviously had substantial impact on British government, his philosophy found greatest application in the principles of the American Declaration of Independence and the United States Constitution.

Natural law.   History's leading classical liberal, Locke believed in natural law. He believed that people were rational beings who could use their reason to perceive the basic pinciples of natural law. Natural law, according to Locke, guaranteed each individual certain rights that could not legally be taken away, or *alienated,* without due process of law. He summarized these inalienable rights as "life, liberty, and estate." However, he was much more explicit than this generalization suggests. He held that individual freedom was an essential right; indeed, its importance to his theory would be hard to overestimate.

While Hobbes and Locke agreed on many points, they also contradicted each other. As we have seen, Hobbes was very pessimistic about human nature. He believed that people were basically evil and that they would harm each other if they were not subject to the control of an outside authority. Hence, Hobbes equated

---

[2]George H. Sabine, *A History of Political Theory,* 3d ed. (New York: Holt, Rinehart & Winston, 1961), p. 540.

individual freedom with restraint by the government. Locke, by contrast, was very optimistic about human nature. He believed that governmental restraints on people were largely unnecessary. In fact, he argued that people were most free when they were left unfettered by government. Thus, to Locke, freedom was found in the absence of restraint. He felt that people would behave decently when left alone and argued that they should be free to exercise their rights without hindrance or regulation as long as they did not interfere with the rights of others.

Individual equality was another right guaranteed by natural law. Locke did not claim that all people were equal in all ways. He recognized that people differed widely in intelligence, physical prowess, and so forth; but regardless of the obvious differences among people he argued that they all had the same natural rights. Thus, no one had a greater claim on liberty than anyone else. Nor did anyone have more, or less, of any other kind of natural right.

Locke was most specific about the individual's right to private property. Like all the early English classical liberals, he believed that private property was essential to people's well-being. The high status he gave to private property rests on two major assumptions. First, he assumed that the accumulation of private property allowed people to provide for themselves and their families the necessities of life. Once freed from the pressures of survival, people could turn to the task of developing their characters. If a society is in the throes of famine, its people care little whether the sun revolves around the earth or the earth orbits the sun. They are not likely to create an important art form, an advanced architecture, a subtle literature, or a sophisticated governmental system. We will see later that Marx adopted this idea, calling for the liberation of people from *compulsive toil* as a major theme of his own ideology.

How property was regarded is of the utmost importance to our study. Property was seen by the English liberal as a means to an end, not as an end in itself. Locke saw private property as a vital first step to an improved human race. Locke's main interest was the individual, and he hoped for a society that would free its people to perfect their characters and their human qualities. The accumulation of property was important to him for the life it made possible, not as an absolute value in itself. Further, the accumulation of private property by any given individual was not to occur unchecked. Locke, as we will see, believed people should be allowed to accumulate only as much as they could use. He did not support amassing huge fortunes in the hands of some people while others lived in poverty. Thus, while he favored a market economy, thinking it most conducive to individual freedom, he would almost surely object to the great disparities in property ownership that exist in today's capitalist societies.

The second assumption of the early English liberals in support of private property involved individual identity. Locke believed that property ownership was more than a simple economic fact. A person's property reflected the individual who owned it. People were identified in part by the things they owned. What they were was modified by what they had.

Although we do not state this concept as often or in exactly the same way as Locke, it is still with us today. A statement such as "clothes make the man" is worth some analysis. In this phrase property and personality are closely related by the implication that owning a particular item can change one's personality. This close link between the self, or the personality, and material items is a very strong feature of Western civilization; indeed, many modern commercial advertisements rely heavily on persuading consumers of this theory. Further, the equation of personality and property ownership helps explain why most important political ideologies have come from the West. You will recall that ideologies tend to offer a better material existence, the promise of a happier or better life. Such values dominate Western thought, whereas Eastern philosophies tend to focus on developing the inner self or finding spiritual contentment. Thus, ideologies are more Western than Eastern.

As one might expect from the importance Locke gave private property, he developed an elaborate theory to explain its origin and value. Not only did these ideas make a vital contribution to democracy, but subsequent thinkers adopted them and applied them to vastly different philosophies. Locke's influence can easily be found in the work of capitalist economists such as Adam Smith and David Ricardo. As we will see, it may also be found in the economics of Karl Marx.

Locke argued that all resources were originally held in common and that people could use them as needed, but he believed that common property became private property when human labor was applied to it. He believed that when people made things from natural resources, they transferred something of themselves into the items produced. The newly created product, the result of a union between human creativity and natural resources, actually became part of the worker and naturally belonged to that person. Thus the right of private property was born. Locke also believed that the value of any item was roughly determined by the amount of labor necessary to produce it. This idea, known as the *labor theory of value,* may be seen in Marx's famous theory of surplus value, discussed in Chapter 7.

As we have seen, Locke assumed that there had been a time when there was no organized society. During this time people interacted with nature, creating private property. Clearly, then, Locke assumed that private property existed before society was organized. In other words, private property was not created by society; society had no special claim on or control over private property. Private property was created by the individual. It was created when individuals passed part of their essence to an object through the process known as work. Thus, we return to the crucial point: *Private property is not important for its own sake.* It takes on importance when part of the essence of a human being has been transferred to it. While this theory seems to make private property equal to life and human equality, property is important only because it has been imbued with the essense of human beings.

That Locke considered property less important than human values is clear from his attitude toward the accumulation of property. Though he thought that people should normally be allowed to gather property without interference from outside agencies, he clearly believed that *property accumulation should be limited.* To begin with, Locke held that no person should be allowed to accumulate more property than could be used before it spoiled. A second restriction on property ownership was more general. Locke argued that people should not be able to exercise their economic rights to such an extent that others were denied the same rights. Since private property helps people define themselves, since it frees people from the mundane cares of daily subsistence, and since it is finite, no individual should accumulate so much property that others are prevented from accumulating the necessities of life. If such a restriction did not exist, it would be possible for one person, through the control of property, to deny others their identities and even their ability to be fully human. On this basis an agency of the society could interfere with an individual's accumulation of property if in so doing the right of others to accumulate property would be protected. Though Locke did not intend it in this way, this principle forms part of the bridge between classical liberalism, which is linked to capitalism, and utopian or humanitarian socialism, discussed in Chapter 8. *The roots of both capitalism and socialism spring from common soil.*

The last principle of natural law about which Locke was very specific has to do with the individual's collective interests. Locke assumed that the basic interests of all people in a given society were the same. Hence, while there might be some minor variations, whatever was beneficial for the society as a whole was probably ultimately beneficial for any particular individual, another belief which can also be found in socialism. This principle led Locke to look toward the majority vote as the most important feature of political decision making. His attitude toward majority rule will be discussed in more detail later; for now it is enough to remark that although Locke considered the individual very important, he viewed people as being united by common interests.

The social contract.   Locke and Hobbes also differed in their views on the condition of people in the state of nature. Rejecting the proposition that people were evil and selfish in the state of nature, Locke believed instead that people were essentially good. Consequently, the state of nature prior to society and government was rather pleasant. Indeed, Locke suggested that the dominant themes in the natural state were "peace, good will, mutual assistance and preservation."

Yet, even though the state of nature was usually peaceful, there were two sources of unrest. Though Locke believed people were basically good, he did not think them perfect. Hence, from time to time some people might try to take advantage of others. Moreover, even when no malice was intended, two people might come into conflict while exercising what they considered to be their just liberties.

Conflict between people, then, could occur in the state of nature; and because there was no third party to arbitrate the dispute, individuals were forced to defend their own liberties. This clash presented a further problem because people were not equal in their ability to defend their rights from attack. Remember, Locke claimed that people are equal only in that they all have the same rights under the laws of nature. The ability to defend their liberties varies from one individual to another. Hence, injustice could occur in the state of nature because the person who manages to prevail over another may succeed only because he or she is stronger and not because he or she is right. The fascists and Nazis, as you will learn in Chapter 10, would scornfully reject this notion. To them force determines justice.

Believing that people were rational, Locke went on to theorize that people saw the need for an agency to dispense justice among them. This led the individuals in a community to make a contract among themselves, thereby creating society and removing themselves from the state of nature.

Hobbes, you will recall, insisted that the king was not a party to the contract that formed the society and thus could not be bound by it. Hobbes held that society and government were distinct elements, thus putting the power of the king above that of the individual and the society.

Locke made the same distinction as Hobbes, but for exactly the opposite reason. The people create the society through the social contract, and then government is created as an agent of the society. Consequently, government is two steps removed from the true source of its power, the individual, and is subordinate to the society, which is, in turn, subordinate to the individual. Also, since government and society are not the same thing, the fall of a government need not mean the end of the community. The community could create a new government to serve it if its original government was unsatisfactory.

The nature and function of government. Though Locke believed that government ought to be strictly limited, he thought it performed a vital function. "The great and chief end of men's uniting into commonwealth," he wrote, "and putting themselves under government, is the preservation of their property." However, Locke also believed that the purpose of government was to serve the people. Hobbes, by contrast, thought that people should serve the government. Locke thought that some things could be done better when people were left alone and that other things were done better by society as a whole or by society's representatives. He believed that most people could act fairly and efficiently by themselves and insisted that government should not interfere with the individual in such cases. *Government functioned solely to increase the individual's rights.* Remember, to Locke freedom meant the absence of governmental restraints on the individual. Yet, there were times when governmental activity was necessary to protect the rights of the people. Locke saw government as a passive arbitrator. Normally it would simply let people pursue their own best interests. When, however, two or more individuals came into conflict over the extent of their liberties, the government was required to step in, arbitrate the dispute, and then step out again and let people go about their business without further interference.

Locke was very positive about natural rights and optimistic about human nature. Unlike Hobbes, who had people giving up almost all their rights to government, Locke believed that people should keep most of their freedoms. The only right that Locke expected people to surrender to government was the right to decide how extensive their individual liberties would be. Even there, however, the only time government should use its power was when individuals came into conflict over the use of their rights. Any other power was denied to government and reserved for the people.

Locke clearly expected that government would be limited. To begin with, he never thought of government as being more than the sum of its parts. Unlike some political theorists, Locke believed that the state or government should never become more powerful than the individuals it served. The government was created by society; society was created by a contract among all the individuals who wanted to join the society. In making the contract, the people agreed to accept the arbitration of the government. Since the power of the government was derived from and therefore dependent on the power of the individuals in the society, the government could not impose its authority on an unwilling individual. That individual would remove himself or herself from the society and from the authority of the government. In so doing, however, the individual would have to return to the state of nature and would forfeit the protection of the government.

Locke was also very particular about the structure and form of government. As pointed out earlier, he assumed that what was good for the society as a whole was good for the individual as well. Further, he believed that people were rational and capable of knowing what was good for them. Consequently, he assumed that the society could use the will of the majority as a formula for deciding correct policy.

Moreover, individuals were expected to accept the decision of the majority even if they disagreed with it.

Besides believing in majority rule, Locke thought that people should be governed by a parliament elected by citizens who owned property. Though he argued that the people were sovereign, Locke thought it best that they not rule themselves directly. He saw members of a parliament as representing their constituents, and he believed that they should vote as their constituents wanted. Hence, the relationship between the government and the governed remained close. Though the people did not actually make the law themselves, the law was a product of their preferences.

Locke also called for separation of the executive and legislative powers. Most important, he believed that the legislature, which was the direct agent of the people, should take precedence over the executive branch. The legislature should decide on the policy of the government, and the executive should dutifully carry out the mandates of parliament. That is why (as we will see in a later chapter), insofar as the concept of parliamentary primacy is concerned, the British system is more directly related to Locke's ideal than is the American system, with its balance of powers among three equal branches, its vetoes, its two-thirds rules, and so forth.

Even though he argued that only property-owning citizens should vote and that the people must obey the government as long as it did not abuse their rights, Locke contended that the people were sovereign and that they had the right to rebel against an unjust government. The government's sole purpose was to serve the individual in such a way as to increase individual rights and liberties. At all other times it was to stay out of the people's business. If the government ever acted otherwise—that is, if it involved itself too much in the affairs of the people, thus reducing their rights and liberties without good reason—then the people had the right to put that government out and to create one that would serve them better. Once again we see Hobbes and Locke on opposite sides. Hobbes opposed popular rebellion against the king, whom he considered the sovereign, or the highest law in the land. Yet, since the king was given power by the people for the sole purpose of keeping order, the people were justified in ousting him and creating a new sovereign if he failed to keep order. In other words, while Hobbes would have the people overthrow the government for failing to keep order, Locke believed such an action was justified when the government tried to regulate people too much. A glance at the spectrum of political attitudes described in Chapter 2 will show that Hobbes's concern for order and Locke's preference for individual liberty are quite consistent with the values of conservatives and liberals, respectively.

Liberal though Locke's ideas were, they too fell short of democracy. Locke was the "spokesman of a middle class revolution." During Locke's time British government was controlled by the aristocracy. Yet a large and wealthy middle class, composed of merchants, manufacturers, bankers, and professionals, emerged on the eve of the Industrial Revolution to demand a share of political power in the society. Although Locke claimed that all people were equally possessed of natural rights, he advocated that political power be devolved only far enough to embrace the middle class by giving Parliament, which the middle class controlled through the House of Commons, the right to limit the monarch's power. He did not advocate that the masses of ordinary people, the poor, be given the right to elect members to Parliament; thus, he denied them political power.

Still, his philosophy was essential to the development of liberal democracy.

Although he chose not to enfranchise the poor, his justifications for giving the middle class political power were equally applicable to people of lower status; indeed, his theories were so sweeping that they could logically be applied to all people. Locke was probably prevented from extending his ideas only by the unquestioned bias for privilege endemic to his era. Thus, democracy had to await a more egalitarian epoch, an era parented when the mass production of goods created the necessary economic and social conditions. Still, it cannot be disputed that Locke's ideas came very close to being democratic; in the next generation, contemporary democratic thought was born.

Jean Jacques Rousseau

After the dramatic political events that stimulated the ideas of Hobbes and Locke, England settled into a period of consolidation and France became the new center of radical thought. Louis XIV (1638–1715) had established an absolutist monarchy and passed it on to his great-grandson, Louis XV. France had made great advances in science and literature. Yet, its political system was harsh, its social structure exploitive, and its government corrupt and unresponsive to the people's needs. These conditions stimulated a surge of literary activity that produced some of the period's best writers. Most were satirists and commentators rather than creators of new political ideas. At best, they built on the basic ideas of the English liberals, restating and popularizing the political ideas of the previous generation. John Locke had an important influence on these writers. Accepting the theories of natural law, individual value, and the social contract largely as Locke had explained them, French writers found much to criticize in Bourbon France. But one thinker, Jean Jacques Rousseau (1712–1778), made such a creative impact as to set himself apart from the others.

While Rousseau is generally considered the founder of contemporary radicalism, it is difficult to place Rousseau on the political spectrum. Generally speaking, his ideas may be classified as radical. Yet, totalitarians cite his belief that the community or state is more important than the individual. Socialists, on the other hand, warm to his preference for limiting private property ownership. Liberal democrats appreciate his emphasis on the common man and the procedure he suggested for decision making.

The community.   Like other social contract theorists, Rousseau believed that there had been a time when neither government nor society existed. People in the state of nature were simple, shy, and innocent. Unlike Hobbes, Rousseau suspected that before society was created people were timid, and that they would avoid conflict rather than seek it out. Such a condition was not unpleasant. Life was peaceful in the state of nature, but it was not fulfilled.

Rousseau believed that people wanted to improve themselves, to make themselves better. This goal, he argued, could not be achieved in the state of nature because, while it was an innocent condition, it was not a moral, fully actualized life. Rousseau was deeply influenced by the ancient Greeks who, you will recall, regarded people as human only if they actually participated in the affairs of state. Pericles, Greece's greatest statesman, expressed this idea quite forcefully: "We alone regard a man who takes no interest in public affairs, not as a harmless but as a useless character."

Rousseau agreed that morals could be developed only in an environment in which people related to and interacted with one another. This relationship did not exist in the state of nature; hence, he concluded that moral life was impossible in the state of nature. Yet, because people wanted to improve themselves, they were compelled to form a community that destroyed the state of nature. The community then established a moral code that made human perfection (and even *becoming* human) possible. In the state of nature people were more animal than human. "We begin properly to become men," Rousseau said, "only after we have become citizens."

Nevertheless, the formation of the community does not necessarily lead to a good life; it only makes a moral life possible. Indeed, Rousseau was convinced that while people had the capacity to be good, they were more likely to become immoral as the community became more sophisticated.

Private property, which Rousseau believed developed only after the community was formed, encouraged greed and selfishness. The most aggressive people in the community gained control of most of the property, and they set up a government to help them maintain that control. Hence, people become prisoners either to their own greed or to that of their rulers. "Man is born free," Rousseau wrote, "and everywhere he is in chains." As we will see later, Marx and other radicals had similar ideas.

The organic society.   Rousseau offered a solution to the dilemma just described. He could not advise a return to the state of nature because that would require people to give up the chance to live moral lives. Instead, people must build a new community that is structured so that a moral existence is possible.

According to Rousseau, people should form a new society to which they would surrender themselves completely. By giving up their rights and powers to the group, they would create a new entity. The society would become an *organism* in which each individual contributed to the whole. By giving up their individual powers, people would gain a new kind of equality and a new kind of power. They would achieve equality because they would all become full contributors to the group. Enhanced power would also accrue to the community, the sum greater than its individual parts.

This new society would actually be a person, according to Rousseau—a "public person." The public person would be directed by the *general will,* that is, the combination of the wills of each person in the society. As such the general will could do no wrong because it would create the right. It could not be bad because it would determine what was moral.

The general will also made individual freedom possible. Freedom, according to Rousseau, meant doing only what one wanted to do. When people join the community, they voluntarily agree to comply with the general will of the community. The general will, created by the majority in the interests of all in society, cannot be wrong. If a person votes with the minority, he or she must still accept the majority decision. If the majority creates the general will, and if the general will can do no wrong, then the minority must be wrong; and since the individual agreed to live by the general will, those who are in the minority are expected to comply with the will of the majority, thus enhancing their freedom. If those in the minority refuse to follow the general will, they are violating their own will and thus are refusing to be free.

People who refuse to comply with the general will, and thus with their own best interests, can be *forced* to comply. Thus, Rousseau argues that the community has the right to force its members to be free. As he put it, "Whoever shall refuse to obey the general will must be constrained by the whole body of his fellow citizens to do so; which is no more than to say that it may be necessary to compel a man to be free."

By asserting that the general will cannot be wrong, Rousseau completed the circle begun by Hobbes more than a century before. It will be recalled that the English philosopher separated the monarch from the agent of moral authority—the Church. Here Rousseau claims that the community, which controls the state, actually creates moral authority itself, thus rejoining moral authority and the state, this time in a secular setting. This theory gave a philosophical justification to the anticlerical features of the French Revolution. It was also used later by Mussolini in developing his notion of the totalitarian state.

An important lesson learned from the example of Rousseau and Hobbes is that sometimes two different ideas, carried to opposite extremes, can result in similar conclusions. Hobbes, on the right of the spectrum, would have society bound to the absolute power of a monarch. Rousseau, on the left, demanded that people subject themselves to the general will in no less absolute fashion.

Economic and political systems. Like Locke, Rousseau gave importance to property, associating it with the foundation of society itself. "The first man who," he wrote, "after enclosing a piece of ground, bethought himself to say 'This is mine' and found people simple enough to believe him, was the real founder of society". Yet, to Rousseau, private property was not a sacred commodity. In fact, he was the first natural law theorist to regard private property as something other than a natural right. Instead, he argued that it was a *social right.* Hence, no one has an unlimited right to accumulate property. Much as Marx would argue later, Rousseau thought that private property could be used to exploit people because it was a source of inequality among individuals. While he never actually supported the elimination of private property, Rousseau objected to an unequal distribution of property among the members of the society. Private property, he believed, should be distributed equally among the individuals in the state. However, Rousseau's motives for supporting equal ownership of private property had nothing to do with the material well-being of citizens. It was purely a political convenience; his goal was individual equality, not well-being.

Rousseau was even more particular about the governmental form he thought the community should use. To begin with, he believed that each individual's will was inalienable; it could not be transferred to another. Consequently, he opposed representative government, since no one could represent another individual. This led him to favor a direct form of democracy, that is, one in which the citizens vote on the laws themselves instead of sending representatives to a legislature. However, because of the limited technology of his time, the direct democracy recommended by Rousseau required that the state be very small. Like the ancient Greeks of whom he was so fond, Rousseau believed that the city-state was the only political entity small enough for all citizens to meet and vote on every law or policy.

Rousseau was also very careful to distinguish between executive and legislative functions and powers. First, he insisted on complete separation of the two. He also demanded that the legislature be more powerful than the executive. The legislature was all of the people, or the community, making the general will. Hence, it was the sovereign or all-powerful body. The executive, according to Rousseau, was merely the government. Rousseau, like Locke, carefully distinguished between the community and the government. The government only served the community. It had no special rights or privileges and, as in Locke's theories, could be changed at any time while the community remained unchanged. The sole function of the executive (the government), in other words, was to carry out the wishes of the community (the general will).

Even as Rousseau established the theoretical basis for radical, or pure, democracy, more conservative thinkers were beginning to modify the ideas of Locke and others, creating a political-economic system known as democratic capitalism. While Rousseau's theories greatly influenced politics on the continent, the more conservative doctrines had an immense impact in England and the United States, only to be followed by the leftist modifications of democratic socialism. In the next chapter, we will study these two variants of democratic theory.

SUGGESTION FOR FURTHER READING

DUNCAN, GRAEME, ed., *Democratic Theory and Practice.* Cambridge, England: Cambridge University Press, 1983.

HOBBES, THOMAS, *Leviathan,* ed. Michael Oakshott. New York: Collier, 1962.

INGERSOLL, DAVID E., *Communism, Fascism, and Democracy.* Columbus, OH: Charles E. Merrill, 1971.

LOCKE, JOHN, *The Second Treatise of Government (An Essay Concerning the True Original, Extent and End of Civil Government) and a Letter Concerning Toleration,* ed. J. W. Gough. New York: Macmillan, 1956.

McDONALD, LEE CAMERON, *Western Political Theory,* Part 3. New York: Harcourt Brace Jovanovich, 1968.

MACPHERSON, C. B., *The Real World of Democracy.* New York: Oxford University Press, 1969.

NELSON, WILLIAM M., On *Justifying Democracy.* London: Routledge & Kegan Paul, 1980.

ROUSSEAU, JEAN JACQUES, *The Social Contract and Discourses,* trans. G. D. H. Cole. New York: Dutton, 1913.

SABINE, GEORGE H., *A History of Political Theory,* 3rd ed. New York: Holt, Rinehart & Winston, 1961.

SCHULTZ, ERNST B., *Democracy.* New York: Barron's Educational Series, 1966.

WEALE, ALBERT, *Political Theory and Social Policy.* London: Macmillan, 1983.

4

Democratic Capitalism, and Beyond

PREVIEW

Economics and politics are inextricably linked in modern society. Hence, two major variants of democracy have developed: *democratic capitalism* and *democratic socialism*. Democratic capitalism combines the economic system developed by Adam Smith, David Ricardo, and Thomas Malthus with the political theories of the neoclassical democrats Edmund Burke, James Madison, and John C. Calhoun. Taking a rather bleak position regarding the nature of people, these democrats favored an economy based on free individual commercial activity, a strong central government, and a relatively paternalistic representative political system.

    Contemporary liberalism developed in the tradition of Jeremy Bentham, John Stuart Mill, Thomas Hill Green, and John Dewey. The positivist approach of these thinkers not only liberalized democracy but turned it toward socialism. This school equates individual happiness with the happiness of society as a whole. Individual contributions are measured and valued in relation to their social effectiveness. Individual liberty is defined in both a negative and a positive sense; that is, government should not act in such a way as to restrict individual liberties, but governmental action

Note: The drawing at the top of the page portrays, from foreground to background, Adam Smith, John Stuart Mill, and James Madison.

is not necessarily equated with restriction of individual liberty. Indeed, government is seen as a potential ally of individual freedom. Because private control of the means of production has been used to oppress large numbers of people, the liberal democrats favor government action, a mild form of socialism if you will, to prevent such oppression. Also, the liberal democrats, who have great confidence in human intelligence, are willing to experiment with social institutions. Believing that people can devise institutions that will serve their needs better than institutions that already exist, they practice social engineering. The victories and defeats of such experiments can be found in the policies of the New Deal and the Great Society, and the reactionary revolution of Ronald Reagan.

CAPITALISM

One of the distinguishing features of modern ideologies is that, since the Industrial Revolution, politics and economics have become inextricably joined. Modern democracy, like all other contemporary ideologies, cannot be divorced from its accompanying economic system. Thus, we find that modern democracy is divided into two major variants, *democratic capitalism* and *democratic socialism*. Accordingly, our study of modern ideologies must necessarily include consideration of economic theory.

The prevailing economic system in Europe during the fifteenth and sixteenth centuries was known as *mercantilism*. It was supposed that the power of a given country was largely determined by its wealth. National wealth at the time was measured by specie—gold and silver. Competing with their rivals for dominance each European monarch reasoned that the state's power would be enhanced if specie could be monopolized, each country attempted to accumulate as much of its adversary's wealth as possible through international trade.

This objective wedded politics and economics. To control the flow of money, monarchs tended to grant trading and manufacturing privileges to only some of their subjects, thus creating highly regulated and monopolistic economic systems. Certain favored people were allowed to produce goods, others to ship them, and so forth. While this system benefited a few fortunate people, it harnessed large numbers of others, preventing them from achieving their economic potential.

The colonial enterprises undertaken by European nations were seen as an important part of the mercantile system. Colonies were created to produce raw materials for the mother country. The mother country, in turn, manufactured the raw materials into finished goods which it sold to its own citizens, to its colonies, and to foreign customers. To lock the system in, the colonies were forbidden to produce certain finished goods and to trade with anyone except the mother country. This arrangement was, of course, seen as exploitative and caused serious dissatisfaction among the colonists. Mercantilist exploitation, a leading issue among the Anglo-American colonists, played a large part in justifying their revolution and eventual declaration of independence.

Thus, the mercantile system was unsatisfactory to many people. Citizens of the mother country who did not enjoy the right to produce or sell as they wished chafed under the arbitrary restrictions. The colonists felt similar pressures and their enmity was increased by the exploitation they endured. Besides these economic problems, mercantilism was not in keeping with the individualist tendencies of the increasingly popular theories of liberalism.

Adam Smith

The economic frustration described above found voice in the writings of a Scottish liberal. In 1776, Adam Smith (1723–1790), the father of modern economics, published *The Wealth of Nations,* in which he set forth economic arguments inspired by classic liberal doctrine. Smith argued that mercantilism actually worked to impoverish the national economy rather than to enrich it. Anticipating mass-production economies, Smith suggested that the wealth of a nation is properly assessed by measuring the value of the goods it produces rather than by piling up specie in the treasury. By imposing artificial restraints on enterprise, mercantilism stifles the economic ingenuity and resourcefulness of people as it protects inefficient monopolists.

Smith advocated a free market system in which the government was to abandon its regulatory functions, thus leaving its citizens free to enter or leave economic pursuits at will. The principle of *laissez-faire* became the paramount feature in capitalist economics and remains even today its most sacred objective.

Smith reasoned that the resources of a nation would be most effectively distributed when each individual in the society could demand and use them as he or she thought best. In this way, Smith suggested, there would be optimum economic development. The "invisible hand" of supply and demand would assure that the best possible quality would be offered at the lowest possible price.

Competition was seen as the driving wheel of the new economic system. People would array themselves against one another in a form of economic combat. Those who offered quality goods at reasonable prices would prosper, while those who did not would find themselves forced out of the market.

The net result of this uninhibited competitive process would be an economic system of unparalleled prosperity, or so it was reasoned. This happy conclusion rested on the assumption that *the good of the whole is best served when each person pursues his or her own self-interest.* Herein lies one of the basic differences between capitalism and socialism. While capitalism assumes that society's best interest is maximized when each individual is free to do that which he or she thinks is best for himself or herself, socialism, as we shall see in Chapter 8, is based on the attitude that the individual's interests are maximized when each person suppresses selfish objectives for the greater good. Socialism asks people to cultivate a social consciousness; capitalism does not, because it assumes that the social good will be achieved automatically.

In the early stages of the Industrial Revolution, the age during which Smith lived, confidence in the therapeutic value of pursuing self-interest may well have been justified. The national economies of the day were badly warped by arbitrary, government-sanctioned monopolies, and it was thought desirable to free economic systems from governmental restraint. The "dead hand of feudalism" still dominated much of the land, even as money began to assume greater importance in the society. Inventions and the application of machinery to production promised to vastly expand the availability of goods, if only people could be persuaded to invest enough capital to make use of them. Indeed, the freewheeling system Smith proposed may have been, as Marx later concluded, the very step necessary to catapult Europe into a new era of human history.

Capitalism after Smith.   Smith, however, was followed by a new generation of economists who were forced to deal with the bleak side of capitalism as well as with its more pleasant aspects. The Industrial Revolution and the need to accumulate capital had visited terrible hardships upon the working class, forcing them to live in the most miserable and oppressive conditions.

In the early 1800s David Ricardo (1772–1823) and Thomas Malthus (1766–1834), two English economists, became capitalism's leading intellectual lights. Ricardo assumed that while human labor created value, it was perfectly appropriate for those who controlled capital to force labor to surrender a large part of the value it created. Otherwise, additional capital would not be forthcoming. On this assumption Ricardo developed the theory of the *Iron Law of Wages,* in which he suggested that the owner of the factory and the machines would be driven by the profit motive to pay the workers only enough to bring them to the factories to work another day. Though this process might be perceived as cruel, Ricardo argued that only in this way would enough capital be created to fund future production. Hence, although the workers' conditions were admittedly miserable, they would degenerate even further unless additional capital was created.

Even gloomier than his colleague, Thomas Malthus became alarmed by the impending disaster he foresaw. Malthus believed that while the production of food increased very slowly, people tended to reproduce much more rapidly. He suggested that food might be expected to increase in arithmetic proportions—from quantities of one, to two, to three, to four, and so on. Population, however, could grow geometrically—from quantities of one, to two, to four, to sixteen, and so on. If such a progression were allowed to take place, the result would soon be catastrophic. Assuming that the population was most likely to increase in good times, Malthus concluded that it was more prudent, and indeed more humane in the long run, to deny the masses more than the bare essentials, thus discouraging a potentially ruinous population explosion. These arguments justified the accumulation of massive amounts of wealth in the hands of a very few, while the suffering among the workers, those who produced the wealth, mounted.

Then, toward the end of the nineteenth century, a new and "scientific" rationale for the possession of great wealth by a few in the face of the misery of the masses was advanced by another Englishman, Herbert Spencer (1820–1903). Loosely extrapolating Charles Darwin's theory of natural selection, Spencer applied it to a concept of social development that became known as *Social Darwinism.* Coining the phrase "survival of the fittest," a phrase often mistakenly attributed to Darwin himself, Spencer suggested that the wealthy were so favored because they were superior to the poor. Thus, according to Spencer, the possession of great wealth set the owner apart as a particularly worthy individual. It also encouraged the rich to redouble their efforts to expand their fortunes, thus asserting their advanced natures over the less worthy poor.

American capitalism.   This theory became most popular in the United States, where capitalist competition and "rugged individualism" had assumed exaggerated proportions. Harkening to the pompous lectures of William Graham Sumner

During the Great Depression of the 1930s, millions of proud unemployed people reluctantly queued up to receive life-saving food from charity organizations.

(1840–1910), a Yale professor and the nation's leading proponent of Social Darwinism, American moguls swaddled themselves in righteous justification while they plundered those less fortunate.

Happily, this brutal phase of capitalism was abandoned with the reforms of the Progressive Era (1901–1920) and, most importantly, with the New Deal of Franklin Delano Roosevelt (1933–1945). Yet, the doctrine of untempered individualism came into vogue once again in the 1980s when Ronald Reagan became President. He limited government involvement in the economy and celebrated the "free market place" as the appropriate arbiter of the distribution of goods and the dispenser of social justice. Ronald Reagan presided over a reactionary revolution which saw businesses deregulated and social programs emaciated by lack of public financial support. The freewheeling entrepreneurial system advocated by Reagan encouraged people to suppress their social consciences, and urged individuals to seek their own advantage. On the positive side, inflation was reduced dramatically, and interest rates and unemployment also fell. But at the same time, homelessness increased disgracefully; the gap between rich and poor widened seriously, the civil rights movement was set back in several important areas, and civil liberties were narrowed. Meanwhile, Reagan's policies of deregulation and his neglectful approach to administering policy saw natural resources pillaged for profit; the toxicity of air and water reached unprecedented levels; and the stock and commodity exchanges descended into unethical and illegal practices that had not been seen since the 1920s. At the same time, the national debt tripled, and the interest on the debt catapulted to the third largest category in the national budget. In only four years, the United States fell from the world's greatest creditor nation to the world's greatest debtor nation. Hundreds of billions of public dollars had to be used to cover losses in the Savings and Loan industry, due in large part to irresponsible investments and outright fraud by some Savings and Loan officials. At the same time, in the government, Pentagon employees were sent to jail for malfeasance in office; Food and Drug Administration officials pled guilty to accepting bribes; high ranking Housing and Urban Development personnel embezzled millions of dollars and diverted government funds to influential Republican Party politicos; and highly placed people in the White House were convicted of influence peddling.

The 1980s fetish with raw individualism seems to have run its course without destroying the foundations of the social–economic system forged by the New Deal, and the electorate voted for the "kinder and gentler nation" pledge of George Bush. We have, it seems, permanently evolved beyond capitalism's most exploitative era, albeit in faltering stages, yet we have not returned to the sanguine age of Adam Smith.

Founded on the principle of unlimited accumulation, American capitalism, most would agree, has been a terribly successful and productive economic system. However, close scrutiny reveals problems and contradictions worthy of consideration.

While affording great opportunity to its citizens, American capitalism reserves many of its greatest advantages for those with enough wealth to buy into the system. The adage "It takes money to make money" is indeed prophetic. For example, the greatest tax advantages to the middle class are usually available through buying a home. Yet, with skyrocketing prices and interest rates, fewer and fewer people can afford the initial amount necessary to buy a house and thus qualify for the tax deductions. The wealthy, on the other hand, can easily afford to buy a home or two—thus receiving this advantage as well; but if President Bush has his way, they will be additionally privileged. Bush has proposed lowering the tax rate assessed against income from capital gains (the profits from investment). Everyone likes the idea of lower taxes, but this proposal will accrue to the advantage of only those people who have surplus wealth that can be invested, and the difference in government revenue presumably must be picked up by the remaining taxpayers: the less well off. "Yes," you might say, "but investors also take the chance of losing their investment." This is true, of course, but do not forget that capital losses are also deductible from taxes, thus the wealthy are insulated from the full gravity of the presumed risk. By the same token, the wealthy enjoy many other tax and financial advantages of which the poor cannot avail themselves. Even the standard practice of volume buying favors the well-to-do. The prime interest rate, that offered to the bank's best customers, is lower than the interest rate assessed ordinary people. Consequently, those who have the greatest amount of money can get more money more cheaply and easily than those who have less money and presumably need it more.

The advantages afforded the wealthy in our system are even more startling when one becomes aware of the tendency for wealth to accumulate in fewer and fewer hands. Recent statistics indicate that the nation's wealth has never before been so heavily concentrated in the hands of a few. The nation's wealthiest people, numbering only 1 percent of the total population, own more wealth than do the poorest 70 percent of our population. This single percent of the people own about one–quarter of the wealth in the United States.[1] Corporate wealth also reflects this trend. Fewer than 500 of the nation's largest corporations account for three quarters

---

[1]Thomas B. Edsall, *The New Politics of Inequality* (New York: Norton, 1984), p. 222.

of the profits earned in a single year. At the same time, we continue to countenance poverty among millions of our citizens. No fewer than 350,000 people are currently homeless street people in the United States. Meanwhile, our cities decay, our poor youth fail to receive decent education, our chronically unemployed become despondent, and our indigent aged lock themselves away trying to weather the assaults of escalating crime and inflation while suffering the terrible pain of loneliness in a society that no longer needs them.

Some people argue that the economic system is malfunctioning when it gives greater advantages to the wealthy than it gives to the poor. They wince at tax laws which give the wealthy vast write-offs until they pay only a small percentage of their income in support of the state, while others carry far heavier burdens. "The rich get richer and the poor get poorer," they grimace. In fact, however, the capitalist system is not malfunctioning when it favors the wealthy—indeed it is doing exactly what it is supposed to do by such bias. Capitalism depends on *private* enterprise. It must have private capital investment if it is to function adequately. The most efficient way of creating private capital is to concentrate huge amounts of money in the hands of a tiny minority of the people rather than spreading it out more equally among the masses. The fortunate few—the wealthy—then put their amassed fortunes into capital investments, increasing productivity. The increased productivity is then divided among the masses in improved living standards and among the wealthy in increased profits. The trick is to divide the nation's productivity properly. If too much money is siphoned off in profits, consumers will lack funds with which to buy, causing a depressed economy and unemployment. If, on the other hand, too much of the productivity goes to the consumer, too little money will be left for capital investment, resulting in aging plants and machinery, reducing efficiency and productivity, and causing inflation.

It is clear, therefore, that capitalism depends on the existence of a tiny, enormously wealthy class. Hence, laws in capitalist societies are structured so as to give their wealthy greater economic benefits than are enjoyed by the rest of their people. Taking advantage of these privileges, the same families are apt to remain wealthy through time. The Rockefellers, Guggenheims, Mellons, Fords, and other families of great wealth, having amassed fortunes at the early stages of our industrialization, are likely to remain wealthy because the law is tilted in favor of their doing so.

This is not to suggest that other people cannot become wealthy or that large amounts of capital investment are not provided by small investors. Clearly, the capitalist system provides enough opportunity to allow for significant social and economic mobility. Yet, the fact remains that over 90 percent of all the stock in the United States is owned by less than 3 percent of its people. In short, capitalism depends upon the monopolization of wealth.

The American system is based upon a high-velocity economy, an economy that depends upon a high turnover of goods and a consequent high frequency of monetary exchange. Hence, a large amount of money must be in circulation and, augmented by high amounts of credit, spent frequently. Enormous numbers of goods are therefore made available to the consumer at relatively affordable prices. Even so, the commitment to moving large numbers of goods tends to encourage terribly wasteful practices. *Planned obsolescence* ensures that consumer goods will be produced at relatively low quality, thus forcing the consumer to replace the easily worn-out objects soon. Many goods are also produced in ways that make repair more costly than replacement.

While such practices may be good for the financial structure of the economy, this approach to the production and exchange of goods squanders national resources and relegates to the junk heap items that might more prudently be saved or reused.

Nevertheless, the negative aspects of capitalism, of which the foregoing are only some examples, should not be dwelled upon at the expense of attention to its positive features. The United States has risen from a relatively poor agrarian country to become the greatest industrial power in the world. Its people enjoy a standard of living unequaled in history. Perhaps even more remarkable, these economic successes have been achieved in a political and economic environment which remains open to personal free expression, affording its citizens a latitude of activity envied by people around the globe. The worst excesses of individualistic aggrandizement have been tempered by government regulation and social welfare programs. In developing programs which mitigate the economic impact on the "losers" in capitalistic competition, however, we have introduced socialist policies. Capitalism, in its purest form, rewards and protects only the "winners." Hence, ours is a mixed economic system.

In any event, capitalism and democracy developed coincidentally, both having been nurtured by confidence in human potential spawned by the scientific method, the Industrial Revolution, and the resulting liberal individualism. Indeed, it was very difficult to distinguish between capitalism and democracy during what one might call the neoclassical period of democratic theory.

NEOCLASSICAL DEMOCRATIC THEORY

The group of theorists who followed Hobbes, Locke, and Rousseau differed from them in a number of ways, though they had much in common with them as well. One of the differences is highly significant, however. The early philosophers were trying to justify a political system that they hoped would become a reality. The *neoclassical democratic philosophers* were trying to design governmental schemes in an environment that was *already* democratic. This single fact made their political views quite different. While Locke and Rousseau were definitely on the left of the political spectrum and were optimistic and hopeful about people, the second wave of democratic theorists tended to be more conservative and pessimistic about human nature, although they did not go to the extreme Hobbes reached.

John Locke, whose ideas have had the greatest impact on the democracies of England and the United States, laid down several specific principles that were modified or rejected by the next generation of political thinkers. These principles include belief in natural law, including the tenets that human reason is the key to the solution of social problems, that the individual is of greatest value in society, that government should be responsive to the will of the majority, that all people are basically equal, and that people should be unfettered in accumulating property unless the property rights of others are abused.

None of these principles would be left unchanged by the neoclassical democrats. The early philosophers were never faced with the problem of applying their theories. Later thinkers, by contrast, had to implement their ideas in the real world, a circumstance that made them more conservative. As time passed, the idea of natural law became less and less credible among scholars and politicians alike. Egalitarianism as well as majoritarianism were set aside in favor of distinctions based on social class. The new generation of thinkers substituted limited voting rights for equal representation, probusiness policies for absolute *laissez-faire,* and in some cases organicism for individualism. Still later, liberal democratic principles reemerged and, as we will see, evolved into one of the two major strains of contemporary democracy. Here, however, we will examine the theories of the second wave of democratic philosophers more closely.

Edmund Burke

There were three major neoclassical democrats. Interestingly, each of the three was a distinguished politician in his own right, and each developed his political theory in response to a political issue that he faced in his public life. The first of the three was Edmund Burke (1729–1797).

Although he was an Irishman, Burke had no trouble being accepted into English society and became an articulate spokesman for the ideals of the English state, crown, and church. Burke was noted for his eloquence in Parliament, where he served for almost 30 years. But his ideas were not universally appreciated. For example, the poet Robert Burns, piqued by the eminent Gaelic conservative, was moved to write:

> *Oft I have wonder'd that on Irish ground;*
> *No poisonous reptile has ever been found;*
> *Revealed stands the secret of great Nature's work:*
> *She preserved her poison to create a Burke.*

Conservative philosophy.   As mentioned in Chapter 2, Burke was the father of modern conservative philosophy. Conservative positions have always existed, to be sure, but Burke was the first to address conservatism as a philosophy, the first to analyze the basic principles and motivations of conservatives.

Burke's attitude was Hobbesian in several ways. Social and political stability were the major goals of his theories. Hence, he believed that a good government is one that keeps the peace. Although Burke was a conservative, he did not always object to change; indeed, he regarded it as a necessary feature of life. However, he felt that any change should be gradual, well thought out, and consistent with the prevailing social environment. He opposed changes that might disrupt the society, believing that the only modifications that should be made are those that will keep things much as they are.

Examples of how Burke applied this theory are found in his positions on the revolutions in England, the United States, and France and in his attitude toward the British East India Company. Burke defended the 1688 revolution in England and the 1776 revolution in the Anglo-American colonies[2] on the ground that each was an attempt to restore to a society constitutional principles that an aggressive king had destroyed. By the same token, however, he opposed the political activities of the

---

[2]Burke's career in Parliament (1765–1794) spanned the period of the American Revolution. British policies in the American colonies had been very controversial. Many members of Parliament opposed the government's attempts to force the American colonies to comply with its will. The British people were also divided on the issue, and their reluctance to fight their American cousins made it necessary for England to hire Hessian mercenaries to fight in the colonies.

British East India Company because he believed that the English had no right to govern India, a civilization that was much older than those of the West. Burke is most famous, however, for his passionate objection to the French Revolution. In his classic work *Reflections on the Revolution in France,* he argued that since the revolution had abruptly cut France off from its past development by replacing its monarchy with a republic, it posed a dire threat to French civilization itself.

Burke's resistance to change stemmed from his assumption that human reason is not competent to improve social or political systems. Burke believed that the institutions of any society are the products of the accumulated wisdom of centuries. No single generation has the ability to produce abrupt changes that will improve the system. Indeed, by meddling with institutions that have been perfected over centuries, people may destroy them completely. Burke viewed civilization as a fragile thing that could be ruined if it were not protected from human folly.

Burke believed that any existing institution had value; that is, an existing institution, a product of the wisdom of successive generations, has proved its value by surviving and should therefore not be trifled with. If they were not useful, institutions would disappear, Burke reasoned. In addition, Burke believed that part of the strength of an institution comes from the fact that it is accepted by the citizens in a society. This popular acceptance could occur only after an extended period. Any proposal for change, regardless of the soundness of the thought that produced it, could not attract the same commitment that an institution could develop over time. Hence, according to Burke, a new institution can never be as valuable as an older one.

Surprisingly, Burke's conservative philosophy led him to develop an attitude toward society similar to Rousseau's. Burke, like Rousseau, believed that there had been a time when people existed as solitary individuals without a society as we know it. They came together, however, out of a need to interact with each other, and in so doing, they formed an institution that has become part of the definition of humanity itself. Burke believed that goodness, morality, even civilization itself became possible only when people had created society. Society thus becomes the context in which people can refine their characters and develop their human traits. Moreover, the society develops an organic character. It becomes a personality in its own right, a "political personality."

Although Burke did not emphasize this point as much as Rousseau, he believed that absolute power came from the society and the state. The society may be a collection of "foolish" individuals, but when those individuals join to form a society, their collective judgment becomes "wise" and "always acts right." Burke's respect for tradition and history, coupled with his assumption that society had almost mystical powers, contributed to an attitude toward society that approached religious devotion. Here, too, he not only followed Rousseau but anticipated the ideas of Georg Hegel (1770–1831).

Theory of government.   As already mentioned, Burke had a conservative attitude toward government. The primary purpose of government, he believed, was to keep order. He was also uneasy about the concept of popular rule. Hence, he made a strong defense for representative government. He argued that the proper governing agency of England was Parliament. Yet, Parliament should not necessarily be controlled by the people. Rather, it was an institution through which the minority would rule the majority, albeit in a benevolent fashion.

Burke maintained that a good ruler must meet three qualifications. *Ability* was of course necessary if the government was to be managed efficiently. Second, Burke believed that only people with *property* should be allowed to govern, since they would be less likely to desire the possessions of others. Burke believed that it was quite natural for property to be distributed unequally among the people in the state. Because people without property are never content, they constantly try to deprive the wealthy of their property. This disruption of society could be avoided if power was granted solely to property holders.

Burke's third qualification for government was *high birth*. While Burke did not argue that the upper class would always rule better than other classes, he pointed out that the nobility tended to have a greater stabilizing influence than any other class and should therefore rule. Note the overriding importance given to stability in each of the last two qualifications. You will remember that the conservative desires order more than anything else.

Burke rejected Locke's belief that members of Parliament should be bound by the wishes of their constituents. Those wishes should be considered, of course, but members of Parliament should not let such pressure sway them from their better judgment. Legislators were elected to make policy for their constituents, but they were not to be thought of as "ambassadors" who could act only on the instructions of their constituents. As Burke put it, "While a member of the legislature ought to give great weight to the wishes of his constituents, he ought never to sacrifice to them his unbiased opinion, his mature judgment, his enlightened conscience."

Burke also rejected another liberal democratic position. *He denied the basic equality of people.* People, he argued, are obviously unequal. They have different abilities and intellects. Consistent with his conservative views, Burke believed that the most important distinctions between people are property and social status. Those who have property and status are simply more important than those who do not. Consequently, the well-to-do, being more influential than the poor, deserve more representation in government.

Burke was also a nationalist. Indeed, his philosophy did much to integrate nationalism with conservative philosophy. As a nationalist, however, Burke rejected the local autonomy of federalism in the United States. He argued that when people were elected to Parliament, they were not required to represent the narrow interests of their constituencies. Parliament, he believed, was a national legislature, not a meeting of local representatives. "You choose a member, indeed," he said in a speech to his constituents, "but when you have chosen him, he is not a member of Bristol, but he is a member of Parliament."

To Burke, then, democracy is a system in which the people choose representatives who will rule them in their best interests. This attitude stems from a pessimistic view of the individual's ability to reason and a denial of the equality of people. Burke's philosophy also implies a nationalism derived from an exaggerated respect for the community or society.

James Madison

James Madison (1751–1836) is the second major neoclassical democratic philosopher. Madison had a long and distinguished political career. His most important political writings, like those of Burke, were responses to the dramatic political

James Madison (1751–1836)

events of his day. Though still a young man in 1787, Madison was an experienced statesman by the time of the Constitutional Convention. It was at this meeting that he made his greatest contribution to government, even though he continued a brilliant career long afterwards.

Because he brought to the Constitutional Convention the fundamental structure on which the United States Constitution was based, Madison is often called the Father of the Constitution. He is also one of our best sources of information on the political intent of the drafters. Sharing authorship of a collection of essays known as the *Federalist Papers* with Alexander Hamilton and John Jay, Madison treats us to a beautifully written, well-reasoned explanation of the political theory upon which the Constitution is based.

Madison's view of politics.   Madison was a very complicated character whose political attitudes vacillated from right to left on the spectrum, depending on the circumstances. With regard to popular government, Madisonian philosophy is definitely conservative. His studies convinced him that the history of democracy was rather unsuccessful. When faced with a crisis, popularly controlled governments usually degenerated into "mob rule," finally ending with the people giving power to a tyrant of some sort. Hence, Madison, like almost everyone present at the Constitutional Convention, had little respect for pure democracy.

Though Madison probably believed in popular sovereignty in theory, he did not trust the people themselves, nor did he have confidence in any form of direct government. In fact, Madison's attitude toward people was somewhat Hobbesian. In *The Federalist* (no. 55) he expressed mixed feelings about the nature of people.

> . . . As there is a degree of depravity in mankind which requires a certain degree of circumspection and distrust, so there are other qualities in human nature which justify a certain portion of esteem and confidence.

In *The Federalist* (no. 10), however, he describes human nature in unambiguous Hobbesian terms. "So strong is this propensity of mankind to fall into mutual animosities that where no substantial occasion presents itself the most frivolous and fanciful distinctions have been sufficient to kindle their unfriendly passions and excite their most violent conflicts."

Despite his Hobbesian disposition toward people, Madison did not share the English philosopher's confidence in strong government as a remedy for human shortcomings. Quite the contrary. Like Locke, he believed that individual liberty was the main goal of a political system. Yet, unlike Locke he was not at all confident of the individual's ability to achieve and maintain liberty in a democratic society. This conflict involved Madison in a dilemma. He believed that people ought to govern themselves in some way, but at the same time experience taught him that popular governments soon degenerated into dictatorships.

Therefore, Madison was convinced that government was necessary, and he preferred a popularly controlled political system. Still, his studies showed that neither the people nor the government could be counted on to maintain "liberty, which is essential to political life." He had observed that government, when left unchecked, was oppressive and cruel. At the same time, however, he believed that human nature was not only aggressive and selfish but *unchangeable* as well. He therefore wanted to construct a system which would play the oppressiveness of government against the avarice of people, hoping that each would check the negative aspects of the other. This mutual negation, he speculated, would result in good government and the greatest amount of individual liberty possible. This, as you will see shortly, is at once the genius and perhaps the greatest failing of James Madison and the American political system.

Madison's political system.   Madison did not fear the individual; indeed, he supported individual rights and liberties. What concerned him was not solitary individuals but groups of individuals in politics. These groups he called *factions.*

Madison noted that in politics people had a habit of combining into factions to pursue mutual interests. This grouping he considered unfortunate but unavoidable. The faction about which he felt the greatest trepidation was the majority. You will recall that he believed people were essentially selfish and that if, in a democratic system, a group was in the majority for a sustained period, it would use its power to oppress the minority.

Using the Constitution to protect the minorities, Madison's system of government is largely an attempt to divide and frustrate the majority. Madison envisioned a political system with the broadest possible power base. For example, he rejected the common belief that a democracy could work only in a very small area, arguing that it could succeed in a large country like the United States. A large population spread over a huge area would make it very difficult to force a permanent majority. Such a society would probably divide into varied and fluctuating minorities, making a long lasting majority unlikely. Instead, majorities would be created out of combinations of competing minorities. Thus, any majority would be temporary, and new ones would be elusive. This system, which political scientists now term *pluralism,* will be discussed in more detail in the next chapter.

Economic disparity was also a necessary component of Madison's scheme. Not unlike Karl Marx, Madison believed that economic factors move people to political activity more than any other single factor. Madison was not as absolute on this subject as Marx; he believed that religion, culture, ideals, and geographic factors also influence people. Still, he argued that economic concerns are the most powerful force in people's lives. "A landed interest, a manufacturing interest, a mercantile interest, with many lesser interests," Madison wrote, "grow up of necessity in civilized nations, and divide them into different classes, actuated by different sentiments and views." Madison's wish for a diverse and competitive economic system, together with his belief that people are by nature combative, led to the conclusion that capitalism is the economic system best suited to the political structure he had in mind.

Madison's view of the nature of a democracy was almost identical to Burke's, with one very important exception. Madison expected that the legislators would represent their districts or their states. Unlike Burke, he wanted to localize rather than nationalize politics, since this process would institutionalize tens, or even hundreds, of local factions. He was very pessimistic about the chance of a successful democratic government. His studies indicated that pure democracy is usually unsuccessful and "can admit of no cure of the mischiefs of faction." On the other hand, he wrote in *The Federalist* (no. 10), "A republic, by which I mean a government in which the scheme of representation takes place, opens a different prospect and promises the *cure* for which we are seeking" (emphasis added).

In short, Madison believed that the people should rule themselves, but only through representatives. What he called a "republic" is more accurately defined as a *representative democracy.* Madison also expected that the representatives would be free to use their judgment rather than being bound to the wishes of their constituents, as Locke had expected. Echoing Burke, Madison wrote in *The Federalist* (no. 10) that a republic would:

> ... refine and enlarge the public views by passing them through the medium of a chosen body of citizens, whose patriotism and love of justice will be least likely to sacrifice it to temporary or partial considerations. Under such a regulation it may well happen that the public voice, pronounced by the representatives of the people, will be more consonant to the public good than if pronounced by the people themselves, convened for the purpose.

Thus, Madison expected that the United States would be governed by an enlightened and benevolent aristocracy that would protect the *interests* of the people but would not necessarily be bound by the people's *will.*

Checks and balances.   Madison's best-known and most creative contribution is the system of *separation of powers* and *checks and balances.* In developing this system, he owed a great deal to two earlier students of government, James Harrington (1611–1677) and Charles Montesquieu (1689–1755). Both of these men were interested in a democratic republic and in developing a way of limiting the power of the government over the people. Using their ideas as a base, Madison created a complex system of institutional and popular restraints.

By separating the powers of government, Madison hoped to make it impossible for any single branch of the government to gain too much power and use it to dominate the others. No person could serve in more than one branch of the government at a time, and each branch was given its own separate and distinct powers. The legislature, divided into two houses, was to make the law, the executive was to carry out the law, and the judiciary was to adjudicate legal disputes and interpret the law. Yet each branch was given some powers that overlapped with those of the other two branches. The legislature controlled the purse strings, and it was also allowed to ratify appointments to the executive and judicial branches. The executive appointed judges and could veto laws. The courts were expected to nullify any law or executive action that violated the Constitution.[3] These are just a few examples of the checks and balances provided for in the American system of government; there are many others, and we shall discuss them in the next chapter.

Another kind of separation or "division of powers" devised by Madison is *federalism*. The powers of government were divided between the state and the national government. In this way Madison hoped to prevent either level of government from gaining too much power. Federalism also divided the people of the United States into several compartments. He hoped that although majorities might develop at the state level, the various majorities would check each other, thus preventing a permanent majority at the national level. "The influence of factious leaders may kindle a flame within their particular States," he wrote, "but will be unable to spread a general conflagration through the other states."

Madison's ultimate check, however, was built into the electoral process itself. To begin with, only members of the House of Representatives were elected directly by the people. Until the Sixteenth Amendment was passed in 1913, senators were elected by the state legislatures. The president and vice president were, and still are, elected by the electoral college, and although the voters elect the electors, the electors are not required by the Constitution to vote for the presidential candidate to whom they are pledged. Judges are even more removed from popular control, since they are appointed to the bench for life.

The people's hold over government is complicated even more because officials are elected to staggered terms from different constituencies. While House members are elected from congressional districts every two years, senators are elected on a statewide basis to six-year terms, with only one-third of the Senate being elected every two years. The president, by contrast, is chosen in a national election to a four-year term. Hence, it takes six full years for voters, in 536 different constituencies, to fill every national elective office. This arrangement was deliberately contrived to soften the effect of popular "passions."

Popular control is also reduced by the fact that the terms of office of elected

---

[3]It is true that the Constitution does not grant the power of judicial review to the courts in so many words, but there can be no question that the founders intended such a power to exist. In *The Federalist* (no. 78) Hamilton wrote: "No legislative act, therefore, contrary to the constitution can be valid . . . . Where the will of the legislature, declared in its statutes, stands in opposition to that of the people, declared in the constitution, the judges ought to be governed by the latter rather than the former. They ought to regulate their decisions by the fundamental laws rather than by those which are not fundamental."

officials are fixed by law and cannot be interrupted except under very unusual circumstances. The people elect many officials, but only when the law calls for elections and not necessarily when the people wish to vote on a particular office. Elections take place on the first Tuesday after the first Monday of November in even years. Why? Because that is when the law calls for them to be held.

It is clear that the American political system, as developed by Madison, is not very democratic in the participatory sense of the term. In fact, it severely limits the ways in which the people actually rule themselves. The people cannot pass laws; they cannot repeal laws. They cannot legally remove a person from office before the expiration of the term. Officials may be impeached, of course, but even this is not done by the people. Congress impeaches; the people do not.

To cap the irony, popular sovereignty, which means that the people are the source of all law and power, is supposed to be the central feature of a democracy. Yet, the Constitution of the United States may not be amended directly by the people of the United States. It may be amended only through their representatives in Congress and the state legislatures.

One should gather from these comments that our political system was not designed to be very democratic in the literal sense of the term. The people formally participate in their government very rarely; their direct control over government officials is limited to election day. It is true that popular control and participation are much more significant than a simple statement of the people's formal powers indicates, but the fact remains that the system was not intended to be very democratic. Even so, the American political system has been liberalized considerably since the Constitution was written. However, the theoretical justification for these changes are founded more in the ideas of Thomas Jefferson than in those of James Madison.

Jefferson's alternative.   A man of reason, Thomas Jefferson (1743–1826) was America's Voltaire. Yet, Jefferson was a man of action as well as a man of thought. His most famous work, the Declaration of Independence, articulated the Spirit of '76, which justified the American Revolution and became a beacon, leading freedom-loving people throughout the world to their goal. America's most articulate statesman, Jefferson may be placed between Locke and Rousseau on the left of the political spectrum. Though he generally leaned toward Locke's version of the social contract and natural law, he shared Rousseau's respect for the common people and for participatory government. More than either of the other natural law theorists, Jefferson favored revolution as a way of bringing about meaningful political change. Arguing that 20 years without a rebellion would be too long if government officials were to remain servants of the people, Jefferson wrote: "The tree of liberty must be refreshed from time to time with the blood of patriots and tyrants."

To Jefferson the Spirit of '76 was a declaration that all people were created equal, that "the Laws of Nature and Nature's God" had given every person a set of rights that could not be legally alienated, and that among those rights were "Life, Liberty, and the pursuit of Happiness."[4] As a social contract theorist, he believed that

---

[4]You will recall from Chapter 2 that in drafting the Declaration of Independence, Jefferson amended Locke's phrase "life, liberty and property" to read "Life, Liberty and the pursuit of Happiness." This distinction is important, since it was intentional. Jefferson put up a spirited defense of the phrase

Thomas Jefferson (1743–1826)

government was the product of a creative act by the people in the society. He agreed with Locke that all "just powers" of government accrue to it from the people and that the government is supposed to serve the people, not the other way around. If the government does not serve the interests of the people, its masters, "it is the Right of

---

against the Second Continental Congress delegates who wanted to change the phrase back to Locke's more familiar one. Though Jefferson was a classical democratic theorist in the tradition of Locke, he, like Rousseau, lived a full generation after the English philosopher and saw a different reality. Locke, the philosopher of a capitalist class that was challenging the dominant feudal class, saw private property as a means of achieving greater freedom. However, by the time of Rousseau and Jefferson the capitalist class had moved much closer to the source of power; some capitalists were actually beginning to use their control of property to deny equality and liberty to others. It will be recalled that Rousseau, the radical, suggested equal distribution of private property as a means by which the equality and liberty of all citizens in the community could be guaranteed. Jefferson sought a milder solution by simply deleting property from the inalienable rights and substituting a more abstract phrase. In either case, however, it is clear that an important change had occurred in leftist thinking about private property. Instead of considering private property a *natural right*, they gave it second-class status as a *social right*. And so it remains today. The left generally deemphasizes the importance of private property and values it only as a contribution to the welfare of the society, while those toward the right of the political spectrum take a more traditionally Lockean position and equate private property with individual well-being and liberty.

One should note, however, that even Locke opposed unlimited accumulation of private property by any individual. The American capitalists' argument in support of unlimited accumulation of private property is acually a perversion of the theories of Locke and Adam Smith rather than a true reflection of their ideas.

the People to alter or abolish it, and to institute new Government, laying its foundation on such principles, and organizing its powers in such form as to them shall seem most likely to effect their Safety and Happiness."[5]

Jefferson's most outstanding characteristic was his love for and confidence in the common individual. No other political theorist has expressed such deep faith in ordinary people. Like Rousseau, Jefferson idealized the common people, yet somehow Jefferson's vision of the sturdy, self-reliant yeoman seems more appealing than Rousseau's "noble savage." True to Rousseau's basic theme, Jefferson avoided the sophisticated society of the cities for the more peaceful and simple rural life of his home in Monticello.

Jefferson's faith in the common people went beyond the romantic notion of an uncomplicated lifestyle, however. His confidence in the strength and wisdom of the ordinary folk was unshakeable. Unlike Hobbes, Burke, Madison, or Hamilton, Jefferson believed that the people were the only competent guardians of their own liberties, and as such they should be in firm control of their government. Discussing the role of the people in a republic, he wrote to Madison from France in 1787 that "they are the only sure reliance for the preservation of our liberties."

Jefferson's democratic ruralism is very close to an early form of populism (an ideology dedicated to the common people). Its impact on our political system has been great. Jefferson's liberal democratic theories have acted as a counterweight to Madison's conservative democratic ideas; indeed, the interplay between these two basic attitudes has dominated American political history. During the American Revolution and under the Articles of Confederation, Jefferson's ideology prevailed. However, for many reasons, not the least of which was the low priority given private property during this period, opposition to the Articles of Confederation began to build, culminating in the adoption of the Constitution of the United States. *The Constitution was, in fact, no less than a conservative counterrevolution to the dominant theme of the American Revolution.*

Put differently, the Spirit of '76 was, for its time, radical and revolutionary. However, because of the apparent failure of the Articles of Confederation (1781–1789), under which it seemed that the economic and political situation was leading the country to disaster, James Madison, Alexander Hamilton, Benjamin Franklin, George Washington, and the other delegates to the Constitutional Convention deliberately stifled the Spirit of '76, replacing it with a much more conservative, less democratic, and more paternalistic system of government. Although most of the nation's founders believed in popular checks on government, they were opposed to *direct* popular control of the basic governmental institutions. Hence, they created a government in which power was much more centralized than it had been under the Articles of Confederation. They also severely limited popular control over the government.

At this point the reader should note that what has just been said is not necessarily a criticism. Certainly, no objective student of American history could argue that the near chaos into which the United States had fallen by 1787 did not warrant some action that would restore tranquility to the land. Nor do I mean to argue that the federal Constitution has not served us well in the past two centuries; quite the

---

[5]From the Declaration of Independence.

contrary. Yet one should not regard the nation's founders as infallible,[6] for while their actions may have been justified and the results of their labors beneficial, some of the steps they took have had unfortunate consequences.

Perhaps the most unfortunate aspect of Madison's work was his conclusion that since human nature is evil and cannot be changed, he had to devise a system that would turn this "fact of life" to advantage. As already mentioned, this compromise was an act of genius. Indeed, the system of government Madison devised 200 years ago has worked remarkably well, and its citizens can take pride in it. Even so, our system works by turning people's greed to advantage; in the process it encourages people to act selfishly, thus making our political system particularly compatible with capitalism. While the material progress accomplished by our system is undeniable, it has done nothing to stimulate people to become better human beings. Actually, it has done quite the opposite. The whole system is predicated on the assumption that human nature cannot be changed; consequently, few people in our society believe human beings can really improve themselves—even in the face of overwhelming evidence to the contrary!

When the Constitution was adopted, the "revolution" was ended, the Spirit of '76 snuffed out, the radical experiment brought to a close, and a different, more conservative, less idealistic experiment begun. What might have existed had the revolution been allowed to run its course is impossible to know. History seems to indicate that we gained a great deal by ending it. One loss, however, was an optimistic attitude toward humanity. Thomas Paine, who understood revolution as did few other people, had expectations for the American Revolution much like Jefferson's, if not even more utopian. "We have it in our power to begin the world all over again," he wrote in *Common Sense*. Even with all our materialistic progress, we must be a bit saddened that Paine's idealism was lost.

The conservative victory was not as absolute as one might think, however. Since 1789, the year the Constitution went into effect, the system has gradually been

---

[6]Historically, one of the most stabilizing features in American political life has been our general confidence in the goodness and wisdom of the Constitution of the United States and its authors. Although I do not challenge this assumption, I offer a word of caution. Our national faith in the validity of the Constitution and its authors is not only justified by historical example but also based on a mystique supported by a number of symbols. The very fact that we capitalize the word *Constitution* illustrates this tendency. Because of our great respect for our early statesmen, we are often tempted to think of them as superhuman and to believe that their judgment was faultless. This is an unfortunate mistake. We will understand the Constitution much better if we recognize that the people who wrote it were practical politicians who had interests to protect and who drafted the document to satisfy those interests, many of which bear little or no relationship to our own lives.

When confronted with a constitutional problem, we are tempted to look back to find out what the nation's founders intended the Constitution to mean. While this practice is sometimes reasonable, we must keep two points in mind: (1) The founders were trying to solve many problems that are of only historical interest to us today. They could not even imagine the synthetics of which our clothing is made, let alone understand the complex fabric comprising our society. Hence, what they intended for their government may not make any sense for us today. (2) The notion that the Constitution was what the founders wanted for their society is incorrect in the first place. Not a single person who participated in the Constitutional Convention got from it exactly what he wanted. Indeed, among the fifty-five men who helped write the Constitution, several refused to support its ratification. Those who did, did so not because it was what they wanted but because the compromise was the best they could hope for and because it was better, in their opinion, than the Articles of Confederation. These two points should temper our attitude toward the nation's founders and help us better understand the Constitution as it applies to our own society.

liberalized. Indeed, George Mason, Jefferson, Samuel Adams, and others insisted, in return for their support, that the conservative Constitution be amended to mention the specific rights of the people under the new system. The original document was concerned primarily with the structure and powers of the central government. Little reference was made to the rights and liberties of the people, and the radicals insisted that they be added. This addition, of course, was the *Bill of Rights*.

Since the passage of the Bill of Rights the country has gone through a series of liberalizing eras that have gradually relaxed the restraints imposed on the people by the new political order. The changing social and economic effects of industrialization demanded political democratization. In the early nineteenth century the administrations of Thomas Jefferson (1801–1809) and Andrew Jackson (1825–1837) extended the vote to almost every adult white male citizen. And the Lincoln epoch (1861–1867) not only liberated the slaves but also brought about the Homestead Act, which made free land available to poor farmers. Other legislation during Lincoln's era promoted federal aid to education and made possible the construction of the transcontinental railroad. The Progressive Era amended the Constitution to provide for women's suffrage and for popular election of United States senators, enacted the progressive income tax, and established the procedures of initiative, referendum, and recall (otherwise known as direct democracy) in many states. The New Deal (1933–1941) brought social security, collective bargaining, and many social-welfare programs. The Great Society (1964–1969) launched a war on poverty and racial bigotry, while the past two decades have witnessed drives to liberate women and gays. Each of these eras produced great change. Nevertheless, each was followed by a period of reaction in which many of the changes were dismantled. The net result is that the liberties of individuals in the system have been gradually, if not completely, equalized and increased. Although much remains to be done, the nation has evolved to something closer to the Jeffersonian political ideal than perhaps Madison and his colleagues intended.

John C. Calhoun

John C. Calhoun (1782–1850) had one of the most distinguished careers of public service in United States history, holding high office almost continuously for nearly 40 years. Devoted to the Union—but also to the principle of *states' rights*—he greatly expanded on a theme earlier initiated by Jefferson and Madison and developed the theory of *nullification* in *The South Carolina Exposition,* written in 1828. In this tract Calhoun argued that the states had created the national government and that the latter was therefore subordinate to the states. Accordingly, no state could be bound to a national law if its state legislature voted to nullify the statute. Thus, in an attempt to define the relationship of the states to the national government, Calhoun insisted that the Constitution was confederate in form and so inadvertently developed the philosophy used by the South in its secession from the Union ten years after his death.

Concurrent majorities.   In the last few months of his life Calhoun, though tired and ill, wrote a brilliant treatise on political philosophy. In this document, entitled *A Disquisition on Government,* he analyzed the essence of democracy, raising questions that have not yet been answered fully.

Calhoun took the social nature of people as fact. People, he argued, instinctively group together. He also assumed that government is necessary when people form groups. While he believed that people are naturally social beings, he argued, not unlike Hobbes, that individuals feel greater concern for themselves than for others in the group. This self-concern causes them to attack one another; hence, the need for government is clear and universal. Yet, Calhoun pointed out that even though government is intended primarily to protect individuals from each other, it is run by people who have the same selfish impulses as other people. Therefore, they can—if unchecked—use the power of government to oppress the very people the government is supposed to protect. Accordingly, government must be limited, and the mechanism by which a government is limited is what Calhoun called a constitution.

Calhoun believed that the people's most important political function was to limit governmental power. He did not concern himself greatly with the concept of government itself because he believed that government was divinely inspired. The job left to mortals was to maintain their liberties by effectively limiting government. "Constitution is the contrivance of man," he wrote in the *Disquisition*, "while government is of divine ordination. Man is left to perfect what the wisdom of the Infinite ordained as necessary to preserve the race."

Because he believed that the governors would naturally use their power to take advantage of the governed, Calhoun saw the governor and the governed as adversaries: "Those who exercise power and those subject to its exercise—the rulers and the ruled—stand in antagonistic relations to each other." As a result he argued that the people must be able to defend themselves against oppressive rulers. Thus, the vote was necessary, he thought, because it gave the people control over the length of time the ruler could rule.

At this point Calhoun turned what appears to be a relatively standard justification of democracy into a piercing analysis of freedom and oppression. In so doing, he filled in many details about the rights of the minority and the nature of majority oppression that Madison had not elaborated.

According to Calhoun, although popular suffrage gave the people some control over the government it did not guarantee justice and good government, as Locke, Rousseau, and Jefferson had believed. All the popular vote did was to transfer power from the few to the many, thus changing the source of governmental authority without changing the tendency of government to oppress. Since every individual has an urge to take advantage of others, government by the many can be just as oppressive as government by one or by a few. The only difference is that government by the majority oppresses the minority, while government by a few oppresses the many. Hence, democracy, while it was the best form of government available, was no guarantee against oppression. Calhoun agreed with Madison that a tyranny of the majority was just as dangerous as any other form of tyranny.

Some philosophers argued that an existing majority would be kept from oppressing the minority because it could find itself out of power and at the mercy of a new majority after the next election. Calhoun rejected this argument on the grounds that the selfish nature of the rulers would force them to oppress all the more when they felt themselves threatened with the loss of their power.

For a solution to this dilemma, Calhoun turned to a Madisonianesque structure of government. He advocated a system in which society should be divided into groups based on economic, religious, regional, and ethnic lines, thus forming several local majorities. At this point, however, Calhoun exceeds Madison's separatism by rejecting the Virginian's belief that the national government should hold sway in disputes with local authorities. Instead, Calhoun insisted that each of the local majorities would have to agree to a national law before it could become effective.

This system of *concurrent majorities* would, Calhoun believed, result in an effective government. The vote would make those who governed responsible to the voters, and the need for a unanimous agreement by the several majorities would prevent government oppression. A perfect government would give representation and a veto to every interest group in the society. This safeguard, however, would be difficult if not impossible to guarantee. Yet, Calhoun reasoned, even if the society were only divided into its major interest groups, each having a veto over the actions of the whole, the goal of protection against oppression might well be achieved. Getting the agreement of several majorities would, Calhoun thought, probably require overwhelming popular approval, leaving a minority too small for the rulers to exploit profitably. As he put it in the *Disquisition,* "For, in such case, it would require so large a portion of the community, compared with the whole, to concur, or acquiesce in the action of the government, that the number to be plundered would be too few, and the number to be aggrandized too many, to afford adequate motives to oppression and abuse of its powers."

Calhoun further justified the system of concurrent majorities by analyzing it in relation to the *numerical majority* used in more standard forms of democracy. As had Burke, Calhoun rejected human equality as sufficient justification for political equality. He argued instead that the numerical majority accounts only for raw numbers and thus implies that everyone in the society has essentially the same interests. This concept, according to Calhoun, is unrealistic. A society, he rightly ventured, is composed of people with many varying interests. Since the numerical majority does not account for these differences, it does not reflect the society in all its complexity.

Concurrent majorities, Calhoun believed, would not only weigh the numerical value of people but also measure people in terms of their interests, thus giving a more accurate accounting of the popular will. The first error that naturally arises from overlooking the differences among individuals is to confuse the numerical majority with the people themselves, and to do this so completely as to regard them as identical. "This *radical* error . . . has contributed more than any other cause to prevent the formation of popular constitutional governments, and to destroy them even when they have been formed" (emphasis added). Here Calhoun makes clear his unwillingness to accept the equality of all the people in the society. Because any single majority could veto the action of the whole, he would obviously give the veto power to a very small number of people. Like Madison, he does not seem to be concerned about the tyranny of the minority, but is it not a tyranny when a tiny part of the whole can prevent the majority of the people from doing what they wish?

Calhoun also argued that a permanent numerical majority would form if his system of concurrent majorities was not used. This seems doubtful, especially in the face of his own correct assertion that the society is made up of a myriad of varying interests. It is more likely that while there could be a group that would find itself always in the minority, the membership of the majority would change from one issue to the next to reflect the varied interest patterns in the society. Moreover, Calhoun seemed to imply that while the society is made up of individuals with various competing interests, each person in the society has only one major interest, and each can be conveniently fitted into one majority or another. But is it not more likely that each person has several interests, and that two or more of those interests may sometimes conflict with each other? How can such a person be represented in the system of concurrent majorities? Can that person vote as a member of each group that reflects his or her interests? In such a case it seems likely that Calhoun's system of concurrent majorities displays at least as many distortions as the simple numerical majority, to say nothing of the possibility that the majority view would often be frustrated by a very small minority.

Calhoun continued his analysis by suggesting that a constitutional democratic government is impossible without the system of concurrent majorities. A constitutional government, which is synonymous with a limited government, allows action by the numerical majority. Such action is positive and is therefore equated with government itself. Apparently forgetting that the numerical majority could vote against a policy just as easily as it could vote in favor, Calhoun further suggested that only the concurrent majorities can veto anything. Moreover, he equated this power of negation or limitation with constitution. "It is, indeed, the negative power which makes the constitution," he wrote, "and the positive which makes government. The one is the power of acting; and the other the power of preventing or arresting action. The two combined, make constitutional governments."

Calhoun argued that a government acted unfairly when it took actions which were unfavorable to any interest group in the society. Those in the minority within their own interest group could be consoled, since at least, they were overruled by people with similar interests and perhaps the majority knew best. However, a simple numerical majority measures quantity, not quality, and thus can abuse the best interests of any part of the society. Calhoun believed that this would be a gross misuse of the power of government and saw it as a form of tyranny no less than any other dictatorship. "The numerical majority is as truly *single power*—and excludes the negative as completely as the absolute government of one, or of the few. The former is as much the absolute government of the democratic, or popular form, as the latter of the monarchical or aristocratical. It has, accordingly, in common with them, the same tendency of oppression and abuse of power."

The neoclassical democrats differ most clearly from the classical democrats in two areas. Locke, Rousseau, Jefferson, and even Hobbes argued that people were basically equal. Further, Locke, Rousseau, and Jefferson agreed that, while property rights were important, they should not be used to deny equal political and economic rights. This assumption of human equality is absent among the neoclassical democrats. Burke and Calhoun were the most clearly elitist, but elitism, or rule by a superior group, is implied by Madison as well. Unlike their predecessors, the neoclassical democrats all agreed that people should have a representative government, but they differed as to the level of government to which the representative should owe greatest allegiance. Burke argued for a national view, but Madison was less adamant about it, and Calhoun was unalterably dedicated to local control of legislation.

Each of the three neoclassical democrats may be considered a democrat because each believed in some kind of popular control over the rulers. Yet, they all rejected direct democracy and favored an elite governing class. Indeed, they even rejected the principle of government by the majority. Burke said least about the concept of rule by the majority; clearly, he did not consider this concept vital, since he supported the preservation of the noble class as a governing group. Madison and

Calhoun were opposed to majority rule as an absolute principle. They feared that the majority would abuse the rights of minorities, and each devised a system for frustrating the majority's wishes. Further, believing people to be essentially self-oriented and rejecting human equality as an important factor, the neoclassical democrats reasoned that capitalism was the most appropriate economic system since it tended to reward people in relation to their contributions. In short, by emphasizing property rights above human rights and by denying majoritarianism and human equality, the neoclassical democrats carried democracy toward the right of the political spectrum. But the passage of time and the evolution of liberal theory eventually restored democracy to the left.

THE RELIBERALIZATION OF DEMOCRACY

During Locke's time people had begun to think that they could use reason to improve social conditions. After all, through science, reason had improved their material existence. They also speculated that if there were natural forces guiding all other creatures, there might also be natural forces guiding people. Hence, liberalism was born swaddled in the natural law theory.

Jeremy Bentham (1748–1832) belonged to a later generation, however. Indeed, he was in the forefront of the second wave of English liberal thinkers. Like earlier liberals, he was a product of the scientific and technological progress achieved since the Enlightenment. He too believed that people could use reason to improve themselves, but he thought that the natural law theory led to a philosophical dead end. Bentham held that as long as the people in a society were confident that there was a "right conduct" that could be found through the active pursuit of "right reason," society would be dynamic and changing. However, as soon as those in power thought that they had found the answer, all the citizens would have to conform to the leader's idea of right conduct. At that point the society would become stagnant and lose its vitality.

Utilitarianism

Bentham did not argue that there was an absolute, eternal, and universal rule in nature by which people should govern their conduct. Instead, he based his liberalism on belief in the value of human self-reliance. He disagreed with the idea of *moral absolutism,* the principle that there was a single source of right and wrong in nature, a good and bad beyond human authority. However, Bentham did not reject the standard of natural law without suggesting his own measure by which to evaluate human activity and conduct: the *moral relativist* philosophy of *utilitarianism.*

"Nature," Bentham wrote in *An Introduction to the Principles of Morals and Legislation,* "has placed mankind under the governance of two sovereign masters, *pain* and *pleasure.*" Human happiness would be achieved when pain was at a minimum and pleasure at a maximum. The value or *utility* of any policy, therefore, can be measured by the amount of pleasure or pain it brings to an individual or to society as a whole. Rejecting elitism, Bentham assumed that one person's happiness is equal to the happiness of any other. Further, Bentham believed that the well-being of society would be maximized by any policy that brought "the greatest happiness to the greatest number." The principle of utility, or utilitarianism, was Bentham's major interest. Almost everything he did or wrote was a variation on that theme, and he developed a theory of law by which to implement it.

Positivist law resulted from the combination of Bentham's rejection of natural law, his utilitarianism, and his conviction that government should take *positive* steps to maximize the happiness of the society. "The business of government," he wrote, "is to promote the happiness of society." The authority of a given law, in Bentham's view, had nothing to do with any concept of eternal good or justice, as natural law theorists believed. As long as the law was made by the legally established agency, it was a valid law. It did not have to meet any other standard. Law was not based on an absolute, unchanging truth. It was *not* a semisacred thing that people should worship and never change. Law, in Bentham's view, was a tool by which the society could modify its social conditions in order to increase its happiness. Thus, Bentham's theory of positivist law took down the pedestal on which law had been placed by the early liberals. It brought law back within reach of the society by calling for change and reform.

Just as positivism was a demand for reform, utilitarianism was the standard on which the value of a proposed policy was to be based. But if a society were to adopt a policy that gave the greatest happiness to the greatest number, it would need a way of measuring utility. To satisfy this need, Bentham developed his *hedonistic calculus*. This elaborate formula included a list of fourteen categories of human pleasure, twelve categories of pain, and seven standards of measurement. These, Bentham suggested, should be used by a *scientific legislature* to determine the wisdom of a proposed policy. Though his hedonistic calculus is impractical and even a bit ridiculous, it stems from a genuine concern for improvement and democratization of the government and the legislative process. Moreover, one should bear in mind that this formula, suggested in a time when people were enchanted with science, was a well-meant attempt to scientifically measure the worth of any policy or law.

Bentham's contribution was important. He had the foresight to lead Western thought out of the trap inherent in natural law. In utilitarianism he gave us a practical standard by which to measure the value of a particular policy. With these ideas he set liberalism on a new course, one that could significantly improve the condition of society. In calling for positive legal and governmental steps to improve the society, he provided motivation for many reforms that were adopted in England between 1830 and 1850: the civil service, the secret ballot, equal representation in Parliament, expanded educational opportunities, humane treatment of animals, and much more. It is perhaps not too much to say that Jeremy Bentham and his followers gave England a new social conscience. In short, Bentham was the founder of contemporary liberalism (see Chapter 2).

Democratic Socialism

The introduction of utilitarianism and positivist law into democratic theory led to a whole new concept of popular government. The relationship of people to their government had changed drastically since Locke's era and even since the time of Madison. In the seventeenth and eighteenth centuries the most likely oppressor of the people was indeed the government. Few other institutions were powerful enough to oppress the masses. Those that were strong enough, such as the Church or the landowning class, almost always used government to dominate the people. Democracy itself was relatively untested at that time. What democracy there was often degenerated into mob rule and eventually turned into a dictatorship of one kind or another.

In the nineteenth century, however, democracy was more successful, and its development was accompanied by the growth of industrialization and capitalism. The new political system was praised as government by the people, yet the economic system seemed to squeeze ownership into the hands of fewer and fewer people. This process continued until a single company became the major employer in a given locale or even owned the town outright. Wages were kept low, hours of work were long, safety features were ignored, and men, women, and children were exploited.

It became clear that people could be controlled by economic forces the way they had been controlled by government in the past. Capitalism, which had long been supported by liberals because it tended to increase individual freedom and equality, became suspect because of its ability to exploit people. Gradually those on the left of the political spectrum began to wonder why, if the government was supposed to be democratic and if the economic forces in the society were exploiting the people, the people did not use their control of government to regulate the economy. *This new emphasis revolutionized liberal democracy, making it more socially oriented and less individualistic.* Although Bentham was the first modern liberal, his thinking only prepared the way for the new attitude toward democracy. It took several later thinkers to bring these new ideas to maturity.

John Stuart Mill.   John Stuart Mill (1806–1873) was a student of Bentham, but his scholarship, logic, and clear writing allowed him to go beyond his teacher. So great were his intellectual powers that he is generally recognized as one of the most important philosophers of the nineteenth century. Like Bentham, he was a political activist, and he even spent three years in the House of Commons. From an early age he supported contemporary movements, such as free education, trade unionism, equal apportionment of Parliamentary seats, and repeal of the corn tariffs. Moreover, he was among the first modern thinkers to advocate the equality of women.

Mill was interested in many areas of thought, including philosophy, logic, morals, and economics. His most important work, *On Liberty* (1859), is perhaps the most eloquent treatment of individual freedom in the English language. In it he argued that although democracy was the preferable form of government, even democracy had a tendency to limit individual liberty. Hence, freedom of speech and thought should be given absolute protection under the law because individual liberty was the surest way of reaching happiness.

Obviously influenced by Bentham's ideas, Mill became a utilitarian. He reasoned that happiness is the principal objective of the society and that happiness can best be achieved when people do good for each other. The original motivation for kindness toward another person, Mill argued, was *enlightened self-interest.* That is, individuals do good deeds because they know that they themselves will ultimately benefit from such acts. However, Mill took his analysis one step further and in so doing was led toward a very different conclusion than that reached by others who supported the enlightened self-interest theory of motivation. Mill argued that, in time, people can become used to doing good and will continue to do so even if they do not expect any particular reward. In other words, Mill came very close to arguing that people are not necessarily selfish, or that if they are, they can change that part of their nature. This optimism about human character is typical of leftist ideologies.

Mill's conclusions gradually led him to attack *laissez-faire* capitalism and made him the first liberal democratic philosopher to attack the "enslaving capacity of capitalism." Mill's arguments were so effective that few liberals have supported *laissez-faire* since his time. Before Mill, *laissez-faire* had been opposed only by the extreme left—by Marx and other socialists and radicals. Under Mill the liberal democrats began a movement to the left that led many of them to prefer socialism over capitalism. That is one of the main reasons for the division among contemporary democratic theorists. These events also led to the conclusion that socialism is an integral part of contemporary liberalism and not, as many people believe, separate and distinct from it. Though there remain radical variants of socialism, that movement was also incorporated into the liberal tradition because of liberalism's natural progression toward social concerns during Mill's time. Capitalism, on the other hand, continued to be preferred by democratic conservatives.

Thomas Hill Green.   Thomas Hill Green (1836–1882), a professor of moral philosophy in England, became a leading liberal thinker. Like Mill, he was concerned with individual liberty. "We shall probably all agree," he wrote, "that freedom, rightly understood, is the greatest of blessings; that its attainment is the true end of our efforts as citizens." Green was careful, however, to point out that freedom did not mean the right to do whatever one wished without regard for others. It was not the same as the absence of restraint, as Locke had suggested. Reacting to the economic and political impediments imposed on most people by industrialization, Green defined freedom as the "liberation of the powers of all men equally for contributions to a common good." Thus, Green's call for freedom in a *positive* and *social* sense represents another major leftward shift in liberal thought.

Green suggested that individual freedom comes not from people being able to contribute to their own welfare but from people being able to contribute to the society as a whole. He argued against a government playing the role Locke envisioned, that is, merely serving as a passive arbiter of disputes between individuals. Instead, he believed that government should take definite steps to increase the freedom of the people. One of the elements in the society that he saw being used to restrict the individual's liberty was private property. The Industrial Revolution had seen wealth concentrated into fewer and fewer hands and people become increasingly dependent on one another. These factors tended to weaken ordinary persons, subjecting them more than ever before to the power of the ownership class. Viewing these trends as undemocratic, Green urged people to use the institutions of government to protect themselves from the powerful economic forces over which they had no other control. This position, of course, is an early philosophical justification of the welfare state. Hence, he gave forceful support to a government that would take *positive* steps to improve the lives of the people through policies promoting free education, labor laws protecting women and children, sanitary working and living conditions, and much more.

Poverty can be a prison as confining as any penitentiary, Green believed. If this assumption is correct, and if the state is responsible for increasing the individual's freedom to the greatest possible degree, as Locke had argued, then it is clear that a government must take responsibility for the material well-being of its citizens. In short, Bentham, Mill, and Green led liberalism beyond the conviction that government had only a political obligation to its citizens. Government must not limit itself to sweeping streets and catching burglars. On the contrary, government has social and economic responsibilities to its citizens besides its strictly civic functions.

Green's ideas were of great importance to the liberal movement. They not only added to the philosophical foundations for positive governmental action to protect the citizens from powers against which they were otherwise helpless, in the tradition of Bentham and Mill, but they also did much more. Green's work directed liberalism away from solitary individualism toward a social conscience and collectivism. This trend will build until eventually liberals support an organic theory of society similar to but less extreme than Rousseau's. Still, Green based his liberalism on Bentham's utilitarianism and Mill's enlightened self-interest, not on any moral view of human rights. It was left to another philosopher to give liberalism the moral depth it has enjoyed in the twentieth century.

John Dewey.   The leading American philosopher of contemporary liberalism, or social democracy, was John Dewey (1859–1952). He stated its goals more clearly than anyone else, putting the final touches on the philosophical principles that find liberals trying to change political institutions for the good of society. Dewey strongly believed in the intelligence and dignity of people and in the power and wisdom of individual contributions to the collective good.

Dewey brought liberalism back to its central theme. He argued that all people are equal in their humanity. This does not mean that there are no differences among people's physical or mental abilities. Such an argument would be foolish. Yet, regardless of the differences among people, no individual is more human than the next, and each person contributes to the society. Consequently, each has a right to

John Dewey (1859–1952)

equal political and legal treatment at the hands of the state. To deny such treatment would be an abuse of the human rights to which each individual has equal claim. Importantly, he argued that precisely because there are physical and intellectual differences among people, equal political and legal treatment becomes necessary. Otherwise, Dewey argued, those who do not have great strength or intellect could be tyrannized by those who do.

Having reestablished this basic assumption, Dewey extended the logic of Bentham, Mill, and Green. Dewey agreed that the happiness of the individual is the primary goal of the society. However, he held that no definition could remain unchanged. Our understanding of all things is determined by our environment and our experiences. This empirical attitude, which of course is the foundation of *pragmatism*, which Dewey supported, tended to make all knowledge tentative and conditional. Hence, the meaning of happiness, society, and human rights, and even of the individual itself, is constantly changing as our perception of the environment changes: "An individual is nothing fixed, given ready-made," Dewey wrote to emphasize his moral relativism. "It is something achieved, and achieved not in isolation, but [with] the aid and support of conditions, cultural and physical, including in 'cultural' economic, legal, and political institutions as well as science and art."

Yet, Dewey did not suggest that we are at the mercy of the environment simply because it creates our definitions. He believed that people could make their lives better by applying their intelligence to the problems they faced.

Dewey's belief in the changing nature of truth and his confidence in human reasoning led him to advocate *social engineering*. Unlike conservatives, who believe that existing institutions have value in themselves and should not be meddled with, Dewey was an enthusiastic supporter of social experimentation. He encouraged people to modify and adjust institutions so as to increase the happiness of the society. He rejected Burke's argument that an institution is the product of the collective wisdom of successive generations and that no single generation is competent to improve that institution by changing it. In contrast, Dewey wrote that liberalism "is as much interested in the *positive construction of favorable institutions* legal, political, and economic, as it is in the work of removing abuse and overt oppressions" (emphasis added). Hence, not only are people able to modify institutions that oppress them, but they should go further by creating institutions that will increase their happiness.

People, Dewey asserted, should study their society and not hesitate to make institutional changes that would improve their lives. They were not to stop there, however. He encouraged them to try to mold individuals themselves, thereby improving human beings and making them more socially compatible. This concept is indeed a far cry from Madison's rather bleak view that human nature is base and unchangeable. "The commitment of liberalism to experimental procedure," Dewey explained, "carries with it the idea of continuous reconstruction of the ideas of individuality and of liberty in intimate connection with changes in social relations."

This dedication to the concept of social engineering by the most influential American philosopher of this century had important effects. Dewey's ideas inspired liberals to create the policies of the New Deal, the Fair Deal, and the Great Society revolution of the 1960s.

This chapter and Chapter 3 have dealt with the theory or principles of democracy. Yet, as indicated in Chapter 3, democracy includes specific procedures as well as principles. In the following chapter we shall consider the most important procedures and institutions found in contemporary democratic systems.

SUGGESTION FOR FURTHER READING

BENTHAM, JEREMY, *An Introduction to the Principles of Morals and Legislation.* New York: Harper & Row, 1952.

BURKE, EDMUND, *Reflections on the Revolution in France.* Chicago: Henry Regnery, 1955.

CALHOUN, JOHN C., *Disquisition on Government and Selection from the Discourse.* Indianapolis: Bobbs-Merrill, 1953.

EDWARDS, RICHARD C., MICHAEL REICH, and THOMAS E. WEISSKOPF, *The Capitalist System,* 2nd ed. Englewood Cliffs, NJ: Prentice-Hall, 1978.

FAIRFIELD, ROY P., ed., *The Federalist Papers: Essays by Alexander Hamilton, James Madison, and John Jay.* New York: Anchor Books, 1961.

GALBRAITH, JOHN KENNETH, *The Age of Uncertainty.* Boston: Houghton Mifflin, 1977.

GARFORTH, F. W., *Educative Democracy: John Stuart Mill on Education in Society.* Oxford, England: Oxford University Press, 1980.

HEILBRONER, ROBERT L., *The Worldly Philosophers,* 5th ed. New York: Simon & Schuster, 1980.

INGERSOLL, DAVID E., *Communism, Fascism, and Democracy.* Columbus, OH: Charles E. Merrill, 1971.

LEVINE, ANDREW, *Liberal Democracy.* New York: Columbia University Press, 1981.

MACPHERSON, C. B., *The Real World of Democracy.* New York: Oxford University Press, 1969.

MILL, JOHN STUART, *On Liberty and Considerations on Representative Government.* Fairhaven, NJ: Oxford University Press, 1933.

————, *Principles of Political Economy.* Toronto: University of Toronto Press, 1965.

5

The Democratic Process

PREVIEW

In the last two chapters we dealt with the theory and principles of democracy. We were concerned with the basic assumptions underlying the democratic system. A discussion of liberal democratic ideology is not complete, however, without a review of the various institutions and procedures used in democratic systems. Put differently, liberal democracy has two facets: *principles,* or a philosophy that justifies and guides the policies of popular government; and *procedures,* or institutions and systems by which people govern themselves. You will recall from Chapter 3, however, that this statement would be challenged by the process democrats, who argue that democracy is no more than a procedure for decision making. They claim that it lacks any important philosophical basis, having no special obligation to particular principles. To these critics a government is democratic as long as it follows the procedures outlined in this chapter. Conversely, other democrats insist that while the procedures used are important, they alone do not make a government democratic. A true democracy, they believe, must be dedicated to the principles discussed in Chapter 3 and 4. Hence, this chapter is devoted to an analysis of the procedures used in various democratic societies.

Note: The drawing at the top of the page portrays Ronald Reagan in the background and Margaret Thatcher in the foreground.

Direct democracy exists when the people make the laws themselves. When representatives make the laws for the people, the government is called a *republic*. *Pluralism* is a variant of the republican form in which pressure groups are the primary link between the people and the policymakers. Some critics, known as elite theorists, argue that the leaders of the various pressure groups actually make policy decisions and that our system is therefore not democratic at all.

Democracy must work within a governmental system. Two systems of government are particularly noteworthy: American *federalism* and the British *unitary* structure. The American system divides power between two basic levels of government: state and national. While the two levels share certain powers, each has some authority not enjoyed by the other.

The American government also uses the *presidential-congressional* system. The most prominent features of the presidential-congressional system are the election of the legislators and the executive to unrelated, uninterruptable terms and the prohibition against serving in more than one branch at a time. Powers are separated among the branches, but some responsibilities overlap and form the basis for the system of checks and balances. While the checks and balances tend to protect the system against the accumulation of power by any single branch of government, they also encourage conflict among the branches.

The British system uses the *unitary* structure, concentrating all governmental power in the central government. Since local governments such as counties and municipalities are created and empowered by the central government, they therefore remain subservient to and dependent upon the national government.

Within the national government, power is further centralized in Parliament through the use of the *parliamentary-cabinet system*. Here Parliament embodies the legislative, executive, and judicial branches. Yet, unlike the American system, the branches are not considered equal in Britain. The legislature, specifically the House of Commons, is at least technically superior to the executive and judicial branches and can pass any law it deems appropriate. The only popular elections held in this system are elections to Parliament. Parliament chooses its leader who forms a government, the Cabinet, which shares administrative powers in a *plural executive*. The Cabinet develops policy as a unit, and takes *collective responsibility* for the consequences. The parliamentary-cabinet system is less stable than the presidential-congressional system, especially if a majority must be achieved through a coalition, but party loyalties tend to be much more binding in the British system.

Democratic systems, regardless of their structure, are largely products of the electoral systems they use. The United States system makes use of a wide variety of nominating procedures, including self-announcement, petition, convention, and primary elections. The single-member district, in which only one seat is available per district, is used in every partisan election in the United States. Because it tends to discourage the existence of more than two major parties, the single-member district usually produces a majority for the winning candidate, a situation that can strengthen government. On the other hand, multimember district tends to encourage the existence of more than two major parties because it gives minor parties a better chance of victory. Hence, more parties win seats in the government, but this arrangement usually diffuses the majority and requires complicated systems of proportional representation and coalition governments.

Directly related to the type of electoral district used is the political party system that evolves. A single-party system exists when only one party has a reasonable chance of gaining control of the government. Although this system can be democratic, it can easily be reduced to a dictatorship. The two-party system tends to produce a majority for the winner and therefore encourages strong government; yet it also allows for a significant opposition party that can check the majority party, thus discouraging abuses of power. The multiparty system, a third alternative, tends to give voice to the various opposing points of view in a political system and gives the voter a variety of specific alternatives among which to choose on election day, but this system can also be unstable because it usually fails to produce a majority party.

The complexity of the issues facing the people has greatly increased since the Constitution was written. In many states the people are allowed not only to vote for candidates but also to pass or veto laws through the initiative and referendum procedures. Often referred to as aspects of direct democracy, these procedures have given the people a much greater voice in the government of their states.

Representation, another controversial subject in any democratic government, raises many unanswered questions. What should be the basis of representation—population, territory, economic functions, ethnic groups, social class, tribes? Are people to be represented equally, or should distinctions be made on the basis of property, social class, race, or sex? Should public officials represent the people's interests or the people's will? Several theories have been developed to answer this last and most important question, but none has prevailed. These theories range from reactionary autocracy to conservative paternalism, to liberal representative government, to radical pure democracy. Regardless what form is used, democracy suffers severe criticism today. Friend and foe alike question its continued viability in a modern technological setting.

SYSTEMS OF DEMOCRACY

When asked to define democracy, most people respond with a statement such as "Democracy means government by the people." While this is a simplistic definition, it is useful as long as it is not taken too literally or considered to be complete. Popular government is indeed the essence of a democratic system. Early liberal thinkers such as John Locke understood this principle, and they saw the policy-making process as the most important democratic procedure. Consequently, they regarded the legislative process as the core of democracy. The executive and judicial functions were thought of as service agencies that carried out the laws made by the people. Accordingly, the democratic process was equated with the policy-making or legislative process, and the relationship between the people and the legislative process became the most important criterion for distinguishing among the various democratic systems.

Democracy and the Legislative Process

The three major democratic procedures are based on the relationship of the people to the legislative, or policy-making, process. In the simplest form, called *direct democracy* or pure democracy, the people act as their own legislature. (See Figure 5–1.) There are no representatives; in other words, the people make the laws

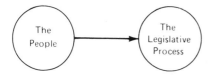

The relationship between the
people and the policy-making
process is direct.

FIGURE 5–1   Direct Democracy

for themselves. You will recall that Jean Jacques Rousseau favored this kind of governmental system. He argued that no one could truly represent another person's will. Hence, all the individuals in the society must represent themselves.

This form of democracy has been used by several societies. Ancient Athens practiced direct democracy, and even today one can find it in some Swiss cantons and in some New England town meetings. Before the advent of modern technology, direct democracy was not possible in an area larger than a city-state; therefore, it has not been very popular. Today, however, it is possible for a society, using computers, television, and the telephone, to govern itself in a much more direct way than was possible in the past. Obviously, more wires would have to be strung across the country, but such a system is certainly possible.

However, any society that has the technological capacity to create a direct democracy through electronics is so complex that the problems it faces may be beyond the understanding of ordinary citizens, given the limited amount of time they could reasonably be expected to devote to policy matters. Some states, however, have adopted limited direct democratic practices by which they allow the people to pass and repeal laws themselves. These procedures will be described later.

A second form of popular government is called indirect democracy, representative government, or *republic*. Each of these terms refers to the same system. However, the word *republic* originally did not necessarily refer to a democratic system. It simply meant government without a king. The Roman Republic, for example, was governed by the aristocratic class (patricians) through the Senate, but most of the citizens of Rome (plebeians) could not serve in the Senate or choose its members. Though it was certainly not a democracy, this system was a republic simply because it was not ruled by a king.

The term *republic* has taken on a somewhat different meaning in the United States. The word is used in the Constitution and was explained by James Madison in *The Federalist* (no. 10). Madison made it clear that *republic* referred to a government of elected representatives who were responsible to the people to some extent. Hence, the term *republic* actually means "democratic republic" in American constitutional law, and the courts have ruled accordingly in the past. A democratic republic is an indirect form of democracy. Instead of the people making the laws themselves, they elect legislators to do it for them. Thus, the people are removed one step from the legislative process, and their relationship to the policy-making process is less direct than under the pure form of democracy. (See Figure 5–2.)

One of the interesting facts about this particular form of government is that there is a negative correspondence between the terms *republic* and *democracy;* that is, the more republican the government, the less democratic it becomes, and vice

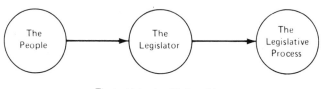

The legislator is added, making
the people's relationship to the
legislative process indirect.

FIGURE 5–2   Republic

versa. Put differently, the more a society gives its representatives to do, the less the people have to do for themselves. Similarly, the more the people participate in their political system, the less power their representatives have.

For instance, a system molded along the lines that John Locke favored would be very democratic and only slightly republican. You will recall that Locke thought that the popularly elected representatives should be bound to vote the way their constituents wanted. A very republican and only slightly democratic form might be one in which the elected representatives were allowed to vote as they wished on any issue and the people could only defeat them in the next election if they disagreed with the way they had voted. This is the procedure desired by Edmund Burke and James Madison. Using the definition we have just developed, one must conclude that the United States' form of government is highly republican but only slightly democratic.

United States citizens do not have a great deal of *formal* control over their political system. We have already learned that we have no direct formal power over who will serve as our judges. We only elect electors, who, in turn, choose the president, and they are not bound to vote for the candidate the people favor. We do have direct electoral control over the members of Congress, but even so we can vote for these officials only when their terms have expired, and some of those terms are as long as six years; none is shorter than two years. Further, elections are not held when the need for them arises; they are held only when the law commands.

You will recall that in a democracy the people are supposed to be sovereign, meaning that they ultimately control the law of the society. Yet, as mentioned in Chapter 4, the people do not propose or ratify amendments to the Constitution of the United States, the country's highest law. The people may not pass or repeal federal statutes, nor may they legally remove public officials before their terms expire. All these responsibilities are granted by the people to their representatives.

To suggest that the political system used in the United States is not very democratic is not necessarily to criticize it, however. It is simply a statement of fact, not a value judgment. Several states do have much more democratic systems than the national government. Some state constitutions cannot be amended without a direct vote by the people, and the initiative, referendum, and recall (discussed later in this chapter) encourage much more direct popular participation in government as well as giving citizens more formal power over the state government than the people enjoy over the national government. Yet, few serious students of government would argue that the state governments that give their citizens such powers make better laws or have finer officials than the national government.

The third major form of democracy, *pluralism,* is not really a different system. Rather, it is a variant of the republican system. Yet, pluralism is such an important variation on republicanism that it should be studied separately.

Pluralism is actually the kind of system foreseen by Madison. He realized that a country as geographically large and as economically, socially, politically, and culturally diverse as the United States cannot attain a single majority on most issues. At the same time, the population of this country is so large that a single ordinary individual is powerless to affect the system. The individual's only hope of protecting his or her interests is to join groups.

The American people have been called a nation of joiners, and so we must be if we expect to further our interests. If, for instance, a person wanted to have a stop sign installed at an intersection, he or she could go to the local officials and petition for the sign. While this procedure might get results, the officials probably would not accede to a request by a single person. Usually, the individual would have to mobilize many other people before the officials felt enough pressure to act.

Pluralism recognizes that the individual must join with other people to achieve his or her political goals. Consequently, in this system the *interest* or *pressure group* is sandwiched between the people and the legislature. (See Figure 5–3.)

Pluralism has certain problems. To begin with, it removes the individual a step further from the policy-making process, creating important philosophical difficulties. As you know, liberal democratic theory argues that the individual is the most important and valuable part of the society; yet, our political practices seem to take the decision-making process further and further from the direct control of the individual—a potentially dangerous situation. Political philosophy is important to any society; it states the society's goals and measures its achievements. If our political theory and practice are contradictory, we run the risk of increasing the dissatisfaction that stems from the unrealistic expectations mentioned earlier.

There are other problems with pluralism. Even if there were no contradiction between democratic theory and pluralistic practice, pluralism would be an imperfect form of representation. For instance, not all the interests in the society are represented equally well. The best-organized and best-financed interest groups can represent their points of view most effectively. The National Rifle Association, for example, is a very well-organized and amply funded group of like-minded individuals; it has been very successful in achieving many of its goals. On the other hand, farm labor, because

FIGURE 5–3   Pluralism

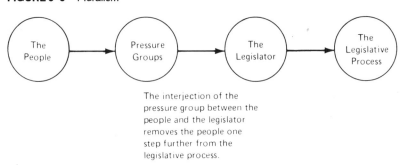

The interjection of the pressure group between the people and the legislator removes the people one step further from the legislative process.

A lobbyist explains his point of view to legislator.

of its migrant nature, its poverty, and its politically disaffected people, tends to be poorly represented. Moreover, even if our major interests are represented by one group or another, it is unlikely that all our concerns are represented. Consequently, pluralism, though it may be necessary in a modern democratic society, is a very imperfect form of representation.

A final aspect of pluralism should be analyzed before we end this discussion. We have seen that the legislative process is affected by a considerable number of pressure groups. When a particular issue arises, however, only a small number of pressure groups take an interest in it. (See Figure 5–4.) Let us assume that only the groups that have a plus or minus sign are interested in a given issue. Let us assume further that those with a plus sign are in favor of a certain policy for dealing with the issue and those with a minus sign are opposed to it. The interested pressure groups are obviously a minority of the total number of pressure groups, and they probably do not represent anything near the majority of the people in the country. Yet, they will be the most influential in determining the fate of the policy. Moreover, we can assume that the number of pressure groups in favor or opposed to the policy will not necessarily

FIGURE 5–4 Pressure Groups in a Pluralist
System

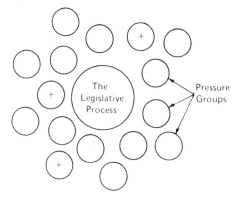

determine what will become of it. Hence, we cannot assume that a policy will pass simply because three pressure groups favor it while only two oppose it. We can also safely assume that the pressure groups that represent the largest number of people will not necessarily have their way.

The victorious side of any issue will not necessarily be the side with the largest following; it will be the side with the greatest power. In other words, pluralism has taken the "body count" out of democratic politics. No longer are issues settled by simply counting those in favor and those opposed to a question, if indeed they ever were decided that way.

Pluralism, to summarize, is a method of decision making that is popularly based and therefore democratic; but in a pluralist system choices are not necessarily determined by the number of people for or against a given question. Many other factors contribute to the power of pressure groups in relation to political issues.

Money is, of course, a major source of power for most successful pressure groups. In fact, money is essential for any pressure group that hopes to succeed for a sustained period of time. Yet, money is not the only, or even necessarily the most important, source of power for pressure groups. Some pressure groups are sustained by *charismatic leaders* such as Dr. Martin Luther King, Jr., Ralph Nader, or Jerry Falwell. Others benefit from an efficient organizational apparatus or an unusually large number of active members.

Of all sources of pressure group power, *knowledge* is undoubtedly the most important most of the time. Politicians often know little about the issues they must resolve and usually look for information which will help them make wise decisions. If a pressure group can establish credibility on a given issue, it can do a great deal to influence policymakers.

Elite Theorism

Among the most persistent and insightful critics of the American political system are the *elite theorists*. As the name implies, these critics argue that the United States government is not a democracy. It is at best an *oligarchy,* or a system ruled by a relatively small number of people. The rulers of this country, the elite theorists contend, are the people who control the large industrial firms and the various pressure groups.

C. Wright Mills, the most influential of the elite theorists, wrote of a *power elite* that controls the political system. He argued that these people maintain their dominant position through social, school, and family relationships. Robert Michels, another elite theorist, suggested a different dynamic when he set forth his theory of the *iron law of oligarchy.* This theory holds that in any organization only a small percentage of members will be active. Hence, the leadership of any body will come from a tiny group of activists. Because the general membership is usually dormant, the leadership will actually run the organization.

Regardless of how the members of the elite rise to their position of control, the elite theorists agree that they, and not the people as a whole, actually run the country. Interestingly, most elite theorists and pluralists do not disagree on the basic structure of the political system. They concur that the system is responsive to pressure groups. The difference between them rests in their definition of democracy. Although pluralists admit that the leadership of various pressure groups has great power, they believe that the general membership has enough control over the leaders to make them responsive, and hence to make the system democratic. The elite theorists see essentially the same reality as the pluralists, but they are not satisfied that the popular power is strong enough to make the system democratic.

Care must be taken that the elite theorists are not confused with people who espouse conspiratorial theories. *Conspiratorial theory* suggests that somewhere in the society a small group of very powerful people is secretly controlling the country or, indeed, the world. There are many such theories. Some suspect an international bankers conspiracy, a Jewish conspiracy, a conspiracy by a cult of satan worshipers, and so on.

Some people are anxious to believe such suggestions because the idea that a secret evil power is responsible for the problems of the world simplifies life. If we can believe that we are manipulated by an unknown force, we can avoid responsibility for our difficulties. Politics is thus reduced to an extremely simple equation.

Yet, the very simplicity of such theories makes them suspect. It is highly unlikely that a few masterminds could be pulling the strings which make all the rest of us dance like puppets without our having overt and clear indications of our situation. Further, to reduce our political system to a simplistic formula betrays a lack of understanding and appreciation for the enormous complexity of our society. To some people, however, believing in an evil force is preferable to coming to grips with the intricacies of a modern political system. In fact, accepting such fantasies represents the ultimate abdication of the personal responsibility so necessary to a successful democracy.

Unlike the conspiratorialists, the elite theorists do not claim that all decisions are made by a single group of unseen people. Each issue generates a different elite. Those with great power on one issue—aerospace, for instance—may have relatively little impact on another, such as farming. The power elite in foreign policy may have relatively little influence in education. Moreover, the elite dominating a policy in a given subject matter may not be able to dominate a second policy in the same field.

Elite theorists suggest that the political system is composed of thousands of elites who coalesce and dissolve coalitions with each new issue as their particular interests dictate. The point is not that a single group dominates every issue; rather, it is that there are several thousand extremely powerful people who populate the elite of the country and who are able to join with others of their number to have their way on particular issues.

SYSTEMS OF GOVERNMENT

No study of the process of democracy would be complete without considering the systems of government in which the process is applied. Although a multitude of governmental systems exists, two forms are particularly important. We will focus on the United States and Great Britain because each developed political systems used, in modified form, in many other democratic societies.

The American System

Federalism. The original structure of American government was *confederate*. Each state was sovereign and independent of the others but voluntarily joined in a compact with the other states for purposes of defense and trade. Traditionally, confederacies are not very successful. Since each participant is sovereign, the central government has no legal way to enforce compliance with national law. Consequently, cooperation among the constituent members is the only adhesive of a confederate compact. Ironically, however, the usual reason for creating a confederate compact of several sovereign and independent entities, instead of forming a single union with sovereignty located in the national government, is that the partners do not completely trust one another—thus making voluntary cooperation difficult. So, this was the situation in the United States under the Articles of Confederation (1781–1789). The individual states were jealous and suspicious of one another and refused to cooperate sufficiently to make the confederate compact successful. The failed American experiment eventually resulted in the drafting of the *Federal* Constitution. (A similar political failure awaited the Confederate States of America during the Civil War [1860–1865]).

Although Calhoun and his supporters argued to the contrary, the United States Constitution initiated an entirely different form of government than that known under confederacy. A federal government is one which divides powers between the states and the national government. Each level is guaranteed certain rights, including the right to exist, so that the states cannot legally destroy the national government or another state government, and the national government may not dissolve the states. Thus, the Union is "one and inseparable."

The states and the national government enjoy certain powers exclusive of each other while sharing other *concurrent powers*. Making war and peace is an example of an *exclusive power* for the national government; education is exclusive to the states. Taxation, besides being as certain as death, is a power exercised concurrently by both levels of government. The division of powers is a complicated matter necessitating a *written constitution,* another innovation of the United States government, so that the rights and prerogatives of each level of government are assured.

The presidential-congressional system. Yet another invention of the American founders is the *presidential-congressional system*. In this arrangement the legislature and the executive are elected separately. Moreover, they are elected to fixed terms that cannot be interrupted. You will recall that the president and vice president are elected to four-year terms, while the members of the House of Representatives serve two-year terms, and the members of the Senate serve for six years. While a citizen may vote for the executive and the legislators on the same day, the elections remain separate, and a vote for one office is unrelated to a vote for another office.

The American electoral process affects our system of government in several important ways. First, although the constituencies of the executives, senators, and representatives are different, each public official is chosen in a popular election. It is true that the executives are chosen by the electoral college, but the electors, with rare exceptions, have traditionally supported the popular choices for president and vice president in their respective states. Since public officials are elected separately, they are not indebted to each other for their election. Also, since only the president and vice president are chosen in a national election, they are the only officials who can claim to represent the nation as a whole. Senators, after all, represent only single states, and representatives represent only districts within the states.

Separate election of principal officials in the United States results in another interesting situation. The people may elect an executive from one party and a majority of the legislature from another. While this situation appeals to the desire of some people for balanced government, it can also cause a serious problem. If the two party platforms reflect definite ideological differences, members of different parties are unlikely to reach agreements readily, a condition that could lead to legislative stagnation, with Congress passing bills and the president vetoing them. Even if the executive and legislative majority are from the same party, the fact that they are elected separately and serve uninterruptable terms tends to diminish the need for party discipline and loyalty. The legislature cannot demand the executive's resignation by a vote of no confidence; similarly, the executive cannot suspend the legislature and force elections. Hence, legislators from the president's party can oppose bills sponsored by the executive because they know that the president will not resign if the bills fail to pass. By the same token, the president does not feel compelled to appoint cabinet members from the ranks of the legislature as the British prime minister must.

Nevertheless, the fact that elected politicians serve terms of office that cannot be interrupted except by extraordinary procedures tends to give stability to the system. That is to say, under the presidential-congressional system officials serve out their terms regardless of what happens (barring death or resignation). True, Congress can impeach officials, but impeachment is an awkward and slow process that has been used only a few times. Several officials have resigned under the threat of impeachment, but still their number is relatively small.

Except under very unusual circumstances, then, our elected officials will complete their terms, come what may. As a result the government does not change suddenly during times of crisis. While this stability is usually considered an advantage of the presidential-congressional system, critics argue that the government seems unresponsive at times. Elections are not called when issues demand them or when the people want a change of leadership; the people get to vote only when the law provides for an election. During the constitutional crisis over the Watergate controversy, many people turned envious eyes toward the parliamentary-cabinet system because under that system unpopular officials can be removed by a general election or a vote of no confidence at almost any time.

As appealing as the quick-turnover feature of the parliamentary-cabinet system may seem, it can cause serious instability. One wonders what turmoil might have erupted if the United States had had a parliamentary-cabinet system between 1966 and 1972. During that period the Indochina War divided the country so badly that no position on our involvement in the war seemed to enjoy majority support. The question dominated our political system, yet it defied solution. In times of such strife the parliamentary-cabinet system can be dangerously unstable, and often the governmental instability brought on by a controversial policy makes the situation even worse, so that a solution is increasingly difficult to achieve.

One final point should be made about the effect of our electoral procedure on the political system. Because elections are held whenever the law calls for them instead of when issues demand them, and also because political party loyalties and discipline are discouraged, our elections tend to be much more personality-oriented and less issue-oriented than those of other systems. When there are few issues and little party identification, candidates generally "sell" themselves rather than popularizing a platform of policies. Some argue that television and Madison Avenue techniques are to blame for our "personality contest" elections, but nonissue, ballyhoo campaigns have been around much longer than modern mass advertising. Of course, modern technology facilitates such campaigns, but programs could be "sold" almost as easily as personalities.

Other distinctive features of the presidential-congressional system are *separation of powers* and *checks and balances*. As mentioned earlier, separate elections make the two branches independent of one another. In addition, the law specifically separates the branches of government from each other. For instance, no person may serve in more than one branch at a time. A member of Congress elected or appointed to the executive branch would have to resign his or her congressional seat.

Further, the executive, legislative, and judicial branches are each given separate powers that only they may exercise. The courts are responsible for adjudicating disputes; they also are the final authority on the interpretation of the law. Only the legislature can pass fiscal legislation—that is, approve expenditures—while the executive is solely responsible for the administration of policy and is virtually unrestrained in foreign affairs.

As Figure 5–5 shows, the basic powers of the three branches are indeed separate and unique; however, some of the powers of each branch overlap with those of the other two. These overlapping powers are called the checks and balances. They are intended to prevent any branch from becoming too powerful and dominating the others. You will recall that James Madison, who devised this system, did not trust government, so he tried to make sure that each branch was relatively equal in power and that each acted as a guardian against abuses by the other two. Yet, we should remember that Madison, like Thomas Hobbes, also had little trust in the people, so he wrote in a number of checks against the majority as well (see Chapter 4 for examples).

FIGURE 5–5   Separation of Powers and Checks and Balances

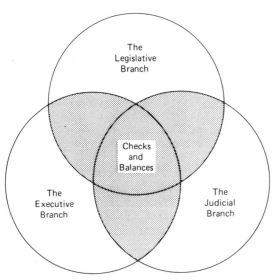

Most of us have a positive attitude toward the separation of powers and checks and balances systems. We normally share Madison's apprehension about government, although perhaps most of us are not as intense about it as he was. There are, however, some undesirable aspects of this feature of our system. By dividing and diffusing power and then causing each of the branches to compete with the others, the presidential-congressional system encourages conflict within the government.

This situation is aggravated by the vagueness of the United States Constitution. Though this lack of clarity has been praised as an advantage that allows the Constitution to adapt to the needs of the society, it sometimes results in a very combative atmosphere. When the built-in division of government is combined with the abstract wording of the Constitution, we find that each branch is encouraged to exercise its powers widely while, at the same time, preventing the other two branches from gaining excessive influence. Such maneuvering leads to constant conflict among the three branches.

A final interesting—though not crucial—feature of the presidential-congressional system is that the positions of head of state and head of government are vested in the same official, the president of the United States. The *head of government,* the country's political leader, develops and administers the policies of the government. While this position is powerful and important, it is strictly political. The office is respected for its power, but the person who holds it does not necessarily have the love and commitment of the people.

The *head of state,* on the other hand, is almost totally lacking in power in most systems. Though the head of state is usually the titular leader of the nation, he or she has no real political power. This official's influence comes from the fact that the office symbolizes the history, tradition, culture, and people of the society. Embodying the essence of the state, albeit lacking formal political power, the head of state enjoys the confidence and devotion of the people.

Such commitment and loyalty to the head of state is not possible, however, when the same person is the head of government, as is true in the presidential-congressional system. This fact has caused an interesting phenomenon. Since the people of the United States cannot give their total loyalty and affection to the president, along with their political support, they have found a different symbol for the state and its traditions. By some historical accident the American flag has been adopted as the symbol of the state. While most countries are quite casual about their flags, giving them no more respect than dozens of other symbols, the United States exalts "Old Glory." Some states still have laws forbidding "desecration" of the flag. Other customs dictate how the colors are to be folded; destroyed if faded, dirty, or torn; burned rather than discarded; and kept from the ground at all costs. Moreover, some citizens, as we learned anew in the 1988 presidential campaign, demonstrate a veritable fetish in pledging allegiance to the flag.

It is not uncommon to hear Americans scoff at the reverence the British have for the monarch, their head of state, as though this were foolish, inexplicable conduct. Yet, how much more amused and mystified must be the European who observes our emotional commitment for the flag. In fact, neither group is really acting strangely. Nationalism, as indicated in Chapter 1, is a powerful force in any society. Emotional attachment for the flag or for the monarch satisfies a human need for patriotic expression.

The British System

Unitary government.   Britain uses a *unitary* structure of government. Older than either federalism or confederacy, the unitary structure is used by most governments in the world. This arrangement centralizes all power in the hands of the national government. Any local governments that exist are created and granted powers by the central government. Local governments, in other words, are dependent on the central government for their powers and have no direct constitutional justifications or guarantees.

The unitary structure seems strange to us because our government uses the federal form. However, the unitary arrangement should not be unfamiliar since it may be seen in the relationship between our state governments and local agencies. Only the relationship between the states and the national government is federal in the United States; that is, both the national government and the state governments are guaranteed by the federal Constitution. City, county, parish, township, and special-district governments are not mentioned in the Constitution and are therefore completely subject to the state governments. As regards the Constitution, the state of Illinois could eliminate the city of Chicago as a political entity if it chose to do so. Illinois could not legally harm the people of Chicago, of course, but the city of Chicago has no guarantee under the federal Constitution and is therefore at the mercy of the state government of Illinois. The same is true of any other local government in any other state. Local governments may be guaranteed by provisions of their states' constitutions, but they have no protection under the Constitution of the United States. The same relationship exists between the central and all lower governments in Britain.

The parliamentary-cabinet system.   Although there are now many variations on the theme, the *parliamentary-cabinet system* was first developed in England, and the British government still provides the best example of this institution. The parliamentary-cabinet system separates the positions of head of state and head of government. The head of government is the prime minister and we will discuss this office in detail shortly. For the moment, we will discuss the head of state which, in England, is the monarch. Other countries that use this system but that do not have a hereditary head of state usually elect someone to the post for a relatively long term, often seven years. Elected heads of state commonly have the title of president. The British head of state has little real power. He or she can dismiss Parliament and call for new elections, appoint ministers, and issue proclamations, but each of these acts is performed only after a request by the prime minister. While some constitutions, such as those of France and India, give the head of state important powers, most give the office a purely symbolic role.

The bulk of the political power in the parliamentary-cabinet system is vested in the Parliament. The British system, which developed out of John Locke's democratic theory, never adopted Madison's structural changes. Hence, separation of powers and checks and balances are less prominent in the British system than in the American system.

A major principle of the British system is *parliamentary primacy.* You will recall that the classical democratic thinkers saw democracy as a process in which the people made policy and thus governed themselves. Therefore, they considered the legislature to be the chief agency of the government. The executive and judicial branches, while important, were only service agencies charged with administering and adjudicating the policies determined by the legislature. The legislature, the primary democratic institution and the agent of the sovereign people, cannot be wrong. Consequently, the British Parliament is, at least in theory, not subject to restraint by the other two branches. No act it passes can be declared unconstitutional. Some scholars argue that the Parliament *is* the constitution. On paper, then, the cabinet becomes nothing more than the executive committee of Parliament and is directly responsible to it. In practice, of course, the relationship between the cabinet and Parliament is quite different, but this is a matter of political practice rather than law.

The principle of parliamentary primacy makes impossible the equality of the three major branches implied in the presidential-congressional system. Hence, the checks and balances cannot work the way they do in the Madisonian model.

Figure 5–6 represent the parliamentary-cabinet system of government: The power of government is not distributed among three separate branches. Actually, each branch of the government is part of the same whole. Parliament, the whole, is made up of the legislature, which is dominant; the executive; and the judiciary. The House of Commons, part of the legislature, is the only body actually elected by the people. Consequently, it acts as the chief agent of the people, and as such it is the major democratic institution in the system. The cabinet, which consists of members of the legislature, is simply the executive committee of the legislature, as indicated earlier. Members of the cabinet need not resign their seats in the legislature before they enter the executive branch. On the contrary, cabinet members must usually be members of Parliament in order to be appointed to the executive body. The courts are also nominally part of Parliament: The Lords of Appeal in Ordinary, Britain's highest court of appeals, is actually a committee of the House of Lords. Its highest magistrate, the lord chancellor, presides not only over the Lords of Appeals in Ordinary but also over the House of Lords, and usually is a member of the cabinet as well. Obviously, no such office could exist in our system.

FIGURE 5–6   The Parliamentary-Cabinet System

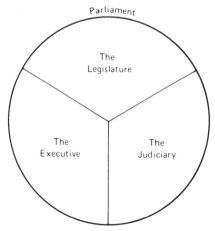

Although some parliamentary-cabinet systems, including Britain's, have bi-cameral (two-house) legislatures, usually the lower house has the greatest legislative power and chooses the prime minister. After all, the lower house is elected by the people. At the beginning of each new legislative term the lower house chooses someone whose leadership the members of Parliament will follow. This individual is, of course, the leader of the majority party and will be *appointed* prime minister by the head of state. Note that there is no popular election for the chief executive in the parliamentary-cabinet system. The prime minister must meet only one requirement: He or she controls the majority of Parliament and can get any bill passed that he or she recommends. If Parliament ever fails to support the recommendation of the prime minister, he or she must resign. Parliament will either hold new elections or pick a new prime minister from the old majority. The decision as to whether or not new elections will be held is usually made by the head of state, who follows the advice of the prime minister.

The fact that Parliament actually chooses the prime minister and that the prime minister decides when elections will be held creates a unique relationship between the executive and the legislature. This relationship tends to increase party discipline and loyalty. The majority party obviously will not choose a member of the opposition to head the government. Also, voting against a policy recommended by the prime minister will not only help defeat the particular policy but may bring down the government as well. Not wishing to help destroy their party's government and loath to stand for reelection prematurely, members of the ruling party in Parliament are encouraged to vote with their executive's policies more regularly than in the presidential-congressional system.

Party loyalty, separation of powers, and checks and balances are obviously features that differ greatly in the presidential-congressional and parliamentary-cabinet systems. Another important area in which the two systems differ is the executive branch. The presidential-congressional system has a *singular executive;* that is, the people of the United States elect only two executive officials, the president and the vice president, and the Constitution gives executive powers only to the president. All other major executive officials are appointed by the president and are given executive powers to administer. Technically, therefore, the president is ultimately responsible for the conduct of the executive branch; all executive powers, regardless of who exercises them, are the president's powers.

The parliamentary-cabinet system, by contrast, has a *plural executive.* The prime minister, as already mentioned, is not elected by the people. He or she controls a majority of the lower house and is appointed prime minister by the head of state. The head of state then appoints to the various other cabinet posts individuals recommended by the prime minister.

The status of the members of the British cabinet is much closer to that of the chief executive than is true in the American system. In the United States the president may give direct orders to cabinet members because they are appointed by the president and exercise the president's powers. In the parliamentary-cabinet system, however, the cabinet members are appointed by the same authority that appoints the prime minister: the monarch. The cabinet members are also more independent of the prime minister, since it is not the prime minister's power they are exercising but the power of the state itself. The prime minister may not give a cabinet minister a direct order because each minister is the sole head of his or her own department.

In the American system the cabinet is a body of advisers to the president. The president has the ultimate power and makes the decisions. If the president delegates this power, he or she is still responsible for policy. In the British system the cabinet is a body of equals headed by the prime minister. The policies of the government are made by the cabinet as a whole. Instead of being flanked by subordinate advisers, the prime minister must get people appointed to the cabinet who can help hold the parliamentary majority together. Thus, the cabinet members are powerful parliamentarians and are influential in party affairs in their own right; clearly, the prime minister does not dominate the cabinet completely.

Not only does the prime minister not dominate the cabinet, but, due to the principle of *collective responsibility*, he or she is not solely responsible for the policies of the government either. Under this principle a governmental decision is arrived at by a consensus of the cabinet. The decision then becomes a policy of the government, and all government ministers (that is, cabinet members) should support it. Although votes are not usually taken in cabinet meetings, a policy is not adopted until it has broad cabinet support. A policy would never be adopted if the members whose ministries were principally involved did not agree to it. Once a policy is adopted, however, any minister who still opposes it must remain silent. If that individual must publicly oppose the policy, he or she is expected to resign his or her cabinet seat.

Unlike our system, the parliamentary-cabinet system tends to centralize the power of government in the hands of Parliament. As already mentioned, the House of Commons can pass any law it chooses. It could end the monarchy, reshape the judicial branch, or suspend elections, thus ending British democracy as we know it. There is no opposing governmental power to prevent such actions, as there is in our system. Instead of encouraging competition and conflict, this system depends on cooperation and trust. If this system is to work well, the people in the country must be well settled and politically mature. The people's belief in democracy must be so strong that public expectation and opinion serves as the ultimate check on abuse of power.

In some ways the parliamentary-cabinet system is more responsible to the citizens, and therefore more democratic, than others. For instance, Parliament is elected to a maximum term; that is, parliamentary elections must be held at least once every four or five years. Yet, elections can be called at any time before the end of the term if the issues require such action. Since this usually occurs and Parliaments rarely remain in office for a full term, issues, and not the calendar, force elections. Consequently, elections tend to be much more issue-oriented in the parliamentary-cabinet system than in the American model.

In 1968, for example, the war in Vietnam was the most pressing political issue in the United States. Yet, neither of the major presidential candidates discussed the topic. Hubert Humphrey avoided it because it had split his party, and Richard Nixon refused to campaign on it, claiming that he had a "plan" to end the war that would be revealed only after he took office. Incredible as it seems, Vietnam was practically ignored by both candidates during most of the 1968 campaign. Similarly, in the election of 1988, the two major party candidates ignored the national debt—our most pressing contemporary problem. George Bush said nothing about it because it was an embarrassment for his party, which had tripled the debt in only eight years. But Michael Dukakis also ignored the issue because he knew that higher taxes must be part of the solution for reducing the annual deficit, and he realized that campaigning to raise taxes would cost him the election.

Such side-stepping of major controversies would be impossible in a parliamentary campaign, since an election would probably have been called to settle the issue. Ideally, elections are held in the British system whenever the government no longer has the confidence of the people or of Parliament. The prime minister will ask for elections when the government's policies seem to lack support. The various parties will usually make definite statements on the issues, campaign actively, criticize their opponents' arguments, and explain their own positions.

The parliamentary-cabinet system is not without its problems, however. Perhaps the greatest problem with this system is that it can be very unstable. As indicated earlier, this system tends to be weak during times of controversy. Elections can be called and governments changed very often. Hence, just when a stable government is needed, this system can be at its most unstable.

The situation is made worse if no majority party is elected. When a single party wins more than half the seats in Parliament, there is very little trouble determining who will form the government. In some cases, however, the seats of Parliament are divided so evenly among three or more parties that no party controls the majority. Then, a *coalition government* must be formed in which two or more parties join to make a majority. They agree on the government's positions on the major issues and divide the various cabinet offices between them.

Coalition governments tend to be very unstable, however. Disagreements often occur between the coalition members, tempers rise, and one or more parties may pull out of the coalition and turn against the government. This reversal of loyalty causes loss of confidence in the government, which must then resign. New elections are held, and if a single party does not win the majority of the seats, a new coalition must be forged—only to begin the process all over again.

At times the divisions among the parties become so severe that they can reach no agreement on which to base a coalition. If such a deadlock occurs, a *minority government* or *caretaker government* is appointed by the head of state. This government simply administers the policies already in effect and awaits new elections. It does not try to pass any major new policies because, without a majority, the bills would fail and elections would have to be called even sooner. Both Britain and Italy had this problem in the mid-1970s, and both countries stagnated until they could produce majorities. You will recall that the presidential-congressional system avoids this problem of instability by using uninterruptable terms of office and by choosing the legislature and the chief executive in separate popular elections.

ELECTIONS

Perhaps nothing is more important in a democratic system than its electoral process. Through elections the people express their will on the issues and choose their leaders. One should not be surprised to learn that elections, vital as they are, are complex, multifaceted processes.

Ballot Issues

In the United States, when we discuss the concept of voting, we often limit our discussion to choosing among candidates for public office. Yet, many states allow their citizens to vote on policy alternatives as well as on the officials who serve them. It should be noted, however, that federal law does not permit similar votes at the national level.

Through the *initiative* process people are able to write and pass laws themselves without going through the legislature. This feature often annoys legislators because basically it allows the people to do for themselves what their elected representatives could not or would not do. The *referendum* is a rather complicated process. There are actually several kinds of referenda. One, the *advisory referendum* or *plebiscite,* is used to submit an issue to the people for their opinion or advice. The *compulsory referendum* is used to decide issues such as school bonds, tax overrides, or constitutional amendments; while these issues are proposed by a government body, they must be approved by the people before becoming effective. A third kind, often called a *petition referendum,* allows the people to veto a law that has been passed by the legislature. Obviously, this particular act is even less popular among legislators than the initiative.

Recall, another method of popular expression permitted in some states, is a way of removing a person from office before the end of his or her term. Usually this procedure can be used only against elected officials, but it is fairly commonplace only at the local level.

The procedures described above are often considered collectively as *direct democracy* and were long resisted as radical and dangerous. They were finally introduced into state governments at about the turn of the century as reforms intended to democratize the governments of the states. Unfortunately, however, these reforms did not equal the expectations of their supporters. They are expensive, thus giving the wealthy a voice in policy that the poor cannot afford. Moreover, they often involve the people in issues so complex that it is very hard to make wise decisions on them. Indeed, some issues are so confusing that citizens complain when these questions are diverted to them.

Nominations

There are several different ways of nominating candidates. Perhaps the least formal of these is the *self-announcement* nomination. Used for many local offices such as school boards and city council seats, self-announcement nomination allows a person to get on the ballot simply by appearing before the proper agency and filing for nomination. Another uncomplicated form of nomination is the *petition* nomination. Also used for local offices, this method of nomination allows the candidate to appear on the ballot after obtaining a specific number of signatures on a petition and filing the petition with the appropriate authorities.

Those who seek high office usually face either nomination by *convention* or nomination by *primary election.* Delegates to a nominating convention may be elected or appointed at the local level to attend the party convention, where they adopt a party platform and nominate candidates for various offices.

Originally adopted as a liberal reform, the convention method is often criticized as undemocratic today. Its opponents argue that the delegate voting before television cameras on the convention floor actually reflects decisions already made by party bosses at secret meetings in a back room of the convention hall. Others believe that even if the convention is not really "fixed," it nevertheless remains an elitist institution that should be replaced by a more democratic method of nominating candidates.

Primaries are elections in which the voters choose the candidates they wish to have listed on the ballot of the November general election. While primary elections are more democratic than other nomination methods, there are some serious drawbacks to them. Primaries extend the election period over several months; costly campaigning must be carried on over this long period. Such added expenditures, it is claimed, have had the effect of limiting public office to the wealthy. Other critics mention the divisiveness of the primary. Partisan primaries (primaries in which candidates must list the political party to which they belong) tend to encourage fights within parties, causing wounds that sometimes do not heal before the general election. Such conflicts weaken the party structure and may cause needless defeats.

One final difficulty with the primary system perhaps deserves the most consideration. Any democrat must believe that when the people are informed, the majority's judgment is usually wise—that the majority is correct more often than any minority group. When the people are not well informed, however, the judgment of the many might not be as good as the opinion of the few who are well informed. The problem of voter ignorance is more serious in primaries than at other times. Nonincumbent candidates, contenders for an office that they do not hold, are usually not well known; moreover, many of them have little money with which to publicize their names and their positions on current issues. Consequently, voters in primaries for congressional and state legislative seats are often poorly informed about the candidates. Under these circumstances the people's choice is not always a good one; the party regulars at the convention would have been able to pick better candidates.

Electoral Districts

The kind of electoral district used largely determines the way a particular political system functions. There are two basic kinds of electoral districts: the single-member district and the multimember district. The *single-member district* is used in the United States in all partisan elections. Regardless of the number of candidates running, only one person will be elected within a single-member district. Members of Congress, for example, are elected from congressional districts, each district having only one seat. Thus, in the 1980s, Massachusetts sent eleven members to the House of Representatives, the state was divided or apportioned into eleven districts, each electing a single individual to go to Washington, D.C.; Florida had nineteen congressional districts; Texas, twenty-seven; Colorado, six; Oregon, five; and so forth.

Since each state's two United States senators are elected at different times, the states are actually single-member districts for Senate elections as well. The states are also single-member districts in presidential elections because *all* the state's electors are awarded to the candidate who wins the most popular votes in that state.[1] Each state, therefore, gives a single prize consisting of a certain number of electoral votes to the winner of its presidential election.

To study the impact of the single-member district, let us assume that parties A,

---

[1]Only Maine divides its four electoral votes, awarding two electors to the candidates who win the largest number of popular votes in each of its two congressional districts. But, since only one person can win electors in each district, these are single-member districts as well.

Party	Vote Distribution
A	41%
B	39%
C	20%

FIGURE 5–7 Elections in Single-Member Districts

B, and C each ran a candidate for Congress in a particular district and that the popular vote in the district was distributed as indicated in Figure 5–7. Because only a *plurality* (the most) is necessary to win in most systems using single-member districts, party A's candidate is the clear winner. At first glance, winning by a plurality does not seem to present any problems, but several interesting features may be seen upon closer scrutiny.

As long as there is more than one candidate for the single seat, the seats will always be distributed disproportionately to the votes cast. In our example, although party A won the largest numbers of votes, a majority of the voters (59 percent) voted against the winner and therefore are unrepresented. Put differently, 41 percent of the voters won 100 percent of the representation. All those who voted for party B or C might as well have stayed home, since their votes do not count toward electing any representatives at all. Consequently, the percentage of congressional seats any party wins is probably not even approximately the same as the percentage of votes it earned. This fact can cause some serious distortions. For example, England, using single-member districts in its Parliamentary elections of 1983, showed returns as indicated in Figure 5–8.

The Conservative Party, led by Margaret Thatcher, carried a substantial majority in Parliament while falling far short of winning a majority of the popular vote. The Labour Party also won more parliamentary seats than the popular vote seems to warrant. The Liberal–Social Democratic Alliance, two parties of similar views which agreed to cooperate during the election, won 25.4 percent of the popular vote (almost as much as the Labour Party); yet because those votes were spread over the whole country instead of being concentrated in only a few districts, the Alliance carried only a small percentage of the seats in Parliament.

The same kind of distortion can occur in the United States because it also uses single-member districts. If, for instance, the Republican Party won very narrow

FIGURE 5–8 Results of British Parliamentary Elections of 1983

PARTY	PERCENT OF POPULAR VOTE WON	PERCENT OF PARLIAMENTARY SEATS WON
Conservatives	42.4	61.1
Labour	27.6	32.2
Social Democratic/Liberal Alliance	25.4	3.5
Other	4.6	3.2

victories for a majority of the seats in the House of Representatives while the Democrats won by large margins in a minority of the districts, the Republicans could hold a majority of Congress even though the majority of people voted Democratic.

The single-member district also works to the advantage of a single-party or two-party system. Looking back at Figure 5–7, we can see that although party A won the election, party B came close. Since party B needs to increase its vote by only two or three percent to win, it will probably remain in existence and enter candidates in future elections. The circumstances are quite different for party C, however. Since it has to more than double its vote in order to win, it does not have much chance of survival. Failing to get even close to victory, all but the most dedicated members will probably soon leave party C for another party whose chances of victory are better, and the two major parties will soon find that they are the only serious contestants. American political history is replete with unsuccessful attempts by minor parties to rise to power, and the use of the single-member district is largely responsible for their failure.

The alternative to the single-member district is the *multimember district*. As the term implies, this system provides for the election of several officials from a given district. This electoral method is used in many countries, including Ireland. Most countries using multimember districts employ a system of *proportional representation* to distribute seats on an equitable basis. For example, let us assume that there are five seats open in an electoral district, and parties A, B, and C entered candidates in the election. If the vote were distributed as indicated in Figure 5–7, each party would win something. Parties A and B would win two seats each and party C would win one seat. Although it would not win dramatically, party C would gain something under this procedure and would undoubtedly remain in existence. In addition, new parties would be encouraged to form simply because the percentage of votes necessary to win is greatly reduced, just as the number of parties is increased. Thus, the multi-member district encourages the existence of a multiparty system.

Political Party Structures

Political parties have several functions. Stating positions on issues, providing candidates, and holding officials responsible for their acts are only a few of their most important responsibilities. The goal of a political party is easily stated: to gain control of the government. Though this may sound harsh, a political party has little reason to exist unless its members take control of the political system. Of course, in a democracy political parties gain and keep control of the government through the electoral system.

There are basically three kinds of political party systems. A *single-party system* exists when one party, over an extended period of time, controls the vast majority of legislative seats and its choice for the chief executive is assured of that office. There may be any number of other parties in the country, but none of them is able to win more than a tiny fraction of the vote.

Care must be taken not to oversimplify the character of the single-party system. Many people equate it with dictatorship. Although dictators often try to hinder their competitors by making opposition parties illegal, a single-party system need not be a dictatorship. Indeed, single-party democracies are not unheard of. During the Era of Good Feelings in the early nineteenth century, the Democrat-Republican Party had no effective opposition in this country. Yet, the period is considered to have been democratic, since leaders were still chosen by the people and the competition that ordinarily takes place between parties occurred within a single party.

A more contemporary example of a single-party democracy can be found in India. Before the usurpation of power by Indira Gandhi between 1975 and 1977, India was a single-party democracy. The Congress Party was favored by an overwhelming majority of the people, often winning as many as two-thirds of the seats in the national parliament and the state legislatures. India, however, provides a dramatic example of the greatest problem of a single-party system. Though such a system can be used in a democracy, the opposition is so small and weak that it can do little to hinder the dominant party if the country's leaders decide to destroy the democratic process. So it was with Gandhi. Feeling her personal power threatened, she imprisoned her opposition, censored the press, intimidated the courts, and eliminated popular liberties. When she had finished, the Indian democracy lay in ruins. To her credit, however, Gandhi restored democracy to India in 1977, accepting her own parliamentary defeat in the process. Displaying amazing political resilience, she was subsequently returned to power by the people of India after the failure of the opposition government, only to be later assassinated in 1984.

A *two-party system* exists when only two parties have a meaningful chance of winning control of the government. Used in several countries, including Australia and the United States, this system has the advantages of the single-party system without running the same risk of becoming a dictatorship. The greatest advantage of the single-party system is that it produces a strong government; its candidates always win with a majority vote of the citizens. If the system has two major parties instead of only one, elected officials also usually win with a majority; yet, the dominant party is checked by a substantial opposition party.

While the two-party system offers the advantage of a majority government checked by a strong opposition, this very factor tends to distort the complexity of politics. Having only two significant parties, such a system implies that there are only two important sides to any issue: the establishment "in" position and the establishment "out" alternative. In reality, there might be many different positions on each issue. Hence, by limiting the opposition to only one significant party, the two-party system tends to limit the full range of alternatives on the issues.

A *multiparty system* exists when there are several parties that have a significant number of seats in the legislature. It best reflects the various minority arguments. In fact, the multiparty system tends to divide the people into so many different factions that the majority is completely lost, leaving only a set of minorities. Many minority parties develop as the willingness or ability to compromise has been lost, and the parties tend to state their differences in very specific terms. This diversity gives the voter many clear alternatives among which to choose, but at the same time it makes producing a majority harder. The proliferation of alternatives and the specificity of debate in this system are admirable, to be sure. However, the lack of compromise as well as the inability to produce a majority party makes this otherwise attractive system less appealing than it might be.

The multiparty system can function reasonably well in a parliamentary-cabinet form of government; it is less compatible with the presidential-congressional system, however. As you have already learned, no party that fails to carry a majority of the seats in a parliament can govern without forming a coalition of minority parties that agree on policy and on selections for the various cabinet positions. Coalition governments are noted for their instability. They usually do not last long because the delicate agreements on which they are founded are soon outdated by new events. When the coalition self-destructs, a new one must be organized; and this process of forming a new government usually requires an election.

Unstable as this procedure may be, the parliamentary-cabinet system can accommodate it because in this system terms of office are not fixed by law. Not so in the presidential-congressional system. Even if there is no majority in the legislature, the executive and legislative officials must serve uninterruptable terms of several years. Governmental stagnation or worse may result.

Perhaps the most poignant example of the dangers of combining incompatible governmental and political party institutions may be found in the events that ended the Allende regime in Chile in 1973. Salvador Allende had won the plurality of the popular vote but not the majority in the elections of 1970, so the election was thrown into the Congress. As a Marxist, Allende was a very controversial figure; the Congress hesitated to elect him. Finally, after much negotiation, an agreement, or coalition, was established and Allende was elected president. But after Allende's inauguration controversies developed over redistribution of farmland and nationalization of foreign-owned properties. Eventually the various parties in the coalition withdrew their support, denying Allende a majority of the Congress. Faced with the prospect of a deadlock that would last for years until his term expired, Allende began to rule by decree, issuing administrative orders that were fiercely opposed by the conservatives and reactionaries in the country. Economic hardship set in; boycotts, strikes, and demonstrations followed. Finally, for the first time in almost half a century, the Chilean army intervened, murdered the president, suspended civil liberties, executed thousands, and imprisoned many more. As would soon happen in India, the most stable democracy in all of South America was destroyed in the name of democracy.

Appealing as the multiparty system might look to people who are frustrated by the seeming lack of difference between the two major American parties, we should be very cautious about opting for the more diverse system. The lack of compromise inherent in the multiparty system bodes ill for a form of government that depends on pluralistic problem solving, as democracy does. The lack of a majority government also tends to make the multiparty system less than desirable; in fact, as we have seen, it is basically incompatible with the presidential-congressional system.

REPRESENTATION

The subject of representation in a democracy is almost as complex as the question of elections. Assuming that the system is not a direct democracy, as Rousseau preferred, the student of politics immediately confronts the question of what the basis of representation should be. Because we are a democratic people by training, our natural inclination is to insist that population be the basis of representation. Further, we would probably agree that all people should be treated fairly by the law and that they should all enjoy equal representation. Yet, there are several foundations on which to base representation besides population. In fact, the United States system does not favor people as much as we assume it does.

Another basis for representation is territory. In the United States, each state—regardless of its population—is represented by two United States senators. As a result

California, the nation's largest state with a population of over 25 million, has the same representation in the upper house of Congress as states one-fortieth its size. This is not very "democratic."

Functional representation is another variant of representation. In some countries institutions such as the church, universities, and labor unions are given representation in the national parliament. Ireland uses this system, as do several other countries. The new Soviet legislative body, the Congress of People's Deputies, also uses functional representation. One-third of its 2,250 members are chosen from various specific groups in the society. For example, the Communist Party is given 100 members, the National Academy of Science has twenty-five members, and the All-Union Temperance Society is entitled to one member. Some governments guarantee representation to their various *ethnic groups*. Switzerland, for example, ensures that its German, French, and Italian populations are each included in its plural executive. Similarly, the Soviet Union guarantees its numerous minority populations seats in one house of the Congress of People's Deputies, in rough proportion to their percentage of the total population. On the other hand, the British government gives its nobles, a social class, representation in the House of Lords, while several African governments guarantee representation in their national legislatures to many of their tribes.

Theories of Representation

Another dilemma is the question of whether public officials should represent the national interest, as Edmund Burke argued, or whether they should reflect the interests of a more local area, as James Madison recommended. If the national interest receives the greatest attention, an unfeeling central bureaucracy can mandate policies that seem to make little sense to local areas. On the other hand, when local interests become paramount, policy tends to become provincial and narrow, working to the disadvantage of a modern state.

Of all the arguments concerning representation in a democracy, none is more controversial than the dispute over whether public officials should represent the people's *will* or their *interests*. This quandary returns us to the question of how democratic a republic should be. If the system is to be highly democratic, the representatives should make every effort to determine how their constituents want them to act and act accordingly. The most republican attitude is that the representatives should use their judgment to determine the interests of the people and then select the course that is best suited to those interests.

The former position assumes that people are rational, able to understand their needs and the various programs that bear on those needs. Further, it assumes not only that people are able to understand the issues but also that they will make the effort to do so. The republican position implies that representatives are somehow better qualified to decide policy than are ordinary people. Because the people may not perceive their interests as clearly as their representatives do, and because they may favor an action that is actually harmful to them, the people's will is not always synonymous with their best interests. Thus, the representative should always vote according to the people's best interests regardless of whether those interests conform to the people's preferences.

The question of how the people should be represented is as old as democracy itself. Many political theorists have grappled with the problem, but none has been persuasive enough to dominate the argument. Although some of this information has already been dealt with in other parts of the book, perhaps a brief outline of the basic theories of representation would be helpful at this point.

The *reactionary theory of representation,* supported by Thomas Hobbes and Alexander Hamilton, is based on the need for order and authority. The executive, preferably a monarch, and the parliament serve the public interest as they perceive it. While they should be open to popular input, being of superior knowledge and judgment they should not be hindered by popular sentiment. The people, for their part, must support the state and accept the government's policies willingly in the confidence that the politicians have acted in the public's best interest.

This elitist position provides for no popular control. Indeed, many people might reject this theory as undemocratic; its only popular aspect is the assumption that the rulers are protecting and benefiting the public interest.

Less extreme is the *conservative theory of representation,* supported by Edmund Burke and James Madison. Conservatives grant popular control without encouraging public participation in the governing process. In this variant the people choose those who are to govern them from an elite group. Yet, the people do not have the right to instruct their representatives or even to compel them to reflect a particular position on a given issue. If, however, the officials do not satisfy the public, the people may replace them with other members of the elite at the next election.

John Locke and Thomas Jefferson subscribed to the *liberal theory of representation,* the most democratic of all the republican theories. According to this theory, all people are essentially equal and all are therefore equally capable of ruling. This mass-oriented theory requires that the representative act as a messenger for his or her constituents rather than as a policymaker. Hence, public officials are obliged to vote the way their constituents want them to.

The *radical theory of representation,* advanced by Jean Jacques Rousseau and the New Left of the 1960s, calls for the greatest amount of popular input. Rejecting representative government altogether, this theory holds that only the people themselves are capable of representing their own views, at least on the important issues. Thus, this theory claims that pure or direct democracy is the most desirable form of government; indeed, it is the only truly democratic form.

SOME CRITICISMS OF DEMOCRACY

Democracy has many critics at every point on the political spectrum. It is attacked by the far left as well as by the far right. Some of the most biting criticisms, however, come from supporters of democracy itself.

Some critics argue that democracy is a hopelessly visionary idea based on a number of impossible principles that can never really work because they are too idealistic. They claim that ideas such as human equality or the actual practice of self-government are futile dreams that can never be carried out. At best, they say, the elite really rules in a "democracy." The fact that the general public believes it is running the system proves that the subtleties of government are beyond the understanding of ordinary people.

Another criticism of democracy is based on the belief that the majority of the people have only average intelligence and creativity. Therefore, a government controlled by the majority would probably be biased in favor of the average or the mediocre. Prejudice against the innovative, the unusual, or the excellent would dominate such a system; laws would be passed to move the society toward the lowest common denominator. The truly superior individuals would suffer as the ordinary people imposed their will on the country. Summing up this position, Russell Kirk, a leading conservative, writes: "Aye, men are created different; and a government which ignores this law becomes an unjust government, for it sacrifices nobility for mediocrity; it pulls down the aspiring natures to gratify the inferior natures."[2]

Democracy is also attacked as slow and inefficient. The mechanism for decision making, which we have just studied, is awkward, unable to make the speedy decisions necessary in a jet-propelled, electronically powered, cybernetic society. The critics also point out that while democracy might have been possible during a simpler era, our technology has complicated society to such an extent that popular government is no longer possible. Ordinary people with everyday concerns are simply not equipped to handle the complexities facing policymakers in the modern state. Our society has evolved faster than we have been able to adjust, and one of the casualties of this development must be democracy itself.

These are just a few of the criticisms of democracy. Many more specific criticisms could be made, but a catalog of these is unnecessary. The general comments made here should be considered carefully, however, because they are supported by some of our most brilliant thinkers. To think of democracy as the best possible form of government is not to make it so. Some questioning of its viability in the face of such challenges as genetic engineering; psychological, chemical, and electronic control of human behavior; computerization; and so forth cannot be delayed any longer. To fail to acknowledge the pressing economic, social, and political changes thrust upon us by technology is to ignore the inevitable and to fail in our responsibilities as citizens of a free society.

As pointed out in Chapter 2, democracy has been adopted by people at virtually all points on the spectrum. To do this, in some cases, it was redefined. Even so, however, the concept which remains consistent in all notions of democracy is self-government. Hence, we now turn to the most extreme theory of self-government: anarchism.

SUGGESTION FOR FURTHER READING

COULTER, EDWIN M., *Principles of Politics and Government*. Boston: Allyn and Bacon, 1981.
CURTIS, MICHAEL, *Comparative Government and Politics: An Introductory Essay in Political Science*. New York: Harper & Row, 1968.
DAHL, ROBERT A., *Dilemmas of Pluralist Democracy*. New Haven, Conn.: Yale University Press, 1982.
DAHL, ROBERT, *Who Governs?* New Haven, CT: Yale University Press, 1961.
DONOVAN, JOHN C., RICHARD E. MORGAN, and CHRISTIAN P. POTHOLM, *People, Power, & Politics*. Reading, MA: Addison-Wesley, 1981.
HARRISON, REGINALD J., *Pluralism and Corporatism*. London: George Allen & Unwin, 1980.
MACPHERSON, C. B., *The Real World of Democracy*. New York: Oxford University Press, 1969.
SCHREMS, JOHN J., *Principles of Politics*. Englewood Cliffs, NJ: Prentice-Hall, 1986.
NORTON, PHILIP, *The British Polity*. New York: Longman, 1984.

[2]Russell Kirk, "Prescription, Authority, and Ordered Freedom," *in What Is Conservatism?*, ed. Frank S. Meyer (New York: Holt, Rinehart & Winston, 1964), p. 34.

6

Anarchism

PREVIEW

Stemming from reaction to the growing power of government and the increasing influence of capitalism, anarchism developed among a small but highly motivated number of people. Poorly understood in our society, anarchism is the *purest expression of individualism in political thought.* Anarchists of all sorts see government as an impediment to human progress and wish to eliminate it in part, or even completely. Agreeing that government should be limited, anarchists tend to disagree on other matters of substance and tactics. *Social anarchists,* those on the left, wish to free individuals from governmental restraint so that the individuals can do the greatest good possible for society as a whole. By contrast, *individualist anarchists,* those on the right of the political spectrum, seek to limit government so that individuals can accomplish the greatest good for themselves alone. Anarchists can be pacifistic or violent, devout or atheistic, socialist or individualist. Indeed, except for the reduction or elimination of government, there are few things on which anarchists agree. After consideration, one might conclude that far more disagreement than agreement should be expected among such diverse individuals.

Note: The drawing at the top of the page portrays, from background to foreground, Emma Goldman, Leo Tolstoy, and Mikhail Bakunin.

DEVELOPMENT OF ANARCHISM

Even as the imperatives of the Industrial Revolution motivated some people to seek more popular participation in government, others agitated for social organization without government. As Europe industrialized, wealth concentrated into the hands of the few, and power centralized in the state. Feelings of impotence and helplessness overcame workers who saw their skills made obsolete by machines and who therefore were put to mindless, repetitive tasks. When once they had actually produced whole products, they now found themselves in assembly lines doing jobs that required little skill and paid a pittance. The simple life of the peasant evaporated as people were forced to enter the squalid ghettoes surrounding the factories. The government, once remote, began to play an increasing role in the lives of the individuals: promulgating restrictions, issuing regulations, giving orders, and making demands. Yet, as the institution of government became more pervasive, the people in government became almost anonymous. Growing with its new tasks, a faceless bureaucracy confronted the common people, imposing its will with vigor, even as it became abstract and ambiguous in form.

Although opposition to organized government can be traced as far back as ancient Greece, anarchism as an ideology and as a political movement did not take shape until the early part of the nineteenth century—with the rise of the Industrial Revolution and improved forms of communication. It was then that the means of social control were complete enough and political power adequately centralized to impose the weight of property and government to the extent that they were perceived as impediments to human development.

DEFINITION OF ANARCHISM

Woefully misunderstood in the United States, anarchism continues to hold a strong attraction for some people in the world. Indeed, anarchism has recently enjoyed a new popularity among the middle class in Western societies and even among rock fans in Britain.

Anarchism is often equated with *anarchy*. This is an understandable mistake, but it results in an unfortunate misapprehension. Anarchy implies chaos, disorder, and confusion resulting from the absence of government. Few, if any, anarchists advocate such a state of affairs. Indeed, they contend that the opposite will result from the elimination of government. The most extreme anarchists do hope to see all institutional government eliminated, leaving individuals to govern themselves; but others view only the national government as a villain and would see it eliminated entirely, or at least considerably reduced. These anarchists, however, support governmental structures at local levels, be they villages, communes, or syndicates.

More expansive than simple antagonism toward government, anarchism also opposes institutions that buttress the state. Private property is criticized since it is viewed as an institution denying people freedom. According to anarchists, property is used to exalt the few and belittle the many, thus becoming an instrument of oppression. Similarly, religion is sometimes condemned. Seen as a tool for mass control, the Church is also eschewed. While most anarchists are atheists, denying the very existence of God, some, like Leo Tolstoy, remained devout but abandoned established religion for a less exploitative interpretation of Christianity.

Many anarchists resist any institution which tends to demand that people conform to accepted behavior. Consequently, schools are often seen as instruments of oppression. All societies use education to socialize their young. Not only do schools teach traditional subjects like reading, mathematics, and music, but they also teach appropriate social behavior. For example, anarchists view teaching elementary students to line up before entering the classroom as an abomination. Such regimentation, anarchists believe, deforms children, squeezing from them their natural spontaneity and robbing them of creativity. Such discipline denies people freedom, forcing them to surrender their individuality and creating slavish automatons of once unspoiled creatures. But schools are only one example. Anarchists view most of society's institutions similarly, including girl scouts and boy scouts, the law, peer group pressure, etiquette and manners, and so forth. All of these institutions are, in the broadest sense, government. The anarchist chafes at its authority, feeling that government places undue restrictions on people, crippling them and denying them their human spirit.

In general terms, anarchists believe that although government and its supportive institutions may have been appropriate at some point in human development, the need for them has long since disappeared. Instead of being a useful institution that helps people accomplish their ends, government now impedes human development and should be drastically reduced, or perhaps eliminated altogether. Viewed from this perspective, anarchism is perhaps not startling to some people. Indeed, although few of us are actually anarchists, many of us harbor some anarchist tendencies. Many of us see some elements of government as detrimental rather than helpful to our interests. Standing in line for hours to have a driver's license renewed, trying to have college transcripts forwarded, paying hard-earned money in exorbitant taxes to support impersonal bureaucracies whose regulations prevent us from doing as we wish, and dozens of other frustrating episodes can kindle within us the desire to see elements of the government reduced or eliminated.

While all anarchists oppose government to some extent, few other generalizations can be accurately applied to them as a group. There are, in fact, several misconceptions about the ideology; for example, in the United States anarchism is seen as a violent movement. This misconception is quite natural because so much violence was attributed to anarchists in this country at the turn of the century. The Haymarket Riot of 1886, the assassination of President William McKinley in 1901, the Great Red Scare of 1919, and the Sacco-Vanzetti hysteria of the mid-1920s were but a few dramatic episodes in which real or alleged anarchistic violence was blamed for the turmoil characterizing the era.

Although it is doubtful that anarchism deserved the full weight of blame ascribed to it in these events, many immigrants to the United States who came from Southern and Eastern Europe at the time were adherents of the violent anarchist theories of Mikhail Bakunin. Thus, the impression developed that all anarchists were bomb-throwing malcontents who should be suppressed for the good of society.

In point of fact, however, anarchism can be violent or nonviolent depending on the particular theory advocated. Indeed, the earliest anarchists eschewed violence and opposed government on grounds that it was the greatest perpetrator of violence in society.

Another misapprehension about anarchism is that it is solely a leftist ideology.

In reality, anarchism can be found on either the far right or the far left of the political spectrum. All anarchists would see government reduced or eliminated, leaving the individual free to pursue his or her best interests. To this extent all anarchists are the same. However, a critical distinction among them is revealed when we investigate exactly why they wish the individual to be freed from governmental restraint. What, in other words, is the individual's relationship to society?

Leftists of other persuasions view the individual in relation to all other individuals. Indeed, they believe that the individual cannot be effectively evaluated apart from the group. Accordingly, anarchists on the left wish to free people from governmental control because they believe that government prevents individuals from making the greatest possible contribution to society as a whole. The state, they believe, is a tool of mass oppression and should be eliminated if humanity is to advance freely to its fullest potential. The state is used by the ruling class to dominate the governed, thus unfairly and artificially restricting the progress of others. For example, laws giving one social class more economic and political rights than others are often found in stratified societies, and these rules invariably benefit those who make them—the ruling class.

Anarchists from the left, known as *social anarchists,* would reduce or eliminate the offending governmental institutions, stripping away the artificial restraints on individual freedom and thus allowing each person, regardless of social class, to make his or her greatest contribution to the society as a whole. Counted among the social anarchists are William Godwin, Pierre Joseph Proudhon, Mikhail Bakunin, Peter Kropotkin, Leo Tolstoy, and Emma Goldman. Some of these social anarchists (Bakunin, Kropotkin, and Goldman) advocated the use of violence, while Godwin, Proudhon, and Tolstoy denounced such practices as immoral or at least counterproductive.

Social anarchism is perhaps the best known form of anarchism because of the prolific literature produced by its adherents and because of their dramatic deeds for the cause. Yet, the anarchists of the far right are probably the most numerous, at least in the United States. Instead of favoring a society in which all individuals advance together, one in which the material differences between individuals are kept to a minimum, the anarchists of the right—*individualist anarchists*—envision a kind of Social Darwinism in which the society will advance best when each individual is encouraged to achieve what he or she can for himself or herself. This principle of "ownness," as Max Stirner called it, suggests that humanity is best served when people advance or fall back in relation to their individual abilities.

Individualist anarchists resist government policies such as welfare programs or progressive income taxes, arguing that these policies protect the weak at the expense of the strong. Such policies artificially warp society, retarding progress, and should be eliminated. Individualist anarchist theories have been expressed by celebrated people such as Max Stirner, Henry David Thoreau, Josiah Warren, S. E. Parker, and Ayn Rand.

PARTICULAR THEORIES OF ANARCHISM

Anarchism has an almost endless number of variations. Some anarchist theories have heralded freewheeling individualistic societies, while others have advocated communist structures. Some anarchists have made atheism an objective; yet others have called for people to forsake government for societies based on religious unions. Violence has often been seen as the vehicle for instituting anarchism, while pacifism has also been counseled. Government has been accused of preventing human harmony, and it has also been challenged by those who see it as impeding the strong and artificially protecting the weak. Because of the diverse views of anarchists, it is difficult to construct generalizations which accurately describe this theory. Anarchism is, indeed, *the purest expression of individualism in politics.* Consequently, rather than generalizing any further, it may be useful to briefly investigate the basic ideas of some of history's leading anarchist thinkers.

The Pacifists

William Godwin (1756–1836) is generally credited with founding modern anarchism. The son of stern Calvinist parents, Godwin followed many of his ancestors into the ministry.[1] Yet, his considerable familiarity with French and English rationalism persuaded him to leave the church to pursue a literary career instead. Godwin was truly a product of his era. Like his contemporary Thomas Paine, he had been schooled in the nonconformist philosophies of radical Protestantism and came to believe in the virtues of human individualism, seeing the church and later the state as conspiracies to benefit a few at the expense of the many.

In 1793 Godwin published his most important work, *The Enquiry Concerning Political Justice,* which immediately established him as a leading social critic. Basically, he suggested that all people are fundamentally equal and rational. If left to their own impulses, people would naturally create a harmonious society in which all would benefit and none would suffer at the hands of another. Unfortunately, however, society had evolved institutions which subdued the natural human impulse, creating a biased and exploitative society.

As you have already learned, these libertarian ideas were not unique to Godwin; Rousseau and other leftists shared this view. However, the English philosopher condemned not only the national government and its centralized institutions, but he also lashed out at schools, organized religion, the family, and other local institutions as purveyors of the biases which threatened individual goodness and accomplishment.

Godwin opposed most laws and institutional restraints imposed upon the individual. In their place he would see the creation of a society which he vaguely described as a community without rules, founded upon the belief that individuals, left to their own inclinations, would conduct themselves with mutual respect and compassion. Those who used social and political institutions for their own advantage—the "imposters," as he called them—were to be "reeducated" to change their values and attitudes.

Godwin's social criticism is far more important than his vague aspirations for a more compatible society. Indeed, his condemnation of the state and other institutions set the tone for subsequent social anarchists (anarchism on the left). Although he launched a spirited defense of the French Revolution in answer to Edmund Burke's

---

[1]Godwin's daughter, Mary, became the wife of the English poet Percy Bysshe Shelly, and it was she who authored the story of Frankenstein.

criticism of it, he generally discouraged the use of violence as unnecessary to bring on needed change.

Incorporating most of Godwin's moralistic objections to the state and its institutions, *Pierre Joseph Proudhon* (1809–1865) gave anarchism the philosophical depth and economic perspective which made it a viable political ideology in the modern world. Largely self-educated, this son of a working man endeared himself to the French public for his modest lifestyle and his sincere devotion to humanitarian principles.

Proudhon professed the *Labor Theory of Value* (all value is created by the workers) and used it to answer the question in the title of his best known book, *What Is Property?*: "Property is theft," he responded on the first page. By this he meant that all unearned property (rent, interest, profits) was stolen from the workers who produced it.

Proudhon, the first person to call himself an anarchist, demanded the elimination of government and other institutions, which he claimed unduly denied the people earned property and human rights so that the governing class might flourish. Denouncing the established order, he advocated restructuring society into voluntary associations of workers. These institutions, *syndicates* they were called, would dispense the necessary services usually provided by government. Thus, *anarcho-syndicalism* was born; it remains to this day a potent influence in the labor movement of France as well as many other countries. Indeed, the "industrial unions"—the United Mine Workers, the United Auto Workers, and many others—in this country are organized on a syndical (industry-wide) basis as opposed to the skilled craftsperson model.

Syndicalism, Proudhon believed, should be voluntary and should be created at the expense of the state. It should liberate the worker from the twin masters of capitalism and government. Frustrated by the growing complexity of modern bureaucracy and decrying the lack of morality in state policy, Proudhon condemned authority as corrupt and decadent. Traditional political authority, he claimed, exists solely to "maintain *order* in society, by consecrating and sanctifying obedience of the citizen to the state, subordination of the poor to the rich, of the common people to the upper class, of the worker to the idler, of the layman to the priest." Since he thought the state exploitative and without moral justification, Proudhon would see it eliminated and replaced with an institution that more accurately reflected the economic and political rights of the people.

Still, however, Proudhon did not call for violent overthrow of the state. Instead, he would have the workers take it upon themselves to ignore traditional authority and organize the syndicates. Thus denied the support of the productive elements in society, the state would collapse, leaving only the voluntary associations of workers.

Leo Tolstoy (1828–1910), Russian noble and literary master, was another noted anarchist. Following a frivolous youth, Tolstoy became troubled by the suffering of Russia's peasants. Equally disturbing to him was the realization that the peasant plight resulted from deliberate policies of the Russian Orthodox Church and the Tsarist regime.

Tolstoy developed a great admiration and respect for the individual and most particularly for the Russian peasant. He saw the peasants confronted with the tremendous power of the state that brutalized them. His sympathy for the peasant deepened when he saw them suffering so desperately, even as they were encouraged to bear exploitation by the Church, which Tolstoy felt manipulated the scriptures to serve the state and its ruling class. The great author's compassion and admiration for the peasant were expressed as early as 1869 in his magnum opus, *War and Peace*. In this exquisite novel about the 1812 Napoleonic invasion of Russia, Tolstoy develops the thesis that the hated aggressor was not turned back by Tsars and generals. Rather, Napoleon was defeated through the dedication, suffering, and sacrifice of millions of lowly individuals who stood to the defense of Mother Russia.

Tolstoy's anarchism stemmed from two fundamental and closely related convictions: his interpretation of Christianity and his commitment to pacifism. Echoing the force theory of the origin of the state, Tolstoy believed that the state resulted from nothing more than the imposition of power by the strong over the weak. Physical violence, he contended, was the basis of political power. A devout Christian who was convinced that Christianity demanded peace and human justice, Tolstoy considered the state illegitimate on the basis of its presumed method of development: the use of force. Yet, beyond this conclusion the state continued its offense by perpetuating violence. Indeed, Tolstoy saw the state as the principal source of violence in society.

On the pretext of having to protect society from aggressive neighbors, the state organized armies. However, in Tolstoy's view, the armies were actually turned against the people they purported to protect. In other words, the state perpetrated violence against its own people. Why did the state use violence against its own citizens? To exploit them, to squeeze the last measure of energy and production from people while denying them the desserts of their labor. The state, then, in Tolstoy's view, was illegitimate from its beginning and continued to assault the individual with orchestrated violence and exploitation. In short, the state was evil and invalid.

To those who argued that the state was the context in which civilization developed, Tolstoy refused to concede the point. But, he argued, even if the state might have been necessary at one time to create the atmosphere in which religion, education, culture, and communication could develop, society clearly had evolved beyond its previous dependence. Arguing that modern people are quite capable of creating and maintaining civilized institutions without the state, Tolstoy indicted the state, charging that it actually hindered rather than encouraged civilized society.

Having thus challenged the legitimacy of this monstrous evil in society, Tolstoy called on the Russian people to destroy the state itself. Yet, he cautioned against the use of revolution for the cause. Instead, he encouraged people to abandon their commitment to the Russian Orthodox Church, which he viewed as the handmaiden of the state. Tolstoy rejected the ceremony, vestments, and clergy as irrelevant trappings of the true faith (he was excommunicated for these beliefs). Rather, he called on each individual to be dedicated to the principles of Christian peace and human fraternity.

He called on people to recognize only one law, the law of God; to be bound only to the dictates of their own consciences; and to ignore any other pretensions to authority. True Christians, he said, could not give their allegiance to the state, for that would mean abandoning their own consciences and the law of God. Christians, he said, were independent of the state because they recognize the law of God as the only true law. Further, they are bound by their faith to follow their own consciences relative to those laws, ignoring other mandates; if they do otherwise, they jeopardize their immortal souls. "Man," Tolstoy wrote, "cannot serve two masters."

The proper response to government, Tolstoy asserted, was simply to ignore it.

When the state issues an order, the people should drop their hands and walk away. Tolstoy believed that this technique, today called *passive resistance,* would spell the doom of government. The power of passive resistance as a political tool was appreciated by many people over the years, but no one has understood its potential like India's great leader Mahatma Gandhi. With unshakeable resolve, Gandhi entreated his people to resist the British colonial government, not with barricades and bullets, but with quiet, firm disobedience.

Russia, Europe's most oppressive state, produced several other important anarchists. Unfortunately, Tolstoy's passive resistance was not seen by many of his compatriots as a viable method of changing the system.

The Revolutionaries

Perhaps history's best known anarchist is *Mikhail Bakunin* (1814–1876) a Russian aristocrat. Preceding Tolstoy, he also resisted the church and the state as exploitative and oppressive institutions. Unlike the venerable author, however, Bakunin also advocated atheism and violence. Indeed, he is credited as being the founder of violent anarchism. Condemning the state as humankind's greatest obstacle to attaining liberty, Bakunin advocated terrorism, destruction, and revolution. More radical even than Marx, who at least called for revolution by honest working people, Bakunin contended that a successful revolution would come about by arming the underworld of society—its vagabonds, pimps, thieves, murderers—the *lumpenproletariat.*

Alternating between long periods of revolutionary activity, imprisonment, and exile, Bakunin was unable to reduce his ideas to organized presentations until the last decade of his life. By then he had gained international notoriety as a revolutionary, and so his reputation remains today. Even so, his writing reveals a logical, if somewhat undisciplined, mind.

Basically, Bakunin rejected all forms of human conformity. He regarded most of society's institutions as devices to enslave the human spirit, denying it the freedom for which it was destined. For example, he rejected religion and belief in God. To believe in a superhuman power necessarily meant the abdication of the free human spirit and the enslavement of people to a supposed divine spirit. Placing total emphasis on human freedom, he challenged God to liberate the people. "If God existed," he wrote, "only in one way could he [sic] serve human liberty—by ceasing to exist." This is an interesting thought, although admittedly not too practical where the Divinity is concerned.

Bakunin had been strongly influenced by the Russian *Narodnik* (Populist) movement, which lionized the Russian peasant. The perfect social arrangement, he opined, would be composed of rural communes in which each citizen freely and voluntarily agreed to work. Unlike Rousseau, however, Bakunin would have nothing to do with the principle of majority rule. Seeing each individual as a free spirit, owing no debt to anyone else, he envisioned that each person in society would remain free either to give or to withhold consent from the norms of the group. Thus maximizing individual freedom, Bakunin expected to liberate people from societal restraints, expecting that they would then be able to make their contributions to the whole as free and willing participants rather than as slaves to the opinion makers of the community.

Although Bakunin failed to depose a government during his lifetime, he is indisputably the most influential anarchist history offers. His ideas are credited with stimulating assassinations, terrorism, and rebellion in many nations. His philosophy had a great impact on subsequent anarchists and other radicals; it was particularly popular among the peasants of Italy, the Ukraine, and Spain. Indeed, the Ukraine in 1917 and Spain in 1936–1939 hosted the only sustained anarchistic experiments, and both were based on Bakuninist theory.

Much less the activist and more the scholarly writer was *Prince Peter Kropotkin* (1842–1921). Like his Russian compatriots Tolstoy and Bakunin, Kropotkin was a noble who profited from the privilege his society afforded that rather arbitrary status. Trained as a scientist, Kropotkin made a number of important contributions to the geographical studies of the Russian Far East and Scandinavia. Captivated by the revolutionary energy of Bakunin, Kropotkin became an activist in the 1870s but returned to the scholarly life after being imprisoned for his illicit activities. From the mid-1880s until 1917 he resided in London, occupying himself with scholarly and philosophical writing. With the Tsar's overthrow in 1917, he returned to Moscow, living there in quiet and honored retirement until his death.

Kropotkin's scientific background encouraged him to dispute the then popular doctrine of Social Darwinism, as put forth by Herbert Spencer. He was convinced that higher animals, and man in particular, had met with the greatest success when acting cooperatively rather than aggressively.

Government, according to Kropotkin, tended to divide person against person, class against class, country against country, and was therefore destructive of human progress. It was the "personification of injustice, oppression, and monopoly" in his view and must therefore be eliminated and replaced with an anarchist society based upon communist principles and voluntary mutual aid among free individuals.

Kropotkin believed that people were essentially social beings and that the state tended to make them antisocial. With its elimination he expected people to seek one another's support and cooperation. Thus, a positive rather than negative atmosphere would evolve and would accrue to the ultimate benefit of all in the society.

Kropotkin's attitude toward revolution was ambivalent. An avowed Bakuninist during his early years, he did engage in revolutionary activities, but he later questioned whether revolution was the most effective method by which to transform society. Although he certainly never became a pacifist, Kropotkin tended to lean increasingly toward the belief that, nourished by the increasing capacity of industrialization to sustain a communist society, anarchism would evolve naturally from the human desire to be free.

Emma Goldman (1869–1940) was the most influential anarchist in United States history. Fleeing Tsarist Russia, she came to America in 1886, only to be brutalized in the sweatshops of the garment industry in Rochester, New York. Disillusioned by harsh economic conditions as well as by the prejudices of the moral strictures of American society, she found herself becoming increasingly radical. *Alexander Berkman*, who became her lifelong lover, introduced her to the theories of Bakunin and to the tiny American anarchist movement.

Soon Goldman became a leading advocate of radical causes ranging from atheism to the use of contraceptives by women. A fiery speaker, she often brought crowds to their feet and the police to her door. Arrested time and again for leftist agitation, Goldman came to be known as "Red Emma."

Few labor laws protected workers in the nineteenth century, and factories were more appropriately called sweatshops.

During most of her career, Goldman was an activist. She led protests, addressed rallies, advocated strikes, published the anarchist journal *Mother Earth,* and even sold her body to get enough money to buy the pistol with which Berkman tried to assassinate industralist Henry Clay Frick. As World War I approached she became a leading opponent of the "capitalist's wars," again finding herself in jail and finally deported to the Soviet Union. Her initial enthusiasm for the Soviet regime soon transformed into bitter disappointment, however, causing her to support the Russian navy's anti-Bolshevik rebellion on the island of Kronstadt in 1921, and ultimately inducing her to leave the country for London.

Continuing her radical activities throughout the 1920s and 1930s, Goldman became a vociferous opponent of fascism and Nazism. She joined the anarchists in Spain resisting the reactionary rebellion of Francisco Franco and ultimately died of a stroke in Canada while trying to raise money for the anarchist cause.

Although she remained an activist to the end, an advocate of "propaganda by the deed," Goldman gradually came to question the violent acts of her youth. Time found her increasingly drawn to the temperate approach of Kropotkin and away from the terrorist methods of Bakunin. In the end, Emma Goldman advocated the elimination of government to be replaced by a network of communes based on mutual trust and consideration among individuals who remained free to think and act as they chose.

Besides the relatively mild Kropotkin and the activist Goldman, history's most extreme anarchist movement also owes a great deal to Bakunin. Unlike their revolutionary mentor, the *Nihilists* remained in Russia, combating Tsarist oppression. Feeling the pressure for change in the nineteenth century, the Tsarist regime responded to demands for reform and modernization with reaction and brutal repression. The government's obstinate intransigence frustrated the radicals and encouraged them to resort to increasingly extreme activities, eventually including conspiracy, terrorism, and assassination.

The most frustrated group of radicals, the Nihilists abandoned all hope of reform and came to believe that government itself had to be eliminated. The term Nihilists was first introduced in *Fathers and Sons,* a novel by Ivan Turgenev. Developing the most chaotic, violent, and destructive variant of anarchistic theories, the Nihilists were prominent between the 1860s and 1880s. Their philosophy contended that government was so rotten, so corrupt, so decayed that it was beyond repair. The only constructive act possible, in the minds of these unhappy people, was the destruction of society. Anything that survived the violent onslaught would perhaps be worth saving. In a single sentence, Nihilist *Dmitri Pisarev* (1840–1918) captured the philosophy of these tortured radicals: "Here is the ultimatum of our camp: What can be smashed, should be smashed; what will stand the blow is good; what will fly into smithereens is rubbish; at any rate, hit out right and left—there will and can be no harm from it."

The most notorious Nihilist was *Sergi Nechayev* (1847–1882). A protege of Bakunin, Nechayev schemed and plotted unscrupulously. Devoted to only one idea, the destruction of the state, he lied, cheated, and even murdered his own co-conspirators. Proclaiming his Nihilist convictions, he wrote: "We must devote ourselves wholly to destruction, constant, ceaseless, relentless, until there is nothing left of existing institutions." Though in practice the Nihilists were amateurish and bungling and were eventually wiped out, their blatant violence terrorized the Russian government and caused it some loss of esteem, since its brutal policies so obviously produced Nihilist extremism.

Individualist Anarchism

Easily the most solitary philosophy among anarchists is *individualist anarchism* (anarchism on the right). The people thus far discussed, whether violent or not, religious or not, socialist or not, were *social anarchists* (anarchism on the left); they opposed government because they believed that it limited people's freedom. However, they were not interested in individual freedom solely for the individual's own sake. Each of the social anarchists recognized that individuals within society are directly related to each other and are somehow responsible to each other. Such is not the case with the individualist anarchists. These ideologues recognize only the individual, denying any obligation or even much value to interrelationships among people. Exceeding the confines of what is usually understood as "individualism," these anarchists promote a concept which might better be termed "individualistism."

The founder of individualist anarchism is *Max Stirner* (1806–1856), a German philosopher and social critic. Stirner led a relatively undistinguished life except for a brief moment of notoriety in the late 1840s, when his most successful work, *The Ego and His Own,* was published. Within its pages Stirner represents humanity as a completely *atomistic* group of individuals who owe no true responsibility to anyone save themselves.

According to Stirner, society's institutions, including government and religion, are artificial props unrightfully forcing the strong to sacrifice in support of the weak. Stirner suggests that all acts, though usually rationalized as being for the greater good, are actually committed out of selfish motives. Thus, he argues that contrary to what people say, they do not really worship God for His [sic] sake, but for their own sake. The worship of God is a protective device intended by the worshippers to save their souls. Yet, they piously represent it as an unselfish act for God's sake. Stirner sees this pretense as a self-deception preventing people from openly and efficiently acting in their own interests.

Stirner demands that people abandon their feeble attempts at mutual responsibility and concentrate on themselves alone. Defiantly proclaiming his thesis of "ownness," Stirner wrote: "*My own* I am at all times and under all circumstances, if I know how to have myself and do not throw myself away on others." In another place in *The Ego and His Own* he restates the point even more bluntly: "I am everything to myself and I do everything on my own account."

Thus establishing to his satisfaction "*the sovereignty of the individual*," Stirner encourages each person to act without regard to the society as a whole. People are justified to take what they wish simply because they desire it. The social good is a hoax created to limit the power of the strong. When society is created by the weak, it destroys individual freedom. Stirner calls upon people to refuse recognition of their supposed obligation to others, thus liberating themselves from the artificial fetters unrightfully imposed upon them. Exalting in his own presumed freedom, he exclaimed, "The *people* are dead. Up with *me!*"

As previously indicated, individualist anarchist ideas can also be found in works by Thoreau, Josiah Warren, S. E. Parker, and Ayn Rand, but such ideas are deeply rooted in the fabric of American society as well. Perhaps stemming from the frontier ethic under which people relied on themselves to carve a life out of the wilderness, the mystique of *rugged individualism* has enjoyed particular popularity in the United States. Thus, the "strong, silent type" who "goes it alone" has often captured the imagination of the American people. The tendency toward an atomistic society in which the individual comes first and society is secondary—almost incidental—has certainly been an important force in our history. Yet, a very real danger is concealed in this approach to modern politics. While a measure of self-reliance is indisputably healthy, we do not live in a society in which people have only a slight relationship to each other. Our society is culturally, politically, and economically integrated. Indeed, the most striking development of the past few decades is the growing interdependence in the world. This state of affairs makes exaggerated individualism paradoxical and even dangerous, for if people in an interrelated context refuse to foster a social consciousness, they will pull at the fabric of society until it is severely damaged, or even destroyed.

At its greatest extreme, individualist anarchism can lead to an attitude of complete self-reliance and a frightening exclusivity. It can become reminiscent of Thomas Hobbes' vision of the natural state: "A war of each against all." Stirner's "ownness" can become a kind of "one, true, and only meism," in which only the self counts. It can isolate people more than any other political theory.

Although Marx would probably not be considered an anarchist because he contemplated using government as a tool with which to bring about the utopia, some of his ideas are very similar to those of the social anarchists. He rejected religion, he condemned property, and he even expected government itself to disintegrate eventually. Not surprisingly, therefore, we find that the same social, economic, and political conditions that motivated the anarchists' rejection of the status quo also evoked the Marxist challenge. Hence, it is appropriate that we now turn to a study of Marxism.

SUGGESTION FOR FURTHER READING

BOWIE, NORMAN E., and ROBERT I. SIMON, *The Individual and the Political Order.* Englewood Cliffs, NJ: Prentice-Hall, 1977.

CARTER, APRIL, *The Political Theory of Anarchism.* New York: Harper & Row, 1971.

FEIERABEND, IVO K., et al., *Anger, Violence and Politics: Theories and Research.* Englewood Cliffs, NJ: Prentice-Hall, 1972.

FORMAN, JAMES D., *Anarchism.* New York: Dell, 1975.

KELLY, AILEEN, *Mikhail Bakunin.* Oxford, England: Clarendon Press, 1982.

RITTER, ALAN, *Anarchism.* Cambridge, England: Cambridge University Press, 1980.

SHATZ, MARSHALL S., ed., *The Essential Works of Anarchism.* New York: Bantam Books, 1971.

TAYLOR, RICHARD, *An Introduction to Freedom, Anarchy, and the Law.* Englewood Cliffs, NJ: Prentice-Hall, 1973.

WARD, COLIN, *Anarchy in Action.* London: Freedom Press, 1982.

WOLFF, ROBERT PAUL, *In Defense of Anarchism.* New York: Harper & Row, 1976.

7

Marxism

PREVIEW

Communism is a very old idea that Karl Marx greatly influenced but certainly did not invent. The basic thoughts that Marx developed can best be understood in the context of the economic, social, and political environment in which he lived. At the time, Europe was going through a period of reactionary repression that was made even worse by the conditions resulting from the Industrial Revolution. Yet, the academic community was progressive and actively sought the formula for understanding human history.

Marx believed that people's ideas are conditioned by their economic environment and that economic change stimulates a dialectic conflict between those ruling and those ruled in society. The rulers use every available resource to keep themselves in power, but this effort is doomed to failure. Eventually the social class controlling the new dominant means of production will win the struggle to create its own political and cultural conditions. According to Marx, the final conflict will find the capitalist and proletarian classes engaged in a struggle that the proletariat will win because, while the capitalist system is productive, it is also exploitative and parasitic. When the proletariat class comes to power, it will establish a dictatorship, which, in turn, will create a socialist economy and eliminate all nonproletarian classes. This

Note: The drawing at the top of the page portrays Karl Marx in the foreground and Friedrich Engels in the background.

development will lead to greater productivity and the elimination of poverty; peace and happiness will prevail. When the last nonproletariat has been eliminated from the society, the state will have "withered away," its few remaining institutions acting only as administrators of the economy. As each country becomes socialist in its turn, national boundaries will disappear and eventually a single utopia of socialist brothers will replace the divided, exploitative, and cruel world of capitalism.

BACKGROUND

Communism is a very old concept, dating back to the beginning of recorded history. Many primitive societies practiced some form of communal ownership, work, and consumption. Almost every advanced Indian tribe in the Western Hemisphere enjoyed rather sophisticated communist institutions. The *ejido* of Mexico, a peasant farm system in which land is owned and cultivated collectively, survives to this day as a relic of primitive communism. Communist tendencies in Europe can be found in as early a work as Plato's *Republic,* in early Christian life, in Sir Thomas More's *Utopia,* in the German Anabaptists, and in the English Levelers and Diggers.

The concept of *communism,* as it was originally meant, did not imply a national economic system. Rather, it meant a local, communal relationship among small groups of people. With the Industrial Revolution, however, two factors evolved that made collective production, distribution, and consumption of goods on a national scale seem feasible. First, the mechanization of production increased output so greatly that some people began to believe hunger and poverty could be eliminated for the first time in history. Second, improvements in technology and communications made possible the organization of a national economy, so goods could be produced, distributed, and consumed collectively.

The realization that technology now made communism possible on a national level, combined with genuine humanitarian compassion, led to the first major "socialist" movement. While communism was originally thought to mean communal living and sharing on a local basis, the term *socialism* was coined by *Robert Owen* (1771–1858), the father of English socialism, to refer to communal living and sharing on a national scale.

Owen was one of a small group of people who thought that simple humanitarianism required the development of a society in which no one would starve while others prospered. These *utopian socialists* were among the first true socialists. Leaders of the movement other than Owen were Charles Fourier, Claude Saint-Simon, Horace Greeley, and Charles A. Dana. The utopian movement will be discussed in more detail in the next chapter; here it is enough to point out that by the middle of the nineteenth century the utopian socialist movement had lost its vitality. People no longer responded to its humanitarian appeal. Its numerous experimental socialist communities in Europe and America had all failed.

Karl Marx was *not* a utopian socialist. Although he was concerned about people's inhumanity to one another, Marx did not believe that people would adopt socialism merely because it was a nice way for one individual to treat another. Marx's theory claimed that socialism was an inevitable result of the Industrial

Revolution. Dubbed *scientific socialism,* Marx's view rescued socialism from oblivion and turned it into one of the most powerful ideas of this century. Marx was also responsible for adding to the meaning of communism. In his introduction to the *Communist Manifesto,* A.J.P. Taylor tells us that Marx used the word *communism* not as a descriptive term but as a polemic intended to arouse people. It excited some and frightened others. *Socialism,* on the other hand, had come to be regarded with ambiguity at best, and indifference at worst. Hence, while Marx espoused *socialism,* that is, a national collectivized economy, he used the word *communist* for the title of his call to revolution, hoping that the substitute term would arouse his audience. For that reason, communism has come to be associated with Marxist socialism.

The complexity of Marx has not been fully appreciated, partly because his ideas and motivations have been distorted by supporters and opponents alike. Misunderstanding, oversimplification, and, at times, deliberate misrepresentation have often obscured his message. Comprehension of his views has also been impaired by the contradictory character of the man himself. Marx was, at the same time, a revolutionary and a Victorian gentleman, a political activist and a brilliant scholar, a philosopher and an ideologue, a historian and a futurist. Making major contributions to many fields of social thought, he developed ideas that are among the most influential of our time. Whatever else can be said in support of or in opposition to Karl Marx, there is no doubt that he was a man whose ideas changed the world.

Marx's Life

Karl Marx (1818–1883) was the oldest son in a Jewish family. Born in Trier, Germany, he came from a prosperous middle-class home. His father was a lawyer who somewhat cynically converted to Christianity for commercial reasons. Yet, his mother remained a strict orthodox Jew and became estranged from her son upon learning he had become an atheist.

In 1835 Marx entered the University of Bonn law school. He was a disappointing student, however, spending much of his time relaxing in the local beer gardens, talking with friends, writing poetry, and dueling. Marx's father was a practical man, however, who soon became disgusted with young Karl's lifestyle and academic performance. In 1836 he insisted that Karl transfer to the University of Berlin, where school life was more disciplined. In Berlin, Marx, still the impressionable youth who had so quickly adopted the romanticism of Bonn, came under the powerful influence of Hegelian philosophy. The young scholar quickly became a serious student, fired by radical ideas of materialism and social justice.

Later Marx moved to the University of Jena, where he completed his doctorate in philosophy. Prepared for a life in academia, the young scholar found the Prussian hand of political oppression heavy indeed. Denied teaching positions by the government because of his radical political views, Marx finally became the editor of a leftist newspaper. The many articles he wrote criticizing the reactionary government incurred its wrath. Unable to tolerate the paper's opposition, the government closed it down in 1843, and Marx was driven into exile.

Paris was the capital of socialism at that time. It hosted dozens of radical groups and was the home of some of the leading socialist thinkers of the day. The young

German scholar was immediately comfortable in this setting, where he met many leftists and even debated with Pierre Joseph Proudhon and Mikhail Bakunin, two leading social anarchists. In 1844 he met *Friedrich Engels* (1820–1895), and they quickly became friends. Each respected the other, and they soon found that they agreed on the basics of a socioeconomic theory of history that would dominate the rest of their lives.

Engels, the son of a wealthy Prussian industrialist family and a scholar in his own right, not only became Marx's lifelong benefactor, supporting him while he studied and wrote, but also collaborated in Marx's work and made several important contributions to it. After Marx's death his loyal friend carried on the work, editing and publishing the second and third volumes of Marx's *Das Kapital* and finally taking up the leadership of the international socialist movement.

Between 1844 and 1848 Marx was forced out of one European country after another. At the same time, the political situation in Europe was growing increasingly tense. Indeed, things had come to such a pass that by 1848 Marx and other socialists belonging to the Communist League were convinced that the proletarian revolution was at hand but that it might be wasted for want of a doctrine. Hence, Marx was commissioned to write a brief essay setting forth the ideology of the impending revolution. This document, hastily written, is the *Communist Manifesto*. It contains a brief sketch of Marx's ideas and includes several important thoughts that Marx adapted from the work of his friend Engels.

The year 1848 was indeed a year of revolution. Uprisings flared in several countries from France to Hungary, but each was suppressed in turn. Marx once again found himself looking for a place to live. At last, in 1849, he took his family to England, where he remained for the rest of his life except for occasional visits to the continent. For the next thirty-four years he studied and wrote in the British Museum. In all of Europe, only England was free enough and sufficiently confident of its political institutions to host this unorthodox and radical thinker.

Marx was so dedicated to his studies that he devoted his entire life to them. For a brief period he worked as a London reporter for Horace Greeley's *New York Daily Tribune,* but the rest of the time he had no income except for some royalties from his books and a modest inheritance. Time and again he watched his beloved family suffer as his financial circumstances brought them to the brink of poverty. However, each time he was rescued by the faithful Engels and was allowed to continue his work.

Despite his scholarly interests, Marx remained active politically. He once wrote, "The philosophers have only *interpreted* the world, the point is to *change* it" (emphasis added). Committed to the revolution he felt sure would soon erupt, Marx corresponded with socialists throughout Europe and in 1864 helped found the International Association of Workingmen, commonly known as the *First International,* about which we will learn more in Chapter 8.

Nevertheless, Marx was not very successful as a revolutionary. Ill at ease in the pragmatic world of applied politics, Marx's revolutionary goal eluded him. Throughout his life he anticipated a great proletarian conflagration which never materialized. Yet, although he modified his theories with the passage of time, until his death he remained convinced of the validity of his analysis. Indeed, his intellectual prowess was so great that he came to dominate the socialist movement. It was only after his death that major variations of his thought attracted substantial followings among socialists.

Europe in the Nineteenth Century

Before we can fully understand Marx, we must acquaint ourselves with the world in which he lived. Only with this kind of perspective can we appreciate the full significance of his work. Europe in the nineteenth century was dominated by three major influences. First, the Scientific Quest, was scholarly; the second, the Concert of Europe, political; and the third, the Industrial Revolution, economic.

The scientific quest. Marx lived during a time when belief in the scientific method was at its peak. Science had revealed secrets of life that were previously unimagined. There was growing confidence that the mysteries of the universe would soon be solved and that humanity was on the verge of a new era of knowledge and understanding of things about which earlier generations could only speculate. Battling with ignorance and superstition, science was close to victory, or so it seemed.

As mentioned earlier, people began to suspect that just as there were laws governing other natural elements, there might also be natural laws governing human beings. A large part of the scholarly society of Europe—including Jeremy Bentham, Herbert Spencer, Auguste Comte, and Sigmund Freud—was indeed persuaded that such laws existed, and Marx was only one of many who sought the "secret" of human motivation. The greatest inspirations in the field of scientific determinism came from Sir Isaac Newton (1642–1727) and *Charles Darwin* (1809–1882). Newton, with his theories of universal gravitation, terrestrial mechanics, and mass and movement, gave us the tools with which to rationalize the universe. Physical phenomena became understandable as well as predictable, and from this foundation, developments in science and technology launched the present era. Darwin, in turn, gave us a theory of

Charles Darwin (1809–1882)

natural selection which provides for biology the foundation that Newton's ideas establish for physics.

Marx believed that he had found the key to human social development; hence, his theories were called *scientific socialism*. Engels, convinced that Marx had done for social history what Darwin had done for biological science, made the following comparison: "As Darwin discovered the law of development of organic nature, so Marx discovered the developmental law of human history."

The Concert of Europe. The Napoleonic conquest of Europe had completely dislocated the established order. When Napoleon was finally defeated in 1815 and sent into exile, the leading statesmen of Europe gathered in Vienna. Although delighted to be rid of their longstanding rival, they were deeply concerned about the legacy he had left them. The Europe they had fought to restore was changed beyond recognition. The map was redrawn, the ancient royal families had lost their domains, and the people of Europe were openly demanding democratic reforms. Major decisions had to be made. Either Europe could be brought closer to the radical goals of the French Revolution or it could be forced to reestablish the old dynastic monarchies. Predictably, Europe's leaders agreed to reestablish autocratic rule. The cruel policies of Nicholas I of Russia (1825–1855) were typical of the era. "Progress," he said, "must be deleted from official terminology."

Thus, three years before Marx's birth, one of the most reactionary periods in history began. This was a time when the crowned heads of Europe cooperated in suppressing their own people. The Quadruple Alliance between Austria, Prussia, Russia, and France guaranteed that Europe's most powerful monarchs would use their forces for stamping out any attempt to establish democracy on the continent and for ensuring that government would remain the private estate of the chosen few.

Yet, the demand for reform would not be quieted. Time and again the flag of rebellion was raised. In 1821, again in 1830, and yet again in 1848, the barricades were thrown up in Belgium, Germany, Poland, Austria, Hungary, Italy, Bohemia, Spain, Portugal, and especially in France. Each time these violent demands for reform were repressed so thoroughly that the next rebellion was inevitable. All the strength of monarchy was set against the irrepressible forces of history. Though democracy won out over monarchy in the end, this inevitable result was postponed for a century at a great cost in terms of human frustration, misery, and death.

This was the political environment Marx encountered during his formative years. Hounded by the police, he fled from one country after another in search of a place that allowed freedom of thought and expression. Little wonder that in his early life he believed that only violence could bring about meaningful changes in society.

The Industrial Revolution. The scientific method had given people a new framework for thought. It also brought on a new technology that mechanized production and replaced human or animal energy with steam. Yet, as machines and energy sources became more sophisticated, their costs exceeded the resources of the individual. Hence, cottage industry was replaced by the factory system. Eventually, family ownership of industry was displaced by stock market investors and professional managers. Each of these developments removed ownership from production and estranged the workers from the owners.

This new economic system allowed people with money to buy up the machinery and factories needed to produce goods. People who had been self-employed, or at least had worked closely with their employers, found themselves forced to work in huge factories. The resulting depersonalization of labor was increased by the new machinery, which tended to make old skills obsolete. Workers were put behind machines to perform monotonous and menial tasks requiring no skills beyond those needed to keep the machine functioning properly, even as wages were suppressed because skilled jobs disappeared.

The factory system brought with it a whole new way of life. People were herded into the cities where housing was cramped and poor. Sanitation facilities were so woefully inadequate that people were forced to live in squalor. The factories themselves were dark, damp, and unventilated. Often they were simply converted basements or barns. If the buildings had windows, the workers were usually forbidden to open them for fear that they would be distracted from their labor. Having isolated the workers from anything that might reduce their productivity, the owners sealed them in stuffy, dimly lighted workrooms. Thousands died of asthma and tuberculosis because the air they breathed was contaminated by smoke, steam, dust, and filth. Many people never saw the sun. They went to work before dawn and returned home late at night, toiling as long as sixteen hours a day in the summer and thirteen and a half hours in the winter, sometimes seven days a week. At times workers could not even leave the factories and were forced to sleep beneath the machines to which they were enslaved. Working people were often crippled and deformed by long hours of hard labor in stooped positions.

Women and children were the most desirable laborers because they could be paid less and were least likely to resist the harsh discipline, beatings, and other cruelties imposed on them. The family unit disintegrated. A working mother might seldom see her children unless they also worked in the factories. Small children were left completely unattended for long periods. Men, usually the first to be fired, sometimes had to depend on the earnings of their wives and children for subsistence. The disgrace and humiliation of these circumstances often drove men to leave home, to dissipate in drunkenness, to perpetrate cruelties on their families, or even to commit suicide.

The owners were often indifferent to the suffering in their factories. Some capitalists rationalized the wretched conditions of the laborers by claiming that industry saved these people from idleness, the greatest sin of all. Others used Social Darwinist arguments, claiming that the laborers were obviously inferior to the owners and *should* be worked hard. They resolved that eventually the inferiors would die out, leaving only the strong. The owners imposed heavy fines and even corporal punishment for whistling or talking at work, for working too slowly, or for being late. The law gave the workers no protection and demanded a heavy penalty for theft. When a woman was put on trial for stealing a few coins to feed her starving children, Thomas Hood, a poet of the time, wrote in anguish, "Oh God, that bread should be so dear and flesh and blood so cheap!" Charles Dickens, however, is probably the best-known author inspired by the plight of the worker. Just a glance at *David Copperfield, Hard Times,* or *Oliver Twist* impresses the reader with the hopeless circumstances of the poor during this era. Given these conditions of political oppression and economic exploitation, and the social evils that accompanied them, it is not difficult to understand how someone as perceptive as Marx could seek nothing less than radical change in the society.

Charles Dickens (1812–1870)

CAPITALIST DEVELOPMENT

Whatever the ultimate validity of his theories, history has shown Marx to have erred in a number of important respects. Our understanding of Marx will be enhanced if we consider a few of his greatest mistakes before studying his theories.

Among the most fascinating paradoxes regarding Marx is that while he was a keen student of history and a perceptive observer of his own time, he badly misjudged certain crucial facts about his era and about the course history would follow. For example, though he saw himself as the founder of a new science of economic history, he was actually the last in a great intellectual tradition—classical economics. The classical economists—including Adam Smith, David Ricardo, Thomas Malthus, Baptiste Say, and Marx himself—were philosophers as well as economists; they were at least as concerned with questions of the social good as they were with the more mechanical aspects of economics. Although some contemporary economists, such as Joseph Schumpeter, Milton Friedman, and John Kenneth Galbraith, have also exhibited philosophical inclinations, most economists since Marx's time have focused on the technical questions in their field. Hence, ironically, we see Marx as the last great thinker of a distinguished line of economists who concerned themselves with the philosophy of value, of work, and of the rightful place of humanity on the globe. Indeed, Marx lived at the end of an intellectual era rather than at the beginning of a new one.

Marx also firmly believed that his generation came at the very end of the capitalist era, and he fully expected the socialist revolution to occur at any moment. Given the despicable conditions of the working class during his life, Marx can be forgiven for expecting that the masses would rise up to cast off their chains should things continue to deteriorate. Perhaps they would have done so had capitalists been as blind as Marx imagined. He was quite wrong, however, in his estimation of both the productivity of capitalism and of its capacity to adjust to threatening conditions. In fact, capitalism far outproduced even the wildest predictions of its nineteenth-century enthusiasts, and the Western capitalists responded to proletarian threats of violence with policies which shared enough of the newly created wealth with the worker to put off a disastrous conflagration.

As it turned out, Marx was seeing the beginning of the capitalist era rather than its end. Preindustrialized (that is, premechanized) economies are usually incapable of producing enough to satisfy all the economic needs of their people. Hence, productivity usually falls below the level we shall call *subsistence*. In these conditions scarcity is a fact of life, causing social anxiety. To escape depravity, a few people in such societies manage to accumulate enough, or more than enough, to satisfy their needs, thus leaving even less to be consumed by the masses. Thus, the portion of production left for the masses to consume falls even farther below subsistence, aggravating the suffering of the majority. (See Figure 7-1).

Industrialization of an economy can eventually increase productivity, but first money must be found to buy the factories and machines. Where does the money come from? Some undoubtedly comes from the coffers of the wealthy, but history shows that the wealthy tend to demand sacrifices from the poor to pay for most technological advances. Wages tend to be suppressed and working conditions tend to decline, thus creating capital to invest in mechanization. Consequently, if the masses are already suffering because they must consume at less than the subsistence level, and are asked to sacrifice more to create enough capital for industrialization, their conditions of life and work must be terrible indeed.

Except for foreign investment, capital comes from a domestic economy which either produces more than it consumes or consumes less than it produces. As we have already seen, preindustrial economies are usually incapable of producing more than must be consumed without incurring great hardship. Hence, force was used to create capital.

To enforce sacrifices on the workers, owners of production used the powers of government, forcing workers to labor for meager wages under terrible conditions.

FIGURE 7-1   Production and Consumption in Preindustrial and Industrializing Societies

Subsistence

Production of a Nonindustrial Economy

Profits and Capital

Consumption Level for the Masses in Preindustrial Societies

Mass Consumption in Industrializing Societies

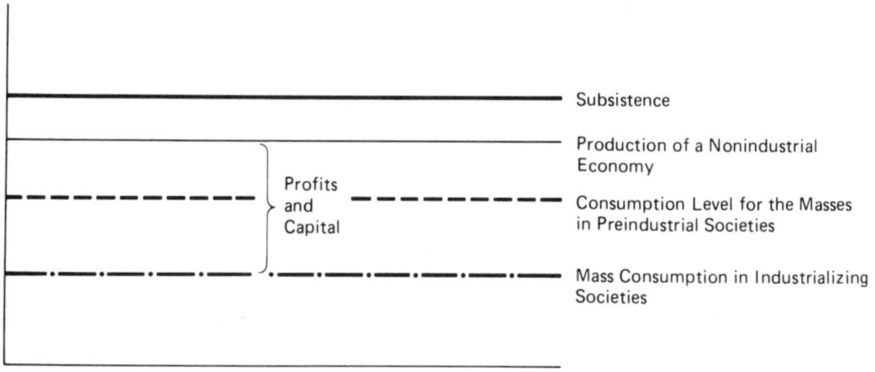

Labor unions were suppressed; strikes were broken by thugs, the police, or the army; and unemployment compensation, worker's compensation, and social security were nonexistent. Collusion between government and the owners of production occurred in every society which industrialized, including England and the United States. The reason for such collusion was that force had to be used to persuade the workers to make sacrifices which they would not otherwise make voluntarily.

This stage of the Industrial Revolution—its most exploitative period—was witnessed by Marx and Dickens. Marx's error was not in decrying these conditions but rather in concluding that the workers' conditions would continue to disintegrate rather than improve. What actually did occur is that, with industrialization, production began to climb, creating capital. Marx anticipated that, driven by the need to increase profits, the capitalists would intensify their exploitation of the workers until the latter could no longer stand their misery: Revolution would then erupt. This bleak prediction has not come to pass in the West. Industrial productivity has grown to such an extent that it has brought huge profits to the owners and, at the same time, vastly improved living and working conditions for the common people. (See Figure 7–2.)

It should be noted, however, that history attests to few instances in which the owners voluntarily shared their wealth with the masses. Perhaps realizing that Marx was indeed correct in predicting their doom if they did not provide improved conditions for the workers, the capitalists have grudgingly accepted collective bargaining, fringe-benefit packages, wage increases, and social protection programs. Each of these benefits, however, followed great struggles by workers for their rights.

Whatever the reason, capitalism has not forced its own doom. Far more flexible and pragmatic than Marx anticipated, capitalism has survived the centennial of his death. Although it has received some very serious blows, the worst of which were the Great Depression and the rise of fascism (1920s–1945), capitalism, albeit in modified

FIGURE 7–2   Production and Consumption in Industrialized Societies

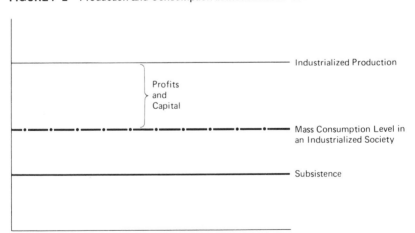

form, survives today as a vital economic system, showing few signs of the demise predicted by its nemesis, while socialism currently appears to be in retreat.

THE BASIC PRINCIPLES OF MARXISM

Wretched as things had become, Marx was still optimistic about the future of humanity. He saw people in historical terms. Individuals, he believed, were destined for freedom and creativity but had been prevented from developing completely because they were slaves to their own basic needs. Before the Industrial Revolution human productivity had not been great enough to provide a sufficient supply of the necessities of life to free people from *compulsive toil* (the necessity to work incessantly just to survive). With the emergence of capitalism, to which Marx gives due praise, people became—for the first time—productive enough to provide an abundance of goods. They could now devote more time to the development of their own humanity. Yet, capitalism failed to distribute its abundance fairly. Indeed, it tended to take away from the workers more and more of the products they created, giving them instead to the capitalist, a nonworker who exploits workers.

The irony of the dilemma that Marx describes is clear: For the first time in history humanity has created an economic system that produces enough for all people so that they may enjoy the spare time necessary to refine their humanity—to be free, in other words. Yet, that very economic system distributes its bounty to a few wealthy people, thus artificially perpetuating the enslavement of the masses. What history had denied people for millennia was now being withheld from them by their fellows. Clearly, in Marx's view, capitalism was to be appreciated for its productivity, but it was also to be despised for its oppression, and it should be abandoned for a more equitable system. Marx was convinced that capitalism was but a necessary step to a new era of social justice. Attempting to explain the world as he understood it, he made important contributions to the fields of sociology, history, politics, economics, and philosophy. Hoping to guide people to a new, more perfect era, he laid down the doctrines we call Marxism.

Marxist Sociological Theory

The most fundamental assumption in Marxism is *economic determinism*. On this premise Marx built the rest of his theory. Economic determinism suggests that the primary human motivation is economic. "It is not the consciousness of men that determines their existence," Marx argues, "but their social existence that determines their consciousness;" that is, what we value and what we do politically is determined by our economic circumstances. Hence, it stands to reason that people in similar economic circumstances will have much in common.

This idea is not unique to Marx. He was introduced to the concept at the University of Berlin, where it enjoyed considerable support. Indeed, even James Madison proceeded from a similar assumption about human motivation. Consider this statement from *The Federalist* (no. 10):

> But the most common and durable source of factions (political adversaries) has been the various and unequal distribution of property. Those who hold and those who are without property have ever formed district interests in society. Those who are creditors and those

who are debtors, fall under a like discrimination. A landed interest, a manufacturing interest, a monied interest, with many lesser interests, grow up of necessity in civilized nations, and divide them into different *classes, actuated by different sentiments and views.* (Emphasis added.)

As a matter of fact, economic determinism has gained general currency in the world today, with most people believing that economics plays an important part in determining political behavior. In this respect at least, Glen Tinder posits that we are all now Marxists.[1]

Marx saw all societies as composed of two basic parts: the *foundation* and the *superstructure.* The foundation of any society, according to this theory, is material. In other words, the economic system is at the base of the society. Marx further divided the economy into two basic factors: the *means of production* and the *relations of production.* The *means of production* are the resources and technology at the disposal of a particular society, and their interrelationship determines the kind of economic system the society enjoys. The *relations of production* (or social classes) are determined by the affiliation between human beings in the society and the means of production. The owners of the means of production enjoy the most beneficial position in the economy, and thus become members of the most influential social group—the ruling class. (The validity of this part of Marx's proposition becomes clear if one tries to imagine a wealthy class which does not have great influence in society.) Thus, in a pastoral society the ruling group would be those who own the most livestock; in an agrarian society the greatest land owners would dominate; and in an industrial society the capitalist class would rule.

The foundation of society (the economic and social class systems) determines the nature of society's superstructure which rests upon the foundation. The superstructure is composed of all non-material institutions in the society, and each is arranged in a way that suits the ruling class. Included in the superstructure are values, ideology, government, education, law, religion, art, and so forth. (See Figure 7–3.) The function of the superstructure is to assure the rulers continued dominance and to keep the ruled in their place.

Consequently, Marx conceived of government as a tool of class oppression that manipulated all the cultural elements in the society to the advantage of those who controlled the economy. "Political power," he wrote, "properly so called, is merely organized power of one class for oppressing another." Marx called religion "the opiate of the people" because he believed that it drugged them, numbing their senses and disposing them to put up with their wretched existence so that they would be rewarded in a "mythical" afterlife. The aphorism "That's the cross I have to bear" illustrates the kind of attitude to which Marx objected. He wanted people to abandon the rationalizations with which they had been programmed by their rulers. When they did, they would become aware of their plight. They would then have taken the first step toward the revolution and freedom.

In specific terms, Marx explained that societies with feudal economic bases (those agrarian societies in which the economy is based on land ownership by a small elite, while the bulk of the population works the land of the great barons) develop similar social and political institutions in their superstructures. Their political sys-

---

[1]Glen Tinker, *Political Thinking,* 4th ed. (Boston: Little Brown and company, 1986), p. 184.

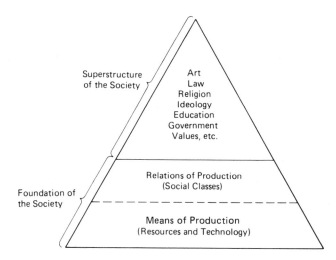

FIGURE 7–3 Marxian Abstract of Society's Structure

tems include monarchies supported by a powerful aristocratic class of landowners. The laws, values, ideologies, and educational systems tend to justify these political and economic systems. The dominant religion tends to be structured in a hierarchical fashion similar to the Catholic Church, and the Church also acts to support the system.

On the other hand, according to Marx, capitalistic systems (those whose economies are based on money and industrial production controlled by a small elite) evolve different institutions in their superstructures. Representative democracies give the illusion of popular control, but the governments are actually captained by the moguls who own the means of production. The laws, values, ideologies, and educational systems encourage sympathetic public attitudes toward these political and economic systems. Protestantism, with its individualistic and egalitarian doctrines, becomes the dominant religious form. Being free of the Catholic bias against usury and commerce, Protestantism is more compatible with capitalist values. Further, espousing the ethic that hard work, industriousness, and frugality result in individual progress, social good, and even (perhaps) eternal reward, Protestantism anoints capitalist activity with moral justifications and would therefore replace Catholicism as the dominant creed.

Although it is certainly not difficult to find circumstances that contradict Marx's sociological views, one would be remiss if he or she failed to recognize that indeed there is much to be learned from Marx's analysis. It is true that the areas which developed extensive capitalist systems—England, Holland, Switzerland, northern Germany, Scandinavia, and the United States—also accepted Protestantism as the dominant religious form. Even in Catholic France, which also built a substantial industrial base, the Huguenots (French Protestants) own a disproportionately large percentage of the capital wealth.

In the United States definite attempts are made to bring about what is called *socialization*. Socialization, a process employed by every society to some extent, is using the society's institutions to "educate" its citizens in the values that society espouses. For example, American Government is a required course in most states at elementary, high school, and college levels. Why is this subject thought to be so important? Other than creating jobs for political scientists (your author included), the study of government assumes that democracy depends upon a well-informed citizenry; thus the requirement. Yet, these courses (especially in the lower grades) do more than simply inform students. Great effort is expended to develop a positive attitude among students about their system of government.

Clearly, the above example illustrates the conscious attempt by society's leaders to inculcate the norms of the society in each new generation. Some may justify this phenomenon as an attempt to help young people become productive and happy citizens, while others may condemn it as propaganda. Whatever the case, the example tends to indicate that Marx is at least partially correct about the function of the superstructure. However, whether or not his assumption about the character of the society's foundation is sound remains debatable.

Marxist Historical Theory

Dialectic materialism is the essence of Marxism. To be a Marxist, one must accept this theory. As the Marxist theory of history, it is the basis for the belief that Marx created a "scientific" theory of socialism.

The dialectic. Part of this theory, the concept of the *dialectic,* was taken from the thinking of Georg Hegel, one of the most important political philosophers of modern history. Hegel's thought not only influenced Marx but also inspired fascist theory, as we will see later. In a general sense, Hegel's most important contribution may have been the idea that change should be viewed in a constructive way. Hegel developed a theory of history in which change is the central theme. Hegel believed that the world was progressing toward a goal that was predetermined by God. He called the goal the *Idea*. History, in other words, was the unfolding of God's Idea.

Since the Idea (or the course of history) was predetermined by God, people could not hope to understand it completely. Nor should they try to adjust the progress of history because that too, for the same reason, was beyond their power. Individuals can, however, be free, and they can find truth. Truth is found when people understand and accept their place in history, or in the divine plan. When they find this truth, they will also be free because they will not imprison themselves in a futile struggle against the will of an all-powerful God. These ideas, far from being liberal, form part of the basis for German nationalism and, more particularly, for fascism. Marx, an atheist with political views on the far left of the political spectrum, obviously did not draw inspiration from Hegel's definition of the Idea.

The concept that Marx did borrow from Hegel was that of the dialectic. Both Marx and Hegel saw the dialectic as a means of achieving historical *progress through struggle*. Hegel believed that history was spiritually motivated. He suggested that the dialectic was a divinely created force by which the Idea (history) was caused to unfold. He believed that any reality is two things. It is itself, and it is part of what it is becoming. Thus, the only consistency Hegel saw was change itself. To Hegel, history was simply the process of change brought on by struggle. In this process no truth was ever lost, since today's reality would become part of a more perfect truth tomorrow.

To better understand Hegel's theory, let us consider the following example. Let us call the existing state of affairs the *thesis*. Eventually any thesis will be challenged by a new idea, which we will call the *antithesis*. A conflict between the thesis and the antithesis will follow; this is called the *dialectic process*. The result of this conflict will, according to Hegel, be a *synthesis* of all the good parts of the thesis and of the antithesis. Then the synthesis becomes the new thesis to which an antithesis eventually develops. Struggle between them ensues, and a new synthesis, and eventually a new thesis evolves, and the process begins again. Hegel believed that the dialectic process always led to something better than what existed previously. He argued that good features were never lost in the dialectic process; rather they became part of a new, more complete good. Negative aspects of the thesis and antithesis, however, were destroyed in the dialectic process. This, Hegel called the "negation of the negative." Hence, Hegel saw history as inevitably progressive, with each new era improved over the last. And he expected the dialectic to continue refining and improving human institutions until the Idea was fulfilled. (See Figure 7–4.)

Dialectic materialism.   Marx rejected Hegel's metaphysical assumptions, of course, but he adopted the dialectic as the fundamental logic of history. He agreed

FIGURE 7–4   Hegelian Dialectic

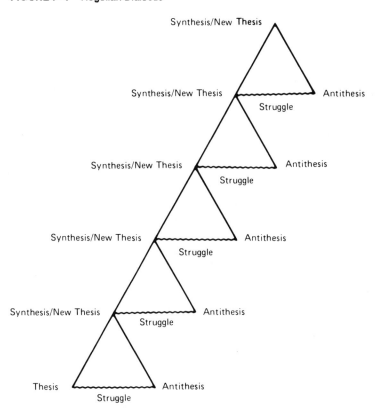

with Hegel that humanity would eventually reach the end of the process of change. In other words, both Hegel and Marx were idealists, each believing that people could develop a perfect social and political existence. However, Marx did not accept Hegel's version of the dialectic but changed it to suit his own view of historical progress. Hegel had argued that the dialectic was a struggle between divinely inspired ideas and that it led to changes in the earthly social or political environment. Marx, it is said, stood Hegelianism on its head by arguing the opposite. Citing economic determinism, Marx claimed that the dialectic was a conflict among worldly interests. Rather than stimulating struggle, ideas were actually the result of the dialectic conflict. *Materialism* not *spiritualism,* inspired the dialectic, according to Marx. He then went on to name the characters in the dialectic drama.

Marx believed that human conflict was caused by social-class differences. In addition, he held that the struggle which occurred at the end of one historical era and led to the dawn of a new one was a struggle between opposing social classes. Further, he believed that humanity had passed through four historical stages and was about to enter its fifth and final era. Each historical era had been characterized by a particular economic system (the means and relations of production) leading to a specific political system (superstructure).

The first era of human history, Marx believed, was based on *primitive communism.* People were unorganized and unsophisticated during this age. There was no occupational specialization, or division of labor. Every person worked at producing, and people naturally shared their produce with one another in order to survive. The antithesis to this system developed as people began to specialize in the production of certain goods. This *division of labor* resulted in more abundant and better quality goods, but it also caused a major division within society. As people focused on producing their specialty, the original collectivism of society was lost. The spears an artisan produced became *his* spears, and he traded them for products which other people produced. Thus, the concept of *private property* was born and with it the nemesis of humankind. Society tended to value various objects differently and the value of the individual was equated with the things he or she owned. This fatal differentation resulted in the beginnings of a class structure that created strife in the society. This strife led to a new era. As the members of a tribe began to differentiate among themselves, they also began to develop prejudices against other tribes. Eventually, after much strife, a new order was born because one tribe, or group of people, came to dominate others. The dominant people forced the dominated people into servitude. Hence, *slavery* became the basis of the economic system in the next era.

Empire was the dominant political system based on the foundation of slavery. The antithesis to the era of slavery and empire was the challenge from the barbarian hordes. When the barbarians finally prevailed over the empire, a new political-economic system had emerged, called *feudalism.* Feudalism was a system in which a landed aristocracy provided police and military protection to the peasants, who soon became *serfs* (people legally bound to the land—"land slaves") and farmed the nobles' lands. Since feudalism depended on a large number of self-sufficient manors, trade was almost completely stopped for a time. Gradually the stability provided by the nobles, the development of new techniques in banking and transportation, as well as the demand for luxury items stimulated a rebirth of trade. The aristocrats, however, usually looked down on commerce, so trade and its profits were left to a new class, the *bourgeoisie*.[2]

The bourgeoisie antithesis grew in strength until it finally toppled the feudal aristocracies in a series of revolutions; the American and French upheavals of the late eighteenth century are among the earliest and best-known examples. The new era initiated by those revolutions featured *capitalism* as its economic system. Marx called the new political systems *bourgeois democracies*. The term *democracy* was given to these political systems because, as Marx explained, there was a pretense of popular government through legislative representation; in reality, however, the capitalists always controlled the system.

Capitalism fostered factory workers, the *proletariat* (or wage slaves), a class which would act as the antithesis in the fourth historical era. Marx believed that the tension between the two classes would build into a new, and this time final, dialectic struggle. Capitalism had increased human productivity to the point at which all basic material needs could be satisfied. Nevertheless, it was exploitative in nature, so that the goods produced were not equally distributed; in fact, the reverse was true. Marx assumed that the victory of the proletariat was inevitable; it would be a victory of the exploited over the exploiter. He also believed that the proletariat itself would not be exploitative. If all other classes were eliminated, the source of all human strife would disappear and a new, classless society holding its goods in common would emerge. In this communist society all people would find peace and happiness. (See Figure 7–5.)

Figure 7–5 is useful for visualizing the Marxist dialectic. However, a fuller appreciation of the integration of the dialectic and economic determinism can be gained if one imagines that each triangle in the illustration represents the composite of a society (as represented in Figure 7–3) as well as part of the dialectic. Each triangle would be divided into a foundation and a superstructure that corresponds to the particular era it represents. In this way we can better visualize the totality of Marx's theory of dialectic materialism.

Marx, however, spent most of his time analyzing capitalism rather than discussing socialism; consequently, his theory is very hazy in places. For instance, he never described the communist utopia in detail. He did say that it was to be democratic, but, as we have already learned, that could mean any number of things. Practically the only specific he mentioned about the utopia was that its economic system would be totally socialist. In other words, in the new society there would be absolutely no private property except for personal effects. Marx is also vague as to what part he expected the peasantry to play in the final revolution. This question is vital to students of Marxism because they note, without exception, the countries that

---

[2]*Bourgeoisie* is a French term that means "middle class" in English. However, one must be careful not to draw any false conclusions from this translation. In the United States almost everyone is considered to be in the middle class. It is true that there are some who are poor and a few who are very wealthy, but traditionally most of the people of the United States see themselves as somewhere between these two extremes. This feeling of economic homogeneity has undoubtedly contributed to the country's political stability, but one wonders if it is not, after all, based on a conveniently broad definition of the label "middle class;" that is, most people are middle class in this country because the definition of the term is purposely expanded until all but the very rich and the very poor are included. The term *bourgeoisie* should not be understood in the same way. Marx meant the word as it is defined in French. The French bourgeoisie was a class of educated, wealthy merchants and tradesmen that developed as trade increased.

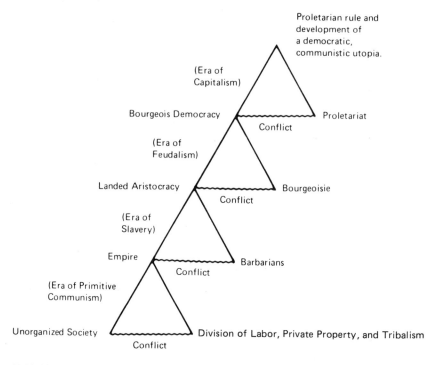

FIGURE 7–5   Marxian Dialectic

have developed Marxist systems as a result of indigenous political movements (for example, Russia, Yugoslavia, China, North Vietnam, and Cuba) have populations consisting largely of peasants. Understandably, there is a great deal of disagreement on this question. Some scholars believe that Marx expected peasants to become an agrarian proletariat and to participate fully in the dialectic. Others think that he did not foresee any significant role for them at all. Vladimir Lenin and Mao Tse-tung, as we will see in Chapters 8 and 9, filled in some of the details of peasant participation in the building of socialism. They have also answered many other crucial questions about the practical application of Marxist theory.

Marxist Economic Theory

As already mentioned, Marx was the last great classical economic thinker. He studied capitalism and the ideas of Locke, Smith, Ricardo, and Malthus very carefully, analyzing them perceptively in *Das Kapital*. In this work he concludes that "capitalism has within it the seeds of its own destruction." In short, Marx believed that the fall of capitalism was inevitable and that it would lead to socialism.

While this belief seems definite enough, it is the subject of considerable debate among students of Marxism. The *orthodox Marxists,* about whom we will learn more later, interpreting dialectic materialism literally, argue that socialism is not possible in any society that has not yet gone from the feudal stage to the capitalist stage. This ideological hair splitting is insignificant only to those who forget that so far Marxism has developed only in precapitalist societies. Obviously, anyone who wished to create the proletarian utopia in agrarian Tsarist Russia in 1917 would have trouble accepting this *two-stage theory*. This issue was, in fact, at the center of the famous dispute between the *Mensheviks* and the *Bolsheviks,* as we will see in Chapter 8. Marx himself confused matters when Vera Zasulich (1851–1919), a famous Russian revolutionary, asked him if the *mir,* an ancient Slavic system of communal farms, could have prepared the Russian people for socialism, allowing them to skip the capitalist stage of the dialectic. Increasingly interested in the possibilities of a Russian revolution, Marx answered that indeed it might be possible for the Russians to go from feudalism directly to socialism, skipping the capitalist stage. Despite this exception to dogma, however, Marxists typically agree that feudalism will eventually give way to capitalism, which will, in turn, inevitably result in socialism. This belief is based on a series of economic principles, to which we now turn.

The theory of work.   Marx, like John Locke, believed that work could be the way in which people might express their creativity. Indeed, both men believed that work is the process through which people develop their humanity and fulfill themselves. By interacting with nature in what is termed labor, individuals develop and change their own character. The essence of human beings, therefore, becomes closely related to their work. To Marx work was a form of "self-creation." Describing the laboring process, Marx wrote, "Man is constantly developing and changing—creating his own nature." In other words, the product of our labor is part of us, and something of us is in our product.

This attitude might appear naive or perhaps even mystical at first glance. Yet, which of us has not felt great satisfaction at having made something by hand? Do we not feel a closer relationship with objects we have made ourselves? Some years ago I had a room added to my house. The person who built it happened to have studied Marxism with me. After the last nail was driven, my former student stood at some distance from the new room and quietly looked at what he had completed. I walked to his side and we stood for a few moments looking at the new addition. Then I asked, "Ken, whose room is that?" "It's mine," he responded, and we both agreed. Though I had paid for the construction of the room, he had created it. He had put part of himself into it, and we both knew that it could never be mine in the same way that it was his.

The theory of self-alienation.   Marx's theory of work and his attitude toward capitalism led him to his theory of human *self-alienation*. This alienation occurs because of three factors. First, since it can be a form of "self-creativity," it should be enjoyable, Marx reasoned. Yet, because the capitalists squeeze every possible cent of profit from the workers, they make the conditions of work intolerable. Hence, instead of enjoying work or the act of self-creation, the members of the proletariat grow to hate the very process by which they could refine their own nature. Consequently, they become alienated from a part of their own selves. Second, Marx believed that capitalists *must* exploit the workers in order to produce a profit. The capitalists force the workers to sell their product and then use that product against the workers to exploit them further. This, Marx claimed, forces the workers to regard their own product, something that is actually part of them, as alien and even harmful to them; thus, it becomes another form of self-alienation. Third, and here Marx is truly paradoxical, the capitalist is criticized for mechanizing production because this process robs laborers of their skills and reduces them to little more than feeders of machines. Hence, all the creativity is taken out of work, making it impossible for people ever to develop their humanity fully: This is the ultimate alienation. Marx is indeed contradictory at this point. Clearly, he saw himself as the prophet of the future. He claimed that socialism was the coming economic system and that it would produce even more than capitalism. Yet, in this theory he seems to resent mechanization and its effects on the proletariat and even appears to look back nostalgically to an earlier era. In a passage from *Das Kapital,* Marx, often a laborious writer, displayed unusual eloquence while discussing human self-alienation.

> Within the capitalist system all methods for raising the social productiveness of labor are brought about at the cost of the individual laborer; all means for the development of production transform themselves into means of domination over, and exploitation of, the producers; they mutilate the laborer into a fragment of a man, *degrade him to the level of an appendage of a machine, destroy every remnant of charm in his work and turn it into a hated toil; they estrange from him the intellectual potentialities of the labor-process in the same proportion as science is incorporated in it as an independent power;* they distort the conditions under which he works, subject him during the labor-process to a despotism the more hateful for its meanness; they transform his lifetime into working-time, and drag his wife and child beneath the wheels of the Juggernaut of capital (emphasis added).

Ironically, the capitalists seem to have learned the lesson of Marx's alienation while the Soviets have not. Capitalists spend millions of dollars each year in efforts to make the assembly line and office more pleasant places in which to work. In capitalist states studies are made of worker satisfaction, walls are painted vivid colors, music is piped in, and workers are frequently rotated on the assembly line in attempts to combat boredom. Yet, in the Soviet Union one finds drab, monotonous working conditions, and worker alienation is painfully obvious. Absenteeism, tardiness, careless or deliberate mistakes, and alcoholism plague Soviet plants to a much greater extent than in the West. Clearly, the workers' paradise has yet to be achieved in the land which claims to be devoted to Marxist ideals.

The labor theory of value.   As you have already learned, the *labor theory of value* was not invented by Marx. It was generally accepted during the eighteenth and nineteenth centuries; in fact, it was openly supported by the great classical economists Adam Smith and John Locke and by no less a figure than David Ricardo. Living as he did at the end of the period dominated by classical economists, Marx is probably the last major economist to support the labor theory of value. In fact, Marx was once called "a Ricardo turned socialist" because he shared so many assumptions with the great capitalist economist yet adapted them to a different conclusion.

The labor theory of value is concerned with the *intrinsic worth* of an object. Value is a complex concept. The value most modern economists are concerned with is the *exchange value* of an item, that is, the amount of money one can get for an item on the market. *Sentimental value* is another kind of worth. Though the market value of one's dog may be high, one may not wish to sell the dog because its sentimental value is greater than anything anyone will offer for it. *Use value* is a third measure of worth. Though the sentimental value one attaches to an old car used to drive back and forth to work may be low and the exchange value little higher, the usefulness of the car might be quite high since it adequately performs a needed function.

By contrast, the labor theory of value is concerned with establishing a standard for measuring intrinsic or absolute value. This concept assumes that there are two kinds of value brought to the production process. Resources, machinery, and finance are termed *constant value;* that is, these factors, when applied to the production of an item, cannot add any value to the item greater than their own intrinsic worth. Only labor is a *variable value* because only labor produces something of greater worth than itself.

Here Marx pays tribute to the genius of human creativity. The materials necessary to produce a watch, for example, can be placed next to the tools and machines used in watchmaking; nevertheless, a watch will not be produced until human creativity—labor—is applied. Similarly, the components of an unassembled piece of clothing have an aggregate value, but when they are combined through labor to become a shirt, something new has been produced, and its value far exceeds the sum of its individual parts.

The intrinsic value of any object, Marx assumed, is therefore determined by the amount of labor—human creativity—needed to produce it. The *price* of the object, the amount of money it will fetch on the market at any given time, is determined by supply and demand. However, the *value* of the object is determined by the labor time needed for its production.

The theory of surplus value. The *theory of surplus value* is based on the labor theory of value and, according to Engels, is Marx's most important discovery. Marx argued that capitalism enslaves the proletariat because people have to work to survive while the capitalist has a monopoly on the means of production—that is, factories and machinery. Hence, the workers must sell their labor at whatever price the capitalist will pay. Marx also adopted Ricardo's *iron law of wages.* You will recall that Ricardo suggested that capitalists, driven by the need to make profits and capital, will pay their workers only subsistence wages—enough to feed themselves and their families—because that much is necessary to bring them back to work the next day. Hence, not only are the workers slaves—"wage slaves"—but their masters pay them only the most meager wages.

Thus, the capitalists force the workers to produce an excess, or *surplus value,* and they keep that sum for themselves as a profit. The surplus value is produced when the workers are forced to produce value greater than their own intrinsic value. The workers' intrinsic value, you will remember, is the money needed to feed themselves and their families. Anything they produce above the subsistence level is extra value. Since under Ricardo's iron law of wages the capitalists pay only a subsistence wage, they keep the surplus value produced by the workers as their profit. For example, let us say that it takes six hours of work to produce the necessities of life for a laborer and his or her family. If the employer forces the laborer to work for thirteen hours, yet only pays a subsistence wage, the capitalist has forced the laborer to surrender seven hours of surplus value. Because the surplus value can be produced only by labor, Marx goes on to argue, it belongs to the laborer by right. Hence, any profit the capitalists make from the labor of their employees is ill-gotten and exploitative. The capitalist is, therefore, a villain, a parasite who lives by sucking the economic lifeblood of the proletariat, and must be erased from society when the proletariat takes over. Needless to say, Ricardo, who was a capitalist economist, would not have agreed with this conclusion. Ricardo believed that the capitalists' control of property distinguished them from other people and justified their exploitation of the worker, for such exploitation created capital thus assuring further productivity.

At this point you might be wondering how Marx expected capital to develop if profits, or surplus value, were not allowed. The answer is simple: Marx did not oppose capital per se, he rejected the capitalist. He did not condemn profit, he opposed private profit. The German scholar knew that capital was necessary for production, but he rejected the notion that it should be controlled by private individuals. Capital, he suggested, was created by all and should be owned by all. Marx certainly did not oppose creating surplus value to be used to invest in increased productivity. What he objected to was that private citizens should be allowed to monopolize the means of production and use that power to force workers—the creators of value—to surrender their goods in order to survive. Put differently, no one should be allowed to profit from the labor of another.

Marxist Theory of Revolution

Marx vacillated over whether violence was necessary to achieve socialist goals. During the early part of his professional life he clearly suggested that one could not hope for a change from a capitalist system to a socialist one without violence. Gradually, however, he began to weaken this position until finally he admitted that certain systems (such as those in England, Holland, and perhaps the United States) might be responsive enough to adopt socialism by nonviolent means. Violence was still necessary elsewhere, however. Later, Lenin would again insist that no meaningful change could occur without violence.

The basis of Marx's argument for violence was his perception of the dialectic process. He believed that technological change cannot be stopped: Resources will become depleted, and new means of production will inevitably evolve, resulting in economic change. When the economy changes, the entire foundation of the society must be transformed, forcing a change in its superstructure as well. In other words, economic change cannot be prevented. Economic change forces social change, which, in turn, drives political change. Violence is necessary in this process because the rulers who control the economy feel their economic and political power threatened by the uncontrollable changes taking place in the means of production. Vainly trying to resist the inevitable, they use their governmental power to keep themselves in control. However, they are resisting the progress of history. History is therefore propelled from one era to another. A series of revolutions punctuates the dialectic dynamic; each new era is born in the victory of those who control the new dominant means of production. In the final struggle the proletariat will confront their capitalist exploiters. The capitalists will have to use force, but their resistance is doomed to defeat at the hands of the irresistible pressure of history.

More specifically, Marx predicted the demise of capitalism. Competition, he argued, would force the capitalists to buy more machinery. Yet, only human labor can produce a surplus value; thus, the capitalists' profits would decline as they employed fewer people. At the same time, unemployment would increase among the proletariat as competition forced increasing numbers of former capitalists into the proletarian ranks. On the one hand, the size of the proletariat and the depth of its misery would increase; on the other, the wealth in the society would be controlled by fewer people. Marx predicted that every capitalist society would be subject to increasingly frequent and ever more serious economic convulsions. Eventually the misery of the proletariat would increase to a point that could no longer be endured and a revolution would erupt, bringing the system to its knees. "The knell of capitalist private property sounds. The expropriators are expropriated."

Marx's attitude toward revolution is of critical importance, since he believed it to be virtually inevitable in most cases. But what kind of revolution did he anticipate, and what did he regard as the proper role for himself and other revolutionary leaders?

Using the French Revolution as his model, Marx envisioned a spontaneous uprising of the workers. Conditions for the common people in prerevolutionary France had degenerated to miserable levels. Yet, little was done in the way of advanced planning for a popular revolt prior to its explosion in Paris in 1789. The precise cause of the French Revolution remains a mystery, but what is clear is that after centuries of aristocratic abuse, the people of France had quietly reached the breaking point; on a hot day—July 14, 1789—some ordinarily trivial event tripped off a public fury which culminated in a frightful period of social and political chaos, and the world was changed forever.

Expecting that the proletariat would rise up spontaneously to cast off its capitalist oppressors just as the French had vanquished their aristocratic rulers, Marx saw a rather passive role for those who first realized the course of history. Marx, Engels, and most other revolutionaries of the period were progeny of middle-class families, not proletarians. Yet, they presumed to herald the advent of a proletarian succession to power. How could this be?

Marx suggested that there were certain people who, by virtue of their perceptive minds, could understand the forces of history long before others. Thus, he and his colleagues were able to predict the new era even before those who were to be its beneficiaries were conscious of their happy future.

The principle of *class consciousness* is critical. Marx assumed that the workers had not yet fully comprehended that they were a group completely separate and distinct from the bourgeoisie. When the proletariat became fully aware of its unique situation in society—when it developed class consciousness—it would realize the full extent of its oppression and the parasitic nature of its rulers. It would then rise up in revolution.

Helping to develop class consciousness is the role Marx saw for himself and his revolutionary colleagues. Calling his followers the *vanguard of the proletariat,* Marx advised that their function was to do what they could to instill in the worker the true nature of a class-ridden society. Importantly, Marx did not advocate that revolutionaries should organize and lead the revolution. He saw their function as more educative than participatory. Once aware of their circumstances, the proletariat would take care of the revolution themselves. Marx's attitude toward revolution and revolutionaries is particularly important because, as we shall see in the next chapter, Lenin, who was supposedly a disciple of the German master, disregarded this rather passive role for a more activist one.

The Marxist Political System

Of all the subjects on which he wrote, Marx is probably least clear in discussing the political system that would exist after the revolution. Basically, he conceived of the proletarian state as developing in two steps. First, he expected that the proletariat would create a dictatorship. The purpose of the *dictatorship of the proletariat* would be to eliminate all but a single proletarian class. Since all human strife emanated from social class difference, according to Marx, human harmony was possible only if class differences could be eradicated. This goal could be achieved through a process of re-education. If that failed, the dictatorship would be justified in removing from the society anyone who opposed it.

Although the purpose of the dictatorship of the proletariat is quite clear, the exact nature of the institution remains shrouded in ambiguity and is the subject of considerable debate. Lenin, who took an elitist attitude, insisted that the dictatorship should be *over* the proletariat as well as superior to all other elements in the society. He argued that not only should the Communist party (the Bolsheviks) lead the revolution, but that it should also become the dictator of the proletariat.

Since Marx insisted on a democratic format in all other things and since he never attempted to form a communist party as Lenin later did, it is highly unlikely that he meant to imply the model Lenin employed. Indeed, Michael Harrington, a noted American socialist scholar, suggested that Marx actually intended something approaching a democracy when he called for the "dictatorship of the proletariat." Marx expected that the overwhelming number of people in society would be among the proletariat when the revolution occurred. Hence, if he meant the dictatorship was to be *by* the proletariat, the situation would indeed be different. The huge majority of people—the proletariat—would impose its egalitarian policies on the tiny corps of remaining capitalists. In popular terms, at least, such a system would be more democratic than that which Lenin used.

In any event, as the dictatorship succeeded in redirecting the society toward the socialist utopia, more and more people would adopt the *socialist ethic,* meaning willingness to work to one's capacity and to share the fruits of labor with the rest of society. This concept is clearly the most revolutionary aspect of Marx's thought. Like all leftists, he believed people could change, redirecting their lives and actions toward more desirable goals. To this end Marx expected the dictatorship to encourage people to abandon their selfish, atomistic ways, adopting collective, or organic, values which accrue to the good of society as a whole. The new society would operate on the principle "From each according to his ability, to each according to his needs."

If people could be encouraged to enjoy their labor, they would become more productive than was possible in a capitalist system. If the productivity was shared equally by all, social anxieties and frustrations would most probably abate, creating a happy, contented populace. Thus, crime, war, and human turmoil would disappear. As strife and anxiety declined, a gradual change in society's foundations would lead to the second Marxist state. The need for the dictatorship would disappear. Eventually, when the last nonproletariat was gone, the state would have "withered away": The police state would have ceased to exist. Then, all the individuals in society would be "free" to *govern themselves* responsibly for the good of all, and the system would have evolved into a *democratic utopia* similar to that desired by many anarchists. Only a skeletal shell of the former state would be left, and it would simply administer the economy. As Engels put it, "In the final stages of communism, the government of men will change to the administration of things."

Internationalism

Since Marx believed that dialectic materialism was a law of historical development, he expected that socialism would be adopted in every country in the world sooner or later. He never suggested a timetable for this development, but there can be no doubt that he believed it was inevitable. The exact schedule for the adoption of socialism in any country depended on its economic development. Though he made no specific predictions, Marx clearly expected that the most industrialized nations of his day (England, Germany, France, Belgium, and Holland) were on the verge of the proletarian revolution.

During Marx's lifetime, the nation-state system was an important political fact, as it is today. Indeed, since the nation-state system had developed along with capitalism, Marx believed that it was part of the capitalist superstructure. He argued that nation-states were organized by the capitalists to keep people who really had a great deal in common separated from one another. People of the same social class from different countries, he reasoned, actually had more in common with each other than people of different classes within the same country. National boundaries were only artificial separations designed to reinforce the capitalist system. Indeed, Marx declared that "workingmen have no country." Consequently, he believed that as various countries became socialist they would recognize the divisiveness of national boundaries and would erase the lines that separated them until finally all national boundaries would have "withered away" and the entire world would be a single socialist brotherhood or worldwide utopia.

Throughout his life, Marx dominated the socialist movement. Yet, socialism existed long before Marx was born, and, following his death, other thinkers developed socialist theories quite different from those of Marx. We shall now turn to a discussion of the various non-Marxist socialist theories.

SUGGESTION FOR FURTHER READING

COHEN, CARL, *Communism, Fascism and Democracy,* 2nd ed. New York: Random House, 1972.

EDWARDS, RICHARD C., MICHAEL REICH, and THOMAS E. WEISSKOPF, *The Capitalist System,* 2nd ed. Englewood Cliffs, NJ: Prentice-Hall, 1978.

FORMAN, JAMES D., *Communism.* New York. Dell, 1974.

HEGEL, GEORG WILHELM FRIEDRICH, *Reason and History,* trans. Robert S. Hartman. New York: Liberal Arts Press, 1953.

HEILBRONER, ROBERT L., *Marxism: For and Against.* New York: Norton, 1980.

HORVAT, BRANKO, *The Political Economy of Socialism.* Armonk, N.Y.: M.E. Sharpe, 1982.

INGERSOLL, DAVID E., *Communism, Fascism, and Democracy.* Columbus, OH: Charles E. Merrill, 1971.

MARX, KARL, and FRIEDRICH ENGELS, *The Communist Manifesto.* Baltimore: Penguin Books, 1967.

MCLELLAN, DAVID, *Karl Marx.* New York: Viking Press, 1975.

MCLELLAN, DAVID, *Karl Marx: His Life And Thought.* New York: Harper & Row, 1973.

8

Socialism

PREVIEW

Socialism has three basic features: (1) public ownership of production, nationalized or cooperative; (2) a social welfare system, with which the society cares for its needy members; (3) the intention of abundance, equality, and sharing that will free people from material want. Combined with one or both of the first two characteristics, the third (social intent) is required to create an authentic socialist state. Some systems have used public ownership and the welfare state without at the same time adopting the social intent. These systems fail to attain the socialist ideal and are actually examples of antisocialist socialism.

Rooted in the Industrial Revolution, the origins of socialism can be traced to prerevolutionary France. Jean Jacques Rousseau, though not a socialist, gave leftists the foundation of egalitarianism and communalism on which socialism is based. François Noel Babeuf anticipated Marx and Lenin with his conspiratorial method and his ideas about class identification. After the French Revolution, a more moderate brand of socialism became dominant. Utopian socialism, supported by Claude Saint-Simon, Robert Owen, and Charles Fourier as well as by several prominent Americans, deplored the suffering caused by early capitalism and claimed that humanity was destined to live communally. To lead the way, they set up a number of communal societies, all of which eventually failed. As a result of these failures the utopians gave

Note: The drawing at the top of the page is of Robert Owen, Edward Bernstein, and Michael Harrington.

way to more radical ideologues. Just as the fortunes of humanitarian socialism were flagging, Karl Marx developed his theory of "scientific" socialism.

Marx helped organize the socialist movement into the First International. Factionalism and government persecution led to the failure of this attempt to defy the pressures of nationalism. The Second International, established by Friedrich Engels after Marx's death, attempted to accommodate nationalism while reflecting the changes in socialist thinking developed by the revisionists. Strongly pacifist, the Second International became an early casualty of World War I. The Third International was dominated by Moscow and became a tool of Soviet foreign policy, ending any pretense of socialist internationalism in the communist sphere. This movement eventually dissipated, but more moderate socialists have reestablished a non-Marxist International.

After Marx's death the socialist movement shattered into three distinct and competitive movements. The *orthodox* school rejected any significant change in Marx's works and rapidly became obsolete. Its collapse was postponed only by the prestige of Engels and by the brilliance of Karl Kautsky. The *revisionists,* led by Edward Bernstein and Jean Jaures, challenged most of the fundamental Marxist theories, preferring more gradual and peaceful development of the socialist goals. Their ideas have had a great impact on almost every modern non-Marxist socialist movement in Europe and America. Developing at about the same time, an even more gradualist movement became prominent in England. The goal of the *Fabian* socialists was to convince the English people of the wisdom of socialism.

Marxism-Leninism is the third major socialist movement that developed after Marx's death. Basically a revolutionary and a practical politician, Lenin proposed a more activist though less consistent ideology than Marx had envisioned. Arguing that the proletariat would not rebel on its own, he created an elite group of dedicated revolutionaries who would lead the rebellion and govern after the capitalist system collapsed.

Troubled by the lack of revolution in the advanced industrial states and pressed to explain why the revolution had occurred first in a less developed capitalist country, Lenin formulated his *theories of imperialism.* Imperialism, he argued, was the final stage of capitalism, but it tended to prolong capitalism by buying off the workers with wealth bled from the colonies. The competitive advantage enjoyed by the advanced capitalist countries required the nonimperialist capitalist countries to exploit their workers even more, forcing them into revolution ahead of their more advanced proletarian counterparts.

When the bourgeois rulers had been replaced by the dictatorship of the proletariat, a system that rewarded people according to their work would be established. Through education, material rewards, and elimination of the worst dissidents from society, the proletariat would grow until it was the only economic class in the society. Then the system would evolve into the classic Marxist utopia.

THE MEANING OF SOCIALISM

Of all the ideologies discussed in this book, socialism is the most vague and controversial. It has been studied in theory and practice, examined as an economic system, and explored as a social, political, and moral philosophy. Some politicians and scholars claim that socialism can be defined very broadly; others believe that there is only one true socialism and that any variation on this model is a sham intended to hoodwink the masses, distracting them from the truth.

In fact, socialism is a complex idea system that cannot be explained in a simple, one-sided way. It is perhaps the most complete political ideology because its goals are all-encompassing. Those who claim that socialism is limited to a particular economic procedure and a specific political system are shortsighted. Socialism is especially poorly understood in the United States. Often equated with Marxism, "socialism" is a buzz word sometimes used to discredit otherwise legitimate ideas and proposals. From the beginning we must keep in mind that while a particular kind of socialism was envisioned by Marx, his is just one variant of that ideology. All Marxists are socialists, but not all socialists are Marxists.

Socialism can be divided into three basic features. Two of them, *ownership of production* and establishment of *the welfare state,* are mechanical and are not necessarily related to each other. The third, however, belief in *the socialist intent,* is the most fundamental aspect of socialism and must exist together with one or both of the mechanical features; otherwise, true socialism cannot be said to exist.

Ownership of Production

As pointed out in the previous chapter, Karl Marx admired capitalism for its productivity. Capitalism made socialism possible by producing enough to satisfy everyone's needs. However, because capitalism distributed goods unfairly due to the existence of profit and private property, Marx proposed that it be eliminated in the new society. Of course, Marx was not alone in this view; the concept of public ownership and control of the major means of production has always been a principle of socialism. The question of ownership of the means of production, exchange, and finance is of central importance to socialism. The traditional way to socialize an economy is by *nationalization.* Nationalization occurs when the government expropriates—takes over the ownership of—an industry. In the Soviet Union and other communist states the former owners were not usually paid for their property. Government officials claimed that the property really belonged to the workers and that the owners had used it to exploit them; therefore, no payment was necessary. In noncommunist socialist states, however, expropriated properties are usually purchased at a fair price.

In Western societies nationalized industries are usually managed by boards or commissions appointed by government officials but insulated in some way from political pressure; that is, the commissioners are usually appointed to office for a specific term and may be removed only by parliamentary or congressional vote. Some good examples of this kind of arrangement are the Tennessee Valley Authority, the British Broadcasting Corporation, and the United States Postal Service.

In the Soviet Union, as in most other communist countries, a government industry is more likely to be closely connected to the society's political leaders than is true in noncommunist countries. No attempt is made to separate the government from the industry because the Soviets do not see the value of such a separation. In the West we usually try to differentiate between the political and economic functions of society. In a Marxist state, however, ideology teaches that politics results from economic conditions and that both are inseparable parts of the same historical era.

Any attempt to separate one from the other is a bad error in policy or a deliberate attempt by the rulers to trick the ruled.

Consistent with their ideology, the Soviets tried to nationalize almost all their property and industries, leaving only clothing and other purely personal property under private ownership. Although peasants are allowed to sell some of their produce on the open market, officially the rest of the economy was totally nationalized. During the past few years, however, led by General Secretary Mikhail S. Gorbachev, the Soviets have pursued reforms called *perestroika,* which allow for private ownership of some small businesses. The ever-present black market is also a hotbed of private enterprise in the Soviet Union.

Although it is the traditional method of socializing the economy, nationalization has gradually lost favor in the Western states, and a different form of socialization has taken its place. Following the Scandinavian model, socialists in the advanced Western states have increasingly turned to *cooperatives* as a means of socializing the economy. A cooperative enterprise is made up of individuals who collectively own the enterprise. They share in both the work and the profits. Usually they elect a board of directors to manage the enterprise. Such cooperatives can become quite extensive. For instance, a village that owned a fleet of fishing boats could expand by buying a cannery, which would become part of the cooperative's assets. With part of the profits from these two *productive co-ops,* the village could buy large quantities of groceries, clothing, hardware, and so forth and create its own *consumer cooperative,* making the best possible price available to its members by buying in volume. Almost any kind of enterprise can be collectivized in this way; there are even cooperative banks similar to our own credit unions.

Cooperatives were developed because serious problems with nationalization became apparent as various enterprises were expropriated by the state. To begin with, not all enterprises can be operated as well under a nationalized structure as in a less centralized system. The size and remoteness of the central government are major drawbacks. No matter how well intentioned it may be, the bureaucracy necessary to run a nationalized enterprise tends to be insensitive to the consumers' needs and to the dynamics of the market itself. Bureaucrats are naturally cautious, anxious to protect their jobs, and unwilling to change their routines—all of which tend to stifle commercial initiative. Indeed, it has become obvious to many socialists that some enterprises work poorly when they are not privately owned. These pragmatic individuals support socializing only those industries which function best under collective management, leaving the rest to private enterprise. The cooperative is an attempt to combine the virtues of private motivation with the benefits of collective ownership.

The political limitations of nationalization are perhaps even greater than its economic problems. When a large part of society's production, exchange, distribution, and employment is controlled by the government, the latter's involvement in the lives of individuals is greatly increased. Totalitarian states are born out of such enormous power. Any free society must be very cautious of centralized power. In addition, free people must be wary of placing all their productivity in the hands of government. To whom would they turn for settlement of economic disputes if all enterprises were owned by the state?

When socialization has been used, however, the cooperative has worked best with the middle to light industries. Farming, retail sales, appliance manufacturing and servicing, and housing construction are examples of industries that have succeeded in

Lido (Lee) Iacocca (1921–   ), Chairman of the Board and Chief Executive Officer of the Chrysler Corporation.

a cooperative setting. Heavy industry and certain nationwide services are usually better socialized by the nationalization process. Basic industries such as weapons production, utilities, transportation, and communication are too vital and perhaps too big to work well under the cooperative structure. Some other industries, such as automobile manufacture, energy production, insurance, and metal production, may also be best suited to nationalization.

Another reason for nationalizing certain industries is that they are important to the national economy but are failing and must be rescued. Some conservatives support nationalization under such circumstances. Indeed, it is not uncommon for a nonsocialist government to nationalize an industry by buying out the stocks and assets of a failing company, thus rescuing friends who would have lost substantially if the company had been allowed to go under. The purchase of Rolls Royce early in the 1970s by the Conservative government of Edward Heath is a case in point. Of course, there are other ways to save failing corporations besides nationalizing the industry. Faced with the possible bankruptcy of the Lockheed Corporation and Chrysler Motors in the 1970s, the United States government guaranteed multimillion-dollar loans for the giant firms, thereby avoiding both business failures and nationalization. Supporters of these policies argued that since these corporations are vital to our national security and prosperity they must not be allowed to collapse. Yet, not a single proposal was made in Congress to nationalize either mammoth company. Instead, Congress voted to countersign notes in order to keep our "free enterprise system" safe from the evils of socialism. Frowning on the irony of similar practices earlier in the decade, 1972 presidential candidate George McGovern once remarked, "American capitalism constitutues welfare for the rich."

Socialist countries not only differ on the method of socializing the economy but also vary greatly in the degree to which their economies are socialized. Just as socialists long ago abandoned the simplistic view that nationalization is the only true method of establishing socialism, so too have they learned that many industries are best run and most productive when left in the private sector. A statement adopted by the Socialist International in 1951 reads, in part:

> Socialist planning does not presuppose public ownership of all the means of production. It is compatible with the existence of private ownership in important fields, for instance, in agriculture, handicraft, retail trade, and small and middle sized industries.

Of all the socialist societies, only the communists still see total socialization as their ultimate economic goal, and even the communist countries have begun to experiment with some limited forms of private enterprise. In all other socialist countries, regardless of how long socialist governments have held power, large portions of the economy remain under private ownership.

The Welfare State

Production is not the central economic focus of socialist thinking. Admittedly, capitalism is a very productive economic system, even though the socialist believes that socialism will ultimately outproduce capitalism. Much more important to the socialist than production is the distribution of the goods produced in the society.

To the capitalist, private property is the reward of individual effort and economic achievement. Consequently, wealthy people are treated with respect, implying that somehow they have accomplished something particularly virtuous. During the 1920s, this country's most capitalistic era, people held the titans of industry in great awe. Moguls such as Ford, Vanderbilt, Rockefeller, Mellon, Insull, Morgan, and Harriman were considered heroes to be admired and emulated. Our enchantment with industrial capitalism was so great that Calvin Coolidge, the spokesman of the age, once said without a blush, "The man who builds a factory builds a temple and the man who works there worships there."

A value system that puts wealth on such a pedestal is not likely to look on poverty with much understanding. The stigma of being poor or even only unemployed was very real during the period just described. People were supposed to make their own opportunities. Those who were "worth their salt" would do well, and anyone who was unemployed was obviously undeserving. The unregulated economy of the United States was allowed to fluctuate with conditions. In good times people would become increasingly confident of making profits, so they made speculative investments and consumed with abandon, thus fueling an economic *boom*. The supply of capital and consumer spending would eventually outstrip the true value of assets and goods. Sooner or later the market would grow wary of the inflation; and suddenly a "panic" would set in, where everyone would wish to sell stock while a few would buy, precipitating a market crash. People then settled down in anticipation of bad times; they stopped spending, demand declined, and factories laid off workers, thus exacerbating the *bust*, until the economy was caught in the throws of high unemployment and depression. These boom/bust cycles continued unabated through our history, with depressions occurring roughly every twenty years during the nineteenth century and then increasing in frequency during the first decade of the twentieth century.

In the 1920s the United States witnessed the quintessential policies of supply-side and *laissez faire* economics. Government fiscal and monetary policies were extraordinarily favorable to big business, while government regulation of the market-place was virtually abandoned. The result was catastrophic. The Great Depression of the 1930s saw a quarter of the work force without jobs, long lines before soup kitchens, lives ruined, and fortunes evaporated.

Dazed and disoriented, the American people were slow to realize that economic and social adversity was caused by forces beyond their personal control and not all people who found themselves out of work were guilty of personal sloth. At first, they refused to confront the problem directly and were embarrassed by unemployment, thinking it was punishment for imagined sins. Gradually, however, they began to realize that they were victims of an irresponsible economic system, captained by people not necessarily devoted to the public interest but rather motivated by personal interests. Once the blinders of the *laissez faire* myth were lifted, the public viewed society in a more realistic way and capitalism was modified, becoming more humane.

Despite all the suffering it caused, the Great Depression had some beneficial effects on American society. It drew people together again, uniting them in poverty and misery. It taught them compassion, which had been forgotten in the materialistic 1920s. It made clear that people were dependent on each other and they joined together and used government to control their economic destinies. Hence, the *New Deal* was born in the 1930s. President Franklin Delano Roosevelt initiated this massive reform program, injecting enough socialism into the system to give capitalism a human face. While the New Dealers stopped short of nationalizing more than a handful of industries, they vigorously regulated business and encouraged workers to organize unions to bargain collectively for better wages and benefits. Their greatest attention, however, was given to creating the welfare state so that the wealth might be more equitably distributed throughout society and individual suffering reduced. At this time, programs were first introduced that have become commonplace in the United States: old age survivors disability insurance (social security), government price supports for agriculture, unemployment and workers' compensation, welfare, federal guarantees for housing loans, government insurance for savings deposits, and so on. Since the 1930s, the welfare state in this country has been expanded to include public health plans for the elderly, job training, federal aid to education, public funding for small business opportunities, etc.

Although the United States is still far from a socialist country, the lessons of the Great Depression led the government to adopt some socialist policies in order to prevent a recurrence of the suffering encountered during the 1930s. We were not alone in this attempt, however. Indeed, many nations went far beyond the United States in developing policies that would redistribute wealth within the society. The communist countries tried to invoke total socialism; but their efforts seem to have failed, and their economies currently are facing collapse. More successful are the Western European countries which have nationalized their banks, utilities, transportation, and some manufacturing, while also developing extensive social welfare policies.

Regardless of the specific programs used, socialism is not always completely egalitarian. It tends to narrow the gap between the haves and the have-nots. Yet, only the most fanatic socialist wants to eliminate all differences in material status. Most socialists recognize that people are different: Some are more talented or hard working than others and should be rewarded for their extra contributions. Still, they believe that all people have a right to a reasonably comfortable life, given the economy's ability to produce enough for all. Consequently, they want to eliminate poverty. Extreme wealth is not necessarily incompatible with a socialist state, however. Indeed, people with great wealth may be found in almost every socialist society except in communist countries, which have the most completely egalitarian systems.

The Socialist Intent

As explained earlier, the first two basic features of socialism (ownership of production and establishment of the welfare state) are mechanical in nature and are not necessarily related to each other. It is conceivable that a society could socialize many, or even all, of its major means of production and still avoid creating a welfare state. Although no state has yet adopted such a policy, it is possible. It is also possible for a government to establish a welfare state without, at the same time, socializing production. In fact, the United States has followed this policy since the Great Depression, although the Reagan Administration's policies slowed this trend significantly.

A third basic feature of socialism, unlike the first two, is essential if the system is to be truly socialist. This is the goal of setting people free from the condition of material dependence that has imprisoned them since the beginning of time.

The true socialist looks forward to a time when the productive capacity of the society will have been increased to the point at which there is an abundance of goods for all. This happy state of affairs, impossible in earlier times, will bring about profound changes in people's conduct, attitudes, and beliefs. In previous eras scarcity made it necessary for people to compete with one another. In this competition for goods they treated each other inhumanely in order to survive. Forced into conflict with each other in order to make a living, people became trapped in a pattern of conduct that not only was harmful to them but also prevented them from developing their nobler aspects.

Now, however, for the first time, technology has created a situation in which people can produce enough to satisfy all their basic needs. If the Industrial Revolution has indeed brought the ultimate freedom, then compulsive toil, the jailor of humanity for millennia, has finally been conquered. People will emerge into a reformed society with new values and new modes of conduct. Competition, formerly the necessary yet destructive mode of human conduct, will become increasingly less effective than cooperation. The replacement of competition with cooperation will lead to a new era of greater productivity, thus improving the lifestyles of individuals even more.

As the general material conditions of the society improve, the specific differences in material status among individuals will decrease. Since there will be plenty for all, traditional property values such as private ownership, the use of money, and the accumulation of luxuries by one class while others live in poverty will disappear. A new society will emerge, one in which the citizens are on an equal footing with one another. As class differences begin to disappear, so too will a major source of social strife, resulting in a happier, more tranquil society. Of course, only Marxist socialists argue that *all* human strife is caused by class differences. Yet, all socialists are convinced that materialism is a major feature in social and political relationships. Removing the cause of material anxieties, therefore, greatly improves social relationships within a particular state.

The equalizing characteristic of socialism is central to our understanding of it. Socialism is an economic equivalent of democracy, if democracy can be equated with individual political equality. Hence, socialism is compatible with democracy, since it is to the individual economically what democracy is to the individual politically. Indeed, some socialists go even further, claiming that democracy is impossible without socialism. Money, they reason, is a major source of political power. Thus, as Rousseau argued, economic systems that distribute wealth unevenly make political equality among their citizens impossible. By the same token, since socialism tends to reduce the material differences among the individuals in the system, some of its supporters argue that democracy is the necessary result of a socialist system.

By this time the perceptive reader is probably wondering about the classification of such obviously undemocratic (in the sense of liberal democracy) systems as those of fascist, national socialist, or communist states. Clearly, these systems use socialist economic techniques such as nationalizing industries and creating the welfare state. Yet, each of these systems, in practice if not in theory, reduces human equality rather than increasing it. In each of these systems the society is highly stratified and popular government is barely a pretense, let alone a realistic goal.

In fact, these systems are not socialist in the true sense of the word because they lack the essential ingredients of socialism. They appear to be socialist because they have socialist institutions, yet they fail the test because they do not aspire to the *socialist intent*. Rather than encouraging equality and democracy, these systems oppose the development of these concepts. They often claim to have egalitarian goals, but in fact, they are only trying to replace old ruling classes with new ones, denying basic human equality in the process. They are, as Michael Harrington wrote, "antisocialist socialisms."

To sum up, socialism is much more than an economic system. It goes far beyond the socialization of the economy and the redistribution of wealth. It foresees a completely new relationship among individuals based on a plentiful supply of material goods. Its goal is a completely new social order in which human cooperation is the basis of conduct and productivity. Individual equality is a major feature of the new socialist order, and this social equality leads directly to a democratic political system. Although few non-Marxist socialists hold that all human strife will disappear with the elimination of social classes, most socialists agree that the elimination of material hardships will relax human tensions as never before, creating a much more pleasant atmosphere in which people can live and develop.

THE DEVELOPMENT OF SOCIALISM

As mentioned earlier, communism has a very long history. Communal living predates written records. As you will recall, Marx argued that the first human lifestyle was communal. As originally used, the word *communism* meant a local, rural, agrarian life. By contrast, *socialism* is traditionally understood to mean the application of communal production and consumption to an entire nation. Technologically impossible before the nineteenth century, socialism became feasible only after the Industrial Revolution, when the resources for national coordination of an economy had come into existence.

From the French Revolution to Marx

The stirrings of socialism began shortly before the French Revolution. Jean Jacques Rousseau, although not a socialist, developed several ideas which became the foundation of the new ideology. You will recall from Chapter 3 that Rousseau opposed great differences in property ownership among citizens because the disparity would create unequal political powers among them. This belief, which is shared by socialists, considers economic equality fundamental to the new society. Both positions assume that only in an environment of economic equality is the full potential of each individual completely free to develop. Hence, though primarily economic in nature, socialism is also a political ideology.

Rousseau's concept of the *organic society* is even more basic to the ideology of socialism. Rousseau viewed people as individual parts of a holistic society. So complete was the union of individuals with the group that the value of their accomplishments would be measured by the amount of benefit the society derived from them. Further, the greatest good for the individual would ultimately be identical with the greatest good for the whole. In Chapter 2 we learned that people on the left of the political spectrum, including socialists, share Rousseau's orientation toward an organic society. Socialism asks individuals to produce as much as they can and to share their product with the society at large. By this means, it is assumed, all will get the greatest benefit, thereby creating the best possible life for all. Further, socialism asks the individual to maintain social consciousness. Subordinating the individual interests to the good of the whole is thereby enhanced.

Influenced by Rousseau's theories, *François Noel Babeuf* (1760–1797) carried their implications to an extreme during the French Revolution. Babouvism represents the first true expression of socialism, though it is an extreme version. While their goal of abolishing all private property and setting up a communist state in which all people were totally equal was very simplistic, the Babouvists' insight into historical trends and their perception of the future were remarkable.

Anticipating both Marx and Lenin, Babeuf founded the revolutionary socialist movement. Even as the French Revolution unfolded, he and his most famous protégé, Louis Blanqui, became convinced that yet another revolution would be required if people were to gain the true freedom desired by the Babouvists. Yet, experience taught that the ultimate revolution could probably not be trusted to ordinary people. Nor could it be expected to occur by itself. On the contrary, the social-class structure, which Babeuf was so early to recognize as the foundation of the state, would probably not improve if it was left to itself.

Calculating that social improvement would not necessarily result from unguided historical development, Babeuf concluded that the masses would have to be led to the revolution by an elite corps of conspirators. Once they won out over the forces of private property, they would need, according to Babeuf, a centrally controlled economy in which the leadership "will always know what each one does, so that he will not produce too much, or too little, but the right thing." Further, the leadership clique "will determine how many citizens will be employed in each specialty . . . everything will be appropriated and proportioned in terms of present and predicted needs and according to the probable growth, and ability, of the community." Thus, Babeuf envisioned a new society, one that he hoped would be based on the principle of mutual production and voluntary sharing of the fruits of labor.

Unfortunately, he did not live long enough to make more than a momentary impact on the left wing of the French revolutionaries. Falling afoul of the revolutionary leaders in France, he went to the guillotine in 1796 at the age of thirty-seven.

Utopian socialism.[1]   After Babeuf's death violent socialism became dormant, awaiting a new generation of radical thinkers. As the time line in Figure 8–1 illustrates, the momentum passed to a far less radical group. The *utopian socialist* movement developed from a sincere desire for equity within the society and from genuine compassion for the masses at the bottom of the social structure. Members of this movement concluded that lavishing fantastic wealth on some while allowing others to languish in squalor was immoral, since the economy produced enough for all to live comfortably if goods were distributed more evenly.

Many utopians believed that there was an ideal egalitarian social order that, if discovered and implemented, would lead humanity to new prosperity and happiness. The value of egalitarianism was obscure to most people, they thought, because no example of a society of equals existed to prove how productive and blissful such an arrangement could be. Accordingly, the utopians decided to create small, local, communal colonies, believing such settlements would be prototypes of the new general social order.

Much more important to the socialist movement than the communal experiments was that the utopians were the first to mobilize the working class. Accepting the labor theory of value, the utopians claimed that only the workers create wealth; therefore, they held that society should adjust its social, economic, and political systems to prevent unequal distribution of wealth. Utopian support of the worker against the owner gave an important boost to the development of trade unionism by giving it an economic doctrine and moral justification.

The utopian socialist movement originated with the help of two unlikely, almost unwilling, founders and a third who was more deliberate. *Claude Henri Saint-Simon* (1760–1825) is sometimes considered the founder of French socialism. Saint-Simon, however, is perhaps more socialist in the reading than in the writing. His followers read into his works a socialist intent that he may not have meant to convey. Besides his wish for mutual human kindness and compassion, Saint-Simon's strongest socialist arguments were his criticisms of capitalism. Capitalism, he concluded, was wasteful because it pitted people against each other and imposed poverty on many to produce wealth for a few. Moreover, certain capitalists made profits far beyond their own productivity, a fact Saint-Simon despised, thereby making himself popular with the French working class.

As a partial solution to the evils he saw in the capitalist system, Saint-Simon proposed a centralized banking system that would make social investments. He also called for the elimination of property inheritance and supported universal education. His ideas did not become generally known until after his death, however, when a cult of admiring followers lionized him and probably credited him with beliefs he did not actually hold. Unaware of the approaching popularity of his theories, he died a disillusioned man, having first mutilated himself in an unsuccessful suicide attempt.

---

[1]The word *utopia* is taken from Sir Thomas More's philosophical romance *Utopia,* written in 1514–1516. Grounded in the philosophy of Plato and the romantic accounts of travelers like Amerigo Vespucci, More's work featured an ideal state wherein private property was abolished.

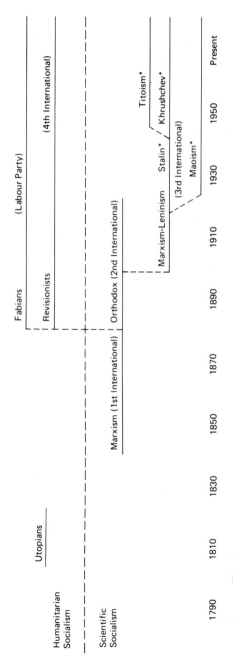

FIGURE 8–1 Time line of the Socialist Movement. The dates are approximates, not to be viewed as exact. *To be discussed in Chapter 9.

A less tragic figure is the second founder of utopian socialism, Robert Owen (1771–1858). A self-made, wealthy industrialist, Owen was basically a conservative man who ardently supported Britain's social, political, and economic system. Yet, his conservatism was tempered by sincere compassion for the human suffering surrounding him. A talented administrator, he had risen from the position of clerk to that of manager of a textile plant before his twentieth birthday. He, however, was concerned about the wretched condition of his employees and became associated with Jeremy Bentham and other social reformers of the day.

Owen was strongly opposed to "dole" programs in which people were simply given money by the government or by charities. However, he realized that capitalism had to be tempered by concern for the basic humanity of people and that it could destroy human dignity when left unchecked. Further, he was unshakeably convinced that exploitation of the worker was ultimately unprofitable and that everyone would be better off if the environment were improved.

Acting on these convictions, Owen reformed the management policies of his New Lanark mill. By raising wages, encouraging trade unionism, avoiding the exploitation of women and children, encouraging universal education, and creating a company store where employees could buy goods at reduced rates, he achieved remarkable results. In less than five years, production at New Lanark had risen markedly, the workers at the mill were far better off than workers anywhere else in England, and Owen had made a fortune. This happy circumstance proved to Owen's satisfaction that, as Marx was later to contend, character was conditioned by the environment. Bad working conditions were not only immoral but simply bad business, unnecessarily depressing the workers and lowering profits as well.

Encouraged by his early success, Owen retired from his business enterprises at the age of fifty-eight and dedicated himself to popularizing and testing his controversial ideas. Traveling widely on speaking tours, he was well received in the United States, even making a speech to Congress. He opposed the imposition of socialism (a term he coined) on a people by its government and warned that the people themselves had to be prepared to adopt it before it could be successful. The worse excesses of capitalism had to be curbed so that the worker would not be exploited. Owen also opposed nationalization of industries, though he favored producer cooperatives.

Perhaps more a liberal capitalist than a true socialist, Owen is still considered the founder of British socialism, and his moderate approach certainly set the tone for England's social reforms. Like most other utopian socialists, Owen was convinced that communal living was the wave of the future and that a few successful examples would prove the attractiveness of this lifestyle. So convinced was he that he invested several years of effort and his entire fortune in unsuccessful attempts to establish communes. Most noted was the effort at New Harmony, Indiana (1825–1828), purchased by Owen after another group had unsuccessfully tried to start a communal colony there. Alas, the Owenite experiment also failed.

A third influential utopian socialist was *Charles Fourier* (1772–1837). Though he found fault with both Saint-Simon and Owen, Fourier became a leading theorist of utopianism. Not only was he a critic of capitalist economics, but he also became a vocal opponent of traditional institutions such as religion, marriage, and the family. Perhaps his most important criticism centered on the structure of society under capitalism. Objecting to the nation-state, Fourier envisioned a society broken up into thousands of small, politically independent, self-sustaining communal entities. These communities could associate with one another in a type of confederacy in which the fundamental independence of each unit remained unchanged. The government of the communes was to be democratic, the labor and its fruits being shared equally by all the members. In such a simple setting, Fourier believed, life would be pleasant and work would become an enjoyable activity in which all would take part willingly.

Although it is difficult to measure accurately, Fourier's influence was significant. Several communes based on his model were started, but each failed and was abandoned. Fourier's thought also influenced many well-known socialists: Charles Dana, Horace Greeley, Nathaniel Hawthorne, and George Ripley were among his American disciples. Fourier also impressed later thinkers such as Proudhon and Marx, and his theories have more recently influenced the collectivization of farms in the Soviet Union.

Because it was a new country when utopianism became popular, the United States was often the scene of communal experiments. Here, it was thought, a new society could be founded, one that was isolated from the prejudices of the old world. Interestingly, America was regarded as the land of new opportunity and hope by socialists as well as capitalists. Although these communal experiments failed, several attained an importance beyond their role as socialist experiments. Intellectual leaders were often drawn to these societies. Important literary and scientific works were sometimes inspired by them, especially by Brook Farm in Massachusetts and by New Harmony in Indiana. Even so, the failure of the communes led to a general disillusionment with the theories on which they were based, and popular attention soon turned from utopianism to more practical concerns.

The internationals.   Important as the utopians were to the development of socialism, their influence is largely limited to their own generation and the one following. Far more important to socialist theory was Karl Marx. Though Marx did not invent socialism, his theory of "scientific socialism" so completely dominated the socialist movement that it may be considered the basis of contemporary socialism. Since we have already discussed Marxist theory, I will limit myself to one brief point: Prior to Marx, though socialist theories differed greatly in details and structure, the basis of the proposed socialist societies had been the humanitarian hope that people would treat each other better as their productivity increased. Furthermore, the development of socialism in any particular society was not seen as inevitable. Rather, socialism was a practice that had to be chosen by the people it was to serve. Though Marx was a compassionate person and certainly not an opponent of free choice, his conclusions were not based on a humanitarian desire for a better life. His theory postulates certain "laws" of human motivation and conduct (economic determinism and dialectic materialism); it concludes that socialism is the unavoidable goal of human historical development. Though his theory was a radical departure from the views of his predecessors, his logic and scholarship were so superior to theirs that he captivated the socialist movement.

Marx was not content to remain cloistered in the British Museum, however. Believing that the revolution would erupt when the proletariat had developed sufficient class consciousness, he organized the vanguard of the proletariat in efforts to help the workers become aware of their place in history. To this end Marx joined other leading socialists in 1864 in establishing the First Socialist International, formally named the *International Association of Workingmen.* The first in a series of

Internationals, this association was the least influenced by the forces of nationalism. Later Internationals fell increasingly under the sway of nationalist ideology and were eventually smothered by it.

The original International did not recognize national parties. Only socialist clubs, societies, or individuals were admitted. Though it was founded amid great fanfare, eloquent speeches, and even more glowing hope, the First International lasted only a dozen years, finally sapped of its vitality by internal bickering and external persecution. Thus weakened, by 1871 the International could not weather the tragedy that befell the *Paris Commune*.

Following France's humiliating defeat in the Franco-Prussian War by Germany in 1871, the people of Paris threw up barricades and called for resistance to the hated *Boche*. They established a socialist government over the city of Paris, proclaiming the dawn of a new era. Thinking the long-awaited revolution had begun at last, socialists of every stripe flocked to Paris from every part of Europe. In opposition, French conservatives and monarchists joined with the Kaiser's troops to stamp out the "Godless" socialist threat. Paris was surrounded and unspeakable carnage ensued. The Paris Commune was obliterated during "Bloody Week" (May 21–28), during which 30,000 people were massacred. The ghastly losses crippled socialism for a generation or more; the First International collapsed in 1876.

In 1883, when it was only beginning to recover some of its former strength, the socialist movement was set back again by the death of Karl Marx. Friedrich Engels became the leader of the socialist movement following Marx's death and the *Second International* was organized in Paris in 1889, establishing its headquarters in Brussels the following year.

Though Engels was very influential, conditions had changed and a new generation of socialists was emerging, its leaders developing followings of their own. Different political circumstances called for an organization unlike the First International. Rather than avoiding a nationalistic orientation, the Second International was set up to accommodate socialist parties as well as private societies and individuals.

The Second International differed from the original organization in two other important respects. Rather than limiting itself to economic issues, the Second International became very heavily involved in political matters. Its members actively tried to bring about reforms through existing political structures instead of insisting that only revolution could effectively change the conditions they opposed. In addition, the socialist movement became much more absorbed than its predecessor in the problem of avoiding war in Europe. As the clouds of World War I gathered, the socialists met repeatedly to discuss what part they could play in preventing war from breaking out. Antiwar efforts ranging from passive resistance to a general strike were proposed and debated, and each conference ended with solemn pledges to avoid war at all costs. Yet, sincere though they were, the socialists could not resist the powerful impulse to join their compatriots in defending their respective countries when the war began in 1914. Regardless of its international and pacifist sympathies, the organization dissolved during the first years of the war as its membership melted away, each individual joining his or her national war effort.

After World War I the socialist parties of Europe reorganized, trying to recapture lost momentum. Faced with fascist pressure before World War II and with Soviet attempts to dominate it, the socialist movement was for many years unable to create an effective international agency. Even so, since World War II socialist parties have enjoyed great success in Scandinavia, Germany, England, France, and most recently in Portugal and Spain. At the same time, socialist movements have had some success in many developing countries in Asia, Africa, and Latin America, although as we will see in Chapter 11, socialism has taken on a distinctly different tone in the developing countries than in industrialized Europe.

The *Third International* arose from a completely different set of circumstances. Organized in Moscow in 1919, after the Bolshevik takeover of the Russian government, the Communist International, or *Comintern,* was structured along Marxist-Leninist lines. Closed to all but the most dedicated Marxists and committed to Leon Trotsky's theory of permanent revolution (which will be discussed in the following chapter), the Comintern was supposed to stimulate Marxist revolutions in all countries. While Lenin was not above using the Comintern to Soviet advantage, it was usually allowed to pursue its revolutionary objectives. Under Joseph Stalin, however, the Comintern lost all traces of independence from Moscow and became a tool of Soviet foreign policy, thus symbolizing *the final conquest of socialist internationalism by the nationalist movement.*

Since World War II the international communist movement in the form of a Comintern has crumbled, finally dissolving in the mid-1950s. Yet, the non-Marxist socialist parties have revived efforts to further their doctrine, organizing the *Fourth International.*

SOCIALIST THEORY AFTER MARX

When Marx died in 1883, the socialist movement became disoriented. In the absence of a firm hand at the helm, conflict began to build within the ranks. Three distinct socialist doctrines emerged from this confusion: Orthodox Marxism, Revisionism, and Marxism-Leninism.

Orthodox Marxism

Guided at first by Engels himself, the *orthodox Marxists* were led by *Karl Kautsky* (1854–1931) after Engels's death in 1895. Besides being a personal friend of both Marx and Engels, Kautsky was a distinguished scholar. His academic skills were not matched by political acumen, however, and he led his followers into a hopeless dilemma.

As the name implies, the orthodox Marxists clung rigidly to Marxist theory and resisted any change in it. The insistence that no significant amendments be made to Marx's ideas made this group inflexible. Such single-minded devotion to a set of ideas stifled imaginative thinking, ultimately spelling its doom among intellectuals.

The same fate awaited this unbending group of loyalists in the arena of practical politics. Looking forward to the revolution that would end the capitalist state forever, Kautsky's followers refused to cooperate in social reform with non-socialist governments. Thinking that if reform was avoided the workers' suffering would be increased, thus hastening the revolution, they persisted in their uncooperative tactics. This attitude badly weakened the orthodox position. Depending on the workers for support, the Kautskyists brought on their own failure by opposing programs that would improve the proletariat's lot. Desperately needing legislation on maximum hours, minimum wages, working safety, and social insurance, and caring little about the expected utopia following the proletarian revolution, the workers abandoned the orthodox socialists for more practical political parties.

By the time of Kautsky's death the orthodox movement was facing challenges that not even his genius could overcome. Forced by the pressure of events to retreat inch by inch from his inflexible position, during the last two decades of his life Kautsky supported liberal reforms and admitted that revolution might not be necessary after all. Eclipsed by the other two socialist schools and driven from his adopted home in Vienna into exile in Amsterdam by the Nazi annexation of Austria, Kautsky died a pauper in 1938.

Revisionism

Edward Bernstein (1850–1932) was the founder of the *revisionist* school of socialist theory. Finding that several Marxist predictions did not match actual historical developments, Bernstein began to develop a revised, more moderate socialist theory. He was aided in this effort by the brilliant French socialist *Jean Jaures* (1859–1914). Bernstein founded social democracy, which is the basis for nearly every major non-Marxist socialist movement in existence today. *However, perhaps the most significant characteristic of the revisionist doctrine is that it represents the return of socialism to its original humanitarian motivations, rescuing it from the moral sterility of "scientific" socialism.*

Bernstein and Jaures were not unappreciative of Marx's contribution to socialist thinking, but they felt compelled to challenge almost every major Marxist principle. Of course, no socialist could deny the importance of economic determinism, but the revisionists believed that Marx had given it too great a role as a motivator of people. Economics, they argued, is an important motivator, but it is not the only one, nor is its impact on human motives constant, tending to decrease as people satisfy their most basic needs. Indeed, it is possible that in more affluent societies economic factors could be a secondary or even weaker source of human motivation.

Noting that Marx had misjudged the development of capitalism, Bernstein pointed out that the capitalist class was increasing rather than decreasing, despite Marx's prediction. Literally millions of people were entering the capitalist class by buying stocks. Further, as more and more governments bowed to the demands of organized labor, the wealth was becoming more evenly spread within the society and the lot of the proletariat was improving instead of growing worse.

These seeming faults in Marxist theory appeared to demand a reappraisal of the tactics socialists should use to bring about their goals. It was obvious to the revisionists that rather than racing toward inevitable self-destruction, capitalism was evolving and adjusting to new circumstances. It was becoming less exploitative and more evenhanded in the distribution of resources. Since Marx had not anticipated this development, Bernstein reasoned that it was proper for socialism to change in response to the new situation.

Revolutionary socialism began to seem inappropriate as a way of ending the evils of capitalism. Would it not be far better to develop evolutionary ways of achieving socialism? This speculation led Bernstein, Jaures, and their followers to conclude that their cause would be better served by abandoning dogmatic theories and supporting pragmatic political policies designed to achieve socialism peacefully and gradually through existing European political systems.

Bernstein's influence did not stop at the shores of the Atlantic. Though Daniel De Leon and Big Bill Haywood proposed militant socialism in their Socialist Labor Party, their efforts met with little success. But, Eugene V. Debs and Norman Thomas carried socialism to modest popularity with the revisionist approach of their Socialist party. Today these two basic trends are still represented in the American Left.

Although not precisely revisionist, a second development in humanitarian nonviolent socialism developed in England during the late 1800s. The *Fabian movement* is peculiar to England because only England combines political and economic maturity with the moderation necessary to the Fabian approach. Founded in the tradition of John Stuart Mill in 1884, the year after Marx's death, the Fabian Society was dedicated to bringing socialism to England.

Like Robert Owen twenty years earlier, the Fabians rejected the policy of forcing socialism on the society. They argued that socialism must be accepted from the bottom up rather than from the top down. Yet, they were confident that socialism would be adopted by all freedom-loving people because they were convinced that only socialism was compatible with democracy. Consequently, if a people were committed to democracy, as the English surely were, socialism could not be long in coming.

Largely consisting of literary figures, including George Bernard Shaw, H. G. Wells, and Sidney and Beatrice Webb, the Fabian Society was particularly well suited to its task. It usually avoided direct political activity and concentrated on convincing the English people that socialism was the only logical economic system for the British nation. The Fabians carried their message to the people in pamphlets, in articles written for journals and newspapers, and in their novels and short stories. Molded as it was to the British style and temperament, Fabianism was very successful. Today's British Labour Party is the direct descendant of the Fabian movement.

Marxism-Leninism

The second son of a well-to-do Russian family, Vladimir Ilyich Ulyanov—*Lenin* (1870–1924)—became a radical at an early age. A brilliant man who ultimately mastered nine languages, Lenin finished school with highest honors and passed the bar without ever entering law school. As a teenager he was profoundly influenced by his brother Alexander, whom he idolized. To the young boy's horror Alexander was executed for an attempt on the Tsar's life, an event Lenin swore to avenge. From that time forward Lenin became increasingly radical, consorting with several of the conspiratorial groups so abundant in Russia at the time.

His revolutionary activities earned him imprisonment and Siberian exile at the end of the century. Allowed to have whatever books friends and family would send, Lenin, like so many other Russian revolutionaries, spent his exile studying and writing radical documents. So common was this activity that internal exile for Russian radical intellectuals could be called "the University of Siberia."

Released in 1900, Lenin went to Switzerland, where he was quickly included among the leadership of the Russian Marxist movement. These expatriots, given to infighting and ideological debate, gradually split into two groups: the *Mensheviks* and the *Bolsheviks*. The Mensheviks were led by the father of Russian Marxism, *Georgi Plekhanov* (1857–1918). They were roughly equivalent to the orthodox Marxists and, subscribing to Plekhanov's *Two Stage Theory,* they insisted that the dialectic had to run its course before a proletarian revolution could take place. Consequently, the revolution would not occur for a long time, since feudal Russia had to pass through the bourgeois stage before developing the proletariat that would eventually come to power. The Mensheviks called upon all socialist revolutionaries to aid the bourgeoisie in coming to power. The capitalists would then begin to exploit the masses, thus "digging their own grave" and provoking the proletarian revolution.

The Bolsheviks, who followed Lenin, rejected Menshevik theory as too dogmatic. They argued that under certain circumstances the proletariat and the peasants could join forces, taking control of the Russian state before it had achieved the bourgeois stage. The Bolsheviks would compress, or "telescope" (as Lenin put it), the bourgeois and socialist stages into a single revolution.

The question of leadership also played a role in these disputes. Plekhanov, the dean of Russian Marxism, considered his young challenger impertinent. He insisted that the final revolution must be a massive one involving the whole society. For his part Lenin was convinced that Plekhanov lacked the imagination and spirit necessary to lead a revolution. He called for an elitist coup to seize power from the decadent Tsarist state.

Thus, the Russian Marxist movement split. Few people had taken these radicals seriously before. With their fragile unity broken and small membership scattered, there seemed little cause for worry that this group of feuding radicals would threaten mighty Russia. As we all know, of course, history proved these expectations quite wrong.

Karl Marx had spent most of his time analyzing capitalism, giving relatively little attention to the coming utopia. Lenin, by contrast, more of a revolutionary and pragmatic politician than Marx, devoted himself to developing a revolutionary doctrine and applying Marxism to a real situation. In so doing, he restored violence to the doctrine, modified the ideas in order to answer certain apparent historical contradictions, amended the theory so that it applied to underdeveloped states, and filled in the blanks which Marx had left regarding the proletarian society that would exist following the revolution.

Theories of revolution and revolutionaries. You will recall that Marx encountered persecution as a young German radical and that this undoubtedly hardened him against the possibility of peaceful change. Experiencing more tolerant treatment in England during the second half of his life, he tempered his attitudes enough to suggest that revolution might not be necessary in some countries. Lenin's experience in his native land had been comparable to Marx's. Easily the most repressive government in Europe, Russia had seen some attempts at reform under Alexander II (1855–1881), only to lapse into a new period of repressive brutalities after his assassination by the *Narodniks* (Populists). From such evidence Lenin drew the same conclusion as Marx: Violent revolution is the only action that will bring about meaningful change. Unlike Marx, however, Lenin never wavered from this conviction, dedicating himself single-mindedly to the cause of revolution.

Marx also taught that the revolution would take place when the workers had developed a class consciousness based upon unity born of misery and exploitation.

Relying on organizations such as the International and trade unions to stimulate the workers' self-awareness, Marx expected that the revolution would erupt automatically, ending the bourgeois state and bringing the worker to power.

Lenin contradicted Marx on this point. He argued that the proletariat would not develop class consciousness without the help of a revolutionary group. Trade unions were helpful in improving the conditions of employment, but they were of no value as revolutionary agents because they did not teach the proletariat the need to bring down capitalism. Lenin believed that a different group was needed to stimulate the revolution. To justify this concept, he expanded on Marx's rather unimportant theory of the *vanguard of the proletariat*. You will recall that Marx believed the vanguard could speed the approach of revolution by helping the proletariat develop class awareness, but he gave the vanguard no other major task. By contrast, Lenin saw the vanguard itself as the principal revolutionary agent that would overthrow the government and establish a socialist state before the proletariat developed self-awareness.

This is what lies behind an important difference in expectations between Marx and Lenin. Marx expected that the proletariat would rebel only after it had become an overwhelming majority in the society and was clearly aware of itself as a class. Consequently, he believed that the *dictatorship of the proletariat* would exist for a relatively brief period during which the small number of nonproletarians would be reeducated or eliminated, creating the classless society.

In Lenin's plan, by contrast, the vanguard would trigger a revolution long before the conditions that Marx anticipated actually existed. In this case, socialism would be imposed on the society by a minority instead of being forced upon the governing elite by the majority. Not only would socialism be hard to attain under these conditions, but the dictatorship of the proletariat would last much longer because such a huge percentage of the population would have to be "proletarianized" before the utopia could be realized.

Lenin was also very specific about the structure of this revolutionary vanguard: a *small, disciplined, totally dedicated* group. It must include only the best in the society because its job of carrying out the revolution demanded total commitment. True to this organizational concept, Lenin was unbending in his arguments with fellow Marxists. This position led to one rupture after another until the party was divided so badly that it seemed doomed. The wisdom of Lenin's seemingly foolish position was demonstrated by the events of 1917 and the years that followed, however, and it is still a major principle in the Soviet Union, where Communist party membership is limited to an estimated 7 percent of the population. Obviously elitist, Lenin's approach is quite different from the more democratic Marxist approach that Plekhanov supported.

The vanguard of the proletariat in Russia was the Bolshevik party (later renamed the Communist party). As implied earlier, it was to do considerably more than just carry out the revolution. You will recall that Marx's statements on the dictatorship of the proletariat were vague. One cannot be sure whether he intended the proletariat to assume the role of dictator itself until only one class existed, or if a dictator was to govern all, including the proletariat. Lenin, on the other hand, was quite specific on this subject. The vanguard of the proletariat was to become a collective dictatorship. In other words, the Bolshevik party would carry out the revolution and then impose a dictatorship on the entire society until it was prepared to enter the utopian stage. Thus, as Lenin saw it, the dictatorship of the proletariat was not to be a dictatorship *by* the proletariat but a dictatorship of Bolsheviks *over* the proletariat.

With the purpose and function of the Bolshevik party clearly in mind, Lenin specified the party's governing procedure, which he called *democratic centralism*. Under this formula, the party would try to function on as broad a base as possible; good government, however, depended on personal responsibility, so the individual had to have the power to make decisions. Hence, democratic centralism had three elements, two of them democratic and the third centrist. According to this plan, the leadership of the party was to be elected by the membership starting from the bottom up. Issues to be decided were to be placed before the general membership for open debate. The leadership was expected to consider the points made in the debate by the membership, but then the leadership would make policy decisions for the party. Actual decisions were not to be made democratically, yet the membership was expected to accept the leadership's judgment without question. Although democratic centralism does not work the way it was intended, it was applied with some integrity while Lenin was head of the party. Even though the ideal has not been achieved, it has remained an important part of the Soviet system.

Lenin also created a structure for the vanguard of the proletariat at the international level. As already mentioned, the Comintern was created in 1919. It was supposed to encourage socialist revolutions throughout Europe. Rebellions in Bulgaria, Hungary, and Germany were successful briefly but were eventually suppressed. These failures were a great disappointment to Lenin and his associates, who were convinced that the Bolsheviks could not stay in power long unless they received some help from the more advanced Western European countries. As it turned out, they not only sustained themselves without help from the West, but they also resisted concerted Western efforts to bring down the Soviet Union. This success, however, was achieved only at the cost of creating a totalitarian dictatorship.

Imperialism.   As the twentieth century began, the pressure from critics of Marxist theory became intense. Marxism was not only attacked by capitalists and conservatives but also questioned by a growing number of socialists. The core of the theory, dialectic materialism, predicted a proletarian revolution that never occurred. Indeed, as the revisionists pointed out, the conditions of labor were improving in the industrial countries, making the revolution appear to be a myth. Hard pressed to explain this seeming contradiction, Lenin studied the trends of capitalism in search of a solution to the dilemma. His conclusion was a clever analysis that went far beyond a simple rationalization of Marx's error.

Since Marx's death a new kind of capitalism had developed. As he predicted, firms became larger though less numerous, their financial needs growing along with their corporate size. But, needing vast amounts of capital to sustain their huge enterprises, the corporations became increasingly dependent on banks for financing, until the bankers themselves gained control of the monopolies. Marx had not foreseen this new financial structure, which Lenin called *finance capitalism*.

Finance capitalism marked a new, much more exploitative stage than the previous condition of *industrial capitalism*. Under these new conditions the owners of the means of production (bankers and financiers) contributed absolutely nothing to the productivity of the plants they controlled. For example, J. P. Morgan, a noted financier, created the Northern Securities Trust in the late 1800s, tying up all the major railroad trunk lines in the United States. He also put together the world's first billion-dollar corporation, United States Steel, in 1901. Morgan and his associates knew nothing at all about the railroad or steel business. Yet, by manipulating capital they gained control of two basic United States industries. Since they contributed nothing to the productivity of those two industries, the labor theory of value held that the fantastic profits of these "robber barons" were stolen from the rightful owners, the proletariat.

In addition, the very fact that the national economies were monopolizing industry was having a profound effect on the international scene. The centralization of ownership was occurring because it was becoming harder to profit from domestic markets. New markets had to be found. At the same time, Lenin believed that the owning class had begun to realize the truth in the Marxist prediction of a revolution by a proletariat whose misery could no longer be borne. This led the owners to find new sources of cheap labor and resources. Thus, they began to *export their exploitation* through colonialism.

The foreign exploitation of which Lenin wrote began in earnest in the 1880s, too late for Marx to assess its significance. The new colonialism, which Lenin called *imperialist capitalism,* also delayed the proletarian revolution. Driven to increase profits, yet needing to protect themselves against a rebellion by their domestic proletariat, the capitalists began to exploit the labor of the colonial people. Then, to relax the tensions created by their previous domestic exploitation, the capitalists shared some of their new profits with their domestic workers. Not only was the domestic proletariat's revolutionary tension reduced by this improvement in living standards, but their virtue was corrupted. Allowing themselves to be "bought off" by profits stolen from the colonial proletariat, the domestic workers became partners in the capitalist exploitation of the unfortunate colonial people. This economic prostitution disgusted Lenin, who saw it as yet another evil policy of the capitalist enemy.

Capitalist imperialism, however, was ultimately self-destructive. Eventually all the colonial resources would be consumed by the various capitalist states. With no more colonies to subdue, the profit-hungry imperialist nations would begin to feed off each other, causing strife and conflict that would end in a general confrontation among the capitalist imperialist powers. *Imperialism,* Lenin declared in 1916, *is the final stage of capitalism.* It will ultimately lead to a conflict in which the capitalists will destroy each other. Thus Lenin concluded that World War I was a giant struggle in which the imperialist nations hoped to finally settle their colonial conflicts, and that socialists should take advantage of this conflict.

In order to take advantage of the turmoil into which the capitalist world had thrust itself, Lenin advised his fellow socialists to follow a policy of *revolutionary defeatism.* Insisting that World War I was a capitalist war, he argued that socialists should remain aloof until the capitalists were defeated. Only after the capitalists had exhausted themselves by warring with each other should the socialists step forward, united and invincible, to establish socialist states across Europe. As we have already learned, however, most socialists did not follow Lenin's advice, preferring to cooperate with their nation's war efforts instead. Only Lenin and his Bolsheviks rejected the appeal of a nationalist war and took advantage of the chaos in Russia to overthrow the state.

However, while Lenin's theory of imperialism explained why the Marxist revolution had not yet occurred among the advanced industrial states in the West, there was still no answer as to why it had occurred in a fifth-rate industrial country such as Russia. Fruitful thinker that he was, Lenin again turned to imperialism for an explanation. Developing his theory of the *weakest link,* he argued that colonialism gave the advanced industrial countries a tremendous competitive advantage over the less developed, noncolonialist capitalist states. If the latter were to compete against the cheap labor and raw materials available to their imperialist opponents, they would have to exploit their own labor force even more. The increased exploitation suffered by the workers in the less advanced countries would naturally push them toward revolution at the very moment when the proletariat of the advanced capitalist countries was being "bought off" with a share of the colonialist spoils. Russia, Lenin concluded, was the weakest link in the capitalist chain, making the first Marxist revolution there quite logical.

Though most evidence indicates that Marx fully expected the revolution to begin in a developed country (perhaps Germany), the possibility of its beginning in a backward country interested him toward the end of his life. Indeed, Marx was so captivated by the revolutionary events taking place in Russia during the 1870s that he attempted to learn the Russian language to facilitate his studies. His premonition about Russia continued to gain strength until in the year before his death he wrote that "the Russian Revolution would give the signal to the proletarian revolution in the West." The reader should note, however, that Marx still thought that the revolution would probably occur first in a highly industrialized state. Further, while he thought it possible for the revolution to happen first in Russia, Marx expected that it would be a peasant uprising rather than a proletarian movement and that it would convert Russia into a socialist state only with the support of later proletarian revolutions in the West. As we will see, Lenin also believed for a time that Russian socialism would be secured only with help from socialist movements in the industrial states.

Lenin's multipurpose theory served yet another, unanticipated function. Early to oppose colonialism, the Soviet followers of Lenin used his theory to contrast their "nonaggressive" policies with those of the "Western capitalist imperialists." Scoring heavily in the propaganda battles of the Cold War, the Soviets condemned imperialist acts and befriended the emerging Afro-Asian states. To defend against these attacks, the West answered that the Soviet policy of absorbing satellite states after World War II was a new form of socialist imperialism. Even so, the Soviet Union benefited greatly from Lenin's theory of imperialism in a way that he had not foreseen.

Achieving the utopia.   Completing his blueprint for the practical application of Marx's sometimes vague theories, Lenin outlined the economic and political development of the future workers' paradise. Like Marx, Lenin believed that the revolution would be followed by a dictatorship. As we have already learned, though Marx was vague on the subject, Lenin stated that the dictatorship would consist of an elite few governing the many and trying to create a classless society.

The economic system to be used by the Bolshevik dictatorship of the proletariat was what Lenin called *state socialism.* According to this theory, the state was to control all elements of the economy. The workers, employees of the state, would produce a profit and the profit, or surplus value, would then be returned to the society by way of investments to increase productivity, social and governmental programs to aid and protect the citizens, and consumer goods to benefit the society.

The formula for the distribution of goods to the citizens is one that colonial Virginia's John Smith would have been proud of: "*From each according to his ability, to each according to his work.*" This formula is even more practical than it appears at first glance. Marx had seen the dictatorship creating a single proletarian class imbued with the socialist ethic by one of two methods: educating the masses to convince them of the wisdom of socialism, or simply removing them from the society. Here Lenin introduced a third technique for achieving the single-class utopia. Because socialists are supposed to enjoy the process of labor, Lenin expected that they would be more productive than those who did not accept socialism. Paying workers according to the labor they performed would reward the socialists, while the slackers would be penalized for lack of productivity.

When the nonconformists had been starved into the socialist mold, all the people would be convinced of the value of labor and the utopian stage would be at hand. As more people became proletariat and socialist, class differences would diminish and strife among the people would be reduced. As human strife disappeared, the need for the state would "wither away," just as Marx had predicted. Eventually there would emerge a utopian existence in which people might live and work in peace. Sharing their labor, they would also share the fruits of their production. In the utopia the economic system would have evolved from "socialism" to "communism," which Lenin, echoing Marx, describes as an economy in which the people give according to their abilities and take back according to their needs.

More practical (or more cynical, if you will) than Marx, Lenin contradicted him several times. More a revolutionary than an ideologue, he was always concerned with the workability of a process, often leaving theoretical inconsistencies to sort themselves out. He ignored the democratic spirit of Marx's theory in favor of an elitist revolution, claiming that its utopian ends justified its extreme means. He violated the dialectic by stimulating an early revolution, which he followed with an elitist dictatorship that Marx almost surely never intended. He used his theory of imperialism to describe a stage of capitalism not foreseen by Marx; he then used it to explain why the revolution happened first in Russia and failed to take place in the highly industrialized countries. Finally, along with state socialism, Lenin proposed a new kind of labor exploitation about which Marx would have had serious qualms. Yet, with all their twists and turns, these modifications and amendments were always intended to bring to fruition the Marxist ideal: a society at peace with itself in a world characterized by human harmony. Never losing sight of this goal, Lenin often surprised his own followers with the depth of his conviction and the totality of his Marxist commitment. However, like Marx before him, Lenin failed to foresee many of the terrible events that followed the establishment of the Soviet Union.

SUGGESTION FOR FURTHER READING

BERKI R. N., *Socialism*. New York: St. Martin's Press, 1975.
BERNSTEIN, EDWARD, *Evolutionary Socialism*, trans. E. C. Harvey. New York: B. W. Heubsch, 1909.
COHEN, CARL, *Communism, Fascism and Democracy*, 2nd ed. New York: Random House, 1972.
CORNFORTH, MAURICE, *Communism and Philosophy*. London: Macmillan, 1983.
CROSSMAN, R. H. S., *The Politics of Socialism*. New York: Atheneum, 1965.
FORMAN, JAMES D., *Socialism*. New York: Dell, 1974.
GARD, ELIZABETH, *British Trade Unions*. London: Methuen, 1970.
HARRINGTON, MICHAEL, *Socialism*. New York: Bantam Books, 1972.
HORVAT, BRANKO, *The Political Economy of Socialism*. Armonk, N.Y.: M.E. Sharpe, 1982.
MCLELLAN, DAVID, *Marxism After Marx*. London: Macmillan, 1983.
WALLER, MICHAEL, *Democratic Centralism*. New York: St. Martin's Press, 1981.
YARMOLINSKY, AVRAHM, *Road to Revolution: A Century of Russian Radicalism*. New York: Collier Books, 1962.

9

Applied
Marxism:
Communism

PREVIEW

Marxism has been put to a great variety of uses and has been given many different, and sometimes contradictory, interpretations. This chapter deals with the application of Marxism in four major settings: the Soviet Union, Yugoslavia, China, and Cuba.

Attempting to socialize the Soviet Union at a single stroke, Lenin saw national productivity fall to dangerous levels as the Bolsheviks fought for their political lives during the Russian Civil War. When the Civil War ended, Lenin, admitting his past mistakes, recapitalized the bulk of the economy with the NEP (New Economic Policy) and tried to introduce total socialism more gradually. Having seen the economy recover somewhat as the Communist party tightened its control over the society, Lenin died without choosing a successor.

Joseph Stalin rose to power by ruthlessly purging friend and foe alike. Once in control, he revolutionized Soviet society by completing the socialization process, dramatically increased production by enforcing enormous sacrifices by the citizens, and created a personal dictatorship through terrorist methods. Weathering World War II and successfully setting the Soviet Union back on the road to economic recovery, Stalin died in 1953 as he was preparing for another bloody purge.

Khrushchev's rise to power resulted in a liberalization program that relaxed restraints on art, literature, and even political commentary. Reforms in industry,

Note: The drawing at the top of the page portrays Joseph Stalin on the left, Josip Tito on the right, and Fidel Castro in the center.

agriculture, and the party were accompanied by increased freedom in the satellite countries. Yet, Khrushchev's policies of de-Stalinization and peaceful coexistence with the West, together with problems in Eastern Europe, cooled Soviet relations with China. These difficulties and Khrushchev's crude, impulsive style led to his removal from power by a vote of the Politburo in 1964.

Khrushchev's expulsion brought a new group to power. Disgusted by Khrushchev's reforms, Brezhnev and his contemporaries executed conservative policies to stabilize the system. Stability soon became stagnation, however, as productivity declined, corruption increased, and spiritual malaise debilitated the Soviet public. As the Soviet leadership aged, the political and economic system sank into the doldrums. Following the brief successions of Yuri Andropov and Konstantin Chernenko, Mikhail Gorbachev, a young and energetic politician, now faces the enormous task of revitalizing the Soviet system. While the record of his reforms is disappointing so far, only time will reveal whether or not his efforts will succeed.

Yugoslavia is unique among Eastern European states because it developed its own Marxist movement, creating a communist government without the help of Soviet troops. This accomplishment gave Josip Tito a degree of independence from Moscow that was not shared by his colleagues. Because Stalin insisted on policies that were quite different from those favored by Tito, Yugoslavia withdrew from the Soviet orbit in 1948. Claiming that there are "many different paths to socialism," Tito made significant innovations. He allowed some capitalism in Yugoslavia and encouraged worker-management programs and other moves toward economic decentralization. Since he believed that the state bureaucracy was likely to grow rather than wither away, Tito also pursued decentralized policies for the Communist party and the government. During the 1970s, however, these antibureaucratic policies were set back by a number of serious economic problems and by the growing ethnic jealousies among the Yugoslav people. Tito's death was met by a smooth transfer of political power, but the economic difficulties have become exacerbated and ethnic rivalries threaten stability.

China has developed yet another major variant of Marxism-Leninism. During its long revolution Chinese communism found a political leader and ideologue in Mao Tse-tung. Modifying Marxism to fit China's rural, oriental character, Mao honored the peasant as he criticized the intellectual and the bureaucrat. He demanded that every citizen periodically return to the farms and "learn from the people." Though his government was cautious at first, as time passed he introduced increasingly radical policies such as the Great Leap Forward and the Cultural Revolution, which were based on the theory of the "mass line." Each of these policies tended to discredit his leadership among government and party leaders, but each time he recovered power only to initiate another radical upheaval.

Tolerating the "loyal" capitalists for practical reasons, Mao applied the concept of permanent revolution to foreign and domestic imperialists. This led him to increasingly militant policies, as did the Sino-Soviet split. Perhaps his greatest impact, however, was in the field of guerrilla warfare. Avoiding defensive engagements, Mao taught guerrillas to befriend the local people, who, in turn, would hold the countryside for the guerrillas, thus "surrounding the cities with the countryside."

Mao's death brought Deng Xiaoping to power. Embarking on major political, social, and economic reform, Deng has vaulted China into a new era of economic progress, but the accompanying political stresses resulted in a bloody crackdown on students demanding faster political liberalization. Whether Deng will be succeeded by a new Maoist radicalization, conservative repression, or a new round of liberalization is impossible to predict.

Cuba, the only communist state in the Western Hemisphere, is unusual in several ways. Having become a Marxist-Leninist after he took power, Castro tends to have more personal influence than his contemporary colleagues. However, Cuba's Communist party has less influence on society than its counterparts in other communist states, even though Castro himself is currently more orthodox than most of his communist colleagues.

Weakened by economic failures, brutalized and isolated by American policy, Cuba was thrust into the Soviet bloc and forced to depend on Moscow for huge amounts of aid. Though it has made many social advances, its economic prospects seem diminished unless the planning process is improved and dramatic increases in productivity are achieved.

In his foreign policy Castro has changed from a radical revolutionary to an established leader of a communist state. While still denouncing Yankee imperialism, sending troops to Africa, and perhaps shipping Soviet arms to Central America, he has shown considerably more moderation in recent years than in the past.

The reforms currently being attempted in the Soviet Union, China, and most Eastern European countries are fundamental in nature. While they do not constitute a rejection of socialism, they are its redefinition in that they inaugurate the abandonment of certain policies of Lenin and Stalin. Stalin's centralized planning is being modified as are Lenin's notions of the inevitability of revolution and the imperative of party dominance.

THE SOVIET UNION

Commenting toward the end of his life on the variety of ways his friend's theories had been interpreted, Friedrich Engels reportedly said: "Marx would not be a Marxist if he were alive today." As we have just seen, time and the influence of new generations brought about many changes in Marxist theory. Yet, varied as the interpretations were, even greater changes were made in the original theory when it was applied to practical political situations. Today Marxism spans the globe, and, as our political leaders have finally realized, it is not the same in any two societies. Its followers have adapted it to every conceivable environment. This chapter looks briefly at some of these multifaceted societies and studies the modifications they have made in Marxism. We will start where it all began—the Soviet Union.

Few people were as surprised by the Bolsheviks' success in 1917 as Lenin himself. As mentioned in the last chapter, he doubted that they could hold onto Russia without the help of sympathetic European states. Yet, always the practical politician, he enthusiastically set about the task of creating the "new socialist man."

Lenin's Policies

War communism. Lenin immediately plunged the Soviet Union into the socialist waters. Destroying the stock exchange and nationalizing the banks, he told the workers to take the factories and the peasants to occupy the land. Ownership became a fluid concept, and, as the White Armies gathered around the Bolshevik-held territory in 1918, the era of *war communism* began.

Friction between the workers and the Bolsheviks developed almost from the start. The pressure of the Russian Civil War (1918–1921) demanded that the economy be centralized. Accordingly, Lenin worked to achieve Bolshevik control over the factories. The proletariat resisted, preferring to run the factories collectively through councils of workers. Strife on the farms was even worse as peasants resisted the confiscation of their crops and animals for the war effort. Meanwhile, any pretense of democracy was abandoned at the end of October 1917, when Lenin dissolved an elected constituent assembly in which the Bolsheviks held only a small minority of the seats. From that moment it was clear that the dictatorship of the proletariat was to function like any other dictatorship, stifling human liberties and ignoring popular preferences.

At the front the ghastly carnage of World War I continued. Seeing that the people were fed up with the war, Lenin knew that there was no practical alternative to making peace with the German government. Though others disagreed, Lenin insisted that peace be made at any price and justified his policy in ideological terms. Lenin argued, as he had argued before, that the conflict was a capitalist imperialist war in which socialists had no interest. Peace negotiations were held, and the Treaty of Brest-Litovsk was signed on March 3, 1918. Although peace had come at great expense to their people and their land, the Soviets, relieved from the pressures of the "capitalist" war, could focus on their looming civil war.

Wretched as it was, the suffering caused by World War I was easily surpassed by the brutality of the Russian Civil War. Both sides demanded incredible sacrifices from their supporters while brutalizing their opponents. The Bolshevik cause seemed lost as the Whites amassed greater supplies of men, weapons, and funds as well as superior leadership. In addition to struggling against the Whites, the Bolsheviks had to contend with an invasion of Russia by Western states, including Britain, France, Italy, Japan, Canada, Poland, and the United States, a fact that did little to make the Allies popular with the new Russian rulers.

With the help of ideological unity and a strategic advantage that allowed them to defend their territory until they were ready to take the offensive, the Bolsheviks managed to rout the White Armies one by one. Military victories were accompanied by economic disasters, however. Poor management and unwilling workers, besides the disruption and destruction of the war itself, combined to reduce industrial production to one-seventh of its prewar level by 1921. Shortages developed in every conceivable item. The peasants, resisting government confiscation, refused to give up their goods. Producing only enough for their own needs, they brought on a food shortage that became a famine in 1920. Despite humanitarian aid from the United States, the resulting starvation claimed 5 million lives, while another 30 million suffered from malnutrition.

The NEP.   With the Civil War ending, the foreign invaders gone, the economy in a shambles, and a rebellion under way in the once loyal navy, Lenin decided to take drastic steps. Accordingly, he claimed that the party had made serious errors in trying to develop a socialist state. Demonstrating his flexibility in times of crisis, he announced his *New Economic Policy* (NEP). Having failed in his attempt at immediate and complete socialization, he took the unexpected step of recapitalizing the bulk of the economy, calling the new system *state capitalism*. Practically everything except heavy industry, finance, communications, and transportation was returned to private ownership and a market economy. Yet, it must be made clear that

Lenin intended the NEP to be only a temporary adjustment to restore economic order so that a better attempt to socialize the economy could be made later.

Even as Lenin relaxed the economy, however, the Bolsheviks, who in 1918 had become the Communist party, began to tighten their political control over the society. Just as James Madison had stifled the American Revolution in favor of order, the leaders of the Communist party betrayed their own revolutionary goals for the sake of power. Opposition parties such as the Mensheviks and the Social Revolutionaries were outlawed and destroyed. The trade unions were brought under state control. The national boundaries began to take shape as the Ukraine and the Transcaucasus states of Armenia, Georgia, and Azerbaijan were brought into the Union. More important, the party gradually became bureaucratically oriented instead of revolutionary in its focus.

Though the political situation was becoming more restrictive, the early 1920s was a time of great social and artistic experimentation in the Soviet Union. A wave of social libertarianism swept through the society. Egalitarianism was popular, stimulating a movement to eliminate the social institutions that imprisoned people in the bourgeois state. Free love was encouraged by Alexandra Kollontai, a leader among radical communists. Also supporting the abolition of the family, easy divorce, and abortions, she became an embarrassment to the puritanical Bolshevik leadership. Equally revolutionary experiments were made in art, films, music, education, literature, and the theater, producing some of the world's most avant-garde art forms. These advances of the postwar era were later squelched by Stalin's conservative notion of *socialist realism,* which required artists to show only the good, progressive side of socialism.

The NEP ended in an important feat for the Soviets. Though he died in 1924, Lenin took comfort in the knowledge that his country was well on its way toward economic recovery. Even more important, the Communist party held unchallenged power over the state, though the choice of a successor for Lenin was certainly not a foregone conclusion.

The Rise of Stalin

Upon Lenin's death the Soviet leadership was headed by a small group of men, including Leon Trotsky, a brilliant revolutionary and commissar of war, and Joseph Stalin (1879–1953), commissar of nationalities and secretary of the Communist party. Before his death Lenin had begun to suspect Stalin's motives, correctly seeing him as a scoundrel who might destroy the revolution in his quest for personal power. Too ill to actively campaign against him, Lenin suggested in his will that Stalin be replaced. Perhaps the most fateful decision in Soviet history was made when the Central Committee (a Communist party ruling body) decided to keep Lenin's will private.

Of the remaining leaders, Trotsky appeared the most likely to succeed Lenin. Brilliant as he was, however, Trotsky was not well liked by the other Communist party leaders, and they feared his rise to power. By contrast, the more placid, unobtrusive Stalin lacked his opponent's energy and seemed to give his colleagues little to fear. However, in underestimating Stalin, his unsuspecting rivals sealed their fate.

Stalin's struggle with Trotsky took place between 1924 and 1928. Besides a personality clash and each man's desire to gain power, three ideological and policy issues divided them. Trotsky attacked his colleague's domination of the party, claiming that Stalin was riding roughshod over it. The second area of disagreement

Joseph Stalin (1879–1953)

between the two was Trotsky's belief that the NEP, which he never accepted, should be immediately reversed and the farms and the marketplace resocialized. Stalin opposed this rash policy, arguing instead that the NEP should be maintained until the Soviet economy had regained its prerevolutionary productivity. The third important dispute is perhaps the most basic. Trotsky, always the revolutionary, deeply believed in the principle of *permanent revolution*. First implied by Marx, this theory suggests that no accommodation between socialists and capitalists can ever be made. Lenin carried this concept a step further in his theory of imperialism by claiming that the exportation of capitalist exploitation not only leads to competition between capitalist states but creates conflict between capitalist and socialist countries as well.

Not content to limit the revolution, Trotsky believed that the Bolshevik's first loyalty was not to any particular national experiment but to encouraging Marxist revolutions around the globe. Consequently, he insisted that Soviet resources should be devoted primarily to stimulating revolutions abroad. Stalin preferred to dedicate all the nation's energies and resources to making the Soviet Union safe from any possible challenge. This policy of *building socialism in one country*, a consuming passion for Stalin, stemmed from his fear of *capitalist encirclement*. Western attempts to frustrate the Bolshevik rise to power, the Allied invasion in 1919 during the

Russian Civil War, and the Allied attempts to strangle the Soviet Union after the Civil War through economic sanctions and boycotts, combined with Stalin's own paranoia, generated in him an exaggerated feeling of national peril. Stalin insisted that any large-scale attempt to stimulate the world revolution must await the development of unconquerable Soviet power. Only then could enough resources be spared to bring Marxism to the rest of the world. In line with this policy, even the Comintern was changed from an international revolutionary movement to a mere instrument of Soviet foreign policy.

The policy of building socialism in one country is of the greatest ideological significance. It effectively nationalizes Marxism-Leninism, a result both Marx and Lenin would certainly have abhorred. This policy is of particular importance, for nationalism is the most powerful political idea of our era. Under Stalin the strongest internationalist ideology in history was completely conquered by the irresistible onslaught of the nationalist trend. Though Stalin was the first to adapt Marxism-Leninism to nationalism, later varieties of Marxism only underscore the grip in which nationalism holds it.

Allying himself with Trotsky's enemies, Stalin saw his rival exiled in the late 1920s. Then Stalin adroitly played each remaining faction against the other to his own benefit. After fifteen years of intrigues, treachery, and bloody purges, Stalin emerged the total victor, having executed or imprisoned his original rivals, hundreds of thousands of his party comrades, and millions of Soviet citizens. Not a single institution escaped his murderous attention: Each new ally became his next victim. Not even Trotsky escaped. In 1940 he was assassinated in Mexico by a Stalinist agent. Ironically, however, he survived most of his fellow revolutionaries, who died at Stalin's hands during the great purges of the late 1930s.

Stalin's Rule

In 1929 Stalin decided it was time to abandon Lenin's NEP and resocialize the economy completely. Thus he initiated the first of the *five-year plans,* a crash program to modernize and industrialize the country. These programs called for the nationalization of all industries, trades, and occupations and included the collectivization of the farms. They also forced enormous sacrifices on the Soviet people so that resources could be diverted from the production of consumer goods to the military and heavy industry. The forced collectivization of the farms and the sacrifice of consumer goods caused incredible misery and millions of deaths. These ruthless policies were not without success, however. Compressing into ten years the advances other states stretched out over several decades, the first two five-year plans catapulted the Soviet Union to the status of a major industrial power.

Stalin's passion to make the Soviet Union unconquerable led him to personalize the dictatorship of the proletariat in a way Lenin would never have approved. The party became the mere servant of his will. Accumulating enormous power, Stalin became the single, unchallengeable head of the state. He increased his power over the party and the government, creating a *totalitarian* state. To accomplish this task, he used terrorism and the secret police, two instruments of government used by Russian rulers since the beginnings of the Russian state. On such foundations Stalin built a *personality cult* seldom equaled in history. Closely linking himself with the memory of Lenin, Stalin made his presence felt throughout the Soviet Union by erecting innumerable statues, pictures, slogans, and monuments to himself. Soviet textbooks taught that only he correctly read the meaning of Marxism-Leninism; he was therefore essential to the Soviet state and personally equated with its welfare.

Stalin's megalomania inspired him to attempt the complete subjugation of the Eastern European states that fell under Soviet influence after World War II. After the grisly siege at Leningrad and the heroic stand at Stalingrad in 1941–1943, Soviet troops drove the Nazi divisions out of their homeland. By the early summer of 1944 Soviet forces had liberated the occupied parts of their land and were preparing to pursue the retreating Nazis across Europe and into Germany itself while the Allies prepared to invade France.

Retreating into Germany, the Nazi armies abandoned Eastern Europe before the Soviet onslaught. One country after another fell under Soviet control, only to find that their liberation from the Nazis was simply the first step in the imposition of a new, equally severe regime. Reeling from the slaughter and pillage that caused the deaths of 20 million Soviets and destruction of one-quarter of the national wealth, Stalin imposed a regime of unparalleled severity on the Eastern European countries, some of which (for example, Hungary and Rumania) had willingly helped Hitler despoil the Soviet Union. Properly called the *satellite countries,* these states were harnessed to the Soviet reconstruction and defense effort. Exporting the principle of building socialism in one country, Stalin forced the satellites to contribute heavily to the Soviet economy and postpone their own recovery.

Khrushchev's Revisions

The long, dark rule of Stalin ended with his death in 1953 and was followed by a four-year power struggle within the top Soviet leadership. Emerging as the dominant, though never absolute, leader in the Soviet system, Nikita Khrushchev (1894–1971) became an important reformer.

Attacking Stalin in February 1956 in a secret speech before the Twentieth Party Congress, Khrushchev listed Stalin's "crimes," many of which Khrushchev himself had helped commit. He called for the *de-Stalinization* of the Soviet Union. Accordingly, Stalin was made a "nonperson": References to him were dropped from history books and his monuments, statues, and pictures were removed.

Khrushchev's de-Stalinization program was part of a series of liberal reforms that revitalized the Soviet state. The Soviet grip on the satellites relaxed, allowing them more liberty and individuality. Khrushchev even accepted Tito's declaration that there are many "different paths to socialism." To say that there was greater freedom in Eastern Europe under Khrushchev is not to suggest that there were no limits on that freedom, however. Those limits were clearly violated by the Hungarian rebellion in 1956: Soviet tanks were sent through the streets of Budapest, brutally suppressing the rebels' futile sprint for liberty.

Khrushchev's domestic reforms surpassed even his liberal policy toward the satellites. Terrorism was abandoned as a technique of governmental control and has not been revived. Khrushchev's adversaries were expelled from the party and the government, but they were not killed. Relaxing the government's censorship policies, Khrushchev unleashed a burst of creative energy (particularly in films and literature) that swept the country, giving vent to the genius of Boris Pasternak and Alexander Solzhenitsyn, among others. A new emphasis on consumer goods resulted in brighter clothing, better housing, and even some private vehicles.

Seeing the need for reform in the party and the government, Khrushchev also pushed for bold new farm programs, a decentralized planning process for industry, and a lean party bureaucracy. He eased out some old, complacent members and promoted a new, well-educated younger generation. His impetuous style and the failure of many of his reforms led to his undoing, however. Threatening the positions of older party members, pursuing agricultural reforms that failed, pounding his shoe on the podium during a United Nations speech, and retreating on the question of missiles in Cuba all weakened Khrushchev's position.

Two of Khrushchev's policies had important ideological implications. He set out on a completely new path when he realized that nuclear weapons made a general war between the Soviet Union and the United States unthinkable. Claiming that Marx could not have foreseen the development of the ultimate weapon that threatened to destroy humanity, he shifted the concept of permanent international revolution to a new arena. The two superpowers, he believed, must settle on a policy of *peaceful coexistence,* since a war between them would be suicidal and victory for either side was impossible.

This modification, however, did not mean that the struggle between the two systems was ended. "We will bury you," he shouted. Yet, he did not mean that we would find ourselves at the bottom of the nuclear rubble heap after a Soviet attack. Rather, he believed that the socialist world, ultimately more productive than capitalist societies, would win out over the West in the marketplace. By suggesting that the competition between the superpowers be shifted from the battlefield to the economic arena, Khrushchev was saying that while a general war between the two giants had become impossible, there was no limit on lesser confrontations. He pledged Soviet aid to struggles for national liberation, especially among the emerging states. Even so, the Soviet plea for peaceful coexistence, coming at the very time that United States Secretary of State John Foster Dulles promised *massive nuclear retaliation* against any infringement on Western interests, created a stark contrast between the policies of the two countries: The Soviets appeared moderate and reasonable, the United States irresponsible and trigger-happy.

Khrushchev's second significant ideological modification came with his announcement that the withering away of the state had begun in the Soviet Union and that the utopia would probably be achieved by 1980. He further predicted that by 1980, Soviet productivity would have surpassed that of the United States. Clearly these predictions did not come to pass. Indeed, Soviet economic growth began to slow in the mid-1970s and since then has continued to decline in comparison with Western productivity. Further, instead of disappearing, the state became even more prominent in Soviet life after Khrushchev's demise because his successors dismantled several of Khrushchev's liberal reforms. Khrushchev's exaggerated expectations did not help his image with his colleagues on the Politburo (the most powerful body in the USSR) and certainly contributed to his ouster in 1964.

The Brezhnev Era and Beyond

Since Khrushchev's fall, Soviet policy has continued to evolve, sometimes in surprising directions. Expecting the worst when Khrushchev was ousted, the world braced for a re-Stalinization of the society. Yet, while some of the most liberal Khrushchev reforms were abandoned, no new terrorist policy followed. In fact, the economic conditions of the people, especially the peasantry, actually improved, at least until the slowdown of the mid-1970s.

At the same time, Soviet foreign policy changed significantly. Reversing its long-held policy of self-sufficiency, the Soviet Union committed itself to long-term grain purchases from the West and to a dependence on Western technology for much of its prosperity. In return, it increased its sale of oil, natural gas, and other raw materials to the West.

A political thaw generally referred to as détente accompanied these economic changes, and for a few years in the 1970s large numbers of Soviet Jews, Armenians, and Volga Germans were allowed to emigrate to the West. However, the Soviet invasion of Afghanistan and the truculence of the early Reagan administration saw rapport between the two countries cool again before Mikhail S. Gorbachev and President Reagan committed their respective societies to better relations, which some people hope signals the permanent cessation of the Cold War.

Politically, the era of Leonid Brezhnev (1964 –1982) was noted for its stability. Reacting to the frenzied reform policies of Khrushchev, the Soviet political elite insisted on stable, conservative policies. Stability soon transformed to political and economic stagnation, however. Job security became almost absolute from top to bottom in the society. With little danger of losing their jobs, long-time government officials became corrupt, and workers became even less conscientious than before: Absenteeism, shoddy production, breakage, and waste increased to serious proportions. Squeezed by low productivity and an enormous defense budget as they tried to equal the United States' military capacity, the Soviets saw shortages of staples as well as luxuries become a serious and constant problem. Shortages in state stores encouraged people to satisfy their needs illegally so the ever-present black market became pervasive throughout the society.

A spiritual malaise set in over the society and ideological conviction declined abruptly in the waning years of Brezhnev's tenure. The decline of popular resolve in response to corruption and scarcity was exacerbated by the growing gerontocracy governing the system. Few of the aging bureaucrats left their powerful positions; hence there was little upward mobility for the younger generations, and the system became sapped of the vitality it had traditionally enjoyed. Hope for reform dimmed as one aging conservative followed another to the pinnacle of Soviet power. (Yuri Andropov ruled from 1982 to 1984, to be succeeded by Konstantin Chernenko until his death in 1985. Both men were aged and infirm during most of their tenures.)

Mikhail S. Gorbachev (born in 1931) was named General Secretary of the Communist Party after Chernenko's death in 1985. Young and dynamic, Gorbachev has embarked on a breathtaking reform package that he calls a "revolution without bullets." *Perestroika* (restructuring), the heart of his reforms, calls for enormous changes in the economy. Plant managers are given more responsibility for production as centralized planning is becoming less comprehensive and intrusive. Small businesses and agricultural enterprises are being returned to private ownership in policies reminiscent of the NEP. Since success is being measured by profits rather than by gross production as it was under the Stalinist model, bankruptcy of inefficient state businesses, greater unemployment, and wage differences based on individual production are now encouraged. The hope is that these reforms, and others like them, will provide the needed incentives to wrest the economy from its fifteen-year stagnation.

A well-educated and progressive thinker, Gorbachev realizes that his reforms must be much broader in scope than just these economic changes, however. Accordingly, he has electrified the world with a series of political and social reforms. Realizing that a high-tech economy rests on a foundation of shared information,

Gorbachev has pushed through *glasnost* (openness), encouraging people to speak freely, the media to publish previously taboo criticisms, and historians and writers to delve into the long-ignored painful truth of Stalin's murderous record. Indeed, a new, more comprehensive de-Stalinization campaign is in progress, accompanied by the rehabilitation of many former Soviet heroes who had been vanquished in dishonor during Stalin's purges.

Accompanying *perestroika* and *glasnost* is a *demokratsiya* (democratization) program intended to strike at the insensitive and corrupt bureaucracy of the Soviet Union. Secret ballots are now used to elect plant managers, trade union officials, government functionaries, and party leaders in contested elections. Assuredly, the nominees for these posts must be acceptable to the party, but at least now the people are enjoying a choice about who rules them. Additionally, Gorbachev has pushed through important changes in the structure of the government, making it somewhat more independent from the party and apparently more responsive to the needs of the citizens.

Capping the entire reform package is an energetic anti-corruption campaign. Striking out at the nepotism and dishonesty of the Brezhnev administration, Gorbachev has seen thousands of people demoted, dismissed, arrested, and even executed for inefficiency, cronyism, negligence, embezzlement, bribery, and so forth. Literally thousands of people in business, government, trade unions, and the party itself have been disciplined.

Since Lenin, the Soviet Union has had two great progressive reformers: Khrushchev and Gorbachev. Khrushchev was able to break the grip of the secret police in the Soviet Union, eliminating terrorism as a means of government. Thus, he dismantled one of the two great pillars that Stalin's legacy rested upon. Khrushchev was unsuccessful, however, in destroying the second buttress of Stalin's legacy, the centralized economic system. It is this edifice that Gorbachev is now trying to replace with a more productive, efficient, and humane system. But doing so means inconveniencing large numbers of people and reducing the power of the immense Soviet bureaucracy. Coupled with several other personal problems, Khrushchev's attempt to reform the economic system put him at odds with the bureaucracy and helped to bring him down. Although Gorbachev is not beset with his predecessor's personal problems, he also faces stiff resistance to his reforms. As of 1990 the performance of the reforms had been disappointing, but whether or not Gorbachev will be more successful than Khrushchev remains to be seen.

YUGOSLAVIA

Tito's Rise to Power

In 1914 Josip Broz Tito (1892–1980) was drafted into the Austro-Hungarian army and sent to fight on the eastern front. The following year he was captured, and he spent two years in Russia as a prisoner of war. In 1917, released by the revolutionary forces, he joined the Red Army to fight in defense of the Bolshevik cause against the Whites.

When the Whites were defeated and the Civil War ended, the young man from Croatia became a member of the Comintern. Having been trained as an infiltrator, he returned to Yugoslavia in 1924. For the next several years he worked as a labor organizer and agitator until he was imprisoned for five years by the Yugoslavian authorities. During the German invasion of his homeland in 1941 he hid in the hills, organizing and commanding a resistance movement.

As World War II progressed, Yugoslavia developed, without Soviet intervention, a communist movement under Tito that was popularly accepted as the ruling group. Stalin sent Tito aid, as did the United States, but the Yugoslav leader was not indebted to the Soviet Union for his power. The nation's clear choice for leader following the war, Tito enjoyed popular support, and Yugoslavia benefited by having a degree of independence from the Soviet Union unique among the European satellite states.

The Evolution of Titoism

At the end of the war Tito was Joseph Stalin's most outspoken supporter. As premier of the new state, he set up a system of economic and political controls based on the Soviet model. Yet, Yugoslav-Soviet ties were not as solid as they appeared. Stalin insisted on Soviet domination of all Eastern European states, including Yugoslavia, causing Tito serious misgivings about the wisdom of a close alliance. Having attained high office on his own, Tito was not enchanted at the thought of being Stalin's puppet. Therefore, he began to resist Soviet pressure to conform.

By 1947 Yugoslavia faced a serious economic crisis, which Tito met with characteristic creativity. Angered by Yugoslavia's failure to follow traditional policies, Stalin began to press Tito to pursue a more orthodox course. Tito's resistance made Stalin even more insistent until relations between the two states were broken off in 1948. Protesting that there are many "different paths to socialism," Tito was cut adrift from the Soviet bloc. To Stalin's dismay this did not lead to Tito's downfall. Instead, the Yugoslav leader, an excellent politician, pioneered the policy of non-alignment with either East or West and profited from trade with both.

By divorcing himself from the Soviet bloc and remaining a Marxist, Tito initiated a second communist line, one that has become the most pragmatic and least dogmatic variant of communist ideologies. He began by warning that just as there are certain fundamental problems in capitalism, socialism is also plagued with internal difficulties that must be faced squarely if they are to be solved.

Lenin's stress on *violence* was a particular problem to Tito. He argued that although violence might have been necessary at one time, it was no longer required for socialist development. Stronger and more fully developed, socialism had gained momentum and could continue to advance without the use of force. This attitude modified the principle of permanent revolution considerably, but Tito changed it even further. Rather than constantly resisting the capitalist states, socialists should coexist with them, he believed. Moreover, he advised that when it was in their interest to do so, Marxists should cooperate actively with the capitalist world.

His fear of capitalist encirclement undiminished after the war, Stalin found Tito's moderate ideas reprehensible. He was already disturbed by Tito's doctrine of different paths to socialism. Tito had insisted that there was no single true interpretation of socialism, making it hard to justify Stalin's attempt to restrict independent socialist thought and to force compliance with Moscow's dictates.

Though Tito's attempt to remain independent of Moscow was the greatest reason for his break with Stalin, his most important ideological revision was concerned not with international relations but with domestic policy. Reaching the conclusion Mao Tse-tung arrived at a few years later, Tito believed that the greatest problem socialism faced was *bureaucratic rigidity*. Accordingly, Tito focused on combating the tendency of over-centralization in the regime. Since socialism requires collectivization of the society as well as organization and direction of the economy on a national scale, Tito believed that conflict could be expected among several legitimate interests within the society. The most vexing of these conflicts would arise from a clash between the individual's interests and those of a society as a whole. Tito also recognized the potential for strife between the preferences of the workers and the economic goals of the state. Perhaps most important of all, however, was the contradiction he saw between the central government and the local agencies in the political arena as well as in the economic field.

Facing the problems of centralization squarely, he concluded that Marx was wrong in suggesting that the dictatorship of the proletariat would wither away as it succeeded in its task of creating the classless society. To the contrary, Tito reasoned, unless it was prevented from expanding, the bureaucracy would grow rather than disappear. Instead of evolving from state socialism to communism, as Lenin had hoped, the political system would be dominated by the bureaucracy. Tito feared that because of its self-protective tendency, the bureaucracy would continue to exploit the worker for its own benefit, and the society would not evolve beyond *state capitalism* to the socialist utopia. He saw the state becoming an end in itself; in other words, the political system would come to resemble fascism, hardly Marx's goal.

Once describing Yugoslavia as "one country with two alphabets, speaking three languages, professing four religions, made up of five nationalities in six republics," Tito moved to decentralize his country. Actually, it was divided into six republics and two autonomous provinces. Its diverse groups find themselves joined in an uncomfortable union required by political realities. They are unable to cooperate fully because of their traditional animosities, jealousies, cultural divisions, isolation, and geographic and economic differences. Such complex problems can be satisfactorily administered only in a federal system, and this structural decentralization sets the tone for other programs intended to relax the grip of the national bureaucracy on the society.

Perhaps the most significant decentralization scheme is found in the Yugoslavian economic system. Under what came to be called *market socialism*, Tito decollectivized most of the farms, returning them to private ownership and control. Even more progressive, however, were the modifications he made in the industrial sector. Reversing his original preference for central control and planning of industrial output, Tito began to encourage the decentralization of industry. Always alert to the encroachments of bureaucracy on the society, he argued that in the most advanced form of socialism the workers would be in direct control of the factories. In his opinion nationalization of industries was only a first and somewhat primitive step toward socialism; *social* control rather than state control was the future condition of the advanced socialist societies. Accordingly, a program to return control of the plants to the workers was inaugurated. Though his program has been only partly successful, it does allow workers to participate in plant management. Workers stand for election to the plant's *workers' council*. Becoming the management team, the workers' council plans and carries out production goals; oversees quality and quantity-control measures, distribution, and sales procedures; and allocates the proceeds to reinvestment, wages, and benefits according to its judgment of the needs of the workers and the enterprise. Of course, the plans and activities of a workers' council must conform to the general needs of the society identified at higher levels, but this process was seen as an experiment in local control and involvement.

Besides the localization of control in industrial production, Tito also allowed private ownership to exist side by side with public enterprise. As already mentioned, agricultural enterprises were largely returned to private hands. Private ownership of small businesses has not only been tolerated, but it has even been encouraged in some cases. Small retail shops, restaurants, repair shops, crafts, and tourist facilities have often been left to private ownership. Even private foreign investment has been encouraged.

The policies of *worker self-management* and recapitalization of some parts of the economy have met with mixed success, however. Despite the economic boom of the 1950s and 1960s, the picture is much less attractive today. Yugoslavia has followed other Eastern European countries into heavy international debt. Yugoslavia's debt exceeded $20 billion in 1986. At the same time it faces an inflation rate of 200 percent (one of the world's highest), its productivity has declined dramatically, causing serious shortages, and its unemployment rate is at 15 percent—Europe's highest.

Accompanying the structural decentralization of federalism and the economic localism of Tito's policies was a reduction of the Communist party's role. Contradicting Marx again, Tito argued that while the economic bureaucracy would eventually evolve away, the party would always remain the leader and guardian of the system. Even so, Tito did not intend to control the party from Belgrade. Renaming the Communist party the League of Yugoslav Communists (LCY), Tito shifted it toward indirect guidance of people and away from direct participation in their affairs. Direct involvement in the citizens' lives was left to the party machinery at the local level.

Decentralization had some unexpected results, however. With the relaxation of control at the national level, the leadership in the various republics became increasingly powerful. Old provincial animosities and problems began to take on new importance. Finally, following student riots in the late 1960s and early 1970s, Tito reversed the trend of political decentralization. A series of purges was begun that replaced dissident party members and intimidated the university system. These moves not only silenced the most vocal separatists but also quieted those who were predicting that Tito, an aging statesman, had actually lost power and was being eased into retirement. In addition, it became obvious that Tito might indeed be the only person who could hold together the feuding and diverse elements of his country. To prevent a disastrous struggle for power when Tito actually did pass from the scene, the Yugoslavs adopted a new constitution that created a plural executive. Eight people, one from each republic and each autonomous province, were to share executive power with Tito as president for life. With Tito's death, it was decided that the presidency is to rotate annually among the eight administrators.

Many people in the West watched the recentralization of power with alarm, fearing that a re-Stalinization of Yugoslavia was in the making. Though understandable, such fears seem ill-founded since the new party dominance is apparently designed to discourage nationalistic separatism rather than to accomplish the centralization of power for its own sake. Indeed, the political circumstances in Yugoslavia have been considerably re-liberalized since Tito's death. Yet the severe, long-lasting economic crisis coupled with the growing animosities among the various ethnic groups gives cause for concern.

With Tito's pervasive and firm influence removed, the Yugoslavs must fall back on their political system for stability. Unfortunately, the political system is weakening. The younger generation chaffs at the absence of upward mobility caused by the unwillingness of the aged leaders to step down. At the same time, the revolving presidency, created to prevent anyone from amassing too much power, is perceived as denying anyone any power at all. Characterized as a game of musical chairs, the revolving presidency leaves the impression that no one is in power, no one is responsible.

The seemingly hopeless economic situation and the increasing political weakness to which Yugoslavia has evolved have caused a general disenchantment with the dominant ideology. Failing to attract young members to the party, the LCY has also suffered a decline of membership as many older members, especially among the working class, have resigned from the party. Indeed, *Milovan Djilas,* one of Tito's close collaborators turned communist critic and outcast, avered that Yugoslavia may be the first European country to abandon communism.

At the same time, the animosity among the Yugoslav nationalities is increasing, placing a strain upon the unity of the country itself. Ancient jealousies among these Balkan people (never far beneath the surface) are exacerbated by contemporary economic problems. Slovenes, Croats, Serbians, Montenegrins, Albanians, Macedonians, and other peoples vie with one another for what each believes is their national rights. Boycotts, strikes, and violent clashes have recently blighted the landscape and the Slovenes, the most affluent national group, threaten to amend their republic's constitution allowing them to secede from the union.

What fate has in store for Yugoslavia is, of course, impossible to predict. Although the once feared Soviet intervention now seems remote, Yugoslavia's major problems come from within. Ultimately, its fate rests in the good will and in the common sense of its own people. They must come to grips with the declining economic situation, and they must free themselves of the debilitating spiritual malaise into which they have settled. Most important, however, they must rise above the factional disputes which plague them and commit to a united national entity. If they are unable to control their ethnic jealousies, their economic difficulties, and their political morale, the Titoist experiment with Marxism indeed may be doomed.

CHINA

Imperial China, one of history's most successful political systems, was based on the principles of Confucianism. Confucianism is as much a political theory as a code of moral conduct. Indeed, in this ancient philosophy moral conduct and an ordered state are equated. Confucius taught that all people should know their place and should accept it, thus maintaining a harmonious society, the most desirable state of affairs. The law, rooted in Confucian teaching, provided that the upper classes would rule and that the peasantry would obey. This sociopolitical arrangement served the Chinese remarkably well for centuries. The Chinese people enjoyed the benefits of an advanced civilization and an ordered society while the West foundered in ignorance and social disorder.

Perhaps because the West was driven to improve the political and economic systems serving it, it took the initiative during the fourteenth and fifteenth centuries. For its part, the Orient turned inward and became isolated from foreign influences. The Chinese placed a premium on tradition, rejecting new ideas as harmful to society.

As a result the West surpassed the East in developing modern technology and political doctrines that accommodated the changes brought about by the new economic order. As the East's resistance was worn down by the pressure of the West's technological superiority, the philosophies of the ancient regimes began to appear less viable and Western ideologies, such as nationalism and later Marxism, became more appealing. Though these Western ideas were modified somewhat, the fact remains that the East has been captivated by Western institutions, economic styles, and idea systems.

The Belligerent Stage of the Chinese Revolution

Though its traditional power seemed antiquated, the imperial system survived foreign invasion and internal pressure for change until early in this century. The inevitable could not be avoided forever, and the belligerent stage of the Chinese Revolution began in 1911 and lasted until 1949.

In 1911 the Manchu Dynasty ended with the child emperor, Pu Yi, abdicating in response to overwhelming pressure. The leader of the victorious republican forces was an unimposing, idealistic man, Dr. Sun Yat-sen[1] (1866–1925). His ideology was a somewhat confused mixture of Western and Eastern theories. Simplifying them for mass consumption, he condensed his goals into the Three Principles of the People: *nationalism,* the unification of China and the liberation of the Chinese coast from foreign colonial powers; *democracy,* which he defined as a popularly elected government; and the *peoples' livelihood,* a kind of welfare state socialism coupled with government-regulated capitalism.

Sun Yat-sen was too idealistic and naive to understand completely the forces he had helped unleash, however, and China's needs went far beyond his simplistic solutions. In the end he was outmaneuvered by the Machiavellians surrounding him. Having been deceived in 1913 into turning over power to an opportunistic lieutenant, he spent the rest of his life struggling with autocratic elements in China.

In the meantime the Communist Party of China (CPC) was founded in 1921. Attending the first party congress was a radical young schoolteacher, Mao Tse-tung (1893–1976). Coming from a well-to-do peasant family, Mao pursued an education and graduated from a teacher's college in 1918. Although he began at a low rank, he attracted the attention of party superiors with his devotion to the cause, his tireless efforts as a union organizer, and his keen insight into the problems of the revolution.

For its part the Soviet Union was becoming increasingly interested in China. As

---

[1]Before 1970 Chinese words in English were commonly spelled using the Wade-Giles system. In 1970 the Peoples' Republic of China adopted the *pinyin* system, and most English publications have since adopted that format. Yet certain names like Mao Tse-tung seem strange and may not be easily recognized in the *pinyin* form (Mao Zedong). Thus, in order to keep confusion at a minimum, I am using the Wade-Giles system for historical names and the *pinyin* system for contemporary names. Also, you will note that Chinese surnames are placed in front of given names. Hence, Mao Tse-tung's surname is Mao; Chiang Kai-shek's is Chiang, and so forth.

we have seen, Lenin was at first convinced that the revolution in Russia could not succeed unless it was quickly followed and supported by revolutions in the advanced states of Western Europe. He had organized the Comintern to encourage such upheavals. Time proved Lenin wrong, however; Europe did not explode in a series of Communist revolutions, and the Bolsheviks survived the Civil War. Lenin's attention turned increasingly to the colonial countries, and he sent Mikhail Borodin to coordinate the Comintern efforts in China. Lenin favored an alliance between the CPC and the *Kuomintang* (Sun's political party) against the reactionary elements in China. More important, Stalin also supported such an alliance, actively encouraging it after Lenin became ill in 1923. Repeatedly rebuffed in his appeals for aid from the United States and Western Europe because he was a socialist, Sun Yat-sen turned to the Soviet Union for support, agreeing to the first Communist-Kuomintang alliance (1924–1927).

The purpose of the first alliance was to break the power of the reactionary provincial warlords who had governed the far-flung provinces of China for centuries. The alliance's initial success was darkened in 1925 when Sun Yat-sen died. He was followed by his lieutenant Chiang Kai-shek (1887–1975), a much more conservative leader. As his armies succeeded in centralizing power somewhat, Chiang began to think about eliminating his troublesome ally. In 1927 he attacked the communists, slaughtering all who fell into his hands. Close to annihilation, the communists fled the cities to seek safety in the provinces.

The ruralization of Chinese communism. Two years before the Kuomintang attacked the communists, Mao had become unhappy with the progress of the revolution. Thus, he had returned to his native Hunan province in southeastern China and studied the peasantry as a revolutionary force. Previously considered a strong supporter of the pro-urban Moscow line, Mao produced his first significant work, *Report on the Human Peasant Movement,* which called upon communists to abandon the cities for the countryside because the peasants were the true revolutionary force in China. With this document he laid the foundation of Maoist ideology and it, together with Chiang's treachery (1927) and the communist failure to rouse the proletariat in the cities, ended the domination of the Soviet Union over the CPC. Though always an important factor, Stalin's influence was clearly secondary in China after 1927 as a distinctly Chinese brand of communism began to develop.

Mao's ideological skill, leadership ability, and shrewd political judgment made him one of the leading party members after 1927. At the same time, a civil war raged between the communists, now recovered from the massacre of 1927, and the forces of the Kuomintang. Finally gaining an almost decisive military advantage over the communists in 1934, the Kuomintang army surrounded them and threatened their destruction.

The Long March. The situation became so desperate that a drastic step had to be taken. To avoid annihilation, the communists broke out of the encirclement—leaving their base behind—and fled to safety in northern China. This epic retreat, called the *Long March,* was the low point of the CPC's history and lasted a full year. About 100,000 people set out on a journey that took them 6,000 miles. Since it was more a running battle than a march, scarcely 35,000 survived. As if the hardships of the trek and attacks by the forces of Chiang and the warlords were not enough, the

Long March precipitated a leadership struggle within the CPC, and Mao gained the top position in the party. Although this position did not give him absolute power, it made him dominant in the movement, a position he would hold until his death. Almost every other important Chinese leader until the late 1970s and early 1980s was a survivor of the Long March.

The march finally ended in Shensi province in north-central China, where a new base was established in 1936. Hostilities between the communists and the Kuomintang would have continued if the Japanese had not become an overriding threat in the same year. Stalin encouraged the Chinese communists to form a new alliance with the Kuomintang because he wanted to preoccupy Japan with a war in China, thus preventing it from invading the Soviet Union. This "alliance" was actually only a truce, however, permitting two antagonists to deal with a third force threatening both. Nevertheless, the war efforts of each partner were restrained, since each saved its energy for the inevitable struggle that would take place when the Japanese were defeated.

When the Japanese were finally vanquished in 1945, the China question emerged once again. The United States, which clearly favored the Kuomintang, tried to negotiate a coalition government between Mao and Chiang. Ironically, Stalin, who believed that the communists could not yet defeat Chiang, also pressured Mao to join in a coalition government. Mao and Chiang were both convinced that they could win the struggle, however, so they each refused to compromise. The upshot was the last phase of the belligerent period of the Chinese Revolution (1946–1949), as the two sides locked in mortal combat. Because he had not been able to control the warlords and because his government was cruel, corrupt, and foolish, Chiang had lost popular support. His military superiority, so obvious on paper, melted away. Mao, on the other hand, enjoyed great popular support in the north and considerable appeal in the south. A series of stunning defeats saw Chiang giving ground until finally, in 1949, all was lost and he fled to the island province of Taiwan.

The Political Stage of the Revolution

The communist regime in China has been marked by a series of important, sometimes traumatic, events. Mao Tse-tung remained a radical force in Chinese politics, often plunging China into tumultuous programs aimed at achieving great goals for his people. When they fell short of those objectives, the reform periods were followed by periods of consolidation that evolved into the staging grounds for the next set of Mao's radical reforms. This behavior pattern was repeated again and again, growing in intensity right up to Mao's death in 1976.

The first years. On the economic front the new regime was surprisingly moderate in its objectives, if not in its methods. Long years of experience in the rural soviets had taught that the peasantry would resist a sudden switch to collectivism. Accordingly, the government decided to achieve socialism on the farms in a series of steps. The landlords, who owned huge estates that they seldom visited, were the targets of the initial social reform, a step that naturally won the support of many peasants. By the end of 1952, after a little more than two years of communist control, the large estates had been dissolved and peasant ownership substituted. Greatly pleased by the agrarian reforms, the peasants felt justified in supporting the new regime. But although it avoided Lenin's mistake of socializing the society all at once, this moderate policy was not without serious abuses. While millions benefited from the redistribution of land, hundreds of thousands, perhaps millions, paid with their lives for resisting the reforms.

The new regime also took bold steps in the area of social reform. Developing the theme of social equality, it condemned great economic differences among citizens. Less popular, but nonetheless strongly pursued, was the issue of women's equality. China, one of the world's most paternalistic societies, had for centuries given women an incredibly narrow role. Never without a male superior, be he father, brother, husband, or son, women were virtually imprisoned in the home, where the drudgery of housework was relieved only by toil in the fields. Perhaps the most poignant symbol of their wretched condition was the ancient tradition of binding women's feet, a painful custom in which the feet were deformed by tight wrappings applied from childhood. Though some aged Chinese women can still be seen hobbling from the effects of foot-binding, the ancient practice has been eradicated.

The next task was to socialize the economy. The first Five-Year Plan (1953–1957) was designed to achieve economic centralization. Its goals were to increase heavy industrial production, socialize light industry and retail enterprises, and collectivize the farms. Though heavy industrial production improved considerably, resistance to the socialization program grew in intensity until forceful measures were used. Although the merchants and artisans were displeased by the takeover of their businesses, the greatest problems faced by the collectivization program arose on the farms. Mindful of the disastrous Soviet experience, however, the Chinese collectivized the farms more gradually. Eventually, private ownership of the land was abandoned altogether, and the peasants found themselves on giant communes.

By 1957 the goals of the first Five-Year Plan had been largely achieved, albeit painfully. Yet, political conditions within the party remained unsettled. Stalin's death in 1954 had brought a new order to the Soviet Union. Khrushchev, as we have seen, liberalized Stalinism and went on to condemn its excesses, particularly the policy of creating a "personality cult." The liberalization of Soviet rule also stimulated rebellions in East Germany and Poland (both in 1953), and in Hungary (1956). Each was ended by stern Soviet measures, including the use of Soviet tanks in Hungary.

These events not only caused stirrings of uneasiness in the West but also had adverse effects within the communist world. The parallel between Stalin's personality cult and the Chinese adulation of Mao was striking, of course. Feeling that the old radical had outlived his usefulness anyway, the moderates in the party, the government, and the army began to maneuver for his retirement. Wishing to divorce himself from the unpopular personality cult policy and also hoping to avoid a disturbance similar to the Hungarian rebellion, Mao surprised his opponents with a sudden liberalization of his own.

The revolutionized revolution.   In 1957 Mao called on the people to criticize the government and its policies and thereby stimulate the rulers to improve the system. "Let a hundred flowers bloom, let a hundred schools contend," he proclaimed, thinking that the malcontents would satisfy themselves with superficial complaints. Instead, the intellectuals took the opportunity to criticize the government, the party, and the leadership at the highest levels. Stunned by their vocal and penetrating outcries, Mao reversed himself after only two months and stifled any further criticism.

Smarting from the failure of the *Hundred Flowers campaign,* Mao was desperate for a way to recover his fading influence. Always the revolutionary, he again took the initiative. A *Great Leap Forward* was announced, based on the twin pillars of Mao's ideology: conquering material want by applying superior willpower (a very un-Marxist idea), and overcoming technological problems by organizing the masses.

Intended to vastly increase the industrial and agricultural output of China, the Great Leap Forward was an immense failure. The society actually took several staggering steps backward. The first Five-Year Plan had centralized heavy industry. Yet, the Great Leap Forward attempted to reverse this trend. Instead of bringing the workers to the factories, the factories were carried to the workers. For example, thousands of families were given small furnaces and iron ore and urged to produce pig iron in their backyards. Unfortunately, the iron was of such poor quality that it was practically worthless.

On the collective farms radicalism was also the order of the day. Attacking the family as a bourgeois institution, Mao tried to destroy it by extending communalism beyond work and ownership. Barracks were built, mess halls raised, and people encouraged to identify with the commune as a whole instead of only with the family. Meanwhile the communes were to become almost entirely self-sufficient by branching out into light industry as well as the usual food and fiber production.

By 1960 all pretense that the new program was succeeding was dropped. Production had fallen drastically and famine threatened the stability of the regime. Mao's prestige reached a new low as the Great Leap Forward was abandoned. Accordingly, he announced that he would retire from government life, preferring, he said, to remain chairman of the Communist party. "Chairman Mao," the official announcement stated, "has retired to devote his time to theoretical questions."

The years between 1960 and 1966 were spent in dismantling the most radical programs of the Great Leap Forward. The backyard industries were abandoned, and the barracks and mess halls gradually disappeared from the collective farms. Though it had been an economic failure, the Great Leap Forward had accomplished one important thing: It had formalized the centrality of the commune in the Chinese society.

During this period the moderates gradually began to regain control of the government and the party. Productivity increased, consumer goods production was expanded, and more moderate foreign policy goals were pursued as Mao remained in the background. In 1966, however, not content with prestige without power and resentful of the moderates, Mao decided to call for yet another radicalization of the revolution. Using his support in the army, the old radical called for rededication of the revolution—a *Great Cultural Revolution*—and for the purge of "reactionaries" who were destroying the movement.

Thus began one of history's most unique and remarkable episodes. A true revolutionary, Mao used revolution to impose his will within a system of which he was a leading part. Inspired by Mao, youthful radicals formed units called the *Red Guard.* Swarming like enraged bees, the Red Guard took over party and government headquarters, schools and factories, communes and collectives. The new revolutionaries subjected officials, teachers, workers, and peasants to rump trials and condemned them for "counterrevolutionary" offenses. The turmoil spread as violence increased, destroying property, purging officials, and disrupting life. Striking out against moderation, the bureaucracy, the intellectuals, and other nonradical elements, the Red Guard made the whole society captive to its destructive fanaticism.

By 1969 the situation had become so bad that even Mao admitted things had gone too far. The army was turned on the Red Guard and order was finally restored. When the dust cleared, China found itself radicalized, but bruised and bleeding as well. Productivity had declined again, and the government and the party were in disarray. Thousands had been purged, including Deng Xiaoping (born in 1904). Others, all radicals, gained power.

The moderates' fortunes, at a low ebb in 1969, began to recover gradually in the early 1970s. Despite radical demands for sacrifice, the Chinese people increasingly expected consumer goods and a better standard of living. Meanwhile the deteriorating relations with the Soviet Union required a modified foreign policy, drawing China closer to an accommodation with the United States.

The Sino-Soviet split, a major event in Maoist China, resulted from a variety of conditions. Because Stalin tried to manipulate events in China to the benefit of the Soviet Union and often to the detriment of China, Mao was careful to maintain a cordial but cautious distance from the USSR. With de-Stalinization, however, Sino-Soviet relations began to decline dramatically: Mao was not pleased by the Soviet's debunking of Stalinism. Khrushchev's policy of peaceful coexistence only aggravated the strain between the two socialist governments. In addition, Mao developed an undisguised contempt for Khrushchev, claiming that he, not Khrushchev, was the senior Marxist and hence the rightful leader of the communist bloc. As attention began to center on the Third World states in the early 1960s, Mao also argued that his country was much more similar to those states than was the industrial Soviet Union. Accordingly, China, not the Soviets, should lead the Third World to prosperity. Besides these ideological concerns, ancient territorial disputes added to the growing conflict between China and the Soviet Union, climaxing in a serious border skirmish between China and the USSR in 1969 and a warming trend in the relations between China and the United States.[2]

These events enhanced the moderates' position, and, led by Chou En-lai, they were resurgent by 1974. So complete was the moderate victory that Chou was able to rehabilitate Deng Xiaoping and designate him as his successor. Yet, the moderate victory was cut short when Chou died in February 1976. Buttressed by the support of an aging Mao, the radicals, led by the *Gang of Four*—including Jiang Quing, Mao's wife—were brought back to power, purging influential moderates, including the recently restored Deng in the process. The radicals failed to win full dominance before Mao's death in late 1976, however, and they were forced to accept a number of compromises before they were finally vanquished completely.

Finally dominant, Deng and his pragmatic associates have initiated far-reaching reforms in the legal system, the bureaucracy, the army, the economy, the party, and even in the commune system itself. Although resisted by the military and the radicals, these reforms have brought major improvements in China's lifestyle and constitute a rejection of the ideological extremes Mao advocated. Among the most important attempted changes, however, are reforms of the political establishment which were designed to strike at the inefficiency, nepotism, and corruption so common at the upper eshelons of the goverment and party. Regrettably, these reforms have not been

---

[2]In the 1980s, however, as China and the Soviet Union have embarked on similar reform programs, relations between the two socialist giants have become warmer.

completely successful and the continuing malfeasance in high office has caused significant concern among the masses.

Meanwhile, reminiscent of the Soviet NEP, the Chinese leadership has encouraged a return to market forces in some parts of the economy. The communes have disappeared and peasants, farming land leased from the state, sell many of their goods on the open market. Private entrepreneurs organize small family businesses, inefficient state enterprises are allowed to go bankrupt, and state workers are paid on the basis of productivity rather than according to Mao's egalitarian policies. As a result, China's productivity has dramatically increased, especially in agriculture. But these economic achievements have been accompanied by many social problems. While some people improve their lot, others—tens of millions of others—remain desperately poor. Inflation has driven formerly fixed prices to unprecedented heights. Crime, juvenile delinquency, and vice are all on dramatic upswings.

Apparently, engaged in another episode of unrest, the society foments and boils in a caldron fired by change. The recent economic and political advances were not won without controversy. Corrupt officials resisted reforms that would reduce their powers; ideologues resented the abandonment of radical goals; conservatives rejected the Westernization of their country; the army disliked the subdued role it has been assigned; and liberal students and intellectuals—impatient for change—agitated for individual rights, free expression, and meaningful elections.

In 1989, matters came to a head. China's university students used the death of a deposed reformer as a pretext to manifest for liberal reforms. For several weeks in May, perhaps as many as one million people occupied Tian An Men Square in central Beijing and others gathered at public places in cities throughout the country, demanding freedom of the press, better treatment for intellectuals, removal of the recalcitrant party and government officials, and the establishment of Western democratic institutions.

At first, the government, apparently engaged in an internal power struggle, did little to remove the students. Some negotiations were held, but the students remained resolute in their demands to which the government continued to be unresponsive. Eventually, troops were brought into the city, but the students confronted them in remarkable demonstrations of outrage and courage. Then, finally, in early June, the Peoples' Liberation Army brutally opened fire and cut down the students in Beijing. Government efforts to justify the crackdown have obscured the numbers killed; but some estimates run into the thousands. After the square was cleared, student protesters were doggedly pursued; some were imprisoned and executed, while others were taken out of school, and, reminiscent of the sent-down movement during the Great Cultural Revolution, thousands of students are now required to spend a year or two in the military or at manual labor in the villages before they can continue their studies.

The power struggle within the party and government resulted in removal of the most progressive elements in China's top leadership, including Zhao Ziyang, the former General Secretary of the Communist Party. In their place, politically conservative people now govern China, although they assert that China shall continue its economic reforms.

Precisely what course China will follow from this juncture is, of course, difficult to say. Clearly, Deng Xiaoping continues to hold sway for the moment. But his efforts to reform China economically and politically and his careful attempts to ensure a smooth transfer of power following his departure from power have been badly damaged by the events of June 1989, and China's future seems much more clouded than it did before the Tian An Men massacre.

The Principles of Maoism

Mao's major contribution to Marxism-Leninism undoubtedly was adjusting it to fit Asian culture. To accomplish this goal, he made certain modifications in the theory itself, focusing on the central concept of social class. An agrarian country lacking even the small industrial base available to Russia in 1917, China was overwhelmingly rural, and so Mao turned to the peasants for political strength.

Populism.   Mao and others realized that the future of the Chinese Revolution was in the hands of the peasantry. The problem of reconciling this practical reality with Marxism inspired him to develop a unique variation on the Marxist theme. Taking a page from the Populists' book, Mao gave the peasant a leading position in the society. Of course, the peasants would eventually have to be proletarianized, but in the meantime their virtues were announced to the world in Maoist literature. Mao believed that the peasants' simple, pure character, unblemished by the evil influences of urban sophistication, was the bulwark of Chinese strength. Later, during the Cultural Revolution, he called on Chinese sophisticates to "learn from the people," as scholars, managers, public officials, and townspeople were forced to the farm to relearn basic values.

Though it was officially a duty and an honor, many people opposed the idea of returning to the farm for spiritual renewal. Resentful of this disruption of their lives, they tried to avoid it in a number of ways, including bribery and deception. Still, millions of people were sent to the villages to toil in the fields, disrupting their lives for a decade or more. The peasants, who did not like the system any better than the city dwellers, found it burdensome to teach their reluctant guests to farm.

Mind over matter.   Populism poses a dilemma. If the peasants are the true foundation of Chinese society, how are they to be proletarianized without destroying their positive features? Mao solved this problem by resorting to a typically Chinese, but very un-Marxist, idea. Much less an economic determinist than Marx, Mao argued that ideological purity was more important than economic experience and that the proletarian mentality could be developed through educational as well as economic stimulation. Hence, he maintained that the peasants might be proletarianized by being taught the socialist ethic, but that they need never leave the farm to complete the transformation. This *mind-over-matter* attitude occurs again and again, not only in Mao's thought but also in his policy—witness the Great Leap Forward and the Cultural Revolution. In each of these events the Chinese tried to overcome massive material problems by sheer ideological commitment and exertion.

Permanent revolution.   Easily the most radical form of Marxism, Maoism's principle of permanent revolution makes the development of a conservative status quo impossible. You will recall that both Marx and Lenin made vague references to the concept of permanent revolution and that Trotsky actually adopted it as a major theme. Mao, however, took the notion even beyond Trotsky's position. He argued that revolution was a means by which people achieved their goals. The road to socialism, he claimed, must be constantly punctuated with violence. This conflict, after all, is the essence of the dialectic. Great progress, born of turmoil and social disruption, is an inevitable fact of life.

The same holds for socialist relations with capitalist societies. There can never be true peace or a permanent accommodation with capitalism because the two systems directly contradict each other. Violent struggle between these two antagonistic systems is therefore unavoidable and can be interrupted only by brief periods of mutual restraint. Peaceful coexistence is a fantasy that can be pursued only at the risk of betraying the revolution itself.

The mass line. Like Tito, Mao feared above all that the Chinese Revolution might fall prey to deadly institutionalization and bureaucratic inertia. Mao placed his hopes in the revolutionary devotion of the masses. Combining his theories of populism, mind over matter, and permanent revolution, Mao rejected Lenin's elitist reliance on the party to lead the revolution. Mao maintained that the people are "intrinsically red" and that given the proper ideological direction, they can be trusted to strive for revolutionary goals. Accordingly, Mao invoked the slogan "red over expert" and he called for the mobilization of the masses again and again, thus visiting a series of sociopolitical thunderbolts on the land. The antilandlord campaign (1949–1952), the first Five-Year Plan (1953–1957), the Hundred Flowers Movement (1957), the Great Leap Forward (1958–1960), and the Great Cultural Revolution (1966–1976) were major events in which the people were mobilized to accomplish the goals of the revolution. Besides these epic movements, literally dozens of campaigns were initiated, and indeed are still being invoked, to reach desired goals: Anti-insect and rodent campaigns, anticorruption movements, sanitary campaigns, and tree planting campaigns are examples of the frequent phenomena of Chinese life which entreat citizens to produce more, conduct themselves properly, and stamp out hazards to health.

Mao's attitude toward the bourgeoisie. When the communists came to power in 1948–1949, the economy was in a sorry state, having been battered by almost four decades of revolution. Regardless of Marxist doctrine, Lenin's experience had taught that immediate socialization of an economy could be dangerous. Though merchants and industrialists were not numerous, Mao and his advisers knew that they were important to the economic stability of China, making their immediate elimination unwise. Hence, he decided that, at least for a time, some members of the bourgeois class had to be tolerated in China.

Such a rationalization for maintaining capitalism has implications far beyond a simple pragmatic accommodation. In Mao's theory of *nonantagonistic contradictions* China was seen to be made up of four harmonious classes: the proletariat, peasantry, the petty bourgeoisie (intellectuals, artisans, and managers), and the national bourgeoisie (patriotic merchants and business owners). These diverse classes could coexist in peace because, while different, their interests were not necessarily in conflict.

By contrast, the evil elements in the society were those that exploited the Chinese people: the landlords and the *imperialist capitalists* (capitalists with foreign ties). In this theory Mao took a stance that was typical of leaders of less developed states. The question of class differences, the feature of utmost importance to Marx, was played down, and foreign exploitation, or imperialism, was stressed. Imperialism is a major theme in Maoist thought, as in Lenin's, though their definitions differ. To combat the evils of imperialism, Mao, like Stalin, turned to nationalism. Never greatly appreciated, capitalists who showed loyalty to the Chinese state were tolerated, while those with foreign connections were considered the worst evils in China. This blatant contradiction of Marx is understandable when we remember that Mao is one of several Oriental theorists who imported Western political ideas, ideas that must always be justified by calls to drive the "foreign devils" from Chinese soil.

Guerrilla warfare. Perhaps the Maoist idea that is most widely applied today is the theory of guerrilla warfare. Both Marx and Lenin believed that power could be seized at a single stroke and that the violent portion of a Marxist revolution would be very short. The two differed only on tactics, Marx believing that the revolution would happen by itself, Lenin supporting a conspiratorial approach. Mao, by contrast, argued that revolutions in the less developed world would have to extend over a long period. Lacking a doctrine to justify such a revolution, Mao developed one himself, setting down its principles in his famous work *Yu Chi Chan* (Guerrilla Warfare). In this book Mao divides guerrilla warfare into two basic parts: *military* and *political.*

Mao saw the military part of a guerrilla war as having three distinct phases. During the first phase the soldiers concentrate on building secure bases, or *safe zones,* in which to rest, refit, and train their troops. A great effort is made at this point to befriend the local people, thus gaining supporters for the cause. The second phase involves numerous small groups attacking the enemy by means of ambush and other guerrilla activities. The final phase begins only after victory is certain and consists of large troop maneuvers and battles similar to those of a conventional war.

The military goal of a guerrilla war is very clear. "The first law of war," Mao wrote, "is to preserve ourselves and destroy the enemy." Mao clearly warns against seeing territorial gains as a major goal. The only real objective must be to destroy the fighting capacity of the opponent. With this in mind Mao also warned that a guerrilla force should carefully choose when it fights, avoiding any battle it is unsure of winning. The only territory essential to the guerrilla is the safe zones. No other territory is worth a fight. In a guerrilla war there may be no defensive battles. If any area is given up to a superior force, with patience and cunning it will be regained later. This strategy is most clearly expressed in Mao's famous dictum, "When guerrillas engage a stronger enemy, they withdraw when he advances; harass him when he stops; strike when he is weary, pursue him when he withdraws." Of greatest importance is the guerrillas' constant field position, from which they always put pressure on the enemy. Never destroyed, always there, the guerrillas give an appearance of invincibility, humiliating the enemy, who in the eyes of the people cannot defeat a ragtag band of jungle fighters.

More important to Mao than military operations are the political activities of the guerrilla force. His often-quoted statement "Political power comes out of the barrel of a gun" should not be taken too literally. Though he was a violent revolutionary, Mao understood the importance of nonviolent political power. A much more helpful quotation in this regard is "The most important victory is to win over the people."

Mao fully expected every soldier to do more teaching than fighting. The war would be won by convincing the peasants of the rightness of the cause rather than by defeating the enemy militarily. This emphasis on converting the people is in reality another expression of the peasant-centeredness of Mao's thought. His strategy, to "surround the cities with the countryside," had little to do with actually holding territory. Rather, it was based on a desire to win the support of the peasants, thus isolating the enemy in the cities and making its defeat inevitable.

Mao was very explicit about the methods that should be used in converting the peasants. First, the soldiers must set a good example. Mao therefore banned the use of opium in the army and insisted that the troops treat the local people with respect. He also commanded that officers live no better than their troops.

When a guerrilla unit first occupied an area, it was to gain the confidence of the peasants by helping them create local governments. This would weaken their political loyalty to the enemy. Moreover, local councils would serve as a base of local resistance if the area ever had to be left to the enemy. Next, the land was to be redistributed—taken from the landlords and given to the people who farmed it—thus giving the peasants an economic stake in the guerrilla cause. Also, the guerrilla soldiers would devote a good deal of time to rebuilding the villages in order to put the peasants on an equal and friendly footing with the soldiers as they shared their labor. During this process the guerrillas would constantly teach the peasants the goals of the revolution, pointing out its benefits and reminding them of the enemy's evil policies.

By such means, Mao believed, the guerrilla force would build an invincible base of support. As peasant support grew, supplies, recruits, and information about the enemy would increase, strengthening the guerrilla units. At the same time, the enemy would grow increasingly isolated and weak as the ring around the cities became tighter and tighter, eventually stifling the enemy's initiative and sapping its power. In time the pressure would become unendurable and would bring about the enemy's collapse.

Successful not only in China, Mao's ideas on guerrilla warfare were applied throughout the developing world. Adapting Mao's military ideas to Latin American conditions, Fidel Castro seized power in Cuba and developed a unique variant of Marxism.

CUBA

In many ways Cuba is unique among Marxist-Leninist states, while in other ways its experience was anticipated in other lands, especially in China. Shrouded in myth, the truth about Fidel Ruiz Castro (born in 1927) is hard to discover. His supporters present one set of arguments and beliefs about him, while his opponents contradict them on nearly every important point.

The Cuban Revolution

Castro, a well-educated man, began the practice of law in Havana and seemed to be on his way to becoming part of the small elite class that controlled most of the wealth in the country. However, his liberal tendencies were set in motion by the return to power of the grisly dictator Fulgencio Batista (1901–1973) after an eighteen-year absence. At the head of a tiny revolutionary group, Castro tried unsuccessfully to seize a military installation in 1953; he and his followers were easily captured and imprisoned.

Released from prison in 1955, Castro went into exile. In Mexico he trained a small group of revolutionaries to invade his homeland. In December 1956 he and his small party landed in Cuba and began to fight the government forces from a base in the Sierra Maestra Mountains. Castro began to build up a following among the peasants, to whom he promised reform and land redistribution. In time his partisans took an ever-greater toll on the ineffective Batista forces. Finally the government collapsed, and Batista fled, leaving the capital open to Castro's occupation in December 1959.

Unquestionably a leftist, Castro was almost certainly not a Marxist during his days in the mountains. Indeed, the Cuban Marxists ignored him until very late, coming to his side, along with almost every other antigovernment group, only after he had begun to succeed. Yet, Castro was influenced from the beginning by a few committed Marxists such as the Argentine revolutionary Che Guevara (1928–1967).

His conversion to Marxism-Leninism after coming to power makes Castro unique. Cuba is the only country to become communist as a result of a movement in which the revolution was not carried out by a cadre of dedicated party members. In fact, the party and its functions are still very limited in Cuba as compared with other communist states.

Whether Castro would have created a communist system on his own is, of course, impossible to say. Certainly, Cuba would have been a socialist state. However, the hostility of the United States government toward the Castro regime from 1959 to 1961 drove Cuba toward communism, forcing Castro to seek the protection of the Soviet Union and thereby wedding Cuba to the Soviet bloc and expanding Soviet interests into the Western Hemisphere.

Fidelismo

In 1961, after hesitating for two years, Castro proclaimed that he was indeed a Marxist-Leninist. Though many critics in the United States thought they had known this all along, Castro's hasty conversion was made obvious by the typical Marxist, but ill-conceived, policies of his government. Setting a goal of rapid industrialization, an almost impossible task for Cuba, the government met with one enormous disaster after another. With production falling drastically and early surpluses depleted, severe rationing became necessary. The situation was so desperate that the Soviet Union had to come to Cuba's rescue with hundreds of millions of dollars per year in aid. Today Cuba still depends on Soviet help, with the total bill amounting to about $5 billion annually.

Failing miserably in his attempt to transform Cuba into an industrial nation, Castro abruptly reversed himself, turning Cuba toward the goal of becoming a prosperous agricultural nation. In the mid-1960s he announced that by 1970 Cuba would produce ten million tons of sugar per year. This goal too proved impossible. Cuba's sugar production barely reached half the projected amount in 1970.

The 1970s witnessed the development of more modest and realistic economic goals. In recent years the Castro government has focused on developing its light industry, especially consumer goods and housing. While still in short supply, these commodities have increased considerably, thus improving the lives of the citizens.

Agricultural research and mechanization have increased the amount of meat, milk, and vegetables consumed, and fish has become an important part of the Cuban diet for the first time. Supported by the Soviets at more than four times the market price, sugar is not only being used for food, but it is also being converted into fuel and cattle feed.

Traditionally, the bulk of Soviet aid to Cuba has come in the form of buying sugar at higher-than-market prices and selling oil to Cuba at much less than the market price. Although no prospect of reducing the sugar subsidy is yet evident, Cuba's recent discovery of oil resources shows promise of making it self-sufficient in energy in the 1990s.

These advances have contributed to several achievements in social progress. The wretched poverty that plagued the vast majority of the peasants has been eliminated. Hunger is no longer a problem, though the unbalanced diet lacks protein and minerals. New construction has improved the still cramped housing conditions, especially in the countryside. The shoeless, ragged peasant dress of former times has been replaced with plain but adequate clothing. The once badly imbalanced distribution of wealth has been corrected with a fairly egalitarian system. Public health has been vastly improved. Increasing from 6 million people who were served by 6,000 doctors in private practice in 1959, the Cuban population, now at about 10 million people, is tended to by 20,000 doctors who dispense medical care and drugs free of charge. And the educational system is perhaps the most successful of all Castro's projects. Once widespread, illiteracy was eliminated in less than twenty years, and today a free education is provided to all.

While many of the most serious social and economic problems have been overcome, Cuba remains an underdeveloped country. Two important factors contribute to its limited progress. First, the planning mechanism employed by Cuban officials has been responsible for numerous egregious blunders. Unappreciative, or unaware, of modern accounting techniques, the people responsible for production schedules have made major errors. Unforeseen demand, pricing inequities, and hoarding of necessities have warped the economy so badly that there is sometimes little relationship between the plan and the reality. While many of the earlier mistakes have been corrected, Cuba still must rely on austerity programs that limit consumption of energy and food.

The second barrier to Cuban prosperity results from the policies of the United States government, policies that were redoubled by the Reagan administration. Since 1960 the United States has boycotted Cuba and has encouraged its trading partners to do the same. This policy has made it very difficult for Cuba to sell its goods outside the Eastern Bloc and to modernize its industrial plant. Additionally, the United States sponsored a "secret war" against Cuba. Saboteurs and terrorists supported by the United States have infiltrated Cuba, burning sugar fields and destroying machinery, to say nothing of repeatedly trying to assassinate Castro himself. Yet, the result of these policies seems to have stiffened Cuban resolve against the United States—anti-Yankeeism is indeed the hallmark of Fidelismo. American militance has also prompted the Castro government to militarize the society, denying Cuban people many human liberties, and it has driven Cuba to even greater reliance on the Soviet Union.

Similar to Mao in his ideological appeal, Castro campaigns vitriolically against imperialism, putting special emphasis on the "colossus of the north," namely, the

United States. In his radical early years he tried to ignite revolutions throughout Latin America by training revolutionaries and sending them to troubled Latin American countries. These moves failed, however, and Castro was rejected and isolated by his Latin American colleagues. The discovery of Soviet missiles on Cuban bases discredited him further in their eyes.

After the 1960s Castro increasingly portrayed himself as a leader of the "establishment" communist world. Far from being a placid leader, he has sent Cuban troops to aid some African countries. It is alleged that he is the source of Soviet arms flowing to Nicaragua, El Salvador, and Guatemala; and Castro continues to condemn Yankee imperialism vociferously. Yet, his demeanor is considerably less truculent than in early years.

Following a brief thaw in relations during the Carter administration, United States–Cuban relations cooled considerably. The Reagan administration assumed a stance reminiscent of the Eisenhower era, when the United States' attitude was so antagonistic that it drove Castro into the Soviet camp. Unfortunately, a similar posture toward the socialist Sandanistas of Nicaragua threatens the same reaction in Central America. Apparently, the lessons of 1959–1961 have not yet been learned by some of our national leaders.

Politically, the Cuban regime is unique among communist states in two related ways. First, because Castro became a Marxist-Leninist only after he had come to power, the Communist party was organized as an instrument of state control only after the revolution and has little identity besides that which it takes from Castro himself. Hence the party's grasp on the Cuban regime is tenuous at best. Although its members head the various public groups like the press, the trade unions, and the social services, the party seems not yet to have established itself as the legitimate organ of authority in Cuba. Accordingly, popular commitment to the party as the instrument of power is not keen.

Second, more than any other contemporary communist leader, Castro enjoys enormous personal power. Not unlike Lenin, Tito, and Mao, Castro is seen as the personification of a popular revolution. Similar to his predecessors, Castro has immense charisma that assures him of a great personal following.

These political circumstances offer both worrisome and happy prospects. Not having established its legitimacy beyond Castro's personal leadership, the Communist party may find it difficult to retain control, or at least to assure an ordered transfer of power, when Castro dies. It is true that Castro's brother, Raoul, is his chosen successor and that he and two other Castro family members hold seats on Cuba's fifteen-member Politburo. Yet, like the Communist party itself, Raoul Castro owes the largest measure of his power to his association with Fidel. It is not at all clear that Raoul or the party will be able to step into Fidel's shoes without considerable difficulty.

On the other hand, enjoying such deep and widespread personal popularity, Fidel is able to act more decisively than his colleagues in other communist states. Although he has often said that he prefers to consult the Politburo before taking action, it is clear that Castro is freer of the bureaucratic impediments with which Gorbachev or Deng must contend.

Over all, it must be said that the Cuban revolution has succeeded. The Castro government and its revolutionary goals enjoy wide popularity. Despite continuing economic problems, it has achieved important social progress for its people. At the same time, however, the regime is guilty of serious human rights violations, and it seems to have little interest in duplicating the reforms of Gorbachev or Deng. While Castro has recently allowed more open criticism of the social ills in his society and has initiated campaigns to improve efficiency and stamp out corruption, he stubbornly resists integrating market techniques and incentives into his economic system and the full scope of *glasnost* is unwelcome. In 1989, his government actually banned the circulation of two progressive Soviet publications (*Sputnik* and *Moscow News*) on grounds that they promoted a bourgeois way of life. Once viewed as the *enfant terrible* of the socialist world, Castro's current defense of orthodox socialist techniques makes him appear much more a stalwart of the "true faith."

RETREAT FROM LENINISM AND STALINISM

Some observers, viewing the transformations in China, the Soviet Union, and Eastern Europe, believe that Marxist socialism is in collapse. While Cuba, North Korea, and Albania continue to resist change, the astonishing events in Poland, Hungary, Yugoslavia, Czechoslovakia, Bulgaria, and Rumania have electrified the world. They have thrown off their orthodox regimes and, indeed, their reforms have been so profound and broad based that they now lead China and the Soviet Union in the pace of change.

Free elections among competing political parties and coalition governments are becoming the norm, while the civil liberties and market economic techniques are being introduced to ameliorate the repressive aspects of these formerly Stalinist systems. At the same time, the East–West axis upon which international relations has been based is beginning to lose its viability; NATO and the Warsaw Pact are each scrambling to adjust to a world in which peace seems to be breaking out all over. If current trends continue, the last decade of the twentieth century will be markedly different from any before it. The ideological divisions which have characterized our world are reduced and some people believe they are disintegrating completely.

But one should take care not to over-generalize the nature of the changes in the communist world. While the reforming societies have each rejected collectivism as the only method of production and adopted some market techniques instead, none has abandoned socialism as the foundation of its systems. True, China's radical egalitarianism is gone and planning has been deemphasized elsewhere, but none has moved away from state ownership of the major means of production, exchange, and distribution. Further, although private enterprise is being allowed at low levels, market incentives are being sanctioned to some extent, and even some relatively high-level joint ventures are being encouraged with foreign capitalist firms, no justification for these measures has been advanced except as methods to increase productivity. Each socialist society remains committed to free education, universal medical care, and an equitable distribution of the nation's wealth. Hence, while the reforming countries have clearly abandoned, at least for the time being, the goal of total socialist egalitarianism, the basic tenets of socialism are still firmly held.

It should be kept in mind that such recapitalization has been initiated before, in order to build productivity so that socialism could be pursued anew. The NEP is a case in point. Just as with Stalin's programs of the 1930s, any contemporary reform could be reversed by a new effort to achieve total egalitarianism. For the moment, however, the reforms seem more permanent. None of the reformers claim that the current changes are only temporary adjustments to garner the resources for a new round of socialization. Gorbachev, Deng, and the other reformers seem to be engaged in developing a new, more flexible, and more variegated definition of socialism—a socialism that allows a measure of private ownership and market incentive unacceptable to earlier Marxists.

In doing so, the reformers are finding it necessary to jettison some fundamental features of their past. Just as Khrushchev eliminated Stalin's governing technique— terrorism—Gorbachev is attacking Stalin's economic model—a highly centralized system that revolves around the all-important economic plan. Although he has voiced no intention of eliminating planning altogether, clearly the plan will be less central to the Soviet economy if he has his way.

Leninism, too, seems destined for change. No communist state currently insists that the world cannot accommodate the co-existence of socialist and capitalist societies. The foreign policies of both China and the Soviet Union lack their former truculence, and all communist states are reaching out to the West for economic cooperation. The Cold War, at least for the present, is indeed ended. Moreover, each of the reforming societies has lashed out at the corruption, inefficiency, and obstructionism of their bureaucracies; and, in each society, the Communist party heads the list of agencies which must be tamed. Hence, if these reforms are allowed to continue, the centrality of the party in communist societies will almost certainly be reduced and individual liberty will be increased. This is not to suggest that the parties will become unimportant in managing these societies, but that their powers will be reduced and their stultifying interference significantly stayed.

The communist world seems to be engaged in a major transformation motivated by its own perception that the mechanisms that created it are no longer adequate to sustain it. It has apparently begun to come to grips with its own failings, and it has also recognized that capitalism, while not the system it chooses for itself, has some features worthy of emulation and need not be obliterated in order to achieve worldwide peace. Socialism, as they have heretofore understood it, must be modified and redefined. But the most significant changes being made to date relate to the instruments of rule about which Marx was silent: those devised by Lenin and Stalin. Only time will tell how far these reforms will go, or if, indeed, they will be allowed to succeed. The strain of change is taking its toll in each of these societies and, so far, the most fundamental reforms—especially in the Soviet Union—have not resulted in the amount of improvement desired or needed to adequately address the crushing social and economic problems that confront these societies. The disruption caused by fundamental change, accompanied by its disappointing payoffs, portend political problems for the reformers and give their conservative adversaries a base of support from which to challenge the reforms and their advocates. Indeed, the prospects for Gorbachev's success, in particular, now appear dimmer than they did only a few years ago.

Communism has indeed presented a formidable challenge to Western democratic systems, yet its claims to support a purer, more refined, democratic order remain unrealized. The twentieth century has witnessed a second major challenge to Western democracy, this time from the reactionary side of the spectrum. Unlike radicalism, fascism and national socialism reject democracy altogether, advocating a political and social order based on elitism, war, and domination—reminiscent of former eras. How these retrogressive ideologies attracted such large followings is the subject of the next chapter.

SUGGESTION FOR FURTHER READING

BARADAT, LEON P., *Soviet Political Society,* 2nd. ed, Englewood Cliffs, NJ: Prentice-Hall, 1989.

BIALER, SEWERYN, *Stalin's Successors.* New York: Cambridge University Press, 1982.

COHEN, CARL, *Communism, Fascism and Democracy,* 2nd ed. New York: Random House, 1972.

COHEN, STEPHEN F., *Rethinking the Soviet Experience.* New York: Oxford University Press, 1985.

CRANKSHAW, EDWARD, *Krushchev: A Career.* New York: The Viking Press, 1966.

GORBACHEV, MIKHAIL S., *Perestroika.* New York: Harper & Row, 1987.

GRIFFITH, SAMUEL B., *Mao Tse-tung: On Guerrilla Warfare.* New York: Praeger, 1961.

GRIPP, RICHARD C., *The Political System of Communism.* New York: Harper & Row, 1973.

HINTON, HAROLD C., *An Introduction to Chinese Politics.* New York: Praeger, 1973.

INGERSOLL, DAVID E., *Communism, Fascism, and Democracy.* Columbus, OH: Charles E. Merrill, 1971.

NETTL, J. P., *The Soviet Achievement.* New York: Harcourt Brace Jovanovich, 1967.

LENIN, V. I., *State and Revolution.* New York: International Publishing, 1943.

MOODY, PETER R. Jr., *Chinese Politics After Mao.* New York: Oxford University Press, 1983.

SINGLETON, FRED, *Twentieth-Century Yugoslavia.* New York: Columbia University Press, 1976.

TOWNSEND, JAMES R., *Politics in China.* Boston: Little, Brown, 1974.

TROTSKY, LEON, *The Permanent Revolution,* trans. Max Shachtman. New York: Pioneer Publishers, 1931.

VON RAUCH, GEORG, *A History of Soviet Russia,* 6th ed. New York: Praeger, 1972.

10

Fascism and National Socialism

PREVIEW

The social stress created by rapid industrialization and urbanization in combination with the economic and political turmoil at the end of World War I caused the collapse of capitalism and the rejection of democracy in both Italy and Germany. The resulting political vacuum was filled by charlatans whose ideas constituted reactionary rejections of modern institutions and values. Men like Mussolini and Hitler called upon their people to forsake reason and prudence, to follow their leaders with unquestioned obedience toward mythical, irrational, and inevitably disastrous goals.

Forming totalitarian states—states in which individualism, human rights, and peace were viewed with disdain—the reactionary leaders built war machines and practiced imperialistic expansion, thus embroiling the world in the greatest human conflict yet experienced. The myths of the state or of the *volk* were used to mobilize people into a frenzy of bigotry, carnage, and genocide. The veracity of the myths were of little consequence, for they were used only as a means for motivation, not as a source of truth.

Under fascism and National Socialism, the shattered economies of Italy and Germany were revitalized and applied toward rejuvenating their military ranks, which had been humiliated during World War I. Once built anew, the martial institutions became the principal instruments of domestic control and of international conquest and imperialism, subjecting weaker states to the role of satellites, servants

Note: The drawing at the top of the page is of Adolph Hitler and Benito Mussolini.

220

of their political masters. The conquered people felt the whip of fascism and Nazism. They were impressed into slave labor for the good of the fatherland. Yet, even this bestial treatment was restrained as compared with the penalties meted out to those who were viewed as a threat to the new order. Leftists, lunatics, Gypsies, and Jews were systematically subjected to heinous medical experiments, sentenced to death in front of firing squads or in specially designed gas chambers, or simply left to die in the labor camps from brutality, overwork, starvation, and untreated diseases.

While some think these theories were left wing concepts, Mussolini's fascism and Hitler's National Socialism were actually reactionary in the sense that they rejected the values and aspirations that had developed in Western civilization over the millennia. In their place warrior states substituted practices that denied human dignity and justified unspeakable horrors. To make matters worse, these primitive impulses were exemplified by leaders who brooked no contradiction, no check. Their lethal policies were carried out with an unprecedented efficiency made possible by modern instruments of mass killing. Yet, reactionary extremism did not die in 1945 with Hitler and Mussolini. Indeed, American authorities and others actually protected some war criminals from prosecution and used them for their own purposes. Today, neo-Nazism is resurgent. The governments in Chile and South African countries openly practice these ideologies and Nazi and fascist movements are again rising in several countries around the world. Even the United States has witnessed a distressing rise in neo-Nazi activity in the 1980s.

THE FAILURE OF DEMOCRACY AND CAPITALISM

It has been said that the rise of fascism and Nazism occurred because liberal democracy and capitalism failed to meet the needs of the people in some industrial states. If democracy did fail, it obviously did not fail everywhere, nor was the failure fatal. Yet, the fact remains that millions of people found that democracy did not provide the policies and solutions so desperately needed in the troubled 1920s and 1930s. Accordingly, we must study these reactionary ideologies so we might come to a better understanding of their causes so that they can be avoided in the future.

The Development of Fascism and National Socialism

Though the historical and philosophical roots of fascism and Nazism can be traced back to ancient times, the conditions in which they finally emerged were created by two events: the Industrial Revolution and World War I (the Great War, as it was then called). The full impact of industrialization was first felt during the Great War. Warfare, once the business of kings and mercenary armies, was democratized as citizens were mobilized for a total war effort. Millions of people were marched to the front, armed with new weapons of unequaled killing capacity. Hideous slaughter ensued as each nation applied the full weight of its technology, energies, resources, and inventiveness to the war.

Expecting a short war, both sides were surprised to find that a stalemate had been reached. Their initial surprise evolved into disappointment and eventually into bitterness as the cruel reality of their situation became clear. Favoring the doctrine of attack (what the French called *élan*), generals carelessly hurled troops at defenders whose withering machine gun and artillery fire cut them down as they became entangled in barbed wire. Thinking that victory would go to the side that pressed the attack, but confronted with invincible defenses, military tacticians squandered human life in senseless battles such as Verdun, where hundreds of thousands fell.

The folly of the Great War was made all the more painful by its irony. Technology had created a plenty never before possible, promising to eliminate poverty, and yet the world's most advanced nations poured their resources into a European blood bath. Similarly, as technology made possible a new mobility that freed people from their provincial bonds, the civilized world found itself engaged in a horrifying stationary slaughter. While the world's youth was dying in the rat-infested trenches of France, large numbers of people came to the realization that science and technology, long considered the solution to all human problems, often created at least as many new problems as they solved.

These disillusioned people entered the 1920s confused and cynical about their previous beliefs, and the postwar world did nothing to restore their confidence. Though the war had marked the end of monarchy as an important political institution, replacing it with democracy, conditions in Europe seemed even more uncertain than they had been under the previous order. Though industrialization had greatly increased productivity, it also tended to centralize wealth. Economic instability increased: Inflation was made worse by unemployment, and personal security evaporated. Millions of people felt defenseless against forces they had never known before. Enticed from the farms to the cities by jobs that soon evaporated, they found

The trenches of World War I.

themselves trapped in situations they did not understand and from which they were powerless to free themselves. Turning to government for help, they found their disillusionment changed to despair as it became obvious that no assistance would be forthcoming from that quarter.

Equally confused by the chaos surrounding them, the parliamentary leaders also lacked solutions. Some leaders desperately tried to restore order and prosperity, while others simply looked for scapegoats. Regardless of their motives, they all became involved in endless debating, bickering, buck-passing, name-calling, and irresponsible procrastination. Popular faith in democracy collapsed as people lost confidence in themselves and in the concept of self-government. Many, having abandoned religion for the new god, science, had been encouraged to support democratic government as a result. Now, however, science was discredited, as was the idea of self-government, and it seemed to this confused and bitter generation that there was no truth left. Is it any wonder that many people put their last faith in the reactionary "flimflam men," men who promised everything to everyone, who simplified life's bewildering complexity by focusing all the blame on a single cause (such as another race or an opposing ideology)? Is it hard to understand why societies that had tried to find reasonable solutions and failed would willingly abandon thought and blindly attach themselves to people who claimed that they alone could find the truth? In an era when morality had been assaulted by war, poverty, national humiliation, and defeat—when rural values had been destroyed by urbanization—when people were so overwhelmed by the complexity of industrialized living that they began to question even their own worth, is it so unlikely that millions of people could become convinced that right and wrong were meaningless and that action was the only true value? Plausible or not, this is exactly what happened, and the world paid an enormous price for this mistake.

Mussolini

Italy, which suffered from almost all the conditions described above, was a prime candidate for fascism. A poor country, Italy joined the war in 1915, on the side of the Allies. But the strain of maintaining a total war effort was too great for this weak kingdom. Massive social and economic dislocation plagued the country, causing serious political problems.

The war's end found Italy in a desperate circumstance. Embarrassed by a poor military showing and by political weakness, the Italians demanded territorial concessions for their part in the war. After all, they had been on the winning side. When they were denied these expansionist claims, they felt betrayed by their allies.

As the veterans returned home, they found few jobs awaiting them, their meager benefits consumed by inflation, and their families displaced. Angry and disgruntled, they became increasingly hostile. With a wary eye on the Soviet Union, where the Bolsheviks were expropriating private property, and anxious about the veterans' discontent, wealthy industrialists and landowners began to fear that a Marxist revolution was brewing, especially since socialism was already popular with Italian labor.

Into this tumultuous situation stepped the unprincipled opportunist Benito Mussolini (1883–1945). Born the year Marx died, Mussolini overcame the terrible poverty of his childhood, obtained an education, and became a teacher. Throughout his early years he was distinguished by a driving ambition to become powerful and famous. Plunging into everything that interested him with total commitment, he was, at the same time, able to reverse himself completely, taking the opposite course if it suited his ambitions.

Drawn to leftist politics by his father's influence, Mussolini joined the Socialist party. He soon gravitated to the extreme left wing of the party and set out to become its leader. Since he was always able to convince himself of the rightness of his position, Mussolini's socialism was probably sincere enough until it became a political liability. He campaigned actively against militarism and condemned nationalism as a relic of a bygone era that should be replaced by internationalism.

Though a socialist, Mussolini consistently rejected egalitarianism as far as leadership was concerned. Heavily influenced by the works of the French philosopher Georges Sorel, Mussolini believed that great historical events were set in motion by the initiative and leadership of a small number of people. Although the masses were expected to progress to new historical eras, they could do so only if they were led by people who were more intelligent and daring than they. This elitism found him agreeing with Lenin's elitist revolutionary ideas during his socialist period. Even after he had abandoned the left, elitism remained a major principle of Mussolini's fascism.

Rising to the editorship of *Avanti*, a leading socialist newspaper, Mussolini used it to increase the popularity of his cause. Yet the elections of 1913, the year immediately preceding the beginning of World War I, denied the socialists a majority of parliament. Its disappointing showing in the elections contributed to Mussolini's growing suspicion that socialism was incapable of unifying his people. Further, since he was personally defeated, Mussolini came to regard elections as an absurd way to choose leadership. Accordingly, with the outbreak of World War I in August 1914 Mussolini carefully observed the political trends as they developed.

Following the traditional policy of the Second International, the Italian socialists campaigned heavily for Italian neutrality. Indeed, of all the national parties in Western Europe, the Italian socialists were perhaps the most loyal to the principle of internationalism. For his part Mussolini, in typical fashion, threw himself into the neutralist campaign with all his might, accusing any colleague who did not completely agree with him of betraying the cause. Although the government hesitated to enter the war, the popularity of this policy melted away as Italy was infected by the war fever that had swept through all of Europe by late August of 1914. Impressed by this change, Mussolini became alert to the potential power of nationalism. Finally, in October 1914, after only two months of war, Mussolini stunned his newspaper's readers by completely contradicting his previous stand and demanding that Italy enter the war. This reversal cost him the editorship of *Avanti* and his party membership.

Quickly finding wealthy interests that would support his newfound militarist and imperialist views, Mussolini organized a newspaper of his own. However, his new pursuits were cut short by the draft; he was severely wounded at the front and discharged upon his recovery in 1917. Still driven by the need to excel, Mussolini returned and became involved in the politics of the war.

A secret treaty bringing Italy into the war had promised it large concessions in what is now northern Yugoslavia, and Italian public opinion became outraged by the Allies' postwar refusal to honor these provisions. This confusion, together with the declining social, economic, and political situations, gave Mussolini the opportunity he desired. He founded a political party, the Fascist Party, offering something to everyone. Supporting an eight-hour day, elimination of class privileges, universal suffrage, and tax advantages, he hoped to attract veterans, labor, and the middle class. Yet, his new party failed to win a single seat in parliament in the 1919 elections.

Twice humiliated at the polls, *Il Duce,* as he was now being called, began to court those on the right side of the political spectrum, hoping that he could improve his strength through ample funding rather than by appealing to the unresponsive lower classes. By advocating laissez faire and opposing the rash of strikes that had swept the land, he drew increasing numbers of wealthy industrialists to his side. Though he publicly condemned anarchy, he used money from his new friends to outfit a gang of thugs who attacked other street gangs supporting republican or communist ideologies. These *Black Shirts* vandalized, terrorized, and bullied, occasionally taking control of municipal governments by force. Paralyzed by this violence, the government did little to combat the fascists. Often the police would either aid them in their fights against the leftists or refuse to interfere with their violent activities.

In the elections of 1921 the fascist fortunes improved slightly with the victory of thirty-five seats in the parliament. Still, this was far from a parliamentary majority. With his third defeat Mussolini began to openly belittle the electoral process. Claiming that the vote was too insignificant to legitimize power, he suggested that only force could put a true leader into power, and what the fascists lacked in votes they made up for in force. Thus, Mussolini began his move toward revolution, bragging that he would force the government to give him control.

A master of bluster and bluff, Mussolini laid his plans for the coup that would bring him to Rome. From Naples he demanded that the government be given to him, warning that he would seize it otherwise. Three days later, on October 27, 1922, his supporters were ordered to take over the local governments, communication and transportation centers, and other strategic points. At the same time, between 8,000 and 30,000 people (estimates vary widely) marched on Rome to demand a fascist government. The government finally decided to restore order by using the army, but King Victor Emmanuel, hoping to save his throne, refused to approve the order calling out the troops. Poorly organized and led, the fascists could easily have been stopped at this point. However, because a fainthearted king tried to preserve his obsolete crown, the fascists prevailed. Two days after the march began, Mussolini received an invitation from the king to form a government. Accordingly, *Il Duce* assumed power, though he later admitted that he had no plans at that point.

Lacking a specific program or even an ideology, he began to react to situations, adopting ideological principles afterwards to justify his policies. Hence, fascism was not created as a coherent, logical theory of government. It was, instead, a collection of rationalizations for policies adopted in reaction to various political problems as they arose. The motivation for these reactions was almost always to increase the personal power of the leader within the state. Almost never positive, the method used to increase the leader's power usually played on the fears and hatreds of the masses, focusing their attention on real or, more often, imagined evils in the society and encouraging them to vent their anxieties in cruel and ignoble ways.

Hitler

At the end of World War I Germany was in even worse shape than Italy. The defeated German government had accepted a harsh peace settlement. The Treaty of

Versailles had unjustly assigned Germany the total blame for the war. Consequently, Germany was forced to give up large amounts of territory to the victorious Allies, who also required ridiculously high reparation payments. Fearing a revival of German military power, the Allies also imposed severe limits on German armament.

The turmoil that followed on the heels of defeat plunged Germany into a five-year period of economic and political chaos. Unemployment reached a high mark and inflation was rampant. Treated as outcasts and bewildered by their economic plight, the German people began to turn to extreme political movements for solutions: The Nazi party was among them.

The moderate Weimar Republic found coping with the tumultuous social, economic, and political problems very difficult. By 1924, however, the situation temporarily improved. The reparation payments were reduced, German industry began to produce again, and prosperity followed. The bubble burst, however, when the Great Depression struck in 1929. Particularly hard hit because of its reparation payments, Germany soon found itself foundering once again amid political and economic chaos. This time the democracy did not survive and the state fell into the hands of an evil genius: Adolf Hitler (1889–1945).

The son of a minor customs official, Hitler had an undistinguished childhood during which he apparently developed an exaggerated sense of German nationalism. Wanting desperately to become an artist, he went to Vienna in 1906, where he remained for seven years, experiencing only rejection, poverty, and humiliation. Ignored by the city's leading art schools, Hitler was soon reduced to painting houses, hanging wallpaper, designing postcards, and taking charity to avoid starvation. During his Viennese period Hitler was influenced by the anti-Semitism that was widespread at the time.[1] An easy target for unreasoning hatred, Jews were blamed for every possible misfortune, and an international Jewish conspiracy was suspected of causing every economic or political problem. Though he would exploit Germanic anti-Semitism to advance his political ambitions, there is no convincing evidence that Hitler's hatred and suspicion of the Jews was merely a political tactic. On the contrary, in his last days he took comfort in the grisly realization that, though the Third Reich had failed, a "better, purer" Europe would evolve because he had exterminated 6 million Jews.

Leaving Vienna for Munich in 1913, Hitler welcomed World War I and joined the German army in 1914. Fighting with some distinction, he was severely wounded by poison gas, was decorated, and spent the last months of the war convalescing. Not having witnessed Germany's domestic turmoil or the collapse of the army at the front, Hitler readily joined the large number of people who claimed that the war was not actually lost, that Germany was instead betrayed by the "Jew-democrats."

In Munich at war's end, Hitler joined a tiny reactionary political party. Easily dominating the other six members, Hitler quickly became the leader of the organization, which called itself the National Socialist German Workers (Nazi) party. Appealing to the dissatisfied elements of Bavarian society, Hitler soon built a following and attracted some important military people to his cause. Seeing Mussolini rise to power

---

[1]Anti-Semitism appears to be a continuing sentiment in Austria in that Kurt Waldheim, former Secretary-General of the United Nations, was easily elected President of Austria in 1986 in spite of, or perhaps because of, serious charges that he was involved in the deportation of Jews to the death camps during World War II.

in Italy and the Weimar government at a low ebb, he attempted to seize the Munich government in 1923, planning to march from there to Berlin and bring down the Republic. Failing to get military support, Hitler's attempted coup, known as the "Beer Hall Putsch," was easily put down; it ended in his arrest, trial, and conviction.

Because he still had the sympathy of some powerful authorities, Hitler received only a five-year sentence, of which he served less than a year. He was given fairly comfortable quarters at Landsberg fortress and spent his imprisonment dictating his political ideology to his private secretary Rudolph Hess. This book, *Mein Kampf (My Struggle)*, stated the basic principles of Nazi ideology several years before Hitler came to power, and even before Mussolini had developed his own ideology completely. A rambling tirade full of irrational outbursts and torrential verbosity, it is nevertheless a reliable guide to the policies that extended over the next two decades. Unfortunately, few people took the book seriously, discounting it as the rantings of a malcontent ne'er-do-well. Yet, fantastic as it seemed at the time, we now know that Hitler not only meant what he wrote but he was able to make it happen.

When Hitler emerged from prison in 1924, he found the country on the road to economic recovery. The new prosperity quieted the political unrest, and the Nazi movement lost popularity. Undeterred, Hitler worked tirelessly to organize the party. Interest in extremist politics was renewed in 1929 as the nation sank into the depths of the Great Depression. Seizing the opportunity to exploit the discontent born of hard times, Hitler spoke out against the "treacherous Jewish democrats and communists." Passions flared on all sides; armed thugs were sent into the streets to do battle with each other. Hitler's force, patterned on Mussolini's Black Shirts, called itself the *Storm Troopers (SA)* or *Brown Shirts*.

Meanwhile the Nazi party, heavily financed by wealthy industrialists, made significant gains at the polls. In 1928 the Nazis held only seven seats in the 608-member Reichstag (the national legislature), but the elections of 1932 gave them 230 seats, the largest bloc of votes in that body. The centrist parties lost power as the communists and other leftist parties also gained larger numbers of seats. Political chaos continued, and governmental indecision became chronic as street violence increased. Finally, thinking they could control Hitler, the conservatives in the government persuaded President Paul von Hindenburg, a heroic general in World War I, to appoint the Nazi leader chancellor in 1933.

Badly underestimating their new chancellor, the conservatives were overwhelmed by Hitler's audacity. He outmaneuvered his rivals in a series of swift, decisive acts. Only a month before the elections in March 1933, the Reichstag building was destroyed in a fire set by the Nazis but which Hitler claimed was started by the communists. Whipping up a hysterical backlash among the people, the chancellor filled the German jails with leftist "traitors" to the Fatherland. His plan succeeded completely: The people flocked to the Nazi banner, giving Hitler a clear majority in the Reichstag.

After this move Hitler quickly consolidated his power. Statutes were passed outlawing opposition parties, strikes, and demonstrations. The Reichstag all but voted itself out of existence by giving legislative authority to Hitler's hand-picked cabinet. Von Hindenburg died the following year, and the *Führer* (leader), as Hitler's followers called him, assumed the office of president as well as chancellor and required all military personnel to take an oath of personal allegiance to him. Thus his power was complete. Adolph Hitler had become the totalitarian dictator of the Third Reich scarcely a decade following Mussolini's success in Italy.

FASCIST AND NAZI IDEOLOGY

Although Hitler developed his ideology in *Mein Kampf* before he came to power, whereas Mussolini developed his after taking control, neither theory was developed into a logical whole. Rather, their principles evolved from pragmatic responses to various issues the leaders faced, guided by a reactionary rejection of the most fundamental principles current in Western civilization: human dignity, the right to freedom, human equality, rationalism, objective truth, and the desirability of peace in human relationships.

National Socialism and fascism are, beyond question, closely related; indeed, they share such concepts as irrationalism, totalitarianism, elitism, militarism, and imperialism. Yet, they differ in several important respects. Due to their philosophical and intellectual traditions, the German people were prepared for a much more complete acceptance of reactionary irrationalism than the Italian people were. Italian fascism[2] employed the corporate state economy, a phenomenon which never fully developed in Germany. And perhaps most important, Hitler focused on racism, while Mussolini emphasized the more abstract theory of the state. Although in 1938 Mussolini belatedly tried to incorporate racism into his ideology in an effort to ingratiate himself with the Führer, it never really gained much importance among Italians.

Irrationalism

Fascism and National Socialism are considered reactionary ideologies because they reject the most fundamental contemporary features of Western civilization, harkening back to values that prevailed in former eras. Since the Enlightenment, as we have already learned, Western civilization has been based on the assumption that people are intelligent beings who can use reason to improve their lives. Indeed, reason is a major characteristic that distinguishes human beings from lower forms of life. The upshot of this emphasis on rationalism was the development of science and technology. Though science has brought us many advantages, perhaps its greatest benefit is the ability to determine objective truth. The scientific method has given us a way to discover the secrets of the universe and better understand the physical world, revealing facts that can be proved.

Fascism and National Socialism reject objective science and reason. Life is so complex and so unpredictable, they argue, that it cannot be understood by ordinary

---

[2]Besides Fascist Italy and Nazi Germany, various authorities have listed the following as fascist states: Japan during the 1930s and 1940s, Spain under Francisco Franco, Portugal under Antonio Salazar, Argentina under Juan Peron (1946–1955), Greece during the late 1960s, Uganda under Idi Amin, and, of course, Chile and South Africa today. Because fascism is a very unpopular term, such regimes do not openly claim to be fascist. For this reason, and because of the vagueness of the ideology itself, it is hard to say with certainty that all these states qualify as fascist regimes. Without question, however, these countries and several others, including Nationalist China, South Korea, and Paraguay, have shown fascist tendencies.

people. Objective truth is either a hoax or unimportant because the really important truths defy rational understanding, being random facts with no logical relationship to one another. Those who believe in reason, therefore, are deluding themselves and grasping at a false reality. Reason, Mussolini once said, is "barren intellectualism," lacking true meaning. The ordinary mind is not fertile; it is a wasteland full of mirages that give only an illusion of reality.

Truth is a subjective quality, available only to a few gifted people whose *will*, or spirit, or personality, is greater than that of the masses. Those with superior will perceive a higher truth than others. They instinctively realize the right, and those who are not so gifted should listen to them, having faith in their leaders' intuitions and following their orders. One should note, however, that not even the specially gifted people in the society realize truth through their intellect or through any other controllable ability. Instead, the source of the higher truth is instinct. The gifted ones simply *know* the truth, acting as neutral conveyers of the righteous energy, from its source to the society.

Selectively citing the theories of Plato, Rousseau, Hegel, and many other philosophers to justify his ideas, Mussolini turned to Georges Sorel (1847–1922) to support his notion of irrationalism. Sorel had developed a theory suggesting that myth (accepted ideas that cannot be proved or disproved) can be used with great political effect. It can unite and motivate the masses, turning millions of individuals into a single entity by giving them a belief to cling to and a goal to work toward.

It was Mussolini and Hitler, however, who used the myth to the greatest political advantage. Mussolini begged his audiences to have faith in the Italian myths, abandoning other loyalties for this higher reality. "We have created our myth," he shouted. "The myth is a faith, it is passion. It is not necessary that it be a reality. It is reality by the fact that it is a goal, a hope, a faith. . . ." Myth, therefore, though it could not be scientifically or objectively proved, was true simply because it existed and served a purpose.

The purpose of myth was to mobilize the masses and channel them into a course of action. Again relying on irrationalism for support, Mussolini argued that the goal of an action was really unimportant. Meaning came from the action itself rather than from its goal. Action, he said, is its own justification; the struggle is as important as the truth or myth that motivated the masses.

Hence, Mussolini admitted that the main goal of his movement was simply to stir the people up and set them on a course of action that might have no provable value. Contemptuous of intellectual conviction, he demanded emotional commitment. "Feel, don't think" was his command to his followers. Desiring only emotional responses, both he and Hitler used every available technique to ignite emotional outbursts in their followers.

Largely ignoring the written word, Mussolini and Hitler much preferred live speeches in which they could use their considerable rhetorical talents, never giving their audience time to think about the true meaning of their inflammatory words. Encouraged to let their emotions outstrip rational restraints, the crowds would be brought to a frenzy, crying, shouting, chanting, and applauding on cue. Such was the hysterical substance of two societies that tried to rule the world.

German mythology. Strong as irrationalism was in Italian fascism, long traditions of mythology and philosophy made it far more potent in Germany. Mythology, or folklore, has always played an important part in the German culture. Tales of the glorious Teutonic peoples have long been the subject matter of storybooks, serious drama, and family entertainment. The theme most often portrayed in German myth is that of the *volk* and its mystical powers. The concept of *volk* has no exact equivalent in English. More than just people or folk, *volk* refers to an inner quality or power residing in the German people. The *volkish essence* is a power possessed by the German people, yet one that goes beyond them as well. It is a spirit, an invincible, invisible force that is constantly engaged in struggle and conflict but emerges victorious after each battle.

Though the volkish essence is part of the German people, it can also be considered part of the German geography. In a mystical communion the people draw strength and courage from nature. Implying that the country is blessed with mysterious, inexplicable powers, German mythology gives particular attention to the deep forest. Mist, which obscures reality, is also a favorite source of power in these stories. Early mornings—crisp, fresh, quiet, still somewhat vague to the mind after a night's sleep—play an important part in these popular legends. Perhaps most vital of all, however, is the soil. Giver of life, mother of plenty, the soil has unmatched mystical properties that nourish and enliven the German people and their volkish essence.

These stories always portray a handsome Teutonic people facing seemingly impossible tasks and challenges. Yet, true to their warrior tradition, they rise to the occasion to do battle, always winning in one way or another. Against heavy odds the mythical Teutonic heroes (usually portrayed as blond and larger than life), fighting, struggling, slashing, and dominating, overcome all difficulties. The Teutonic warrior, heroic and courageous to the end, finds glory and victory even in death, when he crosses over to Valhalla on a blazing funeral pyre.

Mythology and reality thus were never completely separated in the German mind. When in the nineteenth century some philosophers and artists began to lionize mythological figures as *the* source of reality, many people were quick to take up the theme. The philosopher Friedrich von Schilling (1775–1854) managed to attract a following among the early German romanticists, including the famed author Goethe. Von Schilling argued that there was a direct relationship between people and their myths, that mythology unified people, actually creating a social and political unit out of otherwise separate and diverse persons. "A nation," Schilling wrote, "comes into existence with its mythology." Mythology was a "collective philosophy" that expressed the national ethic.

Richard Wagner (1813–1883), a master of the epic drama, gave myth added respectability when he brought it to life in his spectacular operas. Leading a group of artists and scholars in what amounted to a Teutonic fetish, Wagner established an intellectual community at Bayreuth that idealized the Germanic peoples by romanticizing their history and dramatizing their myths. Ancient heroes such as Brünhilde, Hegan, and Kriemhild were immortalized on the German operatic stage. Most important of all was Siegfried, the big, blond warrior who rose above mortal standards of right or wrong and triumphed in his effort to dominate. Hitler later became ecstatic when he heard Wagnerian music and made Siegfried the central hero of the Nazi state. Claiming that the Führer was actually the embodiment of the Teutonic essence and was destined to lead Germany to greatness, Hitler forged a link between himself and the ancient German myth.

Besides teaching the glory of struggle and the destiny of Germany to surpass all other nations, this flirtation with mythology encouraged a turn toward barbarism and a renunciation of Western civilization. Physical strength was prized, as was glorious death. In addition, the exaltation of Teutons or Aryans was soon turned into a justification for unbelievably brutal racism.

German irrationalist philosophy.   Unlike the Italians, who were forced to rely largely on foreigners for most of the philosophical basis of fascism, the Nazis drew from a rich store of irrationalist theory that had accumulated in Germany during the nineteenth century. This was not limited to mythology. A number of German thinkers began to seek explanations of life and nature in areas quite beyond the reach of human reason. However, it is important to note that many of these philosophers' theories were deliberately distorted by the Nazis to give an aura of philosophical respectability to their incredible beliefs.

Johann Fichte (1762–1814), like Georg Hegel, wanted to see the numerous German states unified; hence, both were early German nationalists. Fichte argued that the German people were destined for greatness. Led by a small elite, they would eventually dominate the globe because theirs was a superior race. They would establish a new and more perfect order in which the Germans would rule the lesser races while the leadership elite stood above ordinary morality, tolerating no opposition.

Heinrich von Treitschke (1834–1896), an otherwise obscure writer, was rescued from oblivion by Nazi theorists because his demented ideas suited their cause. Following Fichte's theme, he claimed that the Germans were a superior race. He also adopted Hegel's idea that the state was the platform on which the human drama, the dialectic of history, was played out. Yet, von Treitschke went far beyond Hegel, claiming that people were merely servants to the state and must obey the orders of their political superiors without hesitation. Thinking, he believed, was a futile waste of the ordinary person's time. The leaders supplied the thought while the lesser people simply followed directions.

Important as these three philosophers were to the Nazis, two others were even more central to Hitler's ideology. Arthur Schopenhauer (1788–1860), a contemporary of Hegel, was another irrationalist who rejected Hegel's idealism. To Schopenhauer life was not the unfolding of God's plan (and, therefore, rational and understandable); in fact, it was the reverse. Life was irrational and incomprehensible because it was the product of an uncontrollable impulse. Calling this mysterious energy the *will,* Schopenhauer argued that it was a blind, erratic, unpredictable force that manifested itself in the physical world but could not be analyzed rationally.

Beyond the reach of human reason, the will that produced all physical and intellectual reality made life meaningless. Finding no meaning or rational pattern in life, people were fools to try to resist the will. Any rational explanation of life was artificial, since the will is a senseless fury, a force with no justification. Since their source cannot be understood, the conditions of life cannot be improved by human effort. Life is only a meaningless struggle and resistance is pointless. Faced with such uncontrollable and incomprehensible power, people have no alternative but to submit and let the will have its way.

Most important of all philosophers to the Third Reich was Friedrich Nietzsche (1844–1900). Though he was neither a German chauvinist nor an anti-Semite, his theories were misinterpreted to serve the Nazi cause. Greatly influenced by both

Schopenhauer and Wagner, Nietzsche wrote about a race of supermen who would someday rule the earth. Nietzsche used the word *übermensch,* which may be translated as "over-man." By this he meant a race of people who were stronger and more righteous than the human beings of his generation.

Nietzsche argued that Schopenhauer was mistaken when he said that life was a meaningless struggle. The meaning of life was actually to be found in the struggle itself. Conflict purified humanity because it strengthened the survivors and destroyed the weak, parasitic members of the society. Rather than being a meaningless force, Schopenhauer's will was purposeful. It was a *will to power,* a force that stimulated people to fight and to dominate. Human domination, the will to power, therefore becomes the highest moral expression in life. Accordingly, any attempt to protect the weak or the helpless is immoral. Not surprisingly, Nietzsche found his society corrupted by schemes and plots to protect the weak and the unfit. Especially corrupt, in his mind, were Christianity and democracy. Christianity wrongly shielded the weak from their superiors; democracy favored mediocrity and penalized the excellent. Rather than freeing people, these two institutions created a slave morality. Consequently, Nietzsche proposed a "transvaluation" of societal norms. In place of the Christian values of peace, humility, charity, and compassion, Nietzsche demanded eternal struggle, arrogance, selfishness, and ruthlessness. Instead of the democratic virtues of equality, fairness, and happiness, he demanded an autocracy of strength, deceit, and pain. Anticipating the end of a world dominated by Christian values, Nietzsche defiantly proclaimed "God is dead."

Such a world, he believed, would produce a new race of supermen, "magnificent blond brutes" who would eventually replace the weaker human specimens common in his time. Admiring the Spartan life, Nietzsche argued that people should be hard on themselves as well as ruthless toward others. Pain should not be avoided but rather sought out because it toughened people and strengthened them for the battle. Power, Nietzsche said, was its own justification: "Might makes right." When those with the greatest will to power dominated all others, the most perfect possible existence would have been achieved.

Hitler's attraction to Nietzsche's belief that the strong should be free to dominate the weak became clear very early in his career. In 1926 he said,

> It is evident that the stronger has the right before God and the world to enforce his will. History shows that the right as such does not mean a thing, unless it is backed up by great power. If one does not have the power to enforce his right, that right alone will profit him absolutely nothing. The stronger have always been victorious. The whole of nature is a continuous struggle between strength and weakness, an eternal victory of the strong over the weak. All nature would be full of decay if it were otherwise.

He returned to this theme when he said,

> The fundamental motif through all the centuries has been the principle that force and power are the determining factors. All development is struggle. Only force rules. Force is the first law. A struggle has already taken place between original man and his primeval world. Only through struggle have states and the world become great. If one should ask whether this struggle is gruesome, then the only answer could be: For the weak, yes, for humanity as a whole, no.
>
> World history proves that in the struggle between nations, that race has always won out whose drive for self-preservation was the more pronounced, the stronger. . . . Unfor-

tunately, the contemporary world stresses internationalism instead of the innate values of race, democracy and the majority instead of the worth of the great leader. Instead of everlasting struggle the world preaches cowardly pacifism, and everlasting peace. These three things, considered in the light of their ultimate consequences, are the causes of the downfall of all humanity. The practical result of conciliation among nations is the renunciation of a people's own strength and their voluntary enslavement.

Racism

Although racism is not an important factor in fascism, nothing is more central to Nazism. Hence, we should study the Nazi ideas about race at this point, since so much of the ideology is based on it.

Anti-Semitism stretches far back into German history, but it was no more virulent in Germany than in France, Russia, Spain, and most other European countries before the twentieth century. It is true that German myth and philosophy had long stressed the virtues of Germanic peoples as compared with other groups. Yet, this history of ethnocentrism was not the source of Nazi anti-Semitism. Strange as it may seem, Hitler based his racial theories on the works of a Frenchman and an Englishman. In the nineteenth century the study of linguistics and anthropology had revealed that the languages of many people in Europe and central Asia were related. Though the evidence at the time was sparse, scientists assumed that these related languages had a common origin, and many scholars began referring to the yet undiscovered original people as *Aryans*. These discoveries sparked several theories about the histories of the various peoples in Europe. One of the strangest of all was developed by a French count, Arthur de Gobineau (1816–1882). This intelligent nobleman, who had served as secretary to the brilliant social observer Alexis de Tocqueville, was eventually sent to Germany as a diplomat. Greatly influenced by the German people, Gobineau developed a theory of racial superiority that was to have a profound impact on German history.

Basically, Gobineau argued that the Aryans had been a nomadic people superior to all other races. At various times the Aryans had imposed their will on inferior peoples and had established new civilizations. Unfortunately, the Aryans tended to intermarry with the inferior races, causing the decline of each of these civilizations as their purity became corrupted.

Though the Aryans, blond and blue eyed, had at one time wandered from the north across Europe and Central Asia, by the nineteenth century miscegenation had caused most of their descendants to lose their superiority. Indeed, there was only one area left in which the Aryan blood was pure enough to offer hope for a revival of human civilization. Extending across northwestern Europe, Gobineau's Aryan heaven included Ireland, England, Northern France, the Benelux countries, and Scandinavia. Yet, the purest race of all, Gobineau said, was the German people. Though none of the remaining Aryans could claim to have no trace of inferior blood, the German people were the least mixed racially. This genetic purity gave them an advantage over all other people in fostering the next advanced civilization. This would be possible, however, only if the Germans and other Aryan peoples protected their racial purity against further miscegenation. Not surprisingly, these ideas were ignored throughout most of Europe but they became very popular in Germany.

Among the Germans who were deeply affected by these theories was the great composer Richard Wagner. Wagner's importance in popularizing and dramatizing

German myth has already been mentioned, but his contribution to Nazi ideology is far more significant. In Wagner, three of the major foundations of Nazi ideology—mythology, irrationalism, and racism—are brought together. Wagner had known and admired Schopenhauer and had been briefly associated with Nietzsche. In addition, the German composer had met Gobineau and been deeply influenced by his ideas. Under Wagner's leadership the artistic and intellectual colony at Bayreuth became the center of German irrationalism and racism: The site was made a national shrine when Hitler came to power.

The Bayreuth ethic was carried into the next generation by a Germanized Englishman, Houston Stewart Chamberlain (1855–1927). The son of a British admiral and a nephew of the British prime minister, Neville Chamberlain, this troubled intellectual was attracted to Bayreuth and attached himself to the Wagner household. He became an ardent supporter of Wagner and in 1908, years after Wagner's death, Chamberlain married his daughter Eva.

Chamberlain combined Teutonic mythology, German philosophical irrationalism, and Gobineau's racial theories, achieving on paper what Wagner had tried to accomplish musically. He argued that the Aryan race had created all the world's civilizations, but that each of these advances had been lost as a result of the impurity produced by interbreeding. Chamberlain believed that all races were impure and mixed except the Germans, who were Aryan and good, and the Jews, who were completely evil. History was simply a struggle between the Aryan good and the Jewish evil.

With this "truth" established, the road to the salvation of humanity became obvious. The German people must protect and increase their racial purity and avoid interbreeding with Jews at all costs. This purification, he suggested, would be accomplished when a great leader emerged among the Germans to show them the way. Having set out on a course of deliberate racial purification, the German Aryans would prove their superiority by conquering the world.

These ideas were an instant success in Germany. Kaiser Wilhelm II became an enthusiastic admirer of Chamberlain, and the two men were soon close friends. During World War I Chamberlain supported the German war effort in the hope that it would lead to the Teutonic conquest of the world. After Germany's defeat Chamberlain's fortunes declined, but his belief that a leader would arise to guide a racially pure Germany to world domination never dimmed. So it was that in 1923, when Adolf Hitler was still an obscure politician, Chamberlain recognized Hitler's destiny and predicted that Germany would soon find its true master. Thus, the tradition begun in prehistory was passed through Gobineau, Wagner, and Chamberlain, and was finally adopted by Hitler as the basis of his political theory.

This long tradition of Teutonic superiority, expressed in German mythology, irrationalism, and racism, combined with the hardship and humiliation of the interwar era, made Germany an easy prey for the Nazi movement, and Germanic racism became the centerpiece of Hitler's regime. Following Chamberlain's theories closely, Hitler claimed that history was simply a struggle for domination among the various races in the world. The villain in this drama was the Jew. Hitler used the Jews to his own political advantage, blaming all of Germany's problems on them. His hatred and contempt for the Jews is frightening. "The Jew," he said,

... is a maggot in a rotting corpse; he is a plague worse than the Black Death of former times; a germ carrier of the worst sort; mankind's eternal germ of disunion; the drone which insinuates its way into the rest of mankind; the spider that slowly sucks people's blood out of its' pores; . . . the typical parasite; a sponger who like a harmful bacillus, continues to spread; the eternal bloodsucker; . . . the people's vampire.

Hitler divided the people of the world into three racial categories. The *culture-creating* race was of course the Aryans. This group included the English, Dutch, and Scandinavians, but these peoples were less pure than, and hence inferior to, the German people. These Aryan people, he claimed, were responsible for creating every civilization in the history of the world. Specifically, he argued that the civilizations of India, Persia, Egypt, Greece, and Rome were Aryan creations. Since all cultural achievements were supposedly the products of Aryan peoples, and since Hitler believed that the Germans were the purest Aryans, he saw them as the only hope for humanity. "Man," he said, "owes everything that is of any importance to the principle of struggle and to one race which has carried itself forward successfully. Take away the Nordic Germans and nothing remains but the dance of apes."

Below the Aryans were the *culture-bearing* races such as the Orientals, Latins, and Slavs. These peoples were racially inferior; they could not spawn a new culture, but they could maintain a civilization as long as they did not allow their blood to be corrupted by inbreeding with the lower forms of humanity. The last group, the *culture-destroying* races, included Gypsies, Negroes, and Jews. Because of their destructive tendencies these people were thought to be subhuman. They alone were responsible for the decline of the great civilizations.

Race, the dominant feature of national socialist ideology, was used to explain all aspects of the society. The *volk,* cradled in the German soil, was united in a common destiny: to win the struggle against the evils of the world. Because the Aryan blood was the strongest, the impurities among the German people could be eliminated by strictly avoiding miscegenation. A nation of supermen—of Siegfrieds, if you will—could be created by breeding racially pure people, thus producing Nietzsche's "magnificent blond brutes."

Everything must bend to the imperative of racial superiority. The inferior people of the world must be made to understand and accept their subordination to the master race. If they resist, they must be crushed and forced to comply, for such is the destiny of the world. "Jewish institutions" such as communism and democracy must be destroyed because they protect the weak and thus encourage decay. Objective science also fell victim to racism. "We think with our blood" was the proud, irrationalist slogan of the Third Reich. Hitler and his colleagues rejected any knowledge that did not prove Teutonic racial superiority. "Science," he said, "like every other human product, is racial and conditioned by blood." Accordingly, a new German culture— art, biology, architecture, anthropology, history, genetics, and religion—sprang up, all based on Germanic strength and superiority. Even food raised on German soil was considered superior in taste and nutrition. If others failed to recognize the truth of German supremacy, it was because non-Germans did not have the superior understanding of the world enjoyed by Teutonic peoples.

Much of this would be laughable if German racism had not been taken to other, more pathological, extremes. Racial purity was used as an excuse for sterilizing thousands of people who were mentally or physically lame. Ghastly experiments were performed on "subhuman" people to satisfy morbid Nazi "scientific" curiosity. Millions were marched into forced labor and often were literally worked to death, while others were executed for political and racial crimes. Most horrifying of all, 9 million people, two-thirds of them Jews, were systematically murdered in the extermination camps that dotted the landscape of Hitler's empire. The stench of rotting flesh and burning bodies filled the air as Hitler pursued his "final solution" to the Jewish question.

Totalitarianism

A totalitarian state is a dictatorship in which the political leaders control every institution in the society and use them for political purposes as well as for the functions for which they are ostensibly designed. Hence, a totalitarian dictator dominates not only the government and political parties, but also the labor unions, churches, media, education, social institutions, and cultural and artistic displays. All aspects of society controlled by the state are used as mechanisms of political manipulation.

The term "totalitarianism" was first coined by Mussolini, and he also developed most completely the philosophical justification for it. Even so, his inability to subject the Catholic Church to his will—he was only able to force the church into an uneasy stalemate with his regime—prevented him from exercising totalitarian power in Italy. On the other hand, Hitler was able to do in practice what Mussolini could complete only in theory.

Theory of the state.   Although Mussolini failed to create a completely totalitarian state, he cannot be accused of failing to try. To justify the accumulation of such a huge amount of power in the hands of the state, Mussolini turned again to the German philosopher Georg Hegel. As we have seen, Hegel believed that history was the unfolding of God's plan. The nation-state was the stage on which God's plan was enacted. As the vehicle of God's will, the state had uncommon value, and its people should dedicate themselves to it. The people in the state, also part of God's plan, must take their identity from the state. Like Rousseau and Hobbes, Hegel argued that people derive meaning only through service to the state and that they become free only when they become subject to it. Yet, Hegel did not propose a totalitarian state. Instead, he believed that there were many human pursuits that were not political and that, while people should dedicate themselves to the state in political matters, the state should not interfere in nonpolitical affairs.

Selecting the parts of this theory that suited him and ignoring the rest, Mussolini transformed it into what is today called *statism*. The state had mystical properties; it was at the center of life, with incomparable purpose and meaning. Speaking to a Catholic society, Mussolini used a vocabulary with which they could easily identify. Only the state gave human beings their identity, he claimed, and only through it could they reach the "higher life," a condition he never specifically described.

Making use of the *organic theory of the state,* Mussolini argued that although the state was made up of individuals, it took on an importance that was much greater than the total of its individual parts. As the cells of the body each contribute to a life far greater than their own, so too the state becomes a living being with an importance far beyond that of its individual members. Just as each individual has a personality and a will, the state draws from each, developing a personality and a will of its own. Having the greater will, the state rightfully dominates the individuals within it. The *will of the state* has such power over the society that it actually becomes the measure of all value, virtue, and wisdom. It is the "will of wills," the "good of goods," and the "soul of souls."

Faced with such horrendous power, the individual would be foolish to resist the will of the state. People must conform completely if they are to fulfill themselves. The state can make any demand, give any order, require any sacrifice, and the individual must obey. The power of the state is total, and the loyalty and commitment of the individual must be total. As Mussolini put it, "Everything for the state; nothing against the state; nothing outside the state."

Being the "creator of right" and the "good of goods," the state can tolerate no resistance. Conceiving of a society in which all people had functions—some great, some modest—Mussolini believed that each person must perform the maximum service to the state, no more and no less. Those who did not meet their obligations were of little value to the society and could be removed. Such total subordination of people and human rights to a nonhuman institution flies in the face of the advances of humanity over the past several hundred years and is another reason for fascism's reputation as a reactionary ideology. Yet, the reward for compliance with the will of the state was great indeed. The "higher life" offered the purest, most "heroic" existence possible, even promising immortality in an indirect way. "The State," Mussolini wrote, "is not only present, it is also past, and above all future."

Unlike fascism, Nazi ideology gave the state only secondary importance. It was not seen as the central object in Germany; rather racial purity was most important. The state was only the arena in which the race built its strength and identified its leadership. In foreign affairs the state was the vehicle through which the superior race governed its inferiors. In short, states were jurisdictions into which various races were divided, but the races were of prime importance, not the states.

As in the case of Mussolini, the combination of absolute power with modern technology produced a totalitarian state. True to form, however, Hitler was able to carry the totalitarian concept to a far greater extreme than Mussolini. Structurally, the Nazi government was very similar to the Italian regime. The traditional German state (that is, provincial) governments of Saarland and Bavaria, for example, were dissolved, and power was centralized in Berlin. At the same time, the Reichstag gave up its legislative power to the cabinet, which was headed by the Führer himself. The laws and courts were politicized, along with the military and the civil police. The Gestapo, a secret police force, established a reign of terror that has rarely been equaled.

In addition to these governmental institutions, Hitler mounted the most extensive propaganda campaign in the history of the world. With the expert help of his propaganda minister Joseph Goebbels, Hitler converted every possible medium into a political tool. He used every available technique to get his message across. He destroyed all books and films that opposed his views; he politicized every textbook, newspaper, magazine, novel, movie, radio program, and musical score. Manipulating all the information that reached the people, he followed the formula he had set forth in *Mein Kampf:* Keep the message simple, with little or no regard to its veracity, and repeat it again and again. A master showman, he manipulated people through extravagant, carefully orchestrated mass rallies, using symbols, insignia, regalia, color, emotional outbursts, and patriotic passion to induce mass hypnosis or collective hysteria. Thus, he spurred the German people to levels of barbarity and fanaticism seldom, if ever, matched in modern times.

Elitism

Again referring to Hegel, who argued that people are not equal and that the leaders of society are its heroes and therefore not subject to ordinary moral restraints, Mussolini and Hitler developed theories of *elitism*. People, they argued, are quite obviously unequal: Some are more intelligent, some are stronger, some are more talented, some are more attractive. To act as though people are equal is to ignore the obvious and to fatally deny a basic fact of nature.

Although people vary greatly, they all have an obligation to perform: to serve the state in Italy or the *volk* in Germany. Yet, being unequal, they cannot each make the same level of contributions—some are able to contribute more and some less—and citizens cannot rightfully expect to be rewarded equally for unequal contributions. Therefore, those who give the greatest service deserve the greatest benefit.

Both Mussolini and Hitler envisioned a highly stratified society with each person making his or her maximum contribution. As we have already learned, those who failed to fulfill their potential would be done away with. By the same token, if all did what they were best suited for, the best possible society would result. If, for example, the most able carpenters were allowed to build and the most talented bankers could bank and the most gifted teachers were assigned to the classroom, the society would profit from the best possible construction, finance, and education.

The same logic was applied to society's most important endeavor: government. Rejecting democracy as a sham founded on the false premise of human equality, Mussolini and Hitler were contemptuous of the masses—each calling the people "the herd." Political power must be left to the elite in society if it is to enjoy excellent government. Democracy, it was suggested, reduced government to the lowest common denominator.

Obviously referring to the Fascist Party, Mussolini suggested that in the ideal system the best citizens would emerge. They would be the people most in tune with the will of the state. Relying on racism, Hitler suggested the same dynamic, except that the German elite would be those who enjoyed the greatest amount of the *volkish* essence.

And, they declared, just as there are some people in society who are better than others, so too there is a single person who is qualified above all, and that person should be given total deference as the infallible leader. Truly good people in society would easily recognize their betters and defer to them without qualm.

Il Duce and the *Führer* were endowed with innate power: It could not be acquired. Their claim to power rested in their intuitive, unreasoned oneness with the will of the state or the will of the *volk*. It was not something which could be controlled; it simply existed. Mussolini said that the leader is "the living sum of untold souls striving for the same goal''; he is the embodiment of the state itself. And the Nazi philosopher Ernst Hubber said, "the Führer is no 'representative' of a particular group whose wishes he must carry out. He is no 'organ' of the state in the sense of a mere executive agent. He is rather himself the bearer of the collective will of the *volk*. In his will the will of the *volk* is realized. He transforms the mere feelings of the *volk* into a conscious will."

Thus the leader was to receive total obedience. The people were not to question the leader's commands since his (it was assumed the leader would be male) will is actually that of the society itself. To underscore the point, Italian school children began each day with the assertion "Mussolini is always right!"

The Corporate State

Fascist totalitarianism and elitism manifest themselves economically in the *corporate state*. Though Mussolini announced it as a unique economic system, the corporate state was actually borrowed from other idea systems. Again drawing on the theories of Georges Sorel, Mussolini used syndicalism as the basic structure of his economic system. Actually a radical who would certainly have rejected fascism, Sorel was the foremost philosopher of syndicalism, which would restructure society around giant trade unions. Sorel's movement was basically democratic because he expected that the syndicates would be popularly governed. You will recall that Pierre Joseph Proudhon also advocated syndicalism.

Mussolini stood this concept on its head, reversing the power flow. Instead of the people running the government through the syndicates, Mussolini intended that the government would control the people through the trade unions. The corporate state was based on a foundation of worker and owner syndicates. Strikes and boycotts being illegal, the syndicates were supposed to settle disputes between management and labor. By the same token, prices, profit margins, production standards, and the like were set by the state, leaving very few important decisions to the owners. In fact, though the Italian economy was privately owned, it was actually completely controlled by the state. Membership in the syndicates was technically voluntary, but everyone had to pay dues, and all were bound by the agreements they reached.

The local syndicates were brought together in regional federations, which, in turn, were organized at the national level. Every industry, syndicate, and regional federation was attached to one of twenty-two "corporations." Actually official agencies of the government rather than private firms, the Italian corporations governed the industries, owners, and workers in the economy. The heads of the corporations were members of the National Council of Corporations, by which the economy was centrally controlled and directed. The members of the National Council of Corporations automatically became members of the Chamber of Fasces and Corporations, Italy's highest governing body, which was, of course, headed by *Il Duce* himself. To be assured of absolute obedience at every level, the state appointed the heads of all the corporations, regional federations, and syndicates. Through this process Rome directly controlled the economy.

Besides serving as a tool for directing the economy, the corporate state was the primary means by which the state controlled its citizens. Through this mechanism almost every aspect of daily existence was controlled. Jobs, wages, fringe benefits, social programs, housing, retail goods, recreation, entertainment, and education were all part of this elaborate organization.

The corporate state was also the only vehicle for "valid" popular political comment. Convinced that general policy is too complex a matter for ordinary people, fascists discouraged popular comment on most political affairs. Maintaining that people are suited by nature to different status levels in life and are not qualified to hold valid political opinions on all subjects, fascism limited individuals' political comments to areas in which they had occupational interests. Consequently, farmers were supposed to make formal political statements only in relation to agricultural policy, while carpenters could discuss political questions only in relation to the construction industry, and steelworkers could speak out only on issues directly connected with their occupation. Only the elite, or the party members, were qualified to comment on general political questions, and even they were limited by their party rank. At any rate, the question of popular political activities is an academic one, since the people were seldom given a real opportunity to express their views on political questions.

By these means the state controlled and regulated almost every conceivable social, economic, and political activity of its citizens. This made it relatively easy for the government to reward supporters and punish dissidents. Along with the party and the police, the corporate state was Mussolini's principal mechanism for creating and maintaining control.

Unlike the Italians, the Germans did not establish a corporate state, though there was considerable talk about doing so in the early days of the regime. The economy was tightly controlled by three super agencies. Industrial production was managed by the Estate of Industry and Trade, and the agricultural sector was controlled by the German Food Estate. As in Italy, strikes and boycotts were made illegal and the trade unions were dissolved. In their place Hitler created the Labor Front, a federation of worker and professional associations. Through these mechanisms all economic functions were manipulated by the state.

Imperialism

As we have seen, Mussolini and Hitler viewed society in terms of conflict. Good combatted evil, strength fought weakness. Just as people within society vied with each other for power, so too should nations compete with each other for dominance, until the strongest national will reigned supreme. Mussolini, in an ethnocentric fury, claimed that just as people within society were not equal, states and their wills were not equal, and justice demanded that the most powerful will of the state should achieve supremacy. Applying his racist theories, Hitler concluded the same. Since the German *volk* enjoyed the purist blood, they had the right to impose their will on all lessor races. To shirk this responsibility would be to deny destiny, rejecting rightful heritage, and thus betraying the natural order of things.

Imperialism (one nation dominating others) became the paramount mission for both societies. Exerting power over others within a society is a vital function of those who are best able to rule; imperialism is simply an extension of this principle to a higher, more important level of human relationship. Imperialism, Mussolini claimed, is the most advanced form of this natural regulator, which he called "the will to power." "The highest expression of human power," he said, "is Empire."

Arguing that the "higher life" is possible only when the greatest will dominates all lesser personalities, Mussolini gave imperialism a moral justification. In *The Doctrine of Fascism,* written in 1932, he said "For Fascism the tendency to empire, that is to say, to the expansion of nations, is a manifestation of vitality; its opposite, staying at home, is a sign of decadence: people who rise or re-rise are imperialist, peoples who die are renunciatory."

As one might expect, Mussolini saw Italy as an imperialist state. Once great, Italy was regaining its status as a great power. Accordingly, Mussolini assigned it the task of recreating the Roman Empire. This goal became the national myth, stimulating the Italian nation to action. The absurdity of equating modern Italy with ancient Rome was ignored, since as we have already seen, fascists consider the veracity of a myth unimportant; its value is in spurring people to activity.

Hitler's justification of imperialism was basically the same as Mussolini's except that the Nazi dictator substituted the will of the *volk* for the will of the state. Believing that the strong must dominate the weak in an ongoing process of Social Darwinism, Hitler lusted for territorial acquisition. Sending out an ominous warning of this suicidal tendency in 1929, Hitler said,

> If men wish to live, then they are forced to kill others. . . . As long as there are peoples on this earth, there will be nations against nations and they will be forced to protect their vital rights in the same way as the individual is forced to protect his rights. . . . There is in reality no distinction between peace and war. . . . One is either the hammer or the anvil. We confess that it is our purpose to prepare the German people again for the role of the hammer.

Thus, each expansionist dictator threw his war machine against his weak adversaries even as Britain, France, and the United States appeased them in an effort to placate the aggressive titans. Italian armies were sent to conquer Abyssinia (Ethiopia), Albania, and Greece, while Hitler's *blitzkrieg* (lightning war) was hurled against Poland, and *fifth column* (collaborationist) reactionary movements seemed to rise everywhere. Finally, France and England resolved to allow no more aggression, and World War II began in 1939.

Militarism

The tool of fascist and Nazi imperialism is of course militarism. Yet, according to these ideologies, war is actually much more than simply a means of asserting the national will: War is the prime goal. Rather than something to be used only as a last resort, war is a spiritually creative and positive feature of life. It should occur often and should never be avoided merely to achieve peace. A particular war is ended when the superior national will has dominated its adversaries. Peace is not a positive condition but rather an interlude between national struggles for imperial dominance. Indeed, permanent peace is equated with cowardice and is not to be tolerated because it robs society of its vitality. "Fascism," Mussolini wrote,

> believes neither in the possibility nor the utility of perpetual peace. It thus repudiates the doctrine of Pacifism—born of a renunciation of the struggle and an act of cowardice in the face of sacrifice. *War alone brings up to its highest tension all human energy and puts the stamp of nobility upon the people who have the courage to meet it* (emphasis added).

For Hitler's part, he chose to express the same sentiment with the racist attitudes of von Treitschke. War, von Treitschke believed, was good in itself because states, like people, were driven to dominate each other and warfare was the process by which national domination was achieved. Hence, war was a normal condition of human life. "That war should ever be banished from the world," von Treitschke wrote, "is not only absurd, but profoundly immoral." Permanent peace, he argued, would be a crime, and societies that wanted peace were obviously decaying. The entire society was therefore channeled into preparation for war. Every possible pursuit, be it school, work, pleasure, or whatever, served a martial purpose.

Struggle, conflict, fight, discipline, courage, obedience, the holiness of heroism are among the terms that occur often in fascist literature. Dueling, swordsmanship, pistolry, riding, uniforms, weapons, discipline, and other martial trappings were valued. Masculinity and virility were prized, women being confined to the kitchen and domestic duties. "War," Mussolini said, "is the most important thing in a man's life as maternity is in a woman's."

Fascism's and national socialism's attempt to create *warrior states* is another characteristic that makes them reactionary ideologies. Denying the value of peaceful and friendly human relationships amounts to favoring a return to an ancient era during which those who were physically strong dominated everyone else and people were judged and ranked by their ability to fight. Accordingly, purposeless activities and emotional causes become the goals of such a society, while values such as human refinement, culture, peace, equality, and brotherhood are rejected.

Despite all the rhetoric and emotionalism of these assertions, perhaps the essence of fascism and national socialism was captured in the fascist slogan "Believe, Obey, Fight!" Nothing better expresses the irrationalism, elitism, militarism, or contempt for the masses so prominent in these ideologies. This simple phrase says it all. It demands blind faith rather than intelligent commitment, it insists that people follow the orders of their superiors without hesitation, and it pits people against each other for no other reason than love of struggle itself.

Romantic, emotional, and violent creeds based on a militant rejection of the modern rational and scientific world, these reactionary movements offer little save the perverted sense of glory derived from annihilation and carnage. In a sentence which surely would have enjoyed Hitler's agreement, Mussolini said "Fascism brings back color, force, the picturesque, the unexpected, the mystical; in short, all that counts in the soul of the crowds."

CONTEMPORARY FASCIST AND NEO-NAZI MOVEMENTS

Regrettably, right-wing extremism seems to be resurgent around the world. Perhaps the most powerful movements currently found are in Chile and in South Africa. In Chile, Augusto Pinochet, who leads the military junta governing that country, has created a rigid militarist regime since he forced his way to power in 1973. Idolizing Mussolini, Pinochet destroyed Chilean democracy, South America's most advanced at the time. Thousands of people were arrested, tortured, and killed. Since this usurpation, Chilean civil liberties have been suspended and police-state tactics have suppressed the opposition.

In South Africa the openly racist policy of *apartheid* keeps the white and the dark races separate. Although the government pretends to give home rule to the blacks, all effective political power is monopolized by the tiny white minority. Blacks are forbidden to vote, denied property ownership, and relegated to menial employment at low wages.

Bending to pressure from the international community, the government has made some nominal reforms, which, if allowed to continue and expand, could eventually improve the situation. Yet, one might question the sincerity of these expedient reforms and wonder if they will ever be allowed to develop to the point where blacks are treated equally in the society. At the present rate of change, it would take generations to reach that point.

Regardless of the government's intentions, the reforms seem doomed. Black radicals have taken to the hills and are in open rebellion against this oppressive regime. On the other side of the political spectrum, white supremacists are challenging the government because, in their view, its policies are detrimental to the white cause. The leading right-wing opposition party, the Conservative Party, and its militarized detachments, the *Afrikaner Resistance Movement,* hold rallies reminiscent of Hitler's party congresses. They strut in uniform, use Nazi-style salutes, and display a flag that is strikingly similar to the swastika. With the country torn asunder in this way, consensus for reform seems impossible and the country appears to be drifting toward civil war.

Elsewhere, neo-Nazi and fascist parties are active and growing, but they have not yet attained the prominence of their fellows in Chile and South Africa. There are, however, significant right-wing extremist movements in West Germany, Austria, France, Italy, Britain, Japan, and Argentina.

These movements may seem remote to the average American. Yet, we have our own problems with right-wing extremism, as neo-Nazi appeal is also growing in the country. Recently, the nation was shocked to learn that United States intelligence authorities had shielded high-ranking fugitive Nazis after World War II in exchange for information used in efforts to deal with the threat of the Cold War. Indeed, not only had American officials harbored these war criminals in Europe, but they spirited some of them out of Europe to South America and, indeed, even to the United States itself. For the most part, these refugees assumed apolitical lives and managed to elude extradition. Since 1983, however, the Office of Special Investigation in the Justice Department has engineered the deportation of several Nazi war criminals, including John Demjanjuk, known as Ivan the Terrible, and Andrija Artukovic. These individuals were responsible for hundreds of thousands of deaths in the Nazi camps during World War II, yet they managed to live freely in the United States for decades.

At the same time, indigenous neo-Nazi organizations have sprung up across the country. A partial list of these groups include The Covenant, the Sword, and the Arm of the Lord (CSA) in Missouri and Arkansas; The White Patriots Party in Florida; The White Aryan Resistance in California; and The Aryan Nations—otherwise calling itself the Church of Jesus Christ Christian—in Idaho and Washington state. These new extremist groups have informally allied with older fascist-type organizations like the Ku Klux Klan (KKK), which has increasingly taken to the trappings of Nazi regalia, salutes, and rhetoric. Another, even more recent neo-Nazi movement is found in an element (although certainly not all) of the *Skinheads,* which is composed of youths throughout the country who feel that white culture is being threatened, and who terrorize blacks and Jews on the nation's streets. The Ku Klux Klan has made overtures to these young toughs in an effort to harness and direct their youthful, energetic violence.[3]

Home grown neo-Nazi movements share the anti-Semitism and militance of Hitler's old party, but they are also more viscerally anti-African-American. In addition, these American groups tend to associate with fundamentalist Christian doctrines, so that they righteously proclaim that their beliefs enjoy divine sanction and

---

[3]Tamara Jones, "Violence by Skinheads Spreads Across Nation," *Los Angeles Times,* Dec. 19, 1988.

that their actions, including crime, are justified in the cause of the Lord. For example, consider *The Order*, a spinoff from the Aryan Nations. Convinced that the United States government, which they call the Zionist Occupied Government (ZOG), is controlled by Jewish conspirators, The Order declared war on the United States Government and launched a crime spree during 1984 and 1985. During this rampage members of The Order, whose objective was to establish a homeland for whites in the Pacific Northwest, stole over $4 million in robberies of armored cars; counterfeited currency; bombed the synagogue in Boise, Idaho; engaged in shootouts with the police; and allegedly murdered two people: a suspected FBI informer who was trying to infiltrate the group, and Alan Berg, a controversial Jewish radio talk-show host in Denver, Colorado.

Although most members of The Order have been apprehended and imprisoned, the Aryan Nations continues to function, hosting annual neo-Nazi conferences at its base in Hayden Lake, Idaho. Additionally, many other right-wing extremist organizations continue to thrive, broadcasting anti-Semitic and anti-African-American tirades over radio and television stations — even illegally interrupting the Los Angeles broadcast of the 1989 Super Bowl with an anti-Semitic harangue—and engaging in a brawl with black activists in late 1988 on the nationally televised Geraldo Rivera show. Moreover, former Grand Wizard of the KKK, and viciously racist David Duke, was elected to the Louisiana state legislature in 1989.

Meanwhile, incidences of vandalism and violence against African-Americans and Jews are occurring with increasing frequency across the country. Whether these episodes are the short-lived manifestations of a fleeting fad, or whether they are harbingers of a new prominence for Nazism in this country is, as yet, impossible to say. What can be concluded, however, is that reactionary extremism is far from a dead issue as we move toward the twenty-first century. Indeed, something of a fascist rebirth might also be occurring among societies in the Third World, to which we now turn our attention.

SUGGESTION FOR FURTHER READING

BAYNES, NORMAN H., ed., *The Speeches of Adolf Hitler*. London: Oxford University Press, 1942.
CARSTEN, F. L., *The Rise of Fascism*. Berkeley, CA: University of California Press, 1982. First published in 1967.
COHEN, CARL, *Communism, Fascism, and Democracy*, 2nd ed. New York: Random House, 1972.
GREGOR, A. JAMES, *Fascism: The Classic Interpretation of the Interwar Period*. Morristown, NJ: General Learning Press, 1973.
———, *Fascism: The Contemporary Interpretation*. Morristown, NJ: General Learning Press, 1973.
HALPERIN, S. WILLIAM, *Mussolini and Italian Fascism*, ed. Louis L. Snyder. Princeton, NJ: Van Nostrand, 1964.
HITLER, ADOLF, *Mein Kampf*, trans. Ralph Manheim. Boston: Houghton Mifflin, 1943.
INGERSOLL, DAVID E., *Communism, Fascism, and Democracy*. Columbus, OH: Charles E. Merrill, 1971.
MUSSOLINI, BENITO, *Fascism: Doctrine and Institutions*. New York: Howard Fertig, 1968.
O'SULLIVAN, NOEL, *Fascism*. London: J. M. Dent, 1983.
SHIRER, WILLIAM L., *The Nightmare Years, 1930–1940*. Boston: Little Brown, 1984.
SHIRER, WILLIAM L., *The Rise and Fall of the Third Reich*. New York: Simon & Schuster, 1960.

11

Ideologies in the Third World

PREVIEW

Most newly emerged states are plagued by cultural traditions that stand in the way of modernization. They also have a high rate of illiteracy and lack the skilled and educated workforce necessary for implementing modern technology. With few experienced civil servants and scarce natural resources, these new countries also have limited domestic capital.

While the various Third World countries voice their unique qualities, they tend to exhibit certain ideological traits in common. Being divided along tribal, cultural, religious, and ethnic lines, many newly independent states have adopted an exaggerated nationalistic or even statist posture in attempts to unify the diverse elements within their society and to secure the state's interests against foreign aggression, real or imagined. Struggling against poverty and neocolonialism, Third World states have found socialism and economic nationalism to be compatible with their needs. Although they have rejected capitalism because it demands a competitive social setting which is inconsistent with their traditional values, to say nothing about the pain its exploitation has caused these former colonies, most Third World countries stop short of becoming enthusiasts for Marxism-Leninism. The attitude suggested by Marxism-Leninism—that society is divided into opposing classes—does not adequately reflect reality as it is perceived in the Third World. People in former colonial countries are

Note: The drawing at the top of the page is of Jomo Kenyatta, King Abdel Faisal, and Indira Gandhi.

Hungry people of Northeast Africa.

much more apt to see their society as a single unit which is beset by foreign exploiters.

Holding a different perspective than the capitalist or the communist states, Third World countries tend to evolve unique political and economic systems. Liberal democracy is considered impractical in these struggling societies, while totalitarian dictatorship is also rejected. Hence, Third World countries tend to gravitate toward authoritarian dictatorships. Lacking the individual freedom of the liberal democracies, these systems, sometimes referred to as "guided democracies," vest powerful political controls in the hands of their leaders while denying them complete authority over other elements in the society. Under the most pleasant circumstances, some Third World states may gradually improve their economic and political systems enough to maximize the benefits for all their citizens. Yet, in other cases, the combination of authoritarianism and nationalism may doom their people to fascist equivalents.

THIRD WORLD IDEOLOGIES

To this point we have, with but few exceptions, studied the ideologies that relate to the industrialized nations of the world. Such an approach is completely appropriate given the relationship between modern ideologies and the Industrial Revolution. There are, however, a large number of countries which have yet to undergo the Industrial Revolution, but having not yet developed an industrial base does not prevent these nations from feeling the consequences of industrialization. Indeed, these societies have been very dramatically affected by the Industrial Revolution.

The term one normally hears in reference to these unmodernized states is the *Third World*. Doubtless, this term was not created by the underdeveloped countries themselves, since it implies a subordination to the other two worlds. In fact, the term has gained currency among the Western industrialized community, which refers to itself as the "First World" and to the Soviet Bloc as the "Second World" (an appellation to which the Soviets would surely take exception). In any event, the term *Third World* is generally used today to describe the "have-not" nations, and so will it be applied here as well. Among the Third World states are Bolivia and Nicaragua, Nigeria and Ghana, Libya and Syria, Burma, Indonesia and Malaysia, and many other small, underdeveloped nations.

As with all generalizations, the term Third World suggests a uniformity that in reality does not exist. Including the majority of the world's nations and a huge number of people and cultures, the Third World is composed of a bewildering diversity that virtually defies adequate generalization. There are similarities within the Third World, however, and perhaps the most comprehensive similarity among these countries is poverty. The Malthusian calamity of population growth exceeding the food supply is pressing hard on this sector of the world. The wealthiest nations, numbering fewer than twenty and comprising only 13 percent of the world's population, account for over 60 percent of the world's per capita income. In 1986 the per capita income in the United States was $14,400, while over half of the world's people survived on only $700 each annually.

This reality is startling, and one should not be surprised that feeding the multitudes is the most pressing problem faced by most governments. At the same time, however, some of the Third World countries have recently acquired vast wealth through the production and sale of oil. Hence, even in its most obvious commonality—poverty—the Third World is fraught with contradictions and exceptions.

As difficult as it is to generalize about the Third World without hopelessly distorting the subject, this must be done if such an important element in the world community is not to be ignored. The following, therefore, is intended to be a broad approach to the politics and ideologies prominent among the world's underdeveloped countries.

POLITICS OF THE THIRD WORLD

Essentially, the modern era has seen two stages of colonial expansion, each fundamentally representing the economically advanced powers forcing their domination over other parts of the world. The first colonial era spanned the period from 1492 to about 1785. During this time the trading countries of Portugal, Spain, France, England, and the Netherlands established some outposts in Africa, dominated the Indian subcontinent, and also established themselves in the East Indies and in some port cities in China and Japan. But the most extensive colonization was in the newly discovered Western Hemisphere. The colonies produced some precious metals, gems, and items of trade; but essentially they were consigned the task of providing agricultural goods to their European masters. While some private fortunes were made, the military and administration costs of maintaining the colonies proved to be burdensome for the European powers. Gradually, as Spain, Portugal, and the Netherlands declined in power; as France was vanquished by England from North America and India; and when England lost its most prized colony to the American Revolution, colonialism came to be viewed askance, causing almost a century to pass in which relatively little more colonial expansion took place.

The second era of colonial growth ran from 1875 until 1945. Driven by the wish to feed their newly industrialized economies with cheap raw materials and labor, England, France, Belgium, Italy, and Germany began colonial expansion anew, rushing to take as much of Africa as they could; and, joined by Russia, the United States, and Japan, they also invaded large parts of Asia. By 1914, with the exception of most of Latin America which had won its independence from Spain and Portugal, and Canada, Australia, and New Zealand which had become independent from England, virtually all the world had succumbed to the industrial powers.

In their rush to collect colonies, the industrial powers warred not only with their hapless captives but also with each other. For example, Japan fought with China (1894–1895); the United States warred with Spain (1898); Russia and Japan fought over Manchuria and Korea (1904–1905); and finally, all of the industrial powers entered in the titanic bloodletting of World War I, which was in part motivated by colonial competition. The interwar years saw the rise of totalitarianism and a new spate of colonialism by Italy, Germany, and Japan, even as the Soviet Union expanded Westward, taking the Baltic states and parts of Finland and Rumania.

To the industrialized nations, World War II is viewed as a struggle to conquer fascism, National Socialism, and Japanese militarism; but to the people of the colonies it represented much more. Abandoned to the advancing Axis Armies (Germany, Italy, and Japan) or left to fend for themselves by their preoccupied colonial masters, the colonies saw an awakening of nationalism among their peoples. As the war ended, nationalist movements in the colonies organized to resist continued colonial rule by the industrial powers. Long, bloody wars of national liberation were fought, and in Mahatma Gandhi's India, passive resistance was employed to compel independence.

Without question, the most striking political feature among Third World countries is their enthusiastic *nationalism*. After World War II nationalism lost favor as cooperative internationalism became popular; the United Nations, after all, promised security as a reward for such cooperation. Only a few years later, however, the world was again divided against itself and the Cold War was under way. Even so, nationalism was not the reason for the division between East and West. Instead, the world had become polarized ideologically, with the established states aligning themselves with one of the two great superpowers, the United States or the Soviet Union. Nevertheless, by the mid-1950s nationalism arose once again, this time with new vitality. This revival of nationalism took place in the Afro-Asian states that were just winning independence from their colonial masters.

Used as the rallying cry to drive the hated colonial powers out, nationalism assumed enormous authority in the Third World. Nationalism's importance in the newly emerged states was especially great because they suffered a severe identity crisis. In addition to the wretched economic exploitation of the colonial peoples, the industrial powers also practiced cultural imperialism. Impelled by racism and paternalism, they denigrated the languages, customs, and religions of their colonial charges. The imperial powers paid scant attention to traditional tribal boundaries when they staked out their empires, they ignored the histories of the people they conquered, and they taught that European ways were good and that local traditions were backward.

Thus, when the former colonies emerged as independent states, they found themselves comprised of varieties of tribes, social structures, and cultures and were confused and disoriented about themselves. Grasping for unifying themes, their leaders have pursued contradictory policies of lionizing the traditional languages, art, religions, and cultures, while at the same time championing national unity. Moreover, the weight of nationalism in the Third World is compounded by the insecurity of its leaders. New to independence and power, they are anxious to prove the legitimacy of their rule. This concern often leads them beyond occasional assertion of their national interests to bravado and bombast in world arenas such as the United Nations.

The exaggerated nationalism of the Third World is also a by-product of anti-colonialist feelings. Having experienced the humiliating exploitation of colonialism, the people of the emerging states will not be denied their independence. Yet, the power that foreign investors still have in many developing countries, called *neocolonialism* (dollar, yen, pound, franc, mark, or even ruble diplomacy), frightens the Afro-Asians and the Latin Americans. At the same time, they lack the funds for domestic capital investment and, therefore, are forced to encourage foreign investment. On the other hand, experience has taught that foreign influence can become oppressive. Understandably, this dilemma makes the people of developing countries defensive about their status in world affairs.

While nationalism is used to unify the people in the Third World countries, several factors in these societies also tend to divide them. More often than not, Third World states are composed of a number of different tribal, ethnic, cultural, and religious groups. Forging these diverse people into a single nation requires more than geographic proximity or political and economic necessity. The citizens of these states may be oriented entirely toward their own villages and feel little identification with their newly named country or its government.

In such circumstances leaders use patriotic appeals to awaken national awareness in the minds of their provincial citizens. They often warn that a neighboring regime may take advantage of the new state or that a former colonial oppressor wants to reestablish its control; such warnings are intended to galvanize national spirit. Frequent use of this technique has contributed to strong nationalistic ideologies among the emerging states.

At the same time, however, a true and deeply felt nationalistic attachment cannot be created by such techniques. Nationalism, as explained in Chapter 1, is based on a very personal identification with one's nation-state. For nationalism to develop, a nation must already exist. Shared traditions, history, and territory, while not essential, are very helpful in building a nation. Often the colonial experience has failed to make a unified group out of the various peoples thrown together by European rule and later by independence. Too often a Third World country becomes an independent state without a nation to serve as its foundation. Though the politically aware citizens of such a country are usually united by the effort to liberate their land from the colonial power, the vast majority of the citizens are scarcely aware of the central government and identify only with their immediate area. As a result, while nationalistic appeals may serve to unify the people, local customs and identities may continue to divide them.

This situation creates a political paradox. Not only must the emerging states maintain their independence, sometimes against incredible economic and political odds, but at the same time they must also build a nation. Hence, though the emerging states are often the strongest supporters of nationalism in international affairs, they also often suffer the greatest disunity and separatism within their own borders. Indeed, lacking a united population with which to stabilize the political situation, many Latin American, African, and Asian states have suffered armed coups and militaristic statism. Even neofacism has been substituted for less oppressive regimes.

Disunity within Third World countries is matched by parochialism in international affairs. Although several attempts have been made to create regional international unions, none have succeeded very well. Driven by nationalistic jealousies and historical differences, the Arab states have consistently faltered in efforts to coalesce into larger political units. The Organization of African Unity has seldom been more than a forum in which the various members vent their frustrations, rarely being able to agree on united action. And the Organization of American States, perhaps the most successful of Third World organizations, because it makes no pretense at establishing permanent political unity, is often criticized as being a puppet of the United States.

Currently another, more traditional, phenomenon calls for the unity of some people in the Third World—religious fundamentalism. Muammar Qaddafi in Libya and the Ba'th Party of Syria and Iraq each individually called for Arab unity. They propose to coalesce the traditions of Islam with socialism to modernize their lands and to improve the well-being of their peoples. Yet, the political divisions and economic exigencies of each country have so far foiled their grand schemes, and their governments are held in place by military force and political suppression.

Meanwhile, in what Zbigniew Brzezinski refers to as the "arc of crisis" (Turkey, Iraq, Iran, Afghanistan, and Pakistan), reactionary revolutions threaten to ignite throughout the Muslim world. Yet, in the 1980s, rather than uniting the Muslim people, the awakening of Islam had become the catalyst for bloody divisions in the Third World, as the civil strife in Lebanon and the war between Iraq and Iran have shown. Moreover, with the Soviet evacuation out of Afghanistan, and assuming the defeat of its puppet socialist government, many observers anticipate a brutal civil war among the various Muslim rebel groups in that country. Caught in a crosscurrent between attempts by some to modernize and demands by others to return to traditional beliefs and practices, the Middle East squanders its youth and resources in desperate struggles with the shattering realities of the late twentieth century.

Religion is also playing a major role in the politics of other parts of the Third World. Cypress continues to be divided among its Greek Christians and Turkish Muslims. On the subcontinent, strained relations persist between Muslim Pakistan and Hindu India; and within India itself, Sihks and Hindus have come to bloody clashes over religious, economic, and political issues.

In Latin America, a quite different phenomenon is occurring. Inspired by European liberalism and even Marxism, some Roman Catholic clerics and lay people are becoming political activists in struggles to combat poverty, ignorance, and powerlessness among the masses in Latin America. Harkening to the trumpet call of *liberation theology,* these leftists decry the exploitation of capitalism and neocolonialism and insist that the Church lead the poor in efforts to restructure their societies, and redistribute the wealth and power more equitably. Socialist in concept and sometimes Marxist in rhetoric, this movement has achieved significant followings in Guatemala, El Salvador, Nicaragua, Peru, Brazil, Chile, and Colombia.

In the late 1800s, the Church abandoned its previous posture in focusing only on the spiritual needs of its flock, while remaining uninvolved in social and political questions. Instead, today it recognizes the validity of the Church's engaging in a broader mission. Pope Leo XIII (1878–1903), the greatest of modern pontiffs, wrote a number of public letters (encyclicals) at the turn of the century. These appeals called for social justice (at the time, the primary focus of these thoughts was Europe) and encouraged the Christian socialist movement in Europe, which saw a connection between the egalitarian goals of humanitarian socialism and the teachings of Christ. In the 1960s, the Church gave new impetus to its social and political role with a new set of encyclicals emanating from the work done at the Second Vatican Council (1962–1965) and with subsequent papal comments condemning economic and social exploitation of the poor. While other religions in other areas have also moved toward taking a greater part in redressing the social conditions of the world's poor, the Catholics in Latin America, albeit not unanimously, have taken the leadership. But the Vatican has greeted these activists with ambiguous feelings. The Pope is genuinely committed to social and economic egalitarianism and to an activist Church, but he recoils from the Marxist tendencies of some zealots. Accordingly, he has supported efforts of Latin American priests and nuns to combat poverty and political oppression, but he has condemned their involvement in revolutionary and other directly political activities.

ECONOMICS OF THE THIRD WORLD

Almost all the new states and even some of the older Third World countries (for example, Mexico and Peru) claim to be socialist. Capitalism has few supporters in the Third World, for several reasons. In many cases the customs of the people in these states have no counterparts in capitalist society. Instead of encouraging competition for the sake of self-improvement, traditional ways teach the communal values of the tribe. In many cultures the accumulation of great wealth by individuals is actually frowned upon rather than admired. In addition, capitalism does not recommend itself to former colonial peoples. Having seen at first hand the deprivation and humiliation of imperialistic exploitation, they tend to avoid individualistic, competitive systems in favor of collective, cooperative ones.

A preference for socialism over capitalism does not make the Third World prone to Marxism-Leninism, however. To the extent that Lenin's theories of capitalist imperialist exploitation (discussed in Chapter 8) agree with the Third World's view of colonialism, the emerging states are attracted to communism. This attraction is limited, however. Except for a few communist countries including Albania, Angola, Cambodia, China, Cuba, Ethiopia, Mozambique, North Korea, and Vietnam, the social class conflict stressed by Marxism-Leninism is just as foreign to the Third World as is the competitive individualism of the West. Tribal, religious, and cultural divisions are much more common within newly emerged societies than social-class differences. Further, those who have managed to develop a nationalistic spirit are more likely to see their fellow citizens as members of a single exploited group and to see all foreigners as exploiters. Hence, the conflict between social classes within each society, which as we learned is basic to the Marxist theory of history, is alien to the experience and ideologies of most Third World societies.

Likewise, European socialism offers a serious contradiction to the ideological beliefs of the Third World. We saw in Chapters 7 and 8 that socialist ideology is heavily identified with internationalism. Socialist internationalism stems from the claim that national boundaries are artificial divisions between people, who are far more similar than they are different. Recalling our discussion of nationalism in the Third World, one can easily see the potential for contradiction within the emerging socialist states. Indeed, some observers suggest that the combination of socialism and exaggerated nationalism, or militaristic statism, accounts for both the former Ugandan regime of Idi Amin and Muammar Qaddafi's Libya, as well as several other Third World regimes that resemble fascist or even Nazi states. Liberal institutions such as individual freedom and opposition parties are not tolerated by many Third World leaders, who see such tendencies as dangerously divisive.

Even in other less extreme systems the contradiction between socialism and nationalism is also apparent. Perhaps the best explanation for this contrariety is that the traditional tribal customs of many Third World cultures are communal. Consequently, in the emerging states socialism is often an extension of the tribal-communal ethic to the nation as a whole rather than a commitment to traditional socialist goals. Socialism is seen in the Third World as a means by which to equalize the wealth somewhat. But more important, it is regarded as an instrument with which to engender unity among the people. Hence it is used primarily as a political device. The socialist intent, explained in an earlier chapter, plays only a secondary role among many Third World states.

There are, however, some socialist experiments in the Third World which are genuinely devoted to the economic and social objective of improving the status of all people in the society. Unfortunately, none of these have been successful yet. The experiment with *ujamaa* (familyhood) villages in the United Republic of Tanzania is a case in point. Devised by President Julius K. Nyerere, this program attempted to weld African tradition with socialist goals and, uncommonly, it focused on agricultural development rather than industrialization.

Similar in some ways to the Scandinavian cooperatives and to Mao's communes, Nyerere's communal farms were organized around the extended family. Private ownership of land was eschewed; the group collectively controlled land and produced goods both for its own use and for the market. These familial collectives were to strive for self-sufficiency, providing for their own needs and caring for those in the family who could not work. While major trade and financial concerns were nationalized and managed by the central government, the focus of the economic system rested in the agrarian villages.

Well meaning though it was, the *ujamaa* experiment failed. The crushing poverty of Tanzania, the depressed world market for its goods, the inefficiency and corruption of its political system, and the hesitance of its people to cooperate with a system offering future benefits but few immediate rewards, all combined to defeat the experiment's objectives. Indeed, the economic plight of most Third World countries causes serious questions about the sanguine effect of virtually any effort to modernize and create prosperity.

As pointed out earlier, the economic problems confronting the Third World states are often enormous. Combined with an exploding birthrate, declining infant mortality has produced unmanageable population growth. Two-thirds of the world's population lives in the developing countries; the average age in many of these states is below twenty-five. This overabundance of people is paired with a scarcity of almost every necessity of modern life. Most newly emerged states are plagued by illiteracy, cultural traditions that stand in the way of modernization, few skilled or college-educated people, a lack of experienced civil servants, little modern technology, a small number of natural resources, and scarce domestic capital. Often the problems of Third World countries are made worse by economic dependence upon a single cash crop, such as peanuts, bananas, or sugar.

The feelings of poverty are increased by the awareness, made possible by modern communications systems, that other societies enjoy great wealth and luxurious lifestyles. Television, radio, the press, and films bring distant societies into clearer focus than ever before. The world's have-nots are now painfully cognizant that others enjoy a bounty far exceeding their own meager existence. It would be unnatural for the have-nots to recognize the chasm dividing them from the haves and not want to cross over to the land of plenty.

Indeed, the have-nots are demanding "their share" of the world's material goods with ever-increasing assertiveness, and these demands are creating great tension in world politics. The pressure on national leaders to produce instant prosperity is often disastrous because such demands are impossible to satisfy. The inevitable failure of the leaders to meet the needs of the impatient citizens leads to conflict, resulting in either a rapid succession of unstable governments or in dictatorship. Both of these results, though common, seem equally tragic.

Further complicating this unstable state of affairs is the constant fear that the experiment in independence may fail and that the people of the emerging states may once again be forced into the bonds of colonialism. Accordingly, Third World nations feel an urgent need to succeed economically. This focus on economic success favors the natural tendency of many states toward economic and political centralization.

Meanwhile colonialism has taken on several new faces as it has become more sophisticated to meet the needs of the current era. Though the former colonial powers no longer send troops and bureaucrats to physically govern the developing countries, they have found other ways of controlling them. *Neocolonialism,* in which the industrialized countries own large shares in the basic industries of the Third World countries, is one example. Foreign aid, which often has political strings attached, is another way of manipulating these capital-hungry and technology-starved countries, luring them into economic arrangements similar to colonialism. Called "dollar diplomacy," this phenomenon has been aptly described as imperialism without colonialism.

Perhaps the greatest threat of all to the Third World countries' independence is the role of international corporations in the political affairs of the emerging states. With annual revenues larger than the national budget or even the gross national product of many of the countries in which they do business, these corporations often operate without meaningful legal restraints, protected by their corporate structure and wealth.

The power relationship between the international corporations and the host countries is frequently so uneven that the developing nations find themselves needing the companies more than the companies need them, and they are forced to sell their labor and resources at what they consider unfair rates. Once a corporation has made heavy investments in a Third World country, it understandably becomes interested in its politics. This interest sometimes leads to improper involvement in the domestic and international political affairs of the host country, evoking charges of oppression, exploitation, and neocolonialism. One need only recall the well-publicized involvement of International Telephone and Telegraph (ITT) in the 1973 fall of Chilean president Salvador Allende to appreciate the disquiet the Third World feels when its destiny is manipulated by these corporate giants.

ECONOMIC NATIONALISM

In view of the colonial experience and the economic lessons of colonial exploitation, we should not be surprised to find that the Third World countries themselves often resort to *economic nationalism*—acting in a way that will benefit one's own national economy with little concern for the impact on others. So it is that in this day of scarce natural resources the industrialized nations have felt the sting of boycotts and huge price increases on goods provided by some Third World countries. Although the satisfaction of giving the former colonial countries a taste of their own exploitative medicine is one factor behind economic nationalism, it is by no means the whole story.

To begin with, the industrial nations taught their economic lesson well. Although the imperialist nations are certainly not guilty of the extreme exploitation they are often accused of, it cannot be denied that colonialism is basically exploitative. The colonial powers took the profits extracted from the cheap labor and raw materials of the colonies and transferred them to their own people. The argument that imperialism benefited the colonial people by bringing them the advantages of advanced economic, cultural, and political institutions is of marginal credibility at best. In any case, when economic conditions created a buyer's market, the industrial imperialist states drove hard bargains, using the law of supply and demand as their justification. Today the conditions of some markets have reversed to favor the sellers; the sellers are simply applying the same laws to the industrial states that they experienced under colonialism.

Second, the principle that economics is not far removed from politics is well understood by Third World states. Western nations (plus Japan and Israel) have long had great power because of their ability to produce finished goods. Indeed, until recently their monopoly on industrialization had stabilized the international situation, so few other countries have risen to the status of a great power over the past several centuries. This economic domination has created suspicion in the developing countries. Attempts by industrial states to reduce pollution and conserve resources are interpreted by Third World countries as efforts to hold back their industrial development in order to keep them in a subordinate role. Even détente between the United States and the Soviet Union is viewed by some weak states as a bid to control the world. Realizing that neither giant can win a general war between them, the Third World countries speculate that the superpowers have agreed to cooperate in dividing up the world.

Now that the scarcity of some goods has changed market conditions, however, some Third World states see a chance to convert their newfound economic advantage into political power. The best example of this policy is the oil-rich Arab states' attempt to trade their oil for support of their views on the Middle East problem. Without question, this policy has brought them rich rewards. Almost every Western state, including the United States, whose policies were once clearly pro-Israel, has been forced to become much more friendly to the Arab side in the Middle East dispute.

The third factor leading to economic nationalism is perhaps the least complex. The oil-producing countries of the Third World (the Middle Eastern countries, Indonesia, Nigeria, Venezuela, and others) are well aware that their supply of oil is limited. Unless dramatic steps are taken now, their people could be forced to return to a life of poverty when the oil is depleted. To avoid such a disaster, the leaders of these nations are determined to extract the greatest possible profits from their remaining oil reserves. These profits are then invested in business enterprises throughout the world, hedging against the day the wells run dry.

For these reasons, and not just because they want to twist the lion's tail, the emerging states will continue to pursue their policies of economic nationalism. We can expect ever-increasing prices for scarce raw materials. In addition, the Third World states will take advantage of natural shortages to raise prices and achieve political goals.

DEMOCRATIC DICTATORSHIP IN THE THIRD WORLD

Just as the developing states have rejected capitalism as an economic system, so too have they found that liberal democracy does not meet their needs, except for Latin America, where democracy seems to be gaining in adherents and strength. The Third

Sukarno (1901–1970), the nationalist leader of Indonesia from 1945–1968.

World countries have discovered that the individualism and competitiveness of liberal democracy are incompatible with their culture and traditions.

Still, democracy remains a popular term, and every existing state somehow identifies with it. The term *guided democracies* is often applied to the centralized systems that tend to develop among Third World states. A euphemism for authoritarian dictatorship, this concept is worth some study. Unlike a totalitarian state, in which a ruler controls every aspect of the society—be it cultural, economic, historical, social, or political—an authoritarian dictatorship is less complete. While the authoritarian dictator is in firm control of the political system, he or she has less control over other aspects of the society and is checked by other institutions, such as the church, the military, or a property-holding class.

As I pointed out in Chapter 9, the various communist states tended toward totalitarianism as a result of a mixture of ideological dogmatism, Stalinist influence, and Western hostility. Interestingly, most newly emerged states are no more attracted to totalitarianism than they are to liberal democracy. The centralization of all power in the hands of a small group would be difficult in many technologically backward countries. More important, however, the enormous variety of tribal loyalties, religious beliefs, and traditional attitudes found in many of the emerging states makes national identification shaky and totalitarianism impractical. Recalling the Indonesian experience with the leftist policies of the former Sukarno government, President Suharto recently said,

> We have taken a path that corrects the mistakes we made in adopting open democracy and communism based on class conflict. They may work in other countries but liberalism and communism don't work here.

Guided democracy gets its name from the authoritarian administration of "democratic" policies. As illustrated earlier, in the developing countries political power tends to become centralized for three basic reasons. First, the communal spirit of tribalism encourages a collective rather than a competitive approach. Second, the politically aware people in a Third World state are often united in a single movement organized to liberate the state from colonial control (though such movements do not always develop in countries that are struggling to win independence—consider Angola, which in the early 1970s was the scene of three separate liberation movements). When a single movement does evolve, it becomes easier to centralize power. Since these movements usually benefit from experienced, politically aware, and popular leadership, they often remain in existence after the state has won its independence and tend to dominate the political system.

Third, faced with serious political and economic conditions, together with urgent demands for material progress, many Third World leaders have been forced into a corner. When the government fails to overcome the problems of the new nation, the natural response of the impatient masses is violent and negative. The ruling group must then choose between riding out the period of disorder, taking the chance that the resultant chaos will bring about their fall from power or even lead to foreign intervention, and dealing with the dissidents sternly, thereby stifling free political expression. A brief glance at the governments of the Afro-Asian bloc will reveal a clear preference for the latter policy. Hence, most Third World societies are "guided" by an authoritarian government supported by and often controlled by the military. How can such a system be considered democratic?

The argument is that the people in a developing country are basically united. Although some rule while others are ruled, and while they are divided by tribal, cultural, ethnic, and religious differences, still they remain in the same social group. Regardless of the present status of any individual, all have shared the experience of exploitation by the country's former colonial masters.

True or not, this concept of the basic equality of all the citizens of a Third World country is of great political importance. It tends to legitimize the ruler's power and gives an aura of democratic respectability to the government even as dissent is crushed. Coming from the same origins as the people, the rulers suggest that they are united by common interests and goals. This makes the system democratic in the eyes of some of its citizens. Though most of the people have had little say in developing the nation's policies, they still consider the system democratic. To do otherwise, it is argued, would be to put democratic procedures above the ultimate democratic goal: the common good. Though this vision of democracy is unlike the ideals of the liberal industrial states of the West, we must remember that no society has a monopoly on the political dictionary; hence, other countries' definitions of democracy may legitimately differ from ours.

CONCLUSION

We in the United States are not noted for our attention to philosophy or ideology. Theoretical postulates often appear to be impractical and high-sounding, notions that relate only slightly to the "real world." While pragmatism has contributed significantly to our material success, the fact that we tend to ignore theory makes a full appreciation of politics difficult, denying us the rich satisfaction of completely understanding the world in which we live.

Clearly, however, the centrality of theory to our political lives is undeniable. It is a statement of basic beliefs and goals, and it serves as the yardstick by which we measure success in accomplishing objectives. Without a sound theoretical base a society will wander aimlessly throughout history, groping for meaning, which continues to elude it. Similarly, unless the observer enjoys an understanding of fundamental beliefs and goals, political events can indeed be mystifying.

Difficult as it is to remember at times, many people—probably the vast majority—find politics uninteresting. Politics includes a bewildering array of institutions, traditions, and values. The philosophy of Edmund Burke, the process by which a bill becomes law, or the issues in a particular election seem far removed from daily life and therefore unimportant. This lack of interest in politics is not unusual and is understandable when one realizes that students are seldom shown how such matters relate to their lives.

Acutely aware of this ambivalence I have tried to emphasize the relevance of politics. Quite beyond only examining the abstractions of important political thinkers, I also wanted to develop a setting for the current era, to explain its origins, and to relate these to the political ideas and institutions that influence our everyday lives. In short, my task has involved helping the readers locate themselves in the complex world of politics.

I hope this book has brought its readers a new appreciation for the practical nature of political theory. Serious effort was made to go beyond a simple explanation of each theory to an examination of the causes and consequences of these ideas. To that end, I focused on relevant historical events, social institutions, and economic systems, associating them with political ideologies and relating contemporary political ideologies to political practice.

The world is not only what we have made it but also a product of the efforts of earlier generations. Thus, to fully grasp the present, we must first understand the past. The great thinkers wrote what they did because they had unusual talents, but they were also strongly influenced by their times. Locke, Madison, Bakunin, Mill, Hitler, Mao, and all the others can be fully appreciated only in the light of their historical, intellectual, political, social, and economic circumstances. Yet, although these ideologues were influenced by situations particular to their respective ages, they each responded to a common phenomenon—modernization.

The most fundamental feature of this era, the event that has done more to distinguish this period in history from all others and has contributed most heavily to shaping and molding our environment, is the Industrial Revolution. Industrialization is the latest stage in the chain reaction begun by the scientific method and its application to technology. The shift from handcraftsmanship to mechanized production changed the world dramatically. Work itself was so completely transformed that some, including Marx, argued that people were robbed of their skills and reduced to becoming mere tenders of machines; others, like Adam Smith, reveled in the potential benefits of industrialization; and still more, including Hitler, turned the new productivity into a frightful killing machine in an effort to return the world to primitive values.

As the ideologues struggled with the larger question of social development, the masses met industrialization as individuals. People faced new social problems as they found themselves packed into cities far removed from the land with which they had previously been so intimately involved. New goods in unimagined abundance tended to become an end in themselves; people increasingly turned away from spiritual satisfaction and justification, looking to materialism as the standard by which actions and ideas were judged.

At the same time, new ideas began to develop and to exercise a great impact on politics. Modern ideas of democracy, human equality, and freedom, developed currency. But these new ideas were applied differently by different people at various times. John Locke and Adam Smith, ignoring equality, exalted individual freedom. Rousseau and Marx equated freedom with economic well-being and turned many liberal ideas to radical extremes. The anarchists saw human liberty impeded by institutions of government and therefore demanded that government be abandoned. And the humanitarian socialists insisted that liberal democratic institutions be set to the task of distributing wealth on a more equal basis.

While each of these ideas developed, they were met with resistance by the conservative elements, who feared the potential consequences of trying to take society too far too fast. Yet the twentieth century held in store an even greater resistance to the progressive ideas of the modern era. Indeed, the fascists and the Nazis went beyond resistance to abject and violent rejection of progressivism.

The latter part of the twentieth century has been one of ideological ambiguity. An initial postwar rush toward socialism among the developed states has been checked by inflation and political indecision. The newly emerged states have also found themselves in unclear circumstances. Revolted by the exploitation of capitalism and too insecure politically to allow for liberal individualism, they reject Western institutions. At the same time, the totalitarian model offered by the Soviet Union fails to satisfy their needs. Hence they have adopted a modified socialist system held in place by single-party regimes or, more frequently, by military authoritarianism, which appears uncomfortably similar to a modified form of fascism.

The changes brought about by the Industrial Revolution confronted humanity with some very hard choices. Political problems have become more serious as history has pushed us beyond feudalism toward popularly based social and political structures. Politics truly came into its own in our age. Once the sole province of a tiny elite, government has become the concern of all people regardless of their social status, gender, or race. As technology expanded and people became involved in governing themselves and as new ideologies were met with resistance by those seeking to maintain the status quo and others trying to reverse the progressive trend of history, enormous struggles developed leading to World War I and World War II. These titanic conflicts did not quiet the controversy, however, for we now face the prospect of total annihilation in a third world war. Whether progressive or reactionary, the ideologies people hold are responsible—at least in part—for the dangerous situation we find ourselves in today. And yet, contemporary ideologies are also necessary statements of political aspirations. While they have embroiled the world in devastating conflicts, they have also been the inspiration for some of our most noble and most admirable social accomplishments.

Hence, the record of ideologies is mixed. They cannot be roundly condemned nor can they be uniformly applauded. Good or bad, political ideologies are a fact of modern life. They exist and they exercise an immense impact on our lives. Accordingly, we dare not ignore them. Instead, we must understand them if we are to grasp the full significance of our existence.

Many people feel that it is enough simply to cope with life's problems; understanding them is too much to expect. Nevertheless, some individuals have put much effort into rationalizing the world and understanding its relationship to their lives. Whether we are indeed intelligent enough to grasp the meaning of life, to know truth, and to be just, are questions that will continue to be asked and may perhaps never be answered. What is certain is that we have tried and that while our efforts have fallen short of complete success, they have, at the same time, escaped total failure. What, therefore, remains for us but continuing the quest?

SUGGESTION FOR FURTHER READING

ANGELOPOUS, ANGELOS, *The Third World and the Rich Countries: Prospects for the Year 2000*. New York: Praeger, 1972.
BOFF, LEONARDO, *Church, Charisma and Power*. New York: Crossroad, 1985.
DESFOSSES, H., and J. LEVESQUE, eds. *Socialism in the Third World*. New York: Praeger, 1975.
HUNTING, SAMUEL P. and JOAN M. NELSON, *No Easy Choice: Political Participation in Developing Countries*. Cambridge, MA: Harvard University Press, 1976.
KAUTSKY, JOHN H., *The Political Consequences of Modernization*. New York: Wiley, 1972.
KENNEDY, GAVIN, *The Military in the Third World*. New York: Scribner's, 1974.

MAHAN, BRIAN and L. DALE RICHESIN, eds., *The Challenge of Liberation Theory*. Maryknoll, N.Y.: Orbis Books, 1978.

OTTAWAY, DAVID and MARINA OTTAWAY, *Afro-Communism*. New York: Afrikana Publishing, 1981.

SEGMUND, PAUL E., ed., *The Ideologies of Developing Nations*, 2nd ed. New York: Praeger, 1967.

STODDARD, PHILIP, DAVID C. CUTHELL, and MARGARET W. SULLIVAN, eds., *Change and the Muslim World*. Syracuse, N.Y.: Syracuse University Press, 1981.

VON DER MEHDEN, FRED R., *Politics of the Developing Nations*, 2nd ed. Englewood Cliffs, NJ: Prentice-Hall, 1973.

YOUNG, CRAWFORD, *Ideology and Development in Africa*. New Haven, Conn: Yale University Press, 1982.

Glossary

Anarchism An ideology opposed to all or much of institutionalized government. Some anarchists want to free the individual so that he or she can make the greatest possible personal advancement; they are the *individual anarchists*. Others hope to free people so that they can make their greatest possible contribution to society as a whole; they are the *social anarchists*.

Aryans In Nazi ideology, a race of people who had the best of all human qualities and were the creators of all culture. Science has so far failed to find any proof that this race ever existed.

Atomistic theory of the state The belief that the individuals within the state are of highest importance and that the society itself is only secondary and incidental to its people.

Babeuf, François Noel (1760–1797) A brilliant revolutionary socialist who talked about creating the workers' revolution as early as the 1790s.

Bakunin, Mikhail (1814–1876) The founder of violent anarchism. He also competed with Marx for control of the international socialist movement.

Bentham, Jeremy (1748–1832) The creator of utilitarianism and the founder of modern liberalism. He was also an important force in Britain's early nineteenth-century reform movement.

Bernstein, Edward (1850–1932) A revisionist socialist. See also *Revisionism*.

Bolsheviks Followers of Lenin who believed that violence was necessary to bring about socialism and that Russia could be taken in a coup led by them.

Bourgeoisie The wealthy merchant class that became the dialectical challenge to the feudal society.

Burke, Edmund (1729–1797) An Irish-born British parliamentarian and the father of modern conservative philosophy. His ideas contributed heavily to neoclassical democratic theory, especially in making the property right a dominant theme. He thought that the people ought to be ruled by a benevolent aristocracy elected by them.

Calhoun, John C. (1782–1850) A philosopher for the Southern cause before the Civil War. He believed that the national government should be greatly limited in its powers over the states.

Caretaker government In the parliamentary-cabinet system, when no parliamentary majority can be created by a coalition agreement, it is the minority government appointed to administer existing policy until a majority can be created through either an election or a coalition.

Castro, Fidel Ruiz (born in 1927) A Cuban revolutionary and the founder of the present Cuban regime.

Chamberlain, Houston Stewart (1855–1925) A friend and later the son-in-law of Richard Wagner who shared Wagner's anti-Semitic views and developed a theory based on those views.

Checks and balances   Madison's plan of government, in which each branch of government has the power to influence the others, but no single branch can become too powerful. In addition, through staggered terms of office, indirect elections, and a specific election date, Madison hoped to prevent a permanent majority from controlling the government.

Coalition government   When no single party wins a majority of seats in parliament, sometimes two or more parties will unite to form a government. Such unions are usually unstable and short-lived.

Collective responsibility   In the parliamentary-cabinet system, the notion that the members of the cabinet share responsibility for the government's successes and failures.

Comintern   An organization, also called the Third International, created by Lenin to stimulate communist revolutions throughout the world.

Communism   A very old term that originally meant a local communal relationship among a small number of people. Today it refers to a system based on Marxist-Leninist ideology.

Concurrent majorities   John C. Calhoun's argument that there is not just one majority, but, rather, several majorities that should all agree to a policy before it is put into effect.

Concurrent powers   Powers that both the state and national governments may exercise at the same time. If the two conflict, the laws of the national government prevail.

Confederate system   A compact among several sovereign states. A confederacy exists to achieve certain goals, and any member state, being sovereign, may secede from it at any time.

Conservative   A person who is satisfied with the system as it is and tends to resist change. Some conservatives, realizing that things could be improved, will accept gradual, very superficial, and progressive change. Property rights tend to be very important to conservatives.

Conservative theory of representation   A system in which an elite group is chosen by the people to govern them. Yet while public officials should try to represent their constituents' interest, the people cannot compel them to vote in a particular way.

Conspiratorial theory   The theory that a small group of powerful people are secretly controlling the political and economic events in a country.

Convention, nomination by   A nomination procedure in which the candidate must receive a certain number of delegate votes at a nominating convention.

Cooperatives   Enterprises that are owned and operated by their members, who all participate in the enterprise directly.

Corporate state   The economic system used by fascist Italy. The society was organized into syndicates (unions), regional organizations, and national corporations controlled by the state. Though industry was privately owned, production and prices were controlled by the state through the national corporations; strikes and boycotts were outlawed.

Cultural Revolution (1966–1969)   A revolution in which the radicals in China were unleashed against the moderate bureaucrats and intellectuals. The radicals favored greater personal sacrifice and stronger spiritual commitment to the goals of the revolution, while the moderates wanted to produce more consumer goods.

Democratic centralism   Lenin's theory of party government in which the party's leadership is elected by the general membership. While discussion is to be free and open before a decision is reached, the party leaders have the ultimate power to determine policy, and the rank and file are expected to accept their decisions without question.

Deng Xiaoping (Born in 1904)   A pragmatic reformer who presently enjoys great power in China. Twice purged from the leadership by the radicals, Deng has managed to survive Mao and is responsible for the present modernization of China.

Destutt de Tracy, Antoine Louis Claude (1754–1836)   A French scholar who coined the term *ideology,* calling it the "science of ideas."

Détente   A policy pursued by President Richard M. Nixon in the early 1970s designed to improve relations between the United States and the Soviet Union. The policy gradually lost its luster and then completely collapsed in 1979 with the Soviet invasion of Afghanistan. The current warming of relations between the two superpowers is also sometimes referred to as détente.

Dewey, John (1859–1952)   The philosopher of the New Deal. He called upon people to use their reasoning ability and their control of government to create a better life. He argued that truth was constantly changing and that no institution should be maintained if it was no longer useful. His ideas about social change are often called *social engineering.*

Dialectic   Georg Hegel's concept that historical progress is achieved through conflict between the existing order and challenges to that order.

Dialectic materialism   The Marxist theory of history, which suggests that human progress has resulted from struggle between the exploiters and the exploited. This dynamic, Marx argued, would inevitably lead to socialism.

Dictatorship of the proletariat   A temporary tyranny of the workers that would follow the revolution and last until all nonproletarian classes had been removed, at which time the state would wither away and a democratic utopia would evolve.

"Different paths to socialism"   The slogan under which Tito led Yugoslavia away from Stalin's domination. Tito claimed that each state had to find its own way to socialism.

Direct democracy   A system in which there is no elected legislature and people make the laws themselves.

Divine right of kings theory   The belief that the king had been chosen by God to rule.

Divine theory of the state   The belief that the state was created by God.

Division of labor   Economic specialization, which Marx claimed led to the creation of social classes and to exploitation.

Division of powers   The division of powers between the state and national governments set forth in the federal Constitution; also known as *federalism.*

Economic determinism   The belief that all social and political features are conditioned by the economic environment.

Economic nationalism   Economic policies designed to benefit one state regardless of their impact on other nations.

Elite theorism   A theory suggesting that the political system is controlled by a relatively small number of people who head important pressure groups.

Elitism   The assumption that some people are more deserving and qualified than others and that they ought to govern.

Engels, Friedrich (1820–1895)   The son of a wealthy Prussian textile manufacturer who became a close friend of Marx in 1844 and remained his collaborator and benefactor until Marx died in 1883.

Eurocommunism   A term referring to the policy of independence from Soviet control pursued by the Western European communist parties.

Fabianism   Founded in 1884, the Fabian society was a British socialist movement in the tradition of John Stuart Mill and Robert Owen. The Fabians argued for socialism in a democratic society, insisting that it must be adopted peacefully and gradually.

Federalism   See *Division of powers.*

Federalist Papers   A series of articles written by James Madison, Alexander Hamilton, and John Jay, during 1787 and 1788, urging New Yorkers to ratify the proposed federal Constitution.

Fidelismo   Castro's adaptation of Marxism, which combines dialectic and idealistic rhetoric with anti-Yankee policies to create the new Cuba.

Five-year plans   Plans that direct a state's production and distribution of goods and services over a five-year period; introduced by Stalin in 1929 to replace Lenin's NEP. Also used in China.

Force theory of the state   The belief that the state was created by the forceful conquest of some people by others. One group supporting this theory held that the use of force was evil, while a second group saw force as a positive feature of society.

Foundation of the society (as used by Marx)   Marx argued that economics was the foundation of any society. This economic base was composed of the *means of production* (resources and technology) and the *relations of production* (ownership). The economic base preconditioned the rest of the society *(the superstructure).*

Fourier, Charles (1772–1837)   A utopian socialist. See also *Utopian socialism.*

Führer   The German title for supreme leader, as used by Hitler.

Functional representation   A system that gives legislative representation to institutions such as the Church, universities, trade unions, corporations.

General election   An electoral contest between candidates for public office.

General strike   An action proposed by the syndicalists as the ultimate weapon of the trade unions. When a general strike was called, everyone was to leave work, thus paralyzing the society and bringing the unions to power.

General will   The all-powerful will of Rousseau's organic society.

Gobineau, Arthur de (1816–1882)   A French noble who tried to prove that the French aristocracy was superior to the peasantry and should therefore rule France. In doing so he claimed that the Aryan race was superior to all others. His theories became the foundation of Nazi racism.

Godwin, William (1756–1836)   Once a protestant minister, Godwin eventually became an atheist and founded anarchism.

Goldman, Emma (1869–1940)   The leading anarchist in American history. Sometimes known as "Red Emma."

Gorbachev, Mikhail S. (Born in 1931)   Became General Secretary of the Communist Party of the Soviet Union in 1985 following the death of Konstantin Chernenko.

Great Leap Forward (1958–1961)   An attempt to bring China into the modern industrial age through maximum use of the vast Chinese labor force; it failed miserably.

Green, Thomas Hill (1836–1882)   A liberal philosopher who wrote about freedom in a positive rather than a negative sense. He argued that the government should actively try to provide a good life for its citizens. His ideas offered an early justification for the welfare state, and his work directed liberalism away from solitary individualism and toward collectivity.

Guided democracies   Third World dictatorships in which the leaders claim to be carrying out the popular will.

Head of government   The political leader of a country (e.g., the prime minister).

Head of state   The person who symbolizes the history, culture, people, and tradition of a nation-state (e.g., the King or Queen of England).

Hitler, Adolf (1889–1945)   A German revolutionary leader and the founder of the ideology of National Socialism and the Nazi state.

Hobbes, Thomas (1588–1679)   A social contract theorist who claimed that people had created an ordered society by surrendering their rights to a king.

Human rights   The rights listed in the Declaration of Independence and guaranteed in the Constitution of the United States. The question of whether or not property should be considered a human right is a subject of debate between liberals and conservatives.

Ideology   Any of a number of action-oriented, materialistic, popular, and simplistic political theories that were originally developed as an accommodation to the social and economic conditions created by the Industrial Revolution.

Il Duce   The Italian title for supreme leader, as used by Mussolini.

Imperialism (as used by Lenin)   The most advanced state of capitalism. It followed the stages of industrial capitalism and finance capitalism and represented the exportation of exploitation.

Imperialist capitalists   Members of the Chinese bourgeoisie who had ties to foreign nations. They were held to be the most dangerous element in the society and were to be eliminated immediately after the communists came to power.

Industrial Revolution   A period beginning in the eighteenth century that consisted of several phases: Handcrafted goods produced in cottages or small shops gave way to mechanization (goods produced by machines). Labor then became concentrated in factories and cities. This phase was followed by *automation* (production of goods with machines powered by steam, gasoline, coal, running water, or electricity rather than by humans or animals). Today the United States has reached the *cybernetic* level, in which machines are run by other machines.

Initiative   A procedure in which a law can be proposed by people who do not hold government office and can be enacted by a popular vote.

International Association of Workingmen   An organization, also called the first International, that was formed in 1864 to awaken class consciousness among the proletariat. It was led by Marx.

International, Second   An organization founded in 1889 by Friedrich Engels. It was structured along national party lines but was overwhelmed by the nationalistic pressures of World War I.

Iron law of oligarchy   Robert Michels's theory that only a very few people are active in any organization and that they therefore gain control of the organization. This theory supports the argument that a small elite actually governs the United States.

Iron law of wages   Ricardo's argument that the capitalist would pay the worker no more than a subsistence wage.

Irrationalism   The belief that human reason has definite limits and that people must depend on phenomena that are beyond reason for the explanation and solution of some of their problems.

Jaures, Jean (1859–1914)   A revisionist socialist. See also *Revisionism*.

Jefferson, Thomas (1743–1826)   An American statesman and philosopher in the classical democratic tradition of Locke and Rousseau. He argued for a government that was much more directly controlled by the people than the one proposed in the federal Constitution.

Kautsky, Karl (1854–1931)   A German Marxist who became the leader of the Orthodox Marxists following Engels's death.

Khrushchev, Nikita (1894–1971)   The successor of Stalin and a political reformer in the Soviet Union.

Kropotkin, Prince Peter (1842–1921)   A scientist and a communistic anarchist.

Kuomintang   A Chinese nationalist political party founded by Dr. Sun Yat-sen and taken over by Chiang Kai-shek after Sun's death.

Labor theory of value   A theory developed by David Ricardo and amplified by Marx. It suggested that the true value of any item was determined by the amount of labor it took to produce it.

Laissez faire   The belief held by John Locke, Adam Smith, and David Ricardo that government should stay out of economic matters. This concept is fundamental to capitalism.

Leadership principle   The fascist theory that some people are better able to lead than others and that good citizens will obey their betters.

Lenin, Vladimir (Nikolai) Ilyich (1870–1924)   A Russian revolutionary who first adapted Marxism to a practical political situation; the founder of the Union of Soviet Socialist Republics.

Liberal   A person who favors rapid, substantial, and progressive change in the existing order. Liberals usually use legal means to achieve their goals. The *classic liberals* believed in human reason; to them property was a human right. *Contemporary liberals* reject natural law and count property among the social rights.

Liberal theory of representation   The belief that people should be able to compel their elected representatives to vote in a particular way.

Liberation theology   A movement centered primarily in the Roman Catholic Church in Latin America. Priests, nuns, and lay persons are committed to a socially and politically active Church to bring economic improvement, social advancement, and political power to the poor.

Locke, John (1632–1704)   A social contract theorist and the leading philosopher of classical liberal democracy. He argued that people had created government to serve their needs and that most of the time government should have very little power over the individual.

Long March (1934–1935)   A massive retreat by the Chinese communists from southern to northern China. A power struggle took place during the march, with Mao emerging as the dominant Chinese political figure.

Lumpenproletariat   Vagabonds, prostitutes, and other social outcasts whom Bakunin wanted to mold into a revolutionary force.

Madison, James (1751–1836)   The founder of the American federal system. He believed that people were rather base by nature and that governmental institutions should turn the people's vices into virtues. Hence, he designed a system of separate and diffuse powers with institutions that would check and balance each other.

Malthus, Thomas (1766–1834)   An English economist who postulated that since population increases more rapidly than does food, calamity awaits those nations which do not exercise "moral restraint." His *Essay on the Principle of Population* was very controversial as well as influential. Malthus's work enjoyed wide impact, even influencing Charles Darwin's theory of natural selection.

Maoism   Marxist ideology heavily influenced by populism and traditional Chinese values. Like the ideologies of other developing countries, Maoism is at least as concerned with the problem of imperialist expansion by the advanced states as with the struggle between social classes within the society.

Mao Tse-tung (1893–1976)   A Chinese revolutionary and political leader. He founded the People's Republic of China and adapted Marxism to an oriental peasant society.

March on Rome   A 1922 demonstration in which several thousand supporters of Mussolini marched on Rome to demand that he be given power. The indecisive Italian political leaders became confused and frightened, and finally invited Mussolini to form a government.

Mass Line   A Maoist doctrine calling upon the masses of China to carry out the goals of the revolution.

Massive nuclear retaliation   The United States' nuclear deterrent policy during the Eisenhower administration.

Marx, Karl (1818–1883)   A scholar and the leader of the international socialist movement. He developed a theory of historical development—Marxism—based on the assumption that economic factors were the primary human motivation.

Mensheviks   Followers of George Plekhanov (1857–1918), who believed that socialism would come to Russia only after the nation had been transformed into a capitalist state.

Mercantilism   An economic theory prominent in the 1600s and 1700s. Nations practicing mercantilism used economic monopolies and colonial exploitation in efforts to increase their wealth and political power. Today's vestiges of mercantilism are called "economic nationalism."

Mill, John Stuart (1806–1873)   A British writer who contributed greatly to the development of democratic socialism by questioning the assumptions that people are naturally selfish and that government should have no economic role.

Moderate   A person who is basically content with the system but sees some flaws in it. Accordingly, a moderate will accept a small amount of progressive change.

Moral absolution   The belief that there is a set of absolute truths that apply equally to all people. Natural law is an example of these presumed truths.

Moral relativism   The belief that truth at any given time is subject to the needs of society.

Multimember district   An electoral district in which several people are elected to office. A system of proportional representation is usually employed to distribute the votes in these districts, thus encouraging the development of a multiparty system.

Multiparty system   A system in which there are several parties of roughly equal strength. This system gives the clearest voice to minority opinions but in doing so destroys the majority. Coalition governments and governmental instability may result from the absence of a majority. In addition, the multiparty system demands a certain flexibility that is not possible in a presidential-congressional system.

Mussolini, Benito (1883–1945)   An Italian revolutionary, the originator of fascism and the leader of the Italian fascist state.

Myth   An idea that is believed but cannot be proved. The concept of myth as a political tool was developed by Georges Sorel, who suggested the use of myth to stimulate mass action. The validity of the myth was unimportant as long as it resulted in the desired action.

Narodniki   Russian Populists of the late nineteenth century.

Nation   A sociological term used to refer to a group of people who share a common language, ethnic relationship, culture, or history. The term does not necessarily have a political meaning.

Nationalism   The ideology of the nation-state; the most powerful political idea to emerge in the past 300 years.

Nationalization   Government expropriation of an industry and the later operation and control of that industry by the government.

National Socialist German Workers party   The official name of the Nazi party.

Natural law   Rules in nature governing human conduct that can be discovered through the use of human reason.

Natural theory of the state   The belief that people are political as well as social animals and can develop their humanity only within the context of the state.

Neocolonialism   A condition in which wealthy nations gain control of developing states by making vast economic investments in those states.

New Deal   The 1930s policies of Franklin Delano Roosevelt which tempered capitalism with government regulation of business, collective bargaining for labor, and welfare state institutions including social security, housing loan guarantees, and welfare programs for the needy.

New Economic Policy (NEP)   The failure of War Communism, in which the Soviets tried to rapidly socialize the economy, caused Lenin to initiate the NEP in 1921 to rebuild the economy. Retail, small factories, and agriculture were returned to private ownership; while finance, heavy industry, foreign trade, transportation, and communications remained under state control. Although the NEP revitalized the economy, it was ended by Stalin in 1929 with the introduction of the planned economy.

Nietzsche, Friedrich (1844–1900)   A German philosopher who thought that power and strength were desirable qualities that justified all things.

Nihilism   An anarchist theory of the mid-1800s; its goal was the complete destruction of society.

Nullification   Calhoun's theory that the state legislatures could vote to void a national statute within their jurisdiction.

Organic theory of the state   The belief that the state is similar to a living organism and that people are the cells of that organism.

Original donation theory   The belief that God gave Adam the power to rule the state and that all later kings were his heirs.

Orthodox Marxists   A group of socialists led by Engels and Karl Kautsky who followed the teachings of Marx without significant deviation. The movement was never very successful because of its rigid dogmatism.

Paris Commune   A socialist government established in Paris in 1871, after France's humiliating defeat by Prussia in the Franco-Prussian War. The Commune was quickly overthrown after thousands of socialists had been slaughtered by the conservative forces of Germany and France.

Parliamentary-cabinet system   A system in which the people elect the legislature, which then chooses a leader who is appointed prime minister by the head of state. The head of state also appoints members of the legislature to the cabinet on the recommendation of the prime minister. The cabinet acts as a plural executive, and its members stand (or fall) together on the government's policies.

Passive obedience theory Calvin's theory that people should obey the king because his power came from God.

Patriotism An act or gesture of loyalty or commitment to the nation-state.

Peaceful coexistence Khrushchev's policy of accommodation with the West, based on the recognition that neither side could win a nuclear war.

Permanent revolution A theory, supported by Leon Trotsky and Mao Tse-tung, that favored revolution as the best way to achieve meaningful reform even after Marxists have taken power.

Petition nomination A procedure by which people are nominated to run for office if they can collect a certain number of signatures on a petition.

Plekhanov, Georgi (1857–1918) The founder of Marxism in Russia, Plekhanov broke with Lenin over differences regarding the dialectic and revolutionary tactics. His ideas became the foundation for the Menshevik movement.

Pluralism A decision-making process in which the people's interests are represented by various pressure groups; governmental policy is a compromise between the competing interests of those groups.

Plurality The largest number of votes cast. A plurality is distinct from a majority because it need not be over half; it is simply the most votes.

Popular sovereignty The belief that the people are the sole source of political power; a fundamental idea in liberal democracy.

Positivist law Bentham's theory that the law should serve the people's interests and should be changed when it fails to do so.

Presidential-congressional system A system in which the executive and the legislature are elected separately, resulting in less interdependence between the two branches than in other systems. Officials are elected to uninterruptable terms, a fact that adds stability to the system but tends to reduce popular control over the government.

Primary election An election in which candidates are nominated for public office.

Principle democrats Those who believe that the process of making decisions is only part of democracy. More important are the basic goals of democracy, such as the freedom and independence of the individual.

Process democrats Those who argue that democracy is simply a process by which decisions are made on a popular basis.

Proletariat A class of industrial factory workers who, according to Marxism, are exploited by the capitalist and are supposed to rebel and create a communist democratic utopia.

Proportional representation A method of awarding legislative seats to parties or candidates in relation to the proportion of the vote won. The list system is the least complex form of proportional representation.

Proudhon, Pierre Joseph (1809–1865) A leading anarchist socialist, sometimes called the founder of modern anarchism.

Radical A person who wants immediate, significant, and progressive change in the existing order. Some radicals insist that violence is the only way to bring about meaningful change; pacifist radicals, by contrast, oppose violence altogether.

Radical theory of representation A theory that rejects elected representatives and holds that people should represent themselves in the policy-making process.

Rationalism The belief that human problems can be solved through the use of human reason.

Reactionary A person who would like to see the existing order reversed and favors substituting earlier political institutions for the contemporary system.

Reactionary theory of representation A theory stating that the monarch and parliament should represent the people's interests as they see them without necessarily consulting the people.

Recall A process by which an elected official can be voted out of office before the end of his or her term.

Referendum A process in which the people are asked to vote on an issue. *Advisory referenda* (called *plebiscites* in Europe) request the people's opinion. *Compulsory referenda* are popular votes that must be held before the government can take a particular action. *Petition referenda* allow the people to veto laws by popular vote.

Republic Also called indirect democracy or representative government, a republic is a system in which the people elect representatives to make laws for them. Traditionally the term has meant non-monarchial government.

Revisionism A movement led by Edward Bernstein (1850–1932) and Jean Jaures (1859–1914) that challenged almost every major principle of Marxism. Abandoning scientific socialism, the revisionists returned humanitarianism to a central place in socialist theory.

Revolution   A profound change in the social, political, economic, and cultural patterns of a given society that need not be violent but often is.

Revolutionary defeatism   A policy of neutrality favored by Lenin, who believed that World War I was a war of capitalist imperialism. He hoped that when the war was over the socialists could seize control from the exhausted capitalist governments.

Ricardo, David (1772–1823)   An English economist who applied the capitalistic theories of Adam Smith to the British economy. He is particularly noted for articulating the "iron law of wages" and for his contribution to the theory of profit—"the leavings of wages" as he called it. His major work, *The Principles of Political Economy and Taxation,* earned him the title of the "Newton of economies."

Rousseau, Jean Jacques (1712–1778)   A social contract theorist and founder of modern radical thought. He argued that people are free only when they subordinate their own interests to those of the group.

Rural Soviets   Communist bases of power in the rural provinces of China during the Chinese revolution.

Saint-Simon, Claude Henri (1760–1825)   A utopian socialist. See also *Utopian socialism.*

Satellite countries   A term used to refer to the East European countries that were controlled by the Soviet Union during the Stalinist period.

Schopenhauer, Arthur (1788–1860)   A German philosopher who thought that life was a meaningless struggle beyond human understanding.

Scientific socialism   The term used by its supporters to describe Marxism; they called it scientific because it was based on certain principles of human conduct that Marxists believed were inviolable laws.

Secret war against Cuba   During the 1960s the Central Intelligence Agency funded, trained, armed, and directed Cuban exiles in order to perpetrate acts of sabotage and terrorism against Castro's Cuba. This campaign included numerous attempts to assassinate Fidel Castro.

Self-alienation, theory of   Marx's belief that bourgeois exploitation alienated the workers from themselves in three ways: (1) by making the conditions of labor so harsh that workers were forced to hate their jobs; (2) by forcing the workers to sell the product of their labor at much less than its inherent value; and (3) by robbing the workers of their skills through mechanization.

Self-announcement   A procedure in which a person may be nominated for office by simply filing the appropriate documents with the proper authority.

Separation of powers   The distribution of the powers of the national government among three branches: legislative, executive, and judicial.

Siegfried   The idealization of the Aryan superman. Richard Wagner immortalized this character in his operas, and Hitler made him the symbol of the Nazi racial ideal.

Single-member district   An electoral district in which only one person is elected to office. Since only one person can be elected, those who voted for the losers go unrepresented. Used in the United States, this electoral system also tends to favor a single or two-party system while working against a multiparty system.

Single-party system   A system in which only one party has a reasonable chance of gaining control of the government. Although it can easily be used to create a dictatorship, it may exist in a democracy as well.

Sino-Soviet split   A break in Soviet-Chinese relations dating back to 1959 and based on a number of disagreements between the two communist giants.

Smith, Adam (1723–1790)   A Scottish scholar, he is considered the founder of economics. With the 1776 publication of *The Wealth of Nations,* he first articulated the basic principles of capitalism.

Social contract theory   The notion, outlined by Hobbes, Locke, Rousseau, and others, that people joined together in a contract to create a government that would protect them from the tyranny of the state of nature.

Social Darwinism   A theory developed by Herbert Spencer, who claimed that the wealthy were superior to others and therefore benefited society more than others. Coining the phrase "survival of the fittest," Spencer argued that the wealthy should succeed while the poor should perish because this would strengthen the human race.

Socialism   The application of communistic principles to a national economy. Socialism developed only after the Industrial Revolution increased productivity enough to make it possible to provide plenty for everyone.

Socialist ethic   The hope that true socialists will enjoy work and will voluntarily share the product of their labor with the whole community.

Socialist intent A moral goal that must exist for a system to be truly socialist. This goal is to free people from material need, allowing them to develop and refine themselves as human beings.

Sorel, Georges (1847–1922) A French philosopher who developed the ideology underlying syndicalism and encouraged the use of myth as a tool of mass politics. Though Sorel was a leftist, his ideas were adopted and modified by Mussolini.

Sovereign The highest legal authority in a given society. The term is sometimes used to refer to a monarch.

Stalin, Joseph (1876–1953) A Bolshevik conspirator who succeeded Lenin and became the unquestioned leader of the Soviet Union. Although he made the Soviet Union a first-rate military and industrial power while successfully defeating the Nazi invasion, he imposed a cruel totalitarian system on his country, executing or imprisoning millions of people.

State A political term that includes people, territory, sovereignty, and government. In the United States of America the term has also been used to refer to what are actually *provinces*.

State socialism Lenin's theory that in preparation for the communist utopia, the socialist state will exploit the proletariat and share the proceeds among all the people in proportion to their productivity. The guiding slogan would be "from each according to his ability, to each according to his *work*."

Statism The concept that the state is the focal point of human existence and that all citizens should therefore give it absolute obedience.

Stirner, Max (1806–1856) A leading individualist anarchist.

Sun Yat-Sen (1866–1925) A Chinese physician and revolutionary leader. He inspired the movement which eventually led to the ouster of the Chinese Emperor in 1911.

Superstructure All elements, according to Marx, that are built on the economic foundation of the society, including art, values, government, education, ideology, and the like.

Supply-side economics Pursued by Republican Presidents in the 1920s and again by Ronald Reagan in the 1980s, this policy reduces taxes and government regulation for large corporations while increasing government subsidies and other support for big business.

Surplus value, theory of Marx's argument that the capitalist forced the workers to surrender their product for less than its true worth. The difference between the workers' wages and the true value of the item was the "surplus value" or profit.

Syndicalism A radical theory suggesting that trade unions should become the primary social and political units in the society.

Third World Usually found in Africa, Asia, and Latin America, these states often have marginal economies and are noted for their anticolonialism and nationalism. Many of these countries have avoided too close a relationship with either the United States or the Soviet Union and are sometimes referred to as nonaligned states.

Tito, Josip Broz (1892–1980) A Yugoslavian political and revolutionary leader.

Titoism A pragmatic approach to Marxism that is basically antibureaucratic and has led Yugoslavia to a mixed economy.

Tolstoy, Count Leo (1828–1910) A famed author and pacifist anarchist.

Totalitarian state A state in which the government controls the economic, social, and cultural as well as political aspects of a society. Totalitarianism was not possible before the development of twentieth-century technology.

Trotsky, Leon (1879–1940) A brilliant Bolshevik revolutionary who was Lenin's intellectual equal but was no match for Stalin's ruthlessness; he suffered exile and was finally assassinated at Stalin's order.

Two-party system A system in which the bulk of the vote is divided between two major parties. Though this system has the advantage of loyal opposition, the views of the minority rarely get a fair hearing.

Two-stage theory A question asked by some Marxists, including Lenin, as to whether or not a feudal society must pass through the capitalist stage of the dialectic to reach the communist stage.

Two-swords theory The belief that spiritual and secular powers are both essential and should not be held by a single person.

Ujamaa Meaning familyhood, this policy of Julius K. Nyerere of the United Republic of Tanzania attempted to raise the social and economic conditions of the people by creating self-sufficient familial agrarian collectives.

Unitary system A system of government that centralizes all governmental power in the national government.

Utilitarianism   Bentham's philosophy that the government should do whatever would produce the greatest happiness for the greatest number of people.

Utopian socialism   A humanitarian movement that tried to create ideal socialist experiments that would be imitated by the rest of the society.

Vanguard of the proletariat (as used by Lenin)   A small, dedicated elite of professional revolutionaries who would lead the proletariat to socialism through revolution. The Bolsheviks were the Russian vanguard and the Comintern, the international vanguard.

Vanguard of the proletariat (as used by Marx)   Those who, because of their superior intellect, could recognize the coming of socialism. Marx expected them to organize and awaken the proletariat's class consciousness and thus stimulate the revolution.

Versailles, Treaty of   The treaty ending World War I. It imposed very harsh conditions on Germany and was blamed by Hitler for Germany's severe postwar problems.

Volk   The German people. See also *Volkish essence*.

Volkish essence   A mystical power within the German people that supposedly makes them superior to all others.

Wagner, Richard (1813–1883)   An operatic composer who popularized German mythology and the foundation for anti-Semitism.

War communism (1917–1921)   A period in which Lenin tried to totally socialize the Soviet Union. The experiment ended in failure, and Lenin was forced to shift to his new economic policy (NEP).

Warsaw Pact   A military alliance of communist countries similar to the North Atlantic Treaty Organization (NATO).

Weakest-link theory   Lenin's theory that Russia was the weakest link in the capitalist chain because it had exploited its workers mercilessly to make up for the advantages enjoyed by the imperialist capitalists. This increased exploitation pushed the Russian proletariat to revolution before the proletarian classes of the more advanced industrial states.

Weimar Republic   The democratic government of Germany that existed before Hitler came to power. Although Hitler destroyed the Weimar government when he came to power, he never actually eliminated its constitution.

Welfare state   A society that provides a large number of social programs for its citizens, including social security, publicly supported education, public assistance for the poor, and public health services.

Will of the state   The fascist belief that the state is a living being with a will or personality of its own. The will of the state is more powerful than that of any person or group within the state and must be obeyed without question.

Will to power   An uncontrollable force that inspired people to try to dominate one another. Nietzsche argued that this force was the primary motivator of human history.

Work, theory of   Marx's belief that work was a form of self-creation and self-expression and was therefore good.

Bibliography

SUGGESTION FOR FURTHER GENERAL READING

ABBOTT, LEONARD DALTON, ed., *Masterworks of Economics*. New York: McGraw Hill, 1973, vols. 2, 3.

ADAMS, GEORGE P., JR. *Competitive Economic Systems*. New York: Thomas Y. Crowell, 1955.

APTER, DAVID F., and CHARLES ANDRAIN, eds., *Contemporary Analytical Theory*. Englewood Cliffs, NJ: Prentice-Hall, 1972.

BRACHER, KARL D., *The Age of Ideology*. London: Weedenfeld and Nicolson, 1982.

GOODWIN, BARBARA, *Using Political Ideas*. New York: Johnson Wiley & Sons, 1982.

HARMON, M. JUDD, *Political Thought: From Plato to the Present*. New York: McGraw-Hill, 1964.

JOES, ANTHONY JAMES, *Fascism in the Contemporary World*. Bolder, Colo: Westview Press, 1978.

MACRIDIS, ROY C., *Contemporary Political Ideologies*. Cambridge, MA: Winthrop, 1980.

MAZRUI, ALI A., and MICHAEL TIDY, *Nationalism and New States in Africa from About 1935 to the Present*. London: Heinemann, 1984.

PRESTON, NATHANIEL STONE, *Politics, Economics, and Power*. London: Macmillan, 1967.

RIKER, WILLIAM H., and PATER C. ORDESHOOK, *An Introduction to Positive Political Theory*. Englewood Cliffs, NJ: Prentice-Hall, 1973.

RODEE, CARLTON CLYMER, TOTTON JAMES ANDERSON, and CARL QUIMBY CHRISTOL, *Introduction to Political Science*, 2nd ed. New York: McGraw-Hill, 1967.

ROELOFS, H. MARK, *Ideology and Myth in American Politics: A Critique of a National Political Mind*. Boston: Little, Brown, 1976.

RUSH, MICHAEL, and PHILIP ALTHOLF, *An Introduction to Political Sociology*. New York: Bobbs-Merrill, 1971.

SABINE, GEORGE H., *A History of Political Theory*, 3rd ed. New York: Holt, Rinehart & Winston, 1961.

SARGENT, LYMAN TOWER, *Contemporary Political Ideologies: A Comparative Analysis*, rev. ed. Homewood, IL: Dorsey Press, 1972.

SEERS, DUDLEY, *The Political Economy of Nationalism*. New York: Oxford University Press, 1983.

SHAW, L. EARL, ed., *Modern Competing Ideologies*. Lexington, MA: D.C. Heath, 1973.

SKINNER, B. F., *Beyond Freedom and Dignity*. New York: Bantam Vintage Books, 1971.

271

SPIRO, HERBERT J., *Politics as the Master Science: From Plato to Mao.* New York: Harper & Row, 1970.
TINDER, GLENN, *Political Thinking,* 3rd ed. Boston: Little, Brown, 1979.
TINEY, LEONARD, ed., *The Nation-State.* Oxford, England: Morton Robertson, 1981.
VAN TASSEL, DAVID D., and ROBERT W. MCAHREN, *European Origins of American Thought.* Chicago: Rand McNally, 1969.
WATKINS, FREDERICK M., *The Age of Ideology: Political Thought, 1950 to the Present,* 2nd ed. Englewood Cliffs, NJ: Prentice-Hall, 1979.
ZOLL, DONALD A., *Twentieth Century Political Philosophy.* Scarborough, Ontario, Canada: Prentice-Hall, 1975.

Index

Abortion, 36–37, 41
Absolutism, 54, 56
Abyssinia, 241
Adam and Eve, 16
Adams, Samuel, 88
A Disquisition on Government, 89, 90
Advisory referendum, 117, 267
Aerospace, 107
Afghanistan, 197, 250, 262
Africa, 123, 179, 190, 246, 247, 248, 250, 269
Africa, Cuban troops in, 216
African-Americans, 244
African tradition, 252
Afrikaner Resistance Movement, 243
Afro-Asia, 249
Afro-Asian bloc, 256
Afro-Asian states, 186, 248
Age of Ideology, The, 8
Agrarian reforms, China, 205
AIDS, 5
Air pollution, 73
Albania, 217, 241, 251
Albanians, 202
Alexander II, 182
Allende, Salvador, 122, 254
Allied invasion of France, 195
Allied invasion of Russia, 191, 193–194
Allies, World War I, 223, 224, 226
All-Union Temperance Society, 123
America, 140, 165
  Nazism, 243–244
American,
  Bill of Rights, 37, 88
  capitalism, 45, 72–76, 168
    waste, 75–76
  capitalists, 85
  Civil War, 108, 261
  concentration of wealth, 74
  constitutional law, 102
  Democratic policy, 44–46
  flag, 37, 111
  foreign policy, 43–44
  government, 64, 83, 100, 107, 112, 114, 152
  history, 86–87
  Indians, 28–29
  military, 43
  people, 12, 104, 137, 170

political history, 86, 120
political system, 81, 84, 106
politics, 42–46
society, 31, 170
values, 31
American Revolution, 27, 40, 77, 84, 86, 87, 155, 192, 248
American Socialist Labor Party, 181
American Socialist Party, 181
Amin, Idi, 228, 252
Amsterdam, 180
Anabaptists, 140
Anarchism, 11, 125, 126–138, 261, 263, 264, 266, 267, 269
  definition of, 127–129
  development of, 127
  individualist, 136–137
Anarchist revolutionaries, 133–136
  individualist, 126, 129, 136, 137, 261, 269
  social, 126, 129, 136, 261
Anarcho-syndicalism, 131
Anarchy, 127
  Italy, 225
Andropov, Yuri, 189, 197
Anglican Church, 56
Anglo–American colonies, 77
Anglo–American colonists, 70
Angola, 251, 256
An Introduction to the Principles of Morals and Legislation, 92
Anti-African-American, 243–244
Anticolonialism, 269
Anti-corruption campaign, Gorbachev, 198
Anti-ideology, 8
Anti-Semitism, 226, 231, 233, 243, 244, 261, 270
  Germanic, 226
Antisocialist socialism, 164
Antithesis, 153
Anti-Yankeeism, 215
Apartheid, 242–243
Aquinas, Thomas, 13
Arabs, 14
Arab states, 250, 255
Arab unity, 250
Arctic, 28
Argentina, 228, 243
Aristocracy, 52, 54
Aristotle, 13, 52
Arkansas, 243

Nationalism, 1, 10–19, 38, 40, 79, 111, 178, 224, 246, 248, 249, 250, 252, 266, 269
  Chinese, 203
  economic, 245, 254, 263, 265
  German, 226
  theory of, 17–19
Nationalist China, 228
Nationalities, Yugoslavia, 202
Nationality, 11
Nationalization, 164, 166–167, 266
Nation-state, 1, 12, 17, 18, 163, 266, 267
NATO (North Atlantic Treaty Organization), 217, 270
Natural,
  gas, 197
  law, 30, 50, 65, 84, 92, 266
    Bentham, 93
    Locke, 59–62
  rights, 57, 60, 63, 64, 67
  selection, theory of, 265
  state, 50
  theory of state, 2, 13–14, 266
Nazi, 14, 62, 220, 231, 258, 261, 268 (*See also* National Socialism)
  annexation of Austria, 180
  armies, 195
  death camps, 243
  government, 237
  ideology, 227, 228–242, (*See also* National Socialism)
  imperialism, 241
  invasion of Russia, 195
  party, 226, 266
  racism, 263
  state, 264
  Third World states, 252
  war criminals, 243
Nazism, 135 (*See also* National Socialism)
  America, 243–244
Nechayev, Sergi, 136
Negation of the negative, 153
Negroes, 235
Neoclassical democratic theory, 76–92, 261
Neocolonialism, 245, 249, 250–251, 253, 266
Neo-Nazi movements, 242–244
Neo-Nazism, 221
NEP. *See* New Economic Policy
Nepotism, 208–209
Netherlands, 247–248
New Deal, 42, 70, 73, 74, 88, 98, 170, 262, 266
New Economic Policy (NEP), 188, 191–192, 193, 194, 197, 209, 217, 263, 266, 270
New England, 102
New Harmony, Indiana, 176, 177
New Lanark mill, 176
New Left, 27, 28, 124
New socialist man, 190
New York, 134

New York Daily Tribune, 142
New Zealand, 248
Newton, Sir Isaac, 144, 268
Nicaragua, 29, 216, 247, 251
Nicholas I, 144
Nietzsche, Friedrich, 14, 231–232, 234, 235, 266, 270
  transvaluation, 232
Nigeria, 247, 255
Nihilism, 266
Nihilists, 135–136
Nixon, Richard M., 25, 115, 262
Noble class, Burke, 79
Nominations, 117–118
  convention, 117, 262
  petition, 117, 267
  self-announcement, 117, 268
Nonantagonistic contradictions, 211
Non-Marxist socialist, 165, 172
North America, 12, 15, 40, 248
Northern Securities Trust, 184
North Korea, 217, 251
North, Oliver, 25
North Vietnam, 156
Novum Organum, 6
Nuclear energy, 5
Nuclear war, 267
Nuclear weapons, 5
Nullification, theory of, 88, 266
Nyerere, Julius K., 252, 269

Ochlocracy, 52
Office of Special Investigation in the Justice Department, 243
Oil, 33, 197, 215
  Third World, 247
Oligarchy, 106
  iron law of, 106, 264
Oliver Twist, 145
On Liberty, 94
Order, 34, 35, 57, 131
Order, The, 244
Oregon, 118
Organic,
  society, 263
  theory of society, 13, 17, 77, 173
    Rousseau, 66–67
  theory of the state, 236, 266
Organization of African Unity, 250
Organization of American States, 250
Orient, 203
Oriental people, 235
Original donation theory, 16, 266
Origin of the state, theories of, 13–17
Orthodox Church, Russian, 131–132
Orthodox Marxism, 156, 165, 179–180, 264, 266
Owen, Robert, 140, 164, 176, 181, 263
  capitalism, 176